Religion, Media, and the Public Sphere

Edited by

BIRGIT MEYER

and

ANNELIES MOORS

Religion, Media, and the Public Sphere

INDIANA UNIVERSITY PRESS
Bloomington and Indianapolis

This book is a publication of

Indiana University Press
601 North Morton Street
Bloomington, IN 47404-3797 USA

http://iupress.indiana.edu

Telephone orders   800-842-6796
Fax orders   812-855-7931
Orders by e-mail   iuporder@indiana.edu

Library of Congress Cataloging-in-Publication Data

Religion, media, and the public sphere / edited by Birgit Meyer and Annelies Moors.
      p. cm.
   Includes bibliographical references and index.
   ISBN 0-253-34653-3 (hardcover : alk. paper) — ISBN 0-253-21797-0 (pbk. : alk. paper)
   1. Mass media—Religious aspects. I. Meyer, Birgit. II. Moors, Annelies.
   P94.R4543 2005
   261.5′2—dc22

                                                                2005012165

1 2 3 4 5   11 10 09 08 07 06

Contents

Acknowledgments

This volume is a collective endeavor in many respects. It is the result of a conference we organized in December 2001 at the University of Amsterdam. We would like to express our gratitude to the contributors to this volume as well as to Dale Eickelman, Brian Larkin, Meg MacLagan, David Morgan, Rafael Sanchez, and Peter van der Veer, who also took part in the conference.

The idea for this conference was generated in the Pionier research program, Modern Mass Media and the Imagination of Communities, that has been generously sponsored by the Netherlands Foundation of Scientific Research (NWO), and in the research program of the International Institute for the Study of Islam in the Modern World (ISIM). We would like to thank the Amsterdam School for Social Science Research (ASSR) and the ISIM for providing the financial and logistic support without which this conference would not have been possible.

In developing this book project we have greatly benefited from stimulating conversations with colleagues and friends. Birgit Meyer wishes to express special thanks to the Research Centre Religion and Society (University of Amsterdam), the Pionier program, and others: Gerd Baumann, Marleen de Witte, Peter Geschiere, Francio Guadeloupe, Charles Hirschkind, Lotte Hoek, Stephen Hughes, Michael Lambek, Brian Larkin, Meg MacLagan, Martijn Oosterbaan, Peter Pels, Rafael Sanchez, Patricia Spyer, Mattijs van de Port, Peter van Rooden, Peter van der Veer, Oskar Verkaaik, and Jojada Verrips. Annelies Moors extends her thanks also to the participants in the ISIM research program (especially former fellow Saba Mahmood) and Ph.D. students working on related themes (in particular, Miriyam Aouragh on Palestine in Cyberspace and Nahda Shehada on debates about family law and court practices in Gaza), the Public Discourse section of the Arab Families Working Group (especially Omnia el Shakry with whom she coauthored a piece on media and the family in the Middle East), and the Collaborative Program of the Social Science Research Council on Reconceptualizing Public Spheres in the Middle East (especially Rima Sabban, who writes about the mediated presence of migrant domestic workers and who introduced her to the media world of Dubai).

We also want to mention our involvement with the KNAW-project on Indonesian Mediations directed by Ben Arps and Patricia Spyer, and the Religion and Media Program chaired by Faye Ginsburg and Angela Zito at New York University. We owe special thanks to Saar Slegers for the careful attention she paid to the preparation of the manuscript and for her patience with us. At Indiana University Press we are grateful to Rebecca Tolen for her work on this project.

Religion, Media, and the Public Sphere

Introduction

Birgit Meyer and Annelies Moors

Modernist assumptions about the decline of religion as a public force notwithstanding, religions are thriving all over the world. Pentecostal, Buddhist, Muslim, Jewish, Hindu, and indigenous movements publicize their message through sound and image, and instigate alternative politics of belonging, often in competition with the modern nation-state. How does the accessibility of new mass media, offered by new global infrastructures and media technologies as well as state policies of media liberalization, facilitate the public articulation of religion? What role does the crisis of the modern state play in allowing for the public role of religions?

The relationship between religion and media has recently been subject to more thorough reflection, in academia as well as in public debate. In the 1980s religion and electronic media were by and large seen as belonging to different spheres (belief and the culture industry), with the notable exception of American televangelists, who were, however, dismissed as hopelessly conservative, even ridiculous (Harding 1994) by critical public opinion. Today we witness not only a spread of the televangelical format in Pentecostal-charismatic movements in Latin America, Asia, and Africa, but also the deliberate and skillful adoption of various electronic and digital media—cassettes, radio, video, television, and the Internet—and the formats and styles associated with these media, by Muslim, Hindu, Buddhist, Jewish, or indigenous movements. It seems that, as a *New York Times* article of May 16, 2002, aptly expressed it, at the wake of the third millennium we cannot help but realize that "religion finds technology" (Biersdorjer 2002). At the same time, as we are reminded, for instance, by the prominence of Mel Gibson's *Passion of the Christ* and the rise of religious theme parks worldwide, religion also features prominently in cinematographic and other forms of entertainment.

This volume explores the entanglement of religion and media by focusing on a number of salient examples. Jewish ultra-orthodox Ashkenazim, for instance, have successfully marketed their literature, building on claims to "authenticity" and tradition, whereas ultra-orthodox Sephardim have adopted pirate-radio to reach out to others. The latter, employing a very different style grounded in popular culture, present themselves as an alternative to both the secular establishment and the more textually oriented Ashkenazim. Elsewhere other religious groups have also realized the potential of radio broadcasting to spread their messages. The struggles between religious groups in post-apartheid South Africa over the acquisition of airtime reveal the emergence of new forms of identity politics on the basis of religious affiliation. Public personalities, such as Sharif Haidara, the leader of a charismatic Muslim movement in Mali, turned to broadcasting video- and audio-taped sermons, and in Turkey theology professor Yaşar Nuri Öztürk popularized the notion of "secular Muslims" by appearing regularly on a television talk show. Cassettes that are not broadcast through "big media" (Sreberny-Mohammadi and Mohammadi 1994) but that are circulated instead through popular networks can also greatly impact the formation of new religiously based identities. In Egypt cassette sermons have popularized a particular mix of personal and political virtues and have been employed by the Islamic revival movement to claim its own public sphere. Simultaneously state television has acknowledged the importance of religion, and in programs such as Ramadan riddles, religion makes its appearance in the realm of commerce and entertainment.

Such links between religion and commercial entertainment are widespread. Video-film producers in Ghana and Nigeria have framed their movies in line with Pentecostal concerns, while at the same time the encounter with film and television has transformed Christianity and drawn it into the sphere of entertainment. Hindu nationalist politicians in India also have no problem linking consumerism with spirituality. Modern technology, from cyber-rituals to popularized televised religious serials, is called upon to facilitate the resurgence of Hindu nationalism, both in India itself and in the Indian diaspora. On the other hand, the Indian film industry seems overly involved in multi-ethnic cosmopolitan circuits to be able to afford a narrow identity politics. The politics of making public or visible what remains unsaid in verbal discourse is also evident in situations of strong political contestations. In Palestine documentary films inadvertently reveal what remains concealed in academic writing, that is, the politics of embodied presence. In Indonesia journalists, otherwise protagonists of transparency, refuse to identify the religious belongings of particular groups involved in violence so as to avoid engendering more violence, a move that may actually turn out to be counterproductive. Where mediated visual representations of indigenous culture have been highly contested, such as in the case of the Aboriginals in Australia, the identity politics involved in media productions is crucial.

These cases, discussed in greater detail in this volume, are not isolated examples but rather typify a wider trend. Since the 1990s the increasingly public character of religion, the proliferation of the electronic media, and the crisis of the nation-state have shaped people's life worlds throughout the globe in ever more visible ways and have started to feature strongly in debates in the social sciences and in cultural studies. Scholars in fields as diverse as sociology, political science, anthropology, history, and media studies seek to assess the scope and impact of these changes. Manuel Castells (1996–98) discerned nothing less than "the dawn of the information age," a "new era" characterized by "the rise of the network society." If Benedict Anderson (1991) has shown that the rise and spread of mass-produced print media played a crucial role in forging new imaginations of community geared toward and framed by the nation-state, in the era of the network society imagined communities are no longer confined to the territorial and conceptual space of the nation but are also formed in arenas both wider and narrower than the nation-state. No longer considering the nation-state the privileged space for the imagination of identity, scholars have started to investigate the critical role electronic media play in the imagination and constitution of new links between people and the emergence of fresh arenas of public debate.

While the nexus of electronic media and the crisis of the nation-state has been a key focus of debate for some time (e.g., Anderson 1991; Appadurai 1996; Armbrust 2000; Castells 1996–98; Ginsburg, Abu-Lughod, and Larkin 2002; Morley and Robins 1995; Shohat and Stam 2003), the role of religion in the transformation of the public sphere now also receives increased attention.[1] Alongside research on American "televangelism" (e.g., Alexander 1997; Bruce 1990; Harding 1994, 2000; Hoover 1988) and attempts to reconfigure the relationship between religion and media in the West (e.g., Arthur 1993; Hoover and Lundby 1995; Stout and Buddenbaum 1996), there is a substantial, growing body of scholarly work on the global rise of religious movements such as political Islam, Hindu nationalism, and Pentecostalism. Anthropologists and other scholars increasingly engage in ethnographic studies of the articulation of religious movements in (and their contribution to) the transformation of state-society relationships in postcolonial contexts.[2]

Seeking to further our understanding of the multiple relationships between religion, media, and the public sphere in the context of postcolonial societies, this volume is divided into three parts. The first explores how religious discourses, practices, and forms of organization change as new media are adopted. The second investigates how the presence of mediated religion transforms the public sphere and is played out in the new politics of difference. The main concern of the third part is to analyze how the blurred boundary between religion and entertainment, facilitated by forces of commercialization, offers new possibilities for the proliferation of religion while also addressing questions about the limits of religious representations. To avoid the pitfall of reproducing or misapplying taken-for-granted concepts based on experiences in the West, the essays combine empirical studies with grounded theories. All chapters address the key issue of the public presence of mediated religion and explore it in relation to debates about the crisis of the postcolonial state, the proliferation of electronic media, and the rise of network society, as well as the place and role of religion in contemporary societies.

Religion and/in the Public Sphere

In recent years the notion of the public sphere has often been invoked as an alternative to the concept of civil society, which is critiqued for ascribing Western assumptions of proper state-society relations to postcolonial contexts.[3] The idea of the public sphere, which originates from Jürgen Habermas's pioneering work on the genesis and demise of the *bürgerliche Öffentlichkeit* in European societies (1990 [1962], 1989), can help anthropologists understand the emergence of new arenas of debate that are not fully controlled by the postcolonial nation-state and generate shared ideas, sentiments, and moods among people who do not necessarily have the same cultural or ethnic background (e.g., Barber 1997; Eickelman and Anderson 1999; Meyer 2004a; Probst 1998, 1999). In this, mass media appear to be essential, because around the media evolve alternative notions and possibilities of the public and of what it means to be a person or part of an audience. The point here is not to employ the notion of the public sphere as a universal notion but rather to use it as a starting point in order to develop a more suitable framework for an analysis of the complicated politics of identity in the information age.

Many criticisms have been leveled at Habermas's notion of the public sphere. The concept has been shown to be too normative and universalistic, making use of generalizations based on particular historical developments in England, France, and Germany; to be geared toward an understanding of rationality that excludes other possible registers of critique; and to fail to scrutinize the politics of access to and exclusion from the public (Calhoun 1992; Warner 1992). Moreover, it idealizes the initial stage of the classic public sphere by suggesting that it is constituted beyond the realm of the economy and invokes an emotional nostalgia because of its dilution through the forces of commodification (Hansen 1991; Negt and Kluge 1972). Yet the debates inspired by Habermas's work highlight a number of issues helpful to our understanding of the new conditions in which selves and communities are imagined and the politics of identity to which these imaginations give rise. Such debates point to the importance of the media in facilitating new politics of belonging, which are at times separate from and difficult to co-opt by the nation-state. They underline the crucial relevance of the capitalist economy for carving out a separate sphere of critique and aesthetic expression, and also highlight the complicated and dynamic relationship between the spheres of intimacy, the private and the public, implying both the making public of the intimate and private, and the privatization of the public. These issues and themes generate productive questions for ethnographic explorations of the changing relationship between state, economy, religion, and society, the erosion of boundaries between these domains, and the new arenas in which new links between hitherto unconnected people are imagined and forged.

One issue requiring special attention concerns the presence of religion in the public sphere. Habermas (1990 [1962], 67, 163) saw the emergence of the public sphere and the public decline of religion as dependent on each other. He regarded religion as privatized, stating that religious convictions emerge in public debate only as opinions and thus have to engage with other (non-religiously informed) opinions in line with agreed-upon, rational discursive rules. Although "secularization theory" has come in for severe criticisms (e.g., Asad 2003; Casanova 1994; Martin 1978; van der Veer 1994, 1995), the decline of religion in the public sphere continues to be largely taken for granted as an intrinsic feature of modernity in public debate and in the media. Conversely, if religion assumes a marked public role, this is taken to be a sign of the society's backwardness or at least the backward orientation of the religious movement in question. This perspective on the public sphere as a secular space is intrinsic to a modernist attitude toward society. Such a view was mobilized in the colonial era to legitimize the alleged necessity of the colonial state to control and contain religion, above all Islam. The mobilization of public opinion against "religious fanaticism" in the wake of the events of 9/11 is also reminiscent of this stance (van der Veer and Munshi 2003). Called upon in contemporary debates about the (un)desirability of a public role of religion (Islam, in particular) in the name of the Enlightenment, this perspective is too ideological and normative to be of help in comprehending the changing role of religion and the contests to which this gives rise. In this sense the secular stance engenders a political position that demands as much of scholars' attention as the religious positions critiqued by secularists (Asad 2003).

This viewpoint also informs many scholars' attempts to explain the rise of so-called fundamentalist Muslim, Hindu, or Christian transnational movements, which are perceived as disturbing because they assume a political role and question the authority of the modern state to contain religion. Manuel Castells (1996, 19), for example, understood the rise of Muslim "fundamentalism" as "a reaction against unreachable modernization (be it capitalist or socialist), the evil consequences of globalization, and the collapse of the post-nationalist project." Similarly he argued that Christian American fundamentalists seek to "reassert control over life, and over the country, in direct response to uncontrollable processes of globalization that are increasingly sensed in the economy and in the media" (26). The public articulation of Islam and Christianity, for Castells, is a defensive reaction against the insecurities arising "when the world becomes too large to be controlled" and concerns an attempt of people to shrink it back to a manageable size so as to ground themselves in a delimited place and have a history (65–66).

If Castells sees fundamentalist religion as emerging in reaction against globalization and the proliferation of mass media, Eickelman and Anderson (1999) propound a different perspective. In their investigation of the emergence of a new Muslim public sphere, they argue that the easy accessibility and proliferation of electronic media facilitates the constitution of a new Muslim public able to challenge both the state and conventional religious authorities, build civil society, and engage in transnational relations. Here Islam is shown to thrive and develop not in reaction against but instead *along with* information technology. To Eickelman and Anderson, the Muslim publics "that emerge around these forms of communication [e.g., new media such as cassettes, pamphlets, and the Internet—B.M. and A.M.] create a globalization from below" (10). Their appreciation of Islam's constructive role in the (transnational) public sphere is complemented with regard to Christianity by Susan Harding (1994, 2001) in her analysis of American Christian fundamentalists and by David Martin (2001) in his study of global Pentecostalism. These religious groups eagerly and skillfully employ new mass media in order to, as their self-understanding would have it, "reach out to the world."

Clearly it is inadequate to dismiss the public presence of religion—which is certainly not confined to so-called fundamentalist movements—as being out of tune with the realities shaped by globalization (Marty and Appleby 1991-95; for a well-argued critique, cf. de Vries 2001, 16ff). This dismissal reveals more about scholars' own ideological position than about the phenomenon they seek to explain. Hence it would be a mistake to simply conceptualize the public emergence of religious forms as a "return of the repressed," made possible by the incapacity of the modern state to contain religion. Public religion, in this sense, is not a relic of a premodern past that should ideally be confined to the private sphere. Instead, it is crucial to acknowledge that—religious claims of "returning to the source" notwithstanding—religions tend to be rearticulated with globalization. The role played by the mass media in this rearticulation of Hinduism, Judaism, Islam, and Christianity is a key concern of this volume (cf. chapters 2, 4, 10, 12, and 14).

While Eickelman and Anderson's point that Muslim religious practice transforms through the encounter with new media is well taken, their rather normative understanding of the public sphere as a harbinger of emancipation and rational debate, and of the role of religion therein, is problematic. In the introduction to their edited volume, *Public Islam and the Common Good*, Salvatore and Eickelman (2004, xii) also recognize that the trend toward the fragmentation of religious authority is in fact "uneven and often contradictory." The contributors to this volume are wary to adopt an overtly celebratory tone toward the public sphere out of the realization, noted above, that the public sphere should not be viewed as a universal notion that readily emerges on a global scale once certain basic conditions are fulfilled (see chapters 5, 6, 8, and 9). Rather, this volume suggests that the marked articulation of religion in the public realm destabilizes the narrative of modernity as defined by the decline of the public role of religion, and thus urges us to critically rethink the nexus of religion and media in regard to (trans)national politics and the modern nation-state on the basis of detailed empirical study (cf. chapters 1 and 7). Hence the contributors adopt a rather loose understanding of the public sphere as the space or arena evolving in a host of postcolonial societies in conjunction with some measure of political liberalization and commercialization. These processes run parallel to the decline of the state's power to dominate the media, to assign a place for religion in the sphere of the private, and to govern the production of identity.

Mediated Religion and Its New Publics

Processes of mass mediation impinge on religious organizations as well as on individual experiences, and have major implications for the place and role of religion in society. One may be tempted to think that people's (and "their" anthropologists') turn to the mass media is an intrinsically new phenomenon, triggered by globalization and implying a loss of "authenticity," understood as characterized by the absence of media.[4] Yet anthropology has a long-standing intellectual tradition of studying media. The seminal works of Jack Goody and others explore how the introduction of literacy, as a new media technology, changed existing modes of oral communication and instigated social change. While Goody (1977) asserted, contra Marshall McLuhan, that the message cannot be reduced to the medium, he emphasized the need to investigate changes stemming from the adoption of new technologies in the system of human communication, because these technologies have great implications for the content as well as the social relations through which communication is organized. Although the question of how the mass media impinge on communication in the era of the "information age" is important, as argued above, Goody's work reminds us that the question should be addressed from a historical perspective (see also chapters 1, 3, and 5).[5] Focusing specifically on the development of Muslim publics, Eickelman and Salvatore (2004) also employ a strong historical perspective in their volume, including a section on the historical emergence of publics in the Ottoman Empire. There evidently is a need to shift from a presentist focus on the mass media and their reception as such to a focus on broader, historical processes of mediation, that is, on how the media operate as intermediaries in processes of communication, affirming existing links and creating new ones between people and expressive forms.

If practices of mediation, rather than the (mass) media per se, are taken as a point of departure, it appears that there is nothing entirely new about the link between religion and the media. This may be obvious with regard to so-called book religions such as Islam, Judaism, and Christianity, but it also pertains to other religions that, for instance, employ diviners or spirit mediums in order to contact and know the will of the gods. For, by definition, religions, in one way or the other, claim to mediate the transcendental, spiritual, or supernatural and make these accessible for believers (e.g., Derrida and Vattimo 1998; de Vries 2001; van der Veer 1999). Indeed, "for religious traditions to continue through history they must be translated, or better, transmediated, put in a new form" (Plate 2003, 6; see also Babb 1995). Therefore it is most fruitful, as a starting point, to view religion as a practice of mediation (see also chapter 14). Religion, we argue, cannot be analyzed outside the forms and practices of mediation that define it. This means that the current adoption of electronic and digital media by Islam, Evangelical Christianity, and Judaism—the religions that are central in this section—should not be regarded as an anachronistic combination of matters held to belong to different domains, namely, religion and technology.[6] Rather, the point is to explore how the transition from one mode of mediation to another, implying the adoption of new mass media technologies, reconfigures a particular practice of religious mediation.[7] This raises certain questions: How does the adoption of the media as cassettes, TV, mass-reproduced tracts, or radio impinge on existing modes of religious mediation? What happens to the message when cast through new mass media or broadcast through new, transnational channels of communication? Which conflicts and problems do these transitions evoke, and to what extent are religious leaders able to control the new technologies of transmission? What issues are at stake when believers are addressed as audiences and consumers, and what does this mean with regard to questions of religious authority?

Such processes of reconfiguration have obvious implications for studying the popular appeal of cassette sermons in Egypt, where, as Charles Hirschkind points out in chapter 1 of this volume, the Islamic revival movement has redefined notions of public piety with cassettes playing an important role in the transmission of popular sermons. Grounded in a long tradition of Islamic practice and scholarship, contemporary sermons are put to new uses and are made to speak to the demands engendered by political modernization and the threat of the erosion of the Islamic character of society. Having become increasingly independent of the performances in the mosques, which they set out to reproduce, cassette sermons now circulate transnationally throughout the Arab world, offering comments on a range of topics from ethical standards to politics. They are listened to in public spaces, in the streets, in buses and taxis, in workplaces, as well as at home, engaging friends and strangers in debate. Popularizing the public use of a particular mode of reasoning and ethical speech, cassette sermons are meant to invoke in listeners particular, shared dispositions leading to the ability to change the self and to embrace correct modes of conduct. Thus the adoption of a new medium like cassettes indeed transforms existing practices of mediation in that it popularizes a particular articulation of personal and political virtues addressing contemporary concerns. This adoption takes place within a tradition of Islamic discourse, which points to the existence of a complicated relationship between the new and old media. As a counterpublic, the Islamic revival movement claims its own public space precisely by contesting liberal notions of publicity and the public sphere, and cannot be located within a dichotomy of tradition and modernity with Islam and the state at both sides of the opposition. These categories may play a role in the politics of governance adopted by the state, yet they cannot offer the framework from which to understand the tensions between the state and the Islamic reform movement.

If Hirschkind emphasizes how Islam becomes omnipresent in the public sphere through sound, Patricia Birman, in chapter 2, points out that the *Universal Church of the Kingdom of God* in Rio (Brazil) asserts its presence and power through a strong emphasis on visibility. Also in Brazilian society it appears increasingly difficult to maintain a compartmentalized order, with neat boundaries between the spheres of politics, religion, and the economy that characterizes modernist, liberal visions of society. The increasing public articulation of Evangelical religion occurred in conjunction with the weakening of the power of Catholicism to feature as the hegemonic religion of the nation. Openly denouncing the Catholic Church for its tolerance vis-à-vis other religions (such as *candomblé* and other Africa-oriented cults), syncretism, and idolatry, the Universal Church initially met much resistance. Yet by running its own TV station, newspapers, and magazines, the Universal Church successfully produces itself as an icon of modern media technology, fiercely asserting its public presence and offering an alternative image of the Brazilian nation. Adopting a mode of representation geared to grandiosity and spectacle, the Church strives to organize mass-scale media events such as filling the Maracanã, the world's largest football stadium, or assembling huge crowds in its "Cathedrals of Faith" in Israel or Africa. In doing so, it creates not only a distinct, new style of self-representation but also pinpoints new forms of religious experience that cast believers as spectators, spectacles as miracles, and God's blessing as prosperity. Turning spectators into, albeit mimetic, participants in broadcasted mass rituals that encompass people in different nations through the power of tele-vision, the Universal Church endorses a global orientation. But it not only presents itself as spreading throughout the world (and especially to Africa, the cradle of Afro-Brazilian, allegedly "demonic," cults) but also as being able to master the world and lead people out of poverty. Accepting the marketing and branding methods of corporate business, which shows in the dress style and comportment of its pastors, and emphasizing its links with politics, the Universal Church, like similar Pentecostal-charismatic churches throughout Africa and Asia (Freston 1998; Martin 2002; Meyer 2004b), purports an understanding of religion as being well connected with the world of capital and power.

The adoption of the mass media, although suitable for the spread of religious ideas, raises important questions concerning the maintenance of religious authority. Addressing religious practitioners as audiences may entail cracks in the maintenance of religious regimes, and hence give rise to ambivalent attitudes vis-à-vis new media (Little 1995; Spyer 2001; Meyer, in press; van de Port, 2004). Jeremy Stolow, in chapter 3, discusses the implications of the commodification of Jewish mass-produced literature for the maintenance of ultra-orthodox, religious authority. Judaism is appropriately characterized as a "religion of the book," in that texts play a key role in the production of knowledge, the consolidation of authority, and the social organization of the Jewish community across the diaspora for centuries. Yet changes in the mode of circulation and consumption of these texts impact on the relations between leaders and followers, and raise a vital question: "What has happened to religious authority in the information age?" By analyzing the exchange networks and circuits through which texts published by ArtScroll Publishers circulate, the frictions between ArtScroll's and readers' intentions become evident. ArtScroll, one of the leading Judaica publishers in the English-speaking world with close ties to the *haredi* movement *Agudat Israel*, serves as a vehicle to transmit the voice of ultra-orthodox authorities.

Yet the wish to reach out to "lost Jews" requires the commodification of mass-produced texts, to be circulated in arenas out of ArtScroll's immediate audience and milieu. Its texts are also quite popular among non-*haredi* Jews, such as in the Saatchi synagogue, the "coolest" in London, because of rhetorical strategies employed to claim authenticity. Marketing its texts as markers of Jewish authenticity enables ArtScroll to establish a dominant position in the market for prayer books and religious texts. At the same time, however, it inserts ArtScroll into the logic of commodity exchange. This makes it ultimately impossible to control processes of consumption and to retain religious authority for

ArtScroll's own interpretations. Such an intersection of practices of religious mediation with the logic of commodity exchange in the information society is an important aspect of public religion. It seems that as much as commodification is one of the prime strategies for religions to assert their presence in the neoliberal religious marketplace (see also Moore 1994), outreach in space always implies the risk of loss of control over believers' interpretations and of the message "watering down."

While Stolow focuses on the spread of ultra-orthodox literature throughout the Jewish diaspora, David Lehmann and Batia Siebzehner, in chapter 4, examine the adoption of new media such as pirate radio by ultra-orthodox Sephardi groups in Israel. These groups, represented by the Shas Party, oppose not only the secular state establishment but have found an alternative mode of conveying their message to that used by the more textually oriented Ashkenazi *haredim*. Shas has successfully nestled itself in the *t'shuva* movement that strives to bring "lost Jews" back to religious observance and has established itself as the embodiment of Sephardi identity, and thus is located in one of the many bounded enclaves that characterize Israeli society. By combining with Sephardi identity, the *t'suva* movement seeks to reach beyond its own enclave and to manifest itself in public space by making extensive use of radio. The existence of a great number of pirate radio stations testifies to the incapacity of the Israeli state to control access to this medium and endorse the broadcasting of programs in line with secular imperatives. Developing a distinct style, which is grounded in popular culture and is far more streetwise than traditional expressions of ultra-orthodoxy, the *t'shuva* movement markets the "return" to religious observance as being perfectly compatible with entertainment and matters of everyday life. In attempting to recapture those who are "lost," the movement adopts a new religious style that is more or less in line with the exigencies of the radio format and close to the sphere of entertainment.

This confluence of popular culture, religious renewal, and media not only brings about new styles of being orthodox but also new media personalities such as Amnon Yitzchak. A fervent opponent of television as the prime medium of the secular state, Yizchak runs his own one-man road show which he records and markets as videos and cassettes. In ways similar to the media strategies of the Universal Church in Brazil, he, too, strives for spectacular mass performances aimed to draw people into the *t'shuva* community. Relying on funds from fans, Yitzchak is able to freely distribute a vast number of video and audio cassettes in which he assaults and ridicules secular politicians, from Ben Gurion to the contemporary Israel establishment and even George W. Bush. There are striking similarities between the *t'shuva* movement and the Pentecostal-charismatics in Brazil. And elsewhere a new religious format has emerged as well, evolving around charismatic media personalities that have developed new stylistic repertoires devoted to mass participation. These include the charismatic Malian Muslim Haidara in Mali (see chapter 6); the Turkish divinity professor Yaşar Nuri Öztürk known for his televisual performance (see chapter 11); the Egyptian television personality Amr Khalid, who successfully addresses not only the impoverished middle classes but also a more fragmented public including the privileged groups (Bayat 2002); and the Ghanaian Pentecostal-charismatic pastor Mensah Otabil, whose church runs its own media studio and who fashions himself the teacher of the nation (De Witte 2003).

The new technological possibilities of cassettes, radio, television, and the Internet may be understood by religious leaders or followers as linking up smoothly with existing religious concerns, such as the wish to spread religion to the outside world or to offer a prosthetic device for particular religious practices. Yet, as the examples in part 1 of this volume show, the adoption of new media significantly transforms existing practices of religious mediation. This is not simply a matter of new media allowing for the increased public visibility and audibility of religions. Equally important, the media imply particular formats and styles often taken for granted, and operate in new infrastructures. These factors shape the specific modes by which religions go public, modes that are difficult to control by religious establishments. New media thus have both a destabilizing and an enabling potential for established practices of religious mediation. In this sense, new media may resemble a Trojan horse.

Religion in the Public Sphere and the Politics of Difference

The presence of mediated religion in the public sphere is both constitutive of and constituted by political activism, especially identity politics or the politics of difference. Modern religion refuses to be bound to a distinct religious sphere—as is imagined in modern notions of society as differentiated into separate domains—and appears to be intermingled with politics and sometimes violent political action. Nation-states worldwide are faced with significant problems in attempting to control religion and its inclusion in state-driven imaginations of the nation. Especially pertinent is the link between religions and new electronic forms of mediation in the context of the rise of network society, a connection that evokes important questions regarding the politics of identity. Whereas Castells (1996, 1997, 1998) extensively discussed how the new media technologies have shaped the ways in which identities are generated and anchored—once the privilege of the nation-state but now driven by global processes—he paid little attention to the role of mediated religion (apart from "fundamentalism," as noted above).

This neglect of the potential contributions of mediated religion to the development of a modern public sphere is also evident in the work of Habermas. For him, the distinctive feature of the *modern* public sphere is that individuals are to appear as equals, formally not hindered by an attachment to particular interests or identities, with only the power of rational arguments acknowledged. Following this line of thought, as pointed out above, there is no space for religiously grounded positions in the modern public sphere. Yet, as Habermas's critics have stressed, group identities and interests are always at play in the public sphere.

Rather than employing the notion of a unified public sphere, some have argued that it is more productive to imagine it as a proliferation of publics, as a contested terrain that ought to be thought of in terms of its multiplicity or diversity (a notion employed in Eickelman and Anderson 1999; see also Calhoun 1992; Fraser 1992). Others have proposed a somewhat different take and have emphasized that the central question is how particular groups succeed in presenting their specific interests as universal, as entailing the common good. The principal question, then, is how certain groups succeed in being seen not so much as *in* the public but rather *as* the public (Mah 2002, 167ff). Such a public, as the momentary outcome of the struggle between various groups with specific identities and interests, is always inherently unstable and needs to be continuously reconstituted. With the diminishing capacity of the nation-state for constructing communities of belonging, sub-publics and transnational publics that are grounded in religious convictions, imaginaries, and networks have become increasingly important. Essential for the emergence of these new publics has been the proliferation of new technologies of communication and representation.

A politics of difference is central to the development of such new publics. Particular identities and interests are at play in the contestations between various groups in their attempts to take up a position as the public. This may take the form of highlighting their particular identities and interests in posing as a counterpublic, a sub-public, or an alternative public while at other moments and under different circumstances they may downplay such specificities, normalize their particular positions, and work to appear *as* the public in arguing for the common good (Fraser 1992; Warner 2002). Publics are not bounded entities but rather are involved in continuous processes of construction and reconstruction, of negotiation and contestation. Such contestations do not only refer to positions taken up with respect to the secular versus the religious but refer also to a great variety of positions within an emerging religious public. In this regard certain fundamental questions need to be addressed: What roles do religion and the mass media play in imagining and mobilizing new, and in transforming existing, communities of conviction, producing new identities and politics of difference? What forms of mediation and communication do these more diversified audiences employ, and what styles of communication and persuasion do they use in their engagements in public debate? How are tensions between making public (bringing into the open or making visible) and keeping secret (refusing to reveal) played out in particular political settings? What new forms of inclusion and exclusion are at stake, and which concepts of agency and identity politics are helpful in understanding them?

The ways in which public religion intersects with the politics of difference are addressed in investigations about the inclusion and exclusion of publics in debates about family law reform in Palestine. Debates about what forms of family law to apply in Palestine have been covered both in academic writing and documentary filmmaking. A close analysis of the different types of information these media provide indicate that gender is implicated in more complex ways than is often acknowledged, as Annelies Moors points out in chapter 5. If, in conventional accounts, a secular public sphere of abstracted, free, and autonomous individuals is contrasted with an authoritarian religious world subjecting individuals to uniform models of moral behaviors (see also chapter 1), this is even more so in debates about women and Islam. Such accounts deny to religious subjects the status of agent and also deny that participating in public debate always demands forms of (self-)disciplining. Yet equally unconvincing are accounts that see the emergence of a modern Muslim public sphere largely in terms of the fragmentation of religious authority, and hence as enabling a greater participation of formerly excluded groups, such as "religious women" (Eickelman and Anderson 1999). New Muslim counterpublics may well produce new forms of authority with their own forms of exclusion, not only opposing dominant secular state policies and publics but also subaltern women defined as "traditional" (that is, "not-yet conscious").The complexities of the dynamics of inclusion and exclusion come to the fore not only in verbal debate but are also apparent in other forms of communication such as those embodied in dress codes.

Contestations between a secular state and various contending Muslim counterpublics have been ongoing in urban Mali since the 1990s. Dorothea Schulz, in chapter 6, deals with the workings of broadcast religion as a source of identity construction in the case of a popular Malian charismatic Muslim movement led by Sharif Haidara. Strategies of exclusion that structure public debate in Mali do not so much separate an official secular public from a Muslim counterpublic but rather create and reflect the segmentation of the Muslim discursive field. Whereas "political Islam," working within the institutions of "civil society," plays a relatively minor role, Haidara is highly successful precisely because he distances himself from the field of "politics." Instead, he has succeeded in creating a parallel sphere of discursive engagements by employing video- and audio-taped sermons that are also broadcast on local radio. This points to the importance of forms of mediation and styles of engagement. The diversification of the media landscape has enabled him to reach much wider constituencies while also allowing for forms of persuasion (through an aesthetics of images and sounds) that are based not only on verbal reasoning. Moving toward a new notion of faith, one no longer ethnically based, Haidara requires Muslims to publicly display their individual conviction. Muslim activists, then, not only bring their religious identity into the public sphere but also claim and create their religious identities in public interaction.

Patricia Spyer, in chapter 7, investigates the representation of violence in journalists' narrative strategies in relation to current religious conflicts and identity politics in their writings on the chronic warfare in the Moluccas (Indonesia), inviting us not only to rethink the political effects of publicness but of secrecy as well. These journalists consciously refuse to identify particular groups involved in acts of violence, including references to religious belongings, in favor of presenting a generalized account. Whereas they support the democratic ideals of transparency and are active in a range of *reformasi*-inspired media initiatives, they paradoxically employ a minimalist form of reporting on violence in order to prevent their articles from fueling more hatred and violence. Yet representing occurrences of violence without a clearly identifiable origin risks having the opposite effect from the one intended. If violence is without any signs of identity or responsibility, then violence in different places and circumstances begins to look alike. The more that violence is abstracted from any concrete context and specificity, hence occurring potentially everywhere, the more it may inspire fear and—as a possible response to this—a recourse to more violence. An ironic implication is that, if transparency is sacrificed for the sake of the common good, effacing particular religious identifications actually undermines the peace and civility which this journalistic strategy desperately seeks to evoke.

The relation between religions' mediated presence in the public and identity politics is addressed differently in Rosalind Hackett's discussion, in chapter 8, of the contestations of the various religious communities in South Africa, notably the minority groups, about reapportioning airtime. An investigation of the negotiations over public religious broadcasting at the South African Broadcasting Corporation (SABC; a public service broadcaster), which came to a head as South Africa moved into its post-apartheid phase in the 1990s, brings into view how religious identities are implicated in and transformed through the media politics of the state. The South African case demonstrates the increased centrality of the media for the identity and survival of religious collectivities. Both the identities and actions of religious groups are increasingly located in, and defined by, the interface of modern media. These media have become crucially important for shaping attitudes of religious tolerance or intolerance, and in managing religious diversity, with new religious movements and minority groups particularly vulnerable in this respect. Since the creation of the Religious Broadcasting Panel (RBP) in 1994, the reapportioning of airtime for the country's religious groups has been a key element in the refashioning of the South African state, with these religious groups appealing to their constitutional and international human rights to claim freedom of religion and freedom of expression.

The politics of making visible and keeping secret take on a particular saliency in the case of media representations of Aboriginal traditional practices, where, as Faye Ginsburg points out in chapter 9, mediated representations of indigenous culture in the modern public sphere have been highly contested. The particular claim to visibility upon which media as video and film thrive stands in a strong tension with Aboriginal politics of representation of the sacred and secret. What this means for representing a particular Aboriginal practice depends on the complex ways in which mediation and identity politics interrelate at different historical moments. Ethnographic film projects in Central Australia made in the 1970s representing the spectacular Warlpiri fire used the overvoice of the all-knowing outsider and were based on expectations that Aboriginal traditional practices would disappear. A decade later the fire ceremony was recorded through a community video project in the 1980s as part of an activist project to take control over representation in local terms. Spurred by a desire to block the penetration of Western television, this project also sought to determine the formal, social, and cultural protocols for indigenizing media. By the late 1980s Aboriginal interest in media, fueled by the desire to counter both the absence and the negativity of their media representations, led to the creation of an indigenous presence on state television, through a coproduction between the Warlpiri community and urban Aboriginal producers. Whereas Australian national policies increasingly has granted Aboriginals religious expression, Aboriginal and state practices of visual representation are framed by different understandings of self and memory, and are grounded in power structures that are difficult to align.

Whereas new technologies of mass mediation and communication have enabled the construction of communities of belonging that go beyond the nation-state, the examples presented here and elsewhere also indicate that this cannot be equated with the demise of the nation-state. In various locations the nationalist imagery still has a presence of its own in the field of public culture (Armbrust 1996, 2000; El Shakry and Moors, n.d.). Yet notions of national belonging are not static; they have also been transformed in some ways through the public and mediated presence of other imaginaries, such as those based on ethnicity and religion. Iranian cinema, for instance, is an arena where the rejection of the monopolization of power in favor of political, religious, and ethnic pluralism has become increasingly visible (Tapper 2002).

On Screen: Religious Representations and/as Entertainment

New forms of mediation not only transform religious discourses and practices but religion also features in films, videos, and TV programs in a framework of entertainment or "infotainment." Addressing the links between religion and the "culture industry," it is important to analyze the implications of the commodification and proliferation of media and religion as part and parcel of mass culture while avoiding three pitfalls. The first is to devalue the "culture industry" because it is held to be watering down true culture and to be "refeudalizing the public sphere" (the Frankfurt School perspective; e.g., Adorno and Horkheimer 1993). This view is above all problematic because of its normative, even moralistic point of departure; in contrast, an empirical approach is needed that seeks to investigate the particular form of entertainment in concrete historical contexts and to assess whose voices are privileged through this format. The second danger is to overemphasize the capacity of audiences to appropriate and even subvert the message (e.g., the work of John Fiske [1989a, 1989b] and related audience research, especially in anthropology). In line with much work in the field of popular culture, this view quite uncritically proclaims the people's tactics to circumvent power and tends to overemphasize the agency of audiences inherent in processes of appropriation. This perspective, trapped in an opposition between oppression and resistance, is not very helpful when the focus is on gaining insight in the emergence of new culture industries and the new power structures on which they thrive (cf. Barber 1997). Commercialization and liberalization of the media give rise to new forms of entertainment that entail a repositioning of both the state and the religions represented. Yet focusing on these processes ought not to be equated with flat pragmatism—a third pitfall—which adopts the perspective of neoliberal capitalism and asserts that "this is what the people want," thereby becoming apologetic of commercialization and liberalization of the media.

The emergence in the sphere of entertainment of religion or, better put, the religious—an expression signaling a discontinuity between religion as representing a distinct tradition and disciplinary regime, on the one hand, and more diffuse religious articulations, on the other—evokes important questions as to how religion, as a typically modern notion (Asad 1993), transforms by its deliberate association with mass culture (see also Forbes and Mahan 2000; Mitchell and Marriage 2004; Sanchez 2001). Certainly it would be too simple to understand this process in terms of a gradual watering down of religious content, as many believers themselves would do but would then strive to counter this inflation by an alleged return to religious purity (an issue touched upon by Hirschkind and Armbrust in chapters 1 and 10, respectively; see also van de Port 2005). How can one conceptualize the blurring of religion and media entertainment, and what are the implications of this blurring for the relationship between the "secular" and the "religious," an opposition that has not only dominated the modern social sciences but also informs the ways in which the public sphere is understood in concrete empirical settings? How are media and religion involved in changing politics of representation and visibility, what forms of mediation are involved in these processes, and what are the specific effects of different media for engagements with the public sphere?

Fawazir Ramadan (*Ramadan Riddles*), a popular program broadcast on Egyptian television each evening during Ramadan, just after breaking the fast, blurs the boundaries between religious observances and secular entertainment. As Walter Armbrust shows in his chapter, the program is not Islamic in any strict sense but rather is intrinsic to the glitzy world of commodities, and is geared to the Islamic calendar. For the state, with a monopoly on television, broadcasting *Fawazir Ramadan* entails the capacity to acknowledge Ramadan and at the same time draw it into the sphere of advertisements and entertainment. A detailed study of one particular episode, recorded in 1990, shows how the state managed to synchronize state-sponsored, religious messages with the articulation of corporate-sponsored materialism, showing both to be in full consonance with Muslim piety. Thus the Ramadan riddle operated in the context of a flow in which advertisements for a large variety of commodities and occasional brief religious messages blend into "a veritable sea of commercialism." If, in the course of the 1980s, the mixture of religion and entertainment echoed popular ways of celebrating Ramadan by engaging in excessive consumption, by the mid-1990s this unholy combination has become a target of profound criticism. Whereas the Islamic revival movement, with its emphasis on achieving piety by listening to sermons, stands in opposition to the place assigned to Islam by the state (see chapter 1), through programs such as *Fawazir Ramadan* the state seeks to contain Islam in a context of commercialization. This context makes it difficult to distinguish between religion and entertainment, and yet at the same time triggers the urge to define Islam in opposition to allegedly corruptive forces such as entertainment and commoditization.

In Turkey in the 1990s market forces, energized by liberalization and coupled with a major boom in satellite broadcasting, reconfigured state television and provided new opportunities to disseminate political Islam. As Ayşe Öncü argues in chapter 11, the growing voice and visibility of political Islam in the public realm questions one of the key unifying themes of Turkish nationalism: "We are all secular Muslims." Interestingly the commodified forms and formats of commercial broadcasting have reconfigured the couplet "secular Muslim" as a matter of "free choice," thereby offering an alternative to political Islam. This has become visible in a popular talk show moderated by Ayşe Özgün (as the prototype of a "secular Muslim, Turkish woman"), in which audiences pose questions to Yaşar Nuri Öztürk, a theology professor metamorphosed into a super-personality through commercial broadcasting. Embodying the blended culture of global consumerism, Öztürk's public image oscillates between a man of the world, a scholar, and a fighter involved in a melodramatic conflict between "fake" or "corrupt" Islam and "real" Islam. Opposing both political Islam (although not explicitly) and state bureaucrats in charge of the Directorate of Religious Affairs, Öztürk reanimates and popularizes the notion of a "secular Muslim" through the visual formats and commodity logic of television. There are two opposing tendencies inherent in the current expansion of global media and communication networks. On the one hand, the visual technologies and commodity logic of popular media undermine the normative unity and imagined homogeneity of national cultures by lending voice and visibility to a plurality of alternative political visions. Yet, on the other hand, they foreground new modes of identification with the abstract nation, reaffirming daily the fictive unity of "we the people" through commodified icons and symbols of nationalism. Importantly, as the case of Öztürk as well as that of the Ramadan Riddles indicates, the marked presence of religious entertainment on television may well support, yet at the same time recast, the national project.

Rather than conceptualizing the upsurge of Hindu nationalism as the "return of the repressed," and thus as threatening the triumphant rise of capitalist globalization by resisting linear progress, it can more fruitfully be situated in the context of the ecology of global media in India. Sudeep Dasgupta, in his chapter, argues that in the era of technical reproducibility the aura did not simply disappear but is being reconstructed through new techniques of representation. If the classical aura of a piece of art (as discussed by Benjamin 1978) stems from its perceived temporal and spatial *distance from* the audience, in the era of media globalization the aura is re-embedded and reactivated *in* the place and time of the beholder, through its reception, thereby legitimating social authority through the medium of visual culture. These theoretical reflections are critical to our understanding of how religious images are entangled with consumerism and yet appear supernatural and thus as part of a different order altogether. The Hindu Right relates to modern mass media in complex ways. While media such as the Internet are used to offer the diaspora a pure notion of Hinduness or Hindutva (e.g., by providing cyber-rituals and prayers—"click a deity"—in order to help people reach "back to the source"), in India much energy is devoted to showing that consumerism is perfectly compatible with "Indian spirituality" and with the marketing of religious trinkets (cf. Starrett 1995 on Islamic commodities in Cairo, and numerous religious sites in cyberspace). Vesting commercial items with a new religious aura and religious items with commercial value, Hindutva, visual media, and global capital are engaged in a mutually supportive relationship that surpasses modernist distinctions between the spheres of the economy, politics, and religion, and casts consumers as "gods in the sacred marketplace." Thus the aura of modern technology and the media provides the necessary condition for both the resurgence of narrow identitarian motifs of Hindu nationalism and their articulation within a discourse of globalization and modernization.

The rise of Hindutva also coincides with the invasion of the global media, the rise of new consumer-oriented middle classes, and the popularity of televised religious soap operas such as the Ramayana or the Mahabaratha. Can the argument that Hindutva has encroached upon and grows within public culture be extended to Indian cinema? Fierce criticisms by members of the national secular-oriented bourgeoisie notwithstanding, Rachel Dwyer argues, in chapter 13, that Indian films in general cannot be accused of openly propagating Hindutva (although there are some exceptions). While films, of course, continue to picture signs of Hindu identity as part and parcel of Indian national culture, the film industry is too intrinsic to multi-ethnic and global circuits to propagate a narrow politics of belonging. Not only do Muslims play an important role in the sphere of film production, successful marketing also depends on broad, increasingly international audiences. As religion has always been called upon as a repertoire for imagining the nation and presenting its image through the cinema, the public articulation of religion as such is not new. This raises the question as to why other visual media, television, for example, may be more prone to propagate Hindutva than the cinema.

Finally, in chapter 14, Birgit Meyer explores changes instigated by the shift to audiovisual media in the context of a new mediascape that facilitates the public expression of mediated religion in Ghana. Similar processes occur in many other postcolonial countries, which, often under the pressure of the World Bank, have liberalized the hitherto state-controlled media and turned to democracy. The marked public articulation of Pentecostalism in Ghana was facilitated by the retreat of the state from control over the media and the easy accessibly of cheap media technologies, which gave rise to a new image economy. As shown by the aptitude for business of Pentecostal-charismatic churches and the adoption of Pentecostal motifs or themes by the video-film industry, which has developed over the last fifteen years, Pentecostalism has become a lucrative vehicle for projecting ideas and images. Tracing the importance of vision as a key practice of Christian mediation demonstrates a strong affinity between Pentecostalism and video, cinema and church, miracles and special effects, devotion and distraction (for a similar argument with regard to Catholic charismatics, see D'Abreu 2002). In ways similar to Öztürk's presence on Turkish television and the entanglements of Hindutva and global media, in going public and "taking place" in the era of electronic/digital reproducibility, Christianity is significantly transformed as it spreads throughout the surface of social life, disseminating signs yet having to accommodate to given formats. Its marked public appearance thus occurs in conjunction with new Pentecostal practices of mediation, which thrive on distraction in that they imply mass spectatorship and draw Pentecostalism into the sphere of entertainment, notwithstanding attempts at recasting distraction as devotion.

As Lawrence Moore (1994) has shown in his study of American Christianity, an association with the forces of entertainment appears to be crucial for the survival of religion in the marketplace of culture. At stake here is a change of the shape and form of religious expression not only in relation to its internal organization but also in the sense of diffusing religious forms and elements into public culture. These forms and elements are increasingly difficult to control for the more or less established religious organizations from whose symbol bank these remodeled forms originate and to whom they loosely refer. Instead, they convey a religious flair, a sort of aura, to media entertainment and commodities.

* * *

Focusing on religion, media, and the public sphere, as this volume shows, is not only appropriate to understanding the public presence of religion in the information age but also pinpoints the limitations of overly narrow, discipline-based approaches. The power and popularity of religion cannot be grasped from a perspective of religious studies alone, nor can that which occurs in the public sphere be assessed from the standpoint of narrow and normative political science. New perspectives are needed that are able to surpass the limits of disciplinary approaches toward religion, media, and politics. Such a division of labor among academic disciplines echoes a compartmentalized understanding of modern society that increasingly proves to be out of tune with actual developments (and indeed probably never met realities on the ground). The purpose of this volume is to contribute to the development of new intellectual spaces from which the dynamics of current identity politics may be explored. While the essays in the volume show that the nation-state still matters in framing people's lives (and most probably will continue to do so), equally clear is that religions have come to play an increasingly public role in offering alternative imaginations of communities. At the same time, in the process of going public—by becoming enmeshed with identity politics, by being drawn close to forces of commercialization, and by adopting new media technologies—religions have been transformed. In this sense, public religion, while strong, loud, and visible in certain respects, faces new challenges by having to adjust to styles and formats not necessarily of its own making. The outreach into the world, so advocated by different religious traditions, is certainly facilitated by modern mass media, and yet it implies new challenges, concerning, above all, the maintenance of religious authority.

Notes

We would like to thank David Lehman, Stephen Hughes, and Mattijs van de Port for their comments and suggestions on earlier versions of this introduction.

1. See also *Gazette* 2001, a special issue on mediated culture in the Middle East, and *Middle East Journal* 2000 on the new media; on transnational television, globalization, and the Middle East, see Sakr 2003.

2. On Islam/Muslim movements and media, see Abu-Lughod 1993a, 1993b; Eickelman and Anderson 1999; Hirschkind 2001a, 2001b; Larkin 1997, 2000; Launay 1997; Messick 1996; Öncü 1995; Schulz 2003; and Sreberney-Mohammadi and Mohammadi 1994; for the growth of virtual Islam and cybermuftis and transnational Islam, see Bunt 2000, and Allievi and Nielsen 2003; and for many examples of ongoing research, see contributions to the *ISIM-Newsletter* (renamed *ISIM Review* in 2005). On Hinduism/Hindu nationalism and media, see Babb and Wadley 1995; Dasgupta 2001; Gillespie 1995; Mankekar 1999; and Rajagopal 2001; and on Pentecostal-charismatic movements, see de Witte 2003; Hackett 1998; Lyons 1990; Lyons and Lyons 1991; Marshall-Fratani 1998; and Meyer 2004a. On spirit possession and mass media, see Morris 2000. The question of religion and media is addressed by scholars from different disciplines and thus offers possibilities for future, more interdisciplinary cooperation: for a discussion of media studies, visual arts, and religious studies, see de Vries and Weber 2001; Plate 2003; and Mitchell and Marriage 2004; and for an investigation of Middle Eastern and Asian responses to the events of 9/11 from a perspective of anthropology, media studies, and political science, see van der Veer and Munshi 2003.

3. When applied to postcolonial societies, "civil society" is usually conceptualized as existing in opposition to the state, which is characterized in terms of bad, ineffective governance, lack of legitimacy and accountability, and the absence of democracy. Civil society is expected to cure the ills of the state and to set in motion "development" that will eventually result in political systems replicating Western models. Starting from such an assumption and reproducing this modernization paradigm, the idea of civil society takes far too much for granted (e.g., Bayart 1986, 1993; Comaroff and Comaroff 2000; Hann and Dunn 1996; Mamdani 1995). For a summary of the distinctions between civil society and the public sphere, see Calhoun 1993.

4. Long gone seem the days when anthropologists' attitude toward the media could be captured by the well-known cartoon of some Indians hiding their TVs and VCRs as the anthropologists approach (although the cartoon itself is a misrepresentation, forgetting Powermaker's major work on Hollywood and media in the Copperbelt). Since the fierce polemic between Faye Ginsburg (1994) and James Weiner (1997), anthropologists have struggled hard to rethink notions of authenticity and to turn the media into a respectable field of anthropological inquiry that yielded substantial work. Initially anthropological interest in the media focused on what media studies found difficult to accomplish: the reception side of the mass media such as radio, TV, and film, particularly the

culturally specific ways of producing meaning in media consumption. Although current anthropological work on the media moves beyond this rather limited orientation, the anthropology of media is now still mainly associated with a focus on the mass media, making up, in a way, for the shortcomings of media studies while at the same time adopting its conceptual framework. In the two recent handbooks on media and anthropology (Askew and Wilk 2002; Ginsburg, Abu-Lughod, and Larkin 2002) virtually all contributions focus on modern electronic mass media, film, photography, radio, or TV. Although we sincerely welcome anthropology's turn to the media in the 1990s, we deem it important to realize that the media should not simply be equated with *mass* media and that, if we do so, we conceive of the anthropology of media too narrowly.

5. The importance of mass literacy for the fragmentation of religious authority has been addressed, for example, in Eickelman (1992) and Messick (1993), and in the contributions to *Anthropological Quarterly* 68 (1995) about print, writing, and the politics of religious identity in the Middle East. For a discussion of religious authority in relation to the shift away from orality and literacy, see Probst 1987 (with regard to Africa) and Goody (1977, 41ff.).

6. In this sense the *New York Times* article quoted at the beginning of this introduction is misleading in that it assumes a situation in which religion had not yet found technology.

7. The production and reception of *fatwas* (learned opinions), for instance, is very different under conditions of face-to-face interaction, in the case of radio-muftis broadcasting to an anonymous public (Messick 1996), or in the case of cybermuftis whose identity may well be up in the air. Since the mid-1990s there has been a tremendous growth of Islamic websites, many of which also distribute *fatwas*.

References

Abu-Lughod, Lila. 1993a. Islam and Public Culture: The Politics of Egyptian Television Serials. *Middle East Reports* 23 (1): 25–31.
———. 1993b. Finding a Place for Islam: Egyptian Television Serials and the National Interest. *Public Culture* 5:493–513.
Alexander, Bobby C. 1997. Televangelism: Redressive Ritual within a Larger Social Drama. In *Rethinking Media, Religion, and Culture*, ed. Stewart M. Hoover and Knut Lundby, 194–208. London: Sage.
Allievi, Stefano, and Jorge Nielsen, eds. 2003, *Muslim Networks and Transnational Communities in and across Europe.* Leiden: Brill.
Anderson, Benedict. 1991. *Imagined Communities. Reflections on the Origins and Spread of Nationalism.* Rev. ed. London: Verso.
Appadurai, Arjun. 1996. *Modernity at Large: Cultural Dimensions of Globalization.* Minneapolis: University of Minnesota Press.
Armbrust, Walter. 1996. *Mass Culture and Modernism in Egypt.* New York: Cambridge University Press.
Armbrust, Walter, ed. 2000. *Mass Mediations: New Approaches to Popular Culture in the Middle East and Beyond.* Berkeley: University of California Press.
Arthur, Chris, ed. 1993. *Religion and the Media: An Introductory Reader.* Cardiff: University of Wales Press.

Asad, Talal. 1993. *Genealogies of Religion: Discipline and Reasons of Power in Christianity and Islam.* Baltimore, Md.: Johns Hopkins University Press.

———. 2003. *Formations of the Secular: Christianity, Islam, Modernity.* Stanford, Calif.: Stanford University Press.

Askew, Kelly, and Richard R. Wilk. 2002. *The Anthropology of Media: A Reader.* Oxford: Blackwell.

Babb, Lawrence. 1995. Introduction to *Media and the Transformation of Religion in South Asia,* ed. L. Babb and S. Wadley, 1–20. Philadelphia: University of Pennsylvania Press.

Babb, Lawrence A., and Susan S. Wadley, eds. 1995. *Media and the Transformation of Religion in South Asia.* Philadelphia: University of Pennsylvania Press.

Barber, Karin. 1997. Preliminary Notes on Audiences in Africa. *Africa* 67 (3): 347–362.

Bayart, J.-F. 1986. Civil Society in Africa. In *Political Domination in Africa,* ed. P. Chabal, 109–125. Cambridge: Cambridge University Press.

———. 1993. *The State in Africa: The Politics of the Belly,* trans. C. M. Harper and E. Harrison. London: Longman.

Bayat, Asef, 2002. Piety, Privilege and Egyptian Youth. *ISIM Newsletter* 10 (2): 23.

Benjamin, Walter. 1978. The Work of Art in the Age of Mechanical Reproduction. In *Illuminations,* ed. Hannah Arendt, 217–252. New York: Schocken Books.

Biersdorjer, J. D. 2002. "Religion Finds Technology." *New York Times,* May 16.

Bruce, Steve. 1990. *Pray TV: Televangelism in America.* London: Routledge.

Bunt, Gary. 2000. *Virtually Islamic: Computer-Mediated Communication and Cyber Islamic Environments.* Cardiff: University of Wales Press.

Calhoun, Craig. 1993. "Civil Society and the Public Sphere." *Public Culture* 5: 267–280.

Calhoun, Craig, ed. 1992. *Habermas and the Public Sphere.* Cambridge, Mass.: MIT Press.

Casanova, José. 1994. *Public Religions in the Modern World.* Chicago: University of Chicago Press.

Castells, Manuel. 1996–98. *The Information Age: Economy, Society and Culture.* 3 vols. Oxford: Blackwell.

Comaroff, Jean, and John Comaroff, eds. 2000. *Civil Society and the Political Imagination in Africa: Critical Perspectives.* Chicago: University of Chicago Press.

D'Abreu, Ze. 2002. On Charisma, Mediation and Broken Screens. *Etnofoor* 15 (1/2): 240–259.

Dasgupta, Sudeep. 2001. "Professions of Faith: Hindu Nationalism, Television and the Avatars of Capital." Ph.D. dissertation, University of Amsterdam.

Derrida, Jacques, and Gianni Vattimo, eds. 1998. *Religion.* Cambridge: Polity.

Eickelman, Dale. 1992. Mass Higher Education and the Religious Imagination in Contemporary Arab Societies. *American Ethnologist* 19 (4): 643–655.

Eickelman, Dale F., and Jon W. Anderson, eds. 1999. *New Media in the Muslim World.* Bloomington and Indianapolis: Indiana University Press.

Fiske, John. 1989a. *Understanding Popular Culture.* London: Unwin Hyman.

———. 1989b. *Reading the Popular.* London: Unwin Hyman.

Forbes, Bruce David, and Jeffrey H. Maham, eds. 2000. *Religion and Popular Culture in America.* Berkeley: University of California Press.

Fraser, Nancy. 1992. Rethinking the Public Sphere: A Contribution to the Critique of Actually Existing Democracy. In *Habermas and the Public Sphere,* ed. Craig Calhoun, 109–142. Cambridge, Mass.: MIT Press.

Gazette: The International Journal for Communication Studies. 2001. 63 (2–3). Special issue: *Mediated Culture in the Middle East.*

Gillespie, Marie. 1995. Sacred Serials, Devotional Viewing, and Domestic Worship. A Case-Study in the Interpretation of Two TV Versions of the Mahabharata in a Hindu Family in West London. In *To Be Continued . . . Soap Operas around the World*, ed. R. C. Allen, 354–380. London: Routledge.

Ginsburg, Faye. 1994. Culture and Media: A (Mild) Polemic. *Anthropology Today* 10 (2): 5–15.

Ginsburg, Faye, Lila Abu-Lughod, and Brian Larkin. 2002. *Media Worlds: Anthropology on New Terrain*. Berkeley: University of California Press.

Goody, Jack. 1977. *The Domestication of the Savage Mind*. Cambridge: Cambridge University Press.

Habermas, Jürgen. 1990 [1962]. *Strukturwandel der Öffentlichkeit. Untersuchungen zu einer Kategorie der bürgerlichen Gesellschaft*. Frankfurt: Suhrkamp.

———. 1989. *The Structural Transformation of the Public Sphere: Inquiring into a Category of Bourgeois Society*. Boston: MIT Press.

Hackett, Rosalind I. J. 1998. Charismatic/Pentecostal Appropriation of Media Technologies in Nigeria and Ghana. *Journal of Religion in Africa* 28 (3): 1–19.

Hann, Chris, and Elizabeth Dunn, eds. 1996. *Civil Society: Challenging Western Models*. London: Routledge.

Hansen, Miriam. 1991. *Babel and Babylon: Spectatorship in American Silent Film*. Cambridge, Mass.: Harvard University Press.

Harding, Susan F. 1994. The Born-Again Telescandals. In *Culture/Power/History: A Reader in Contemporary Social Theory*, ed. N. B. Dirks, G. Eley, and S. B. Ortner, 539–579. Princeton, N.J.: Princeton University Press.

———. 2001. *The Book of Jerry Falwell: Fundamentalist Language and Politics*. Princeton, N.J.: Princeton University Press.

Hirschkind, Charles. 2001a. Civic Virtue and Religious Reason: An Islamic Counterpublic. *Cultural Anthropology* 16 (1): 3–24

———. 2001b. The Ethics of Listening: Cassette-Sermon Auditioning in Contemporary Egypt. *American Ethnologist* 28 (3): 623–649.

Hoover, Stewart M. 1988. *Mass Media Religion: The Social Sources of the Electronic Church*. Newbury Park, Calif.: Sage.

Hoover, Stewart M., and Knut Lundby, eds. 1997. *Rethinking Media, Religion, and Culture*. London: Sage.

Horkheimer, Max, and Theodor Adorno. 1993. The Culture Industry. Enlightenment as Mass Deception. In *The Dialectic of Enlightenment*, 120–167. New York: Continuum.

Larkin, Brian. 1997. Indian Films and Nigerian Lovers: Media and the Creation of Parallel Modernities. *Africa* 67 (3): 406–440.

———. 2000. Hausa Dramas and the Rise of Video Culture in Nigeria. In *Nigerian Video Films*, ed. Jonathan Haynes, 209–241. Athens: Ohio University Center for International Studies.

Launay, Robert. 1997. Spirit Media: The Electronic Media and Islam among the Dyula of Northern Côte D'Ivoire. *Africa* 67 (3): 441–453.

Little, John T. 1995. Video Vacana: Swadhyaya and Sacred Tapes. In Media and the Transformation of Religion in South Asia, ed. Lawrence A. Babb and Susan S. Wadley, 254–283. Philadelphia: University of Pennsylvania Press.

Lyons, Andrew P. 1990. The Television and the Shrine: Towards an Anthropology of Mass Communication. *Visual Anthropology* 3: 429–456.

Lyons, Andrew P., and Harriet D. Lyons. 1991. Religion and the Mass Media in Nigeria. In *Religion and Society in Nigeria*, ed. J. Olupona, 97–128. Ibadan, Nigeria: Spectrum.

Mah, Harold. 2000. Phantasies of the Public Sphere: Rethinking the Habermas of Historians. *Journal of Modern History* 72:153–182.

Mamdani, Mahmood. 1995. A Critique of the State and Civil Society Paradigm in Africanist Studies. In *African Studies in Social Movements and Democracy*, ed. M. Mamdani and E. Wamba-dia-Wamba, 602–616. Dakar: Codesria Book Series.

Mankekar, Purnima. 1999. *Screening Culture, Viewing Politics: An Ethnography of Television, Womanhood, and Nation in Postcolonial India*. Durham, N.C.: Duke University Press.

Marshall-Fratani, Ruth. 1998. Mediating the Global and the Local in Nigerian Pentecostalism. *Journal of Religion in Africa* 28 (3): 278–315.

Martin, David. 1978. *A General Theory of Secularization*. Oxford: Blackwell.

———. 2001. *Pentecostalism: The World Their Parish*. Oxford: Blackwell.

Marty, Martin E., and R. Scott Appleby, eds. 1991–95. *The Fundamentalism Project*. 5 vols. Chicago: University of Chicago Press.

Messick, Brinkley. 1993. *The Calligraphic State: Textual Domination and History in a Muslim Society*. Berkeley: University of California Press.

———. 1996. Media Muftis: Radio Fatwas in Yemen. In *Islamic Legal Interpretation: Muftis and Their Fatwas*, ed. Muhammad Khalid Masud, Brinkley Messick, and David Powers, 311–320. Cambridge, Mass.: Harvard University Press.

Meyer, Birgit. 2004a. "Praise the Lord": Popular Cinema and Pentecostalite Style in Ghana's New Public Sphere. *American Ethnologist* 31 (1): 1–19.

———. 2004b. Christianity in Africa: From African Independent to Pentecostal-Charismatic Churches. *Annual Review of Anthropology* 33: 447–474.

———. In press. Mediating Tradition: Pentecostal Pastors, African Chiefs and Priests in Ghanaian Popular Films. In *Christianity and Social Change in Africa: Essays in Honor of John Peel*, ed. T. Falola. Durham, N.C.: Carolina Academic Press.

Middle East Journal. 2000. Special issue: *The New Media. Middle East Journal* 54 (3).

Mitchell, Jolyon, and Sophia Marriage, eds. 2004. *Mediating Religion: Conversations in Media, Religion and Culture*. London: T&T Clark.

Moore, R. Lawrence. 1994. *Selling God: American Religion in the Marketplace of Culture*. Oxford: Oxford University Press.

Morley, David, and Kevin Robins. 1995. *Spaces of Identity: Global Media, Electronic Landscapes, and Cultural Boundaries*. London: Routledge.

Morris, Rosalind C. 2000. *In the Place of Origins: Modernity and Its Mediums in Northern Thailand*. Durham, N.C.: Duke University Press.

Negt, Oskar, and Alexander Kluge. 1974. *Öffentlichkeit und Erfahrung. Zur Organisationsanalyse von bürgerlicher und proletarischer Öffentlichkeit*. Frankfurt-am-Main: Suhrkamp.

Öncü, Ayşe. 1995. Packaging Islam: Cultural Politics on the Landscape of Turkish Commercial Television. *Public Culture* 8 (1): 51–71.

Plate, S. Brent. 2003. Introduction: Filmmaking, Mythmaking, Culture Making. In *Representing Religion in World Cinema: Filmmaking, Mythmaking, Culture Making*, ed. S. Brent Plate, 1–15. New York: Palgrave.

Port, Mattijs van de. 2005. Candomblé in Pink, Green and Black: Re-scripting the Afro-Brazilian Religious Heritage in Salvador, Bahia. *Social Anthropology* 13 (1): 1–24.

Probst, Peter. 1987. The Letter and the Spirit: Literacy and Religious Authority in the History of the Aladura Movement in Western Nigeria. *Sozialanthropologische Arbeitspapiere* 4, Freie Universität Berlin, Institut für Ethnologie.

———. 1998. Auf der Suche nach dem Publikum. Prolegomena zu einer Anthropologie der Öffentlichkeit im sub-saharischen Afrika. In *Kulturen des Performativen*, ed. E. Fischer-Lichte and D. Kolesch, 291–305. Berlin: Akademie Verlag.

———. 1999. Mchape 95 or the Sudden Fame of Billy Goodson Chisupe: On Healing, Social Memory and the Enigma of the Public Sphere in Post Banda Malawi. *Africa* 69 (1): 108–138.

Rajagopal, Arvind. 2001. *Politics after Television. Religious Nationalism and the Reshaping of the Indian Public.* Cambridge: Cambridge University Press.

Sakr, Naomi. 2001. *Satellite Realms: Transnational Television, Globalization and the Middle East.* London: I. B. Taurus.

Salvatore, Armando, and Dale Eickelman, eds. 2004. *Public Islam and the Common Good.* Leiden: Brill.

Sanchez, Rafael. 2001. Channel-Surfing: Media, Mediumship, and State Authority in the Mariá Lionza Possession Cult (Venezuela). In *Religion and Media*, ed. H. de Vries and S. Weber, 388–434. Stanford, Calif.: Stanford University Press.

Schulz, Dorothea. 2003. "Charisma and Brotherhood" Revisited: Mass-Mediated Forms of Spirituality in Urban Mali. *Journal of Religion in Africa* 33 (2): 146–171.

el Shakry, Omnia, and Annelies Moors. N.d. "Mass Mediated Public Discourse: Constructing the Family and Youth." Paper to be published in *Framings: Rethinking Arab Families*, ed. AFWG.

Shohat, Ella, and Robert Stam, eds. 2003. *Multiculturalism, Postcoloniality, and Transnational Media.* New Brunswick, N.J.: Rutgers University Press.

Spyer, Patricia. 2001. The Cassowary Will (Not) Be Photographed: The 'Primitive,' the 'Japanese,' and the Elusive 'Sacred' (Aru, Southeast Moluccas). In *Religion and Media*, ed. H. de Vries and S. Weber, 304–219. Stanford, Calif.: Stanford University Press.

Sreberny-Mohammadi, Annabelle, and Ali Mohammadi. 1994. *Small Media, Big Revolution: Communication, Culture, and the Iranian Revolution.* Minneapolis: University of Minnesota Press.

Starrett, Gregory. 1995. The Political Economy of Religious Commodities in Cairo. *American Anthropologist* 97 (1): 51–68.

Stout, Daniel A., and Judith M. Buddenbaum eds. 1996. *Religion and Mass Media: Audiences and Adaptations.* London: Sage.

Tapper, Richard, ed. 2002. *The New Iranian Cinema: Politics, Representation and Identity.* London: I. B. Taurus.

Veer, Peter van der. 1994. *Religious Nationalism: Hindus and Muslims in India.* Berkeley: University of California Press.

———. 1995. The Secular Production of Religion. *Etnofoor* 8 (2): 5–14.

———. 1999. Religious Mediation. In *Media and Social Perception*, ed. E. R. Larreta, 345–356. Rio de Janeiro: UNESCO/ISSC/Educam.

Veer, Peter van der, and Shoma Munshi, eds. 2003. *Media, War and Terrorism: Responses from the Middle East and Asia.* London: Routledge Curzon.

Vries, Hent de, and Samuel Weber, eds. 2001. *Religion and Media.* Stanford, Calif.: Stanford University Press.

Warner, Michael. 1992. The Mass Public and the Mass Subject. In *Habermas and the Public Sphere*, ed. C. Calhoun, 377–401. Cambridge, Mass.: MIT Press.

———. 2002. Public and Counterpublics. *Public Culture* 14 (1): 97–114.

Weiner, James. 1997. Televisualist Anthropology: Representation, Aesthetics, Politics. *Current Anthropology* 38, 2: 197–236.

Witte, Marleen de. 2003. Alta Media's *Living Word:* Televised Christianity in Ghana. *Journal of Religion in Africa* 33 (2): 172–202.

Part One | *Mediated Religion and*
Its New Publics

1 Cassette Ethics: Public Piety and Popular Media in Egypt

Charles Hirschkind

A preacher's voice reverberates through the rusted speakers of a tape player in the Karim Coffee Shop in Bulaq-Dukrur, a lower-middle-class quarter of Cairo. The owner of the shop wipes down the counters while listening to the preacher's passionate evocation of the current suffering of Bosnian Muslims at the hands of Serbian aggressors. His three clients, all men from the neighborhood, accommodate to the languorous rhythm of their water pipes as the account of Serbian atrocities and European indifference echoes around them. At a certain point the preacher, his voice now straining with grief, halts his description to ask: "Where are the Muslims?! Where are the Muslims, while Muslim girls are being raped, mosques are being burned?! Where?!" "Enough, O' Shaykh," the man sitting closest to the counter calls out, "they're not Muslims; they're Europeans!" Turning now to the owner of the shop, he continues, "Why all these tears for the Bosnians; they dress like Europeans, they act like Europeans. There is nothing Islamic about them." "How can you say that?" the shop owner retorts as the preacher continues behind him, "Didn't you hear? They have mosques; they pray; they stand in the same line [*nafsi saf*] as we do. They worship . . . " His client cuts him short: "No, no, no. They may have been Muslims once, but they became Westerners long ago [*yatagharrabu min zaman*]. Whatever little Islam they had was extinguished by the Communists." One of the other clients, an acquaintance of the first and visibly irritated by his comment, weighs in: "Shame on you, Ahmed [*Haram alaik, ya Ahmed*]. Muslims are Muslims, wherever they are. The shaykh is right: the shame is on us that we sit by and do nothing while our brothers [*ikhwanina*] are being slaughtered. The mosques collect a little money, the prime minister says, 'we support the rights of the Bosnians,' and nothing is done." Ahmed again rejects the argument: "We Arabs have enough problems. Palestinians are being murdered, and you want us to save the Bosnians?! Maybe the Bosnians are our cousins, but our brothers, the Arabs—the Iraqis, the Algerians, the Palestinians—they're the ones we should be concerned with." As the preacher begins a collective prayer calling for an end of Bosnian suffering, the shop owner returns again to the theme of Muslim solidarity: "So we should only help Arabs. That's exactly the reason why Muslims are so weak today. That's exactly what our enemies want us to do: 'Those Muslims are different from us; those over there don't speak our language; those there, their clothes are strange.' No. If you say 'There is no God but the one God,' then you are a Muslim. That's in the Quran. The Serbs destroy houses of God, full of people praying, and you say, 'It's not my business' [*mᶜlish daᶜwa*]! Listen to the Shaykh, Ahmed." Attempting to bolster the shop owner's argument, the third man cites a well-known prophetic tradition [*hadith*] on the equality of Arab and non-Arab Muslims: "No Arab is superior to an Ajami [non-Arab] except by righteous conduct." The exchange is interrupted as a boy from the store next door calls out for the shop owner to bring over another round of tea. Ahmed returns to his water pipe, while, echoing from the dusty electronics of the tape recorder, the weeping of the supplicants rises up to engulf the preacher's voice as he continues to lead the collective prayer.

In Cairo, where I conducted fieldwork for two years, cassette-recorded sermons of popular Islamic preachers, or *khutabaᵓ* (sing. *khatib*), have become a ubiquitous part of the contemporary social landscape. The recorded voices of these orators can be heard echoing from within grocery stores, cafes, butcher shops, private homes, and most forms of public transportation throughout the city. Through the multiple practices of audition, exchange, and dialogue they mediate, these tapes have contributed to the formation of what I will call an Islamic counterpublic, one that often finds expression in informal exchanges of the sort described above and that are now a common element of daily experience for many Egyptians. Although shaped in various ways by the structures and techniques of modern publicity, the counterpublic I discuss here exhibits a conceptual architecture that cuts across the modern distinctions between state and society, public and private, that are central to the public sphere as a normative institution of modern democratic polities. In contrast to a space for the formation of political opinion through intersubjective reason, the discursive arena wherein cassette sermons circulate is geared to the deployment of the disciplining power of ethical speech, a goal, however, that takes public deliberation as one of its modalities. Within this context, public speech results not in policy but in pious dispositions, the embodied sensibilities and modes of expression understood to facilitate the development and practice of Islamic virtues and therefore of Islamic ethical comportment. This unique entwining of the deliberative and the disciplinary, as I describe, owes to the way Islamic notions of moral duty and practices of ethical cultivation were mapped onto a national civic arena by Muslim reformists over the course of the last century, in the context of an engagement with the institutions, concepts, and technologies of modern political life. As mosques in Egypt became the site for new kinds of social and political organization and expression, everyday practices of pious sociability gradually came to inhabit a new political terrain, one shaped both by the discourses of national citizenship and by emerging transnational forms of religious association. In the course of this shift, forms of practical reasoning tied to the tradition of the virtues became oriented not simply toward a notion of moral community but toward what we would recognize as a modern public as well: the practice of the virtues and the deliberation of issues of public concern were increasingly linked together in a unique fusion. The cassette sermon provided the discursive vehicle in which this interdependency was most extensively and intensively worked out.

Cassette-Da'wa

From their inception in the early 1970s the production and consumption of sermon tapes has been associated with the broad movement known as *al-da'wa* (literally, a summons or call), and almost all the preachers who make use of this medium refer to themselves, and are referred to by others, as *du'at* (sing. *da'iya*), that is, those who undertake *da'wa*. The term *da'wa* has historically encompassed a wide range of meanings. As found in the Quran, it generally refers to God's invitation, addressed to humankind and transmitted through the prophets, to live in accord with God's will. Over the early centuries of Islam's development *da'wa* increasingly came to be used to designate the content of that invitation, and in the works of some classical jurists it appears to be interchangeable both with the term *shari'a* (the juridical codification of God's message) and *din* (often translated as "religion").[1] *Da'wa* also, however, carried another sense from early in Islam's historical career, one that has been central to contemporary Islamic thought: that of a duty, incumbent upon some or all members of the Islamic community, to actively encourage fellow Muslims in the pursuance of greater piety.

The notion of *da'wa* seems to have received little systematic elaboration from the late medieval period until early in the twentieth century. While the "rediscovery" of the notion cannot be tied to any particular figure or institution, its current salience is the result primarily of its development within Islamic opposition movements earlier in the century, most notably the Muslim Brotherhood.[2] From the late 1920s Hassan al-Banna, the founder of the Brotherhood, revived the classical notion of *da'wa* to define the goals of the organization, namely, the restoration of the Islamic community (*umma*) in the face of its increasing secularization under khedival rule (Mendel 1995, 295). The Brotherhood was particularly critical of the marginalization of Islamic doctrines and practices within the projects of social and political reform being promoted by nationalist thinkers, as well as the failure of the established institutions of Islamic authority to oppose this process. By employing such modern political methods as media campaigns, large-scale rallies, and training camps for Islamic activists, the Brotherhood quickly went from a local grass-roots association aimed at encouraging pious conduct to becoming an international organization embodying considerable religious and political power and authority.[3]

As elaborated by al-Banna, *da'wa* defined the mode of action by which moral and political reform were to be brought about. Brotherhood members were advised to go to mosques, schools, cafes, clubs, and other public locations so as to speak with whomever would listen about Islam, the Brotherhood, and the task of building a pious Muslim society. The Brotherhood also encouraged the Islamic practice of *istiᵓdhan*, wherein a member of the mosque assembly asks permission to address the gathering on matters relevant to the Muslim community. This practice, one that became increasingly widespread during subsequent decades, had the effect of enhancing the dialogical structure of social discourse within the mosque, thereby expanding its role as a key site of public discussion. Mass media also became central to the Brotherhood's effort. Books, short tracts, pamphlets, and flyers by Muslim reformers, as well as magazines covering national and international events considered relevant to Muslims, were widely circulated and competed with the more secular-oriented publications of the nationalist movement. For *daᶜwa* speech and print—and later audio—media, the sermon provided a paradigmatic rhetorical form, a practice that stood in contrast to the European models of political oratory increasingly adopted by Egyptian secular nationalists. Al-Banna's sermons, in particular, became massively popular in Egypt and other Arab countries and were widely distributed in book and pamphlet form.

While the Brotherhood was eventually banned by the Egyptian state and many of its members imprisoned or driven underground, *daᶜwa* itself did not disappear. On the contrary, over the last half-century *daᶜwa* has increasingly become a space for the articulation of a contestatory Islamic discourse on state and society, a discourse embodied in a diversified array of institutional forms including educational centers, preaching associations, thousands of private mosques, and an expanding network of publishing houses and other media. As a result of the activity of these publishing houses and various media, there now exists a vast literature offering instruction in the practice of "individual *daᶜwa*," understood as an ethical form of speech and action aimed at improving the moral conduct of one's fellow community members. The concept has also become a key point of reference for a wide variety of other activities in some way oriented toward promoting and fortifying the ethical practices that constitute Islamic modes of piety and community—from providing social services to the poor, to tutoring children at mosques, to selling religious books or tapes. *Daᶜwa*, in other words, has come to describe a particular way of linking public activism with moral reform. Placed under the rubric of this notion, a wide range of commercial, educational, and welfare activities essential to the reproduction and maintenance of modern society were assigned moral significance, as contributions to the goal of building a community oriented around the practice of the virtues.

Taxi Talk

The kind of discursive arena I am suggesting here can be illustrated through a conversation I overheard during a taxi ride through downtown Cairo, a scenario that is rather typical of the kind of public interactions for which cassette sermons have played a constitutive role. Taxis in Cairo frequently pick up more than one passenger. In this case I was sharing the ride with two other people, a teenage boy and a young woman who wore the *hijab* (head scarf). The

Fig. 1.1. "The Earthquake," a sermon by ʿAbd al-Hamid Kishk, a pioneering figure of the *daʿwa* movement.

taxi driver, who had a long beard and was dressed in a *jalabiyya*, was listening to a sermon tape by the popular preacher ʿUmar ʿAbd al-Kafi. At a certain point during the ride, as the tape came to an end, the boy sitting in front next to the driver asked him if he had any music he might put on instead. After a few moments of awkward silence, the driver responded that music was *haram* (forbidden) in Islam. The boy looked surprised and irritated but kept quiet and turned away. The driver, noting the boy's irritation, said, "Don't just look away, tell me what you're thinking. We can talk, there's no problem." "How can singing be *haram*?" said the boy, "Who told you that?" The driver replied, "Do you or don't you believe in the Quran and the *sunna*?"[4] The boy responded that of course he did. "Shouldn't we do everything in our lives to follow the *sunna*? Doesn't it tell us not only the rules of God, but, as Muslims, isn't it also a model for us?" Again the boy, now getting impatient, concurred. On a roll, the driver moved to clinch the argument by means of a *hadith*, an account of one of the Prophet's deeds or sayings: "When the Prophet used to hear songs, he would put his fingers in his ears, and considered music to be one of the devil's snares [*madkhal al-shaitan*]." The boy quickly retorted that the driver's *hadith* was *daʿif*, a classificatory term referring to a category of *hadith* whose authority is of the weak-

إنتبه الموت قادم

مجموعة
علماء

Fig. 1.2. "Beware: Death Is Coming," a tape compiled from the sermons of various religious scholars.

est kind. Not ready to concede the point, the driver continued: "Do you believe there is nothing that is *haram* in religion [*din*]?" "Of course not," the boy countered, "but I must know where the proof [*dalil*] is for the *haram*. Someone can tell you today that driving a car is *haram,* and you'll stop driving. Then later you'll find out it was wrong, and start to drive again, unless you found out from the beginning whether what was called *haram* was really *haram* or just an erroneous invention." The driver, realizing now that he had better take another tack, asked: "Don't you think that drinking alcohol is *haram*? Do you know why? Because it interferes with prayer. It's the same with songs, when you hear songs your mind goes somewhere else and you can't pray." The boy retorted vigorously: "Alcohol is one thing, but the Quran says nothing about music. I pray, fast, and do all my obligations of worship [*iᶜbadat*], and what is wrong if I hear songs as well? I am not doing anything *haram!*" At this point one of the women sitting in the back next to me entered the debate:

> But all the words of songs are about love and all of these things, so that when you go out you think about that rather than think about God. Your ears get used to hearing the songs, until you don't like to listen to the Quran. Well, then songs are prohibited so that at an adolescent age you don't think about things that would lead you to illicit desire [*shahwat*] and sin [*al-dhanb*]. Especially in this era and time, when the world is full of seductions that are always seeking to occupy your

thoughts [*tishaghallak ʿala tul*]. The sermon, on the other hand, makes you think of God, and brings you feelings of humility [*khushuʿ*] and regret [*nadam*].

The woman then quoted a verse from the Quran, but the boy immediately pointed out to her that the verse made no mention of music. "Yes," she concurred, "but it leads you to the reasoning of why music is *haram*." The driver nodded in agreement. The boy, not to be defeated, countered, "Love is not *haram* in Islam."

This conversation reveals a number of characteristics of a kind of public deliberation that has become increasingly prevalent in Egypt in recent decades. Note, to begin, the rather unstructured and informal character of this exchange. Circulating outside the boundaries of prescribed ritual practice, cassette sermons have helped to create the context for this type of public argument, one that, as we see here, cuts across generational and gender lines in ways not possible within the ordered, sex-segregated space of the mosque. The relation between the speakers is not that of teacher to pupil nor of social superior to social subordinate but rather that of coparticipants in a common moral project, their speech structured around an orientation to correct Islamic practice. As opposed to the position of *khatib* within the mosque, which is reserved only for men, the duty of *daʿwa* falls to both men and women.[5]

In addition, and contrary to what has often been suggested, reference to authoritative Islamic sources does not close debate. Instead, the lines of argument pivot precisely upon the proper interpretation of those sources. Whereas in liberal society religious authority is generally understood to impose undue constraints on free and open discussion and is thus unwelcome within the secular public sphere, here it provides the foundation upon which opposing viewpoints are articulated.

The exchange also points to a new familiarity with bases and styles of Islamic argumentation, evidenced, for example, in the boy's knowledge of the specific *hadith* as well as its classification within the authoritative traditions. The advent of modern mass education, literacy, and the wide availability of written texts has equipped recent generations of Muslims in the Middle East with new competencies in styles of scholarly argumentation and their associated textual materials, both classical and modern (see Eickelman 1999, 1992). Cassette sermons and recorded mosque lessons, likewise, enable listeners to expand and bolster their knowledge of Islamic traditions in moments of the day when the sort of concentration demanded by written texts would be impossible—and to do so, moreover, without the literacy skills required by such texts. All the men I worked with had sought to acquire competence in these traditions, a task that has become easier with the proliferation of new institutions of Islamic learning associated with the revival movement, such as mosque study groups, private Islamic institutes, *daʿwa* centers, and a vibrant market in Islamic books and tapes.

For many of those I worked with in Cairo and who participated in the fashion of listening to cassette sermons, *daʿwa* entailed a commitment both to learn Islamic virtues and to encourage those around them through personal appeal to abide by Islamic moral standards—an activity they understood to be a duty placed upon them as Muslims. Sermon tapes helped one pursue both these commitments. Sermons are listened to as a disciplinary practice geared to ethical self-improvement: a technique for the cultivation and training of certain forms of will, desire, emotion, and reason, conceived of as intellectual and bodily aptitudes or virtues that enable Muslims to act correctly as Muslims in accord with orthodox standards of Islamic piety. In addition, cassette sermons provide a point of reference when discussing religious issues with acquaintances, or an inexpensive and easily accessible media form through which others might be encouraged to attend to their religious duties. Tapes are frequently exchanged between friends or acquaintances, both informally and in the context of mosque study groups, a type of association that many of the young men I worked with had at some point been involved in. Indeed, it is the difficulty of controlling a media form that can be so easily and inexpensively reproduced and circulated that has enabled the cassette tape to evade, to an extent far greater than other media, the regulatory purview of the state.

While the commercial aspect of the cassette sermon should not be ignored, I would caution against overemphasizing it for the following reasons. First, the majority of the *khutaba*ʾ whose sermons are available on cassette have no formal contractual relations with the tape companies and receive no remuneration from the sales of their tapes. Indeed, many *khutaba*ʾ encourage people to record, reproduce, and disseminate their sermons, and even commercially produced tapes usually include a written statement prompting the buyer to copy the tape and make it available to others as part of doing *daʿwa* work and as a means of receiving beneficence from God. Moreover, the majority of tapes listened to in Egypt circulate outside the structures of sale and marketing, through the practices of borrowing and exchange mentioned above. Many mosques in Egypt are now equipped with tape libraries that regular attendees can borrow from without charge.

In this way cassette sermons played an important role in the transformation of *daʿwa* in Egypt since the 1970s from being an organizing principle within specific institutions to becoming a popular form of public practice and participation. Owing largely to the mass popularity achieved through cassette circulation, popular preachers—most notably Shaykh ʿAbd al-Hamid Kishk (d. 1996) —became rallying points and exemplary figures within an emerging counterpublic of *daʿwa* practitioners. A number of the young men I worked with explicitly identified cassette sermons as an alternative to the televisual and press media promoted by the state. As one of the men told me, pointing to his cassette recorder: "This is the only mass media [*al-iʿalam*] I need. The [state-controlled] television and the newspapers never discuss the important events and issues. We would never find out about what is really going on even here in Egypt without these tapes."

Here, however, I want to draw attention to how *daʿwa*, as developed first within the Muslim Brotherhood and later in many other institutional locations, became the conceptual site wherein the concerns, public duties, character, and

سوء الخاتمة

الشيخ/محمد حسان

Fig. 1.3. With a title that might be loosely translated as "Road to Destruction," this tape explores the unpleasant consequences that await the impious in the afterlife.

virtues of an activist Muslim citizen were elaborated and practiced. In the case of the men I worked with in Cairo, this practice was woven into their daily activities. When speaking with colleagues at work, one might remind the others to thank God for their successes. While riding a bus, one might point out to a fellow passenger the error of getting angry with the slow driver. *Daʿwa* may even take the form of conversations among friends, in discussions over whether one may pray in a mosque built over a tomb, or whether donations collected at the mosque should go to Bosnia or be used to buy schoolbooks for the needy in the neighborhood.

The *Daʿiya* as Muslim Citizen

While the ethical and social norms of conduct of such a citizen are oriented around the notion of a broad unity of practicing Muslims, an *umma*, they are also grounded in political technologies of modern national citizenship. That is, while *daʿwa* has provided conceptual resources grounded in a long tradition of Islamic practice and scholarly inquiry, these resources have been put to novel uses within a contemporary situation shaped by modern political institutions, pedagogical techniques, and media forms, as well as by notions of civic respon-

Fig. 1.4. Muhammad Hassan's tape on the Day of Reckoning, a common sermon topic.

sibility grounded in the idea and experience of national citizenship. As in other modernizing states, in Egypt the process of recruiting citizens into the structures of national political life produced expectations, aspirations, and participatory demands before the administrative, ideological, and security apparatuses that could accommodate these demands had been fully developed. In this context, *da'wa* has become one of the critical sites for the expression of those demands engendered by political modernization, especially among those ill-versed in the literacy of newsprint. Resituated in this way, these demands have given new impetus and direction to a project aimed at fortifying the bases of the Islamic community. The elaboration of *da'wa* as a civic duty, in this sense, has involved neither what has been termed "retraditionalization" nor, on the other hand, simply the instrumentalization of a traditional category within a modernizing or secularizing project.

As opposed to the national public sphere centered around the press and televisual media, the *da'wa* public reveals a more marked supranational focus, evident, for example, in the considerable attention given within sermons to the plight of Muslims worldwide as well as the interest shown by cassette-sermon audiences in such issues. As one man told me after hearing a tape by an Egyptian *khatib* on Muslims in the U.S.:

When one hears these things, like that people in the U.S., or in Bosnia are taking up Islam, one is stirred. You ask yourself, if they are turning to Islam there, how is it that I as a Muslim am not even committed in my practice? What do they have over me? We are all equals after all. So hearing this moves me toward committing to Islam, and reforming my practice.

In this way, as numerous scholars have pointed out, mass media have transformed the political and religious context wherein Islamic virtues are cultivated and practiced, endowing it with a distinctly transnational focus for participants of this movement, a point underscored in the coffee shop conversation I began with. This tendency has been further enhanced, first, by the fact that many of the *khutaba'* whose tapes are listened to in Egypt are from other Muslim countries, particularly Saudi Arabia, and, somewhat less so, Jordan and Lebanon; and, second, insomuch as the leading contemporary *khutaba'* and other significant figures of the *da'wa* movement have ongoing associations with mosques and *da'wa* centers not only in other Arab countries but also in Europe, the U.S., and Canada.

Note also that this practice does not map onto the constitutionally demarcated separation of public and private but rather traverses this distinction in a way that is often uncomfortable to those with secular-liberal sensibilities. *Da'wa* is undertaken in the street, on public transportation, at the workplace, or in the home. It may take place between friends or coworkers but also between total strangers, as in the case of the taxi ride cited above. From a liberal perspective, *da'wa* is seen as encouraging an unwarranted intrusion into the privacy of others, especially as it entails entering into what are considered to be personal matters of religious faith. *Du'at* render public issues that the liberal state relegates to the private sphere of individual choice—the modesty of one's dress, the precision of gesture in prayer, the danger of gossip, the proximity of unrelated men and women in both the workplace and the home, as well as questions of Quranic interpretation and religious authority. For liberals, these issues tend to be viewed as either insignificant (e.g., precision in prayer, gossip) and thus unworthy of public attention; or, alternatively, as matters of individual preference (e.g., dress, gender relations), and, as such, protected by private law. *Da'wa* for this reason constitutes an obstacle to the state's attempt to secure a social domain where national citizens are free to make modern choices, as it *re-politicizes* those choices, subjecting them to a public scrutiny oriented around the task of establishing the conditions for the practice of Islamic virtues.

Politics and Ethics

The media and associational infrastructure put into place by the *da'wa* movement has created the conditions for a kind of publicness, one grounded in certain classical Islamic concepts but reformulated in response to a variety of contemporary conditions;[6] that is, reformers like al-Banna and 'Abd al-Hamid Kishk revived a notion of *da'wa* as a civic duty the performance of which, conceptually and historically, had long been defined as a condition for the vitality of the Muslim collective. In its contemporary elaboration, *da'wa* defines a kind of practice involving the public use of a mode of reasoning whereby the correctness of an action is argued and justified in the face of error, doubt, indifference, or counterargument. I say "public" precisely insomuch as to assume the position of *da'iya* (the one who does *da'wa*) is to adopt the rhetorical stance of a member of the Islamic *umma* acting on behalf of that particular historical project (and thus not simply as an individual concerned for his or her own moral conduct). In this sense, although such a *da'wa* public has only become possible with the contemporary emergence of a range of Islamic institutions, it is less an empirical entity than a framework for a particular type of action. It is constituted whenever and wherever individuals enter into that form of discourse geared toward upholding or improving the moral condition of the collective as a whole, as illustrated, for example, in both the conversations described above. As a type of activity aimed at shaping other practices through persuasion, exhortation, and deliberation, it is fundamentally a political practice, and hence is distinct from both the web of personal relationships and public representations of cultural identity (e.g., public ceremonies, Islamic media productions), neither of which are grounded in processes of deliberation. Indeed, *da'wa* emerges not at a point of commonality but precisely at one of difference, where a discrepancy in practice makes argument necessary.

While *da'wa* frequently takes the form of discussion and deliberation, its paradigmatic speech genre is the sermon. Notably the interpretive norms informing Islamic homiletic traditions foreground the capacity of ethical speech—particularly one imbued with the language of the Quran and the teachings of the *sunna*—to move the sensitive heart toward correct practice. A well-crafted sermon is understood to evoke in the listener the affective dispositions that underlie ethical conduct and reasoning, and which, through repeated listening, may become sedimented in the listener's character. Enabled in part by the mediatization of sermons on cassette, the norms governing sermon practice have been extended by the *da'wa* movement to the dialogical context of public discourse. Within this arena speech is deployed in order to construct moral selves: to reshape character, attitude, and will in accord with contemporary standards of pious behavior. The efficacy of an argument here devolves not solely on its power to gain cognitive assent on the basis of its superior reasoning, as would be the case in some versions of a liberal public sphere, but also on its ability to move the moral self toward correct modes of being and acting. A language ideology foregrounding poetic and affective aspects, sensory modes of understanding outside the realm of semantics narrowly construed, provide conceptual scaffolding here. In other words, what joins the practice of delivering or listening to a sermon with that of arguing with a neighbor is a conception of the rhetorical force of ethical speech to shape character. Deliberative and disciplinary moments are thoroughly interwoven and interdependent within this arena.

As conceived by its participants, the *da'wa* public constitutes that space of communal reflexivity and action understood as necessary for perfecting and sustaining the totality of practices upon which an Islamic society depends. For the *duᶜat* (those undertaking *daᶜwa*) I spoke to over the course of my fieldwork in Cairo, this practice has been necessitated by the erosion of the Islamic character of society under the impact of what is most often referred to as "*al-ghazwa al-fikri*" (ideological conquest, i.e., Western cultural imperialism), and particularly its forms of consumerism and sensualism that are seen to be corrosive of the virtues enabling one to live a Muslim life. In this context, *daᶜwa* responds to the need for an individual and communal praxis to uphold what is perceived to be an enfeebled Muslim community. The scope of this practice is not limited to issues of personal piety but necessarily extends to address such matters as the methods and content of education, appropriate styles of popular entertainment, modes of public conduct for men and women, and even appropriate forms of employment. In short, as a project aimed at securing the conditions necessary for the practice of Islamic virtues, *daᶜwa* entails an intervention into, and transformation of, the activities and institutions that constitute the community. By promoting the cultivation of sensibilities and the adoption of certain goals, the movement shapes the form of collective life and culture that its adherents, as Muslims and national citizens, will endorse, the arguments they will find persuasive, the projects to which they will contribute their energies.

Contestatory Religion

Although the practice of *daᶜwa* does not presuppose the idea of the nation so much as that of the collective of those who practice Islamic virtues, national institutions are a necessary object of the *daᶜiya*'s discourse insomuch as they shape the conditions of social existence for Muslims in Egypt. As we know, through the processes central to modern nation building, such institutions as education, worship, social welfare, and family have been incorporated to varying degrees within the regulatory apparatuses of the modernizing state. Whether in entering into business contracts, selling wares on the street, disciplining children, adding a room to a house, in all births, marriages, deaths—at each juncture the state is present as overseer or guarantor, defining limits, procedures, and necessary preconditions. As a consequence, in Egypt as elsewhere, modern politics and the forms of power it deploys have become a condition for the practice of many personal activities. When the state acts in ways that foreclose the possibility of living in accord with the Islamic standards promoted by the movement—such as forbidding schoolgirls from wearing headscarves, broadcasting television serials that show what are considered indecent public behavior (e.g., kissing), or cutting back on the amount of time dedicated to learning the Quran in schools[7]—*khutaba'* use the mosque sermon to publicly criticize these actions, a critique that is then quickly distributed on tape.

The Egyptian state is anxious about the loyalties and sensibilities of the religious subject being forged within the *daᶜwa* movement and has sought, in response, to establish a network of secular cultural institutions as a prophylaxis. Thus, within the government-controlled press, we find numerous articles calling for the development and expansion of after-school cultural activities—music, literature, debating clubs, arts, and sports. As discussed within such writing, Islam—as individual spiritual practice—should stand as a brief interlude between the two primary modes of existence around which the times and spaces of daily life are arranged, work and leisure. Indeed, it is precisely this disjuncture between the kind of public subject fashioned within the *da'wa* movement and one who will perform the role of national citizen inhabiting a private domain of unconditional immunity that has made culture a site of considerable struggle. For *khutaba'* and their audiences, the danger of Western cultural forms and popular media entertainment lies in the fact that they engender emotions and character attributes incompatible with those that, in their view, enable one to live as a Muslim. As a *khatib* I worked with told me, echoing a widely held opinion, "the enemies of Islam use *fann, adab, thaqafa,* and *muda* [art, literature, culture, and fashion] to attack Islam," a comment explicitly acknowledging the Western and secular genealogy of these categories of discourse and practice. Much of the criticism found in cassette sermons is directed at media entertainment, film stars, popular singers, and television serials. Thus, Shaykh Kishk's most well-known sermons are his critiques of the immensely popular national icons, the singers Umm Kulthum and Muhammed 'Abd al-Wahab, while the *khatib* 'Umar 'Abd al-Kafi is best known for having convinced a number of famous film actresses to give up their acting careers.

The state's attempt to control *da'wa* has met with two serious obstacles. One is grounded in the limited resources and capacities of the economically enfeebled Egyptian state. The second, on the other hand, owes to the very heterogeneity of the state itself. Many of the state-administered religious organizations include sizable factions sympathetic to the same religious arguments that their own institutions have been called on to officially denounce and combat. It is also notable that most of the well-known Egyptian *khutaba'* of recent years—for example, Muhammed Mitwalli al-Sha'arawi, Muhammed al-Ghazali, 'Abd al-Sabbur Shahin, and 'Abd al-Hamid Kishk—have all been affiliated at some point in their careers both with state institutions *and* with major opposition movements, primarily the Muslim Brothers. Shayhk Kishk, one of the most unequivocally oppositional public voices in the last thirty years, was never entirely outside the official structures he so powerfully criticized. While Kishk worked for a brief period as an itinerant *khatib* within the system of mosques belonging to the private *da'wa* association *al-Jam'iyya al-Shar'iyya,* for most of his life he preached for the Ministry of Religious Affairs at the al-Malik mosque in the al-Hada'iq al-Qubba quarter of Cairo. Notably he retained his position as *khatib* at this mosque from 1964 until 1981, despite having become one of the most virulent critics of the Egyptian government and having been subject to all forms of state repression, including two periods of imprisonment.

In short, while the state has tried to harness the Islamic pedagogical, juridical, and homiletic institutions to a variety of national goals (many now tied to issues of state security), this has not led to the wholesale abandonment within these institutions of practices and discourses that articulate with the field of *da'wa*.[8]

As a result, many of those active in *da'wa* do not categorically identify the state as an enemy or antagonist. Rather, among those involved in the movement one finds a plurality of arguments and opinions in regard to the state, ranging from outright condemnation to distrust and ambivalence to indifference.

While in practice *da'wa* may entail an oppositional stance regarding the state in the various ways I have described, this type of public does not in its present form play a mediatory role between *state* and *society*. In other words, the practice of *da'wa* does not take place within, nor does it serve to uphold, that domain of associational life referred to as civil society. While the nation inhabits the *da'iya*'s discourse as a necessary object of reflexive self-identification, it is as an object embedded in (and subordinate to) the broader moral project of an Islamic *umma*. As performatively enacted within *da'wa* discourse, the nation's claims on loyalty and identity are relativized in light of the demands of this moral project, one understood to be irreducible to the concepts of territory, ethnicity, and collective historical experience upon which the nation is founded. In this regard, when asked where the effect of the *da'wa* movement was most evident, rarely did those I worked with refer to "Egyptian society" or "the nation." Instead, when indicating the positive impact of *da'wa*, most of them would refer to specific popular neighborhoods where in their view residents' neighborly conduct accorded with Islamic standards: assistance was provided to the sick and poor by the community, those behaving improperly (e.g., drinking, swearing, fighting, or dressing inappropriately) were readily confronted by community members, and most people prayed and attended mosque regularly. While participants of this movement clearly considered themselves to be Egyptian citizens, they also cultivated sentiments, loyalties, and styles of public conduct that stood in tension with the moral and political exigencies, and modes of self-identification, of national citizenship. In this sense they constitute what I have called a counterpublic.

Dialogic Conditions

Cassette sermons have played a central role in the creation of the public domain I have thus far described. By allowing the sermon to move outside the more rigid framework of the mosque, the cassette medium enabled this oratorical form to become a key instrument of *da'wa*. Traditionally the Friday sermon occurs within a highly structured spatial and temporal frame, as a duty upon the Muslim community as established in the exemplary practices of the Prophet.[9] As a traditional and obligatory component of Muslim weekly routine, the *khatib*'s performance anchors its authority in its location and timing, in the *khatib*'s competent enactment of a tradition-required role as established within the instituted practices of Muslim societies. During the initial years of their use, taped sermons permitted an infinite extension and replication of this performance but remained beholden to it, a mere supplement, and not a departure or transformation, of a long-standing authoritative Islamic oratorical form. Sermon speech was now displaced outside its assigned locus but only as a re-

Fig. 1.5. Muhammed Hassan's "Death of the Apostle," probably the most popular tape in Egypt in the 1990s.

presentation of an original founding performance to which it referred. However, with the increased popularity of such tapes, the development of tape markets, new practices of listening, association, commentary, and tape-based *khutaba'*, taped sermons have become increasingly independent of the mosque performances which they reproduce: a signifying practice of their own, related to but not subsumable within mosque sermons.

Notably the fact that taped sermons may be widely distributed and repeatedly listened to has meant that they are now subject to a higher degree of public scrutiny both in terms of scholarly rigor and general argument, and this has further accentuated the dialogicality of the practice. For example, in late 1996 the widely acclaimed Egyptian *khatib* Muhammed Hassan put out a re-recording of his most popular sermon, on the death of the Prophet, which was prefaced by a studio-recorded apology for certain errors in *hadith* citation he had made in the original. The question of an error in a *khatib*'s discourse, which previously would have been solely a concern of religious specialists, has become a topic to be addressed before the mass public of sermon listeners, many of whom now take an active interest in these issues. In this way *khutaba'* are now subject to assessment by increasingly well-informed audiences.

Hassan's apology illustrates the way the contemporary sermon, as the privileged rhetorical form of the *da'wa* movement, has come to reflect the set of de-

Fig. 1.6. A tape on "Washing and Enshrouding the Corpse," by Shaykh Ismail Humaidi.

mands placed on it by the new public context wherein it now circulates. Within this sphere, taped sermons mediate multiple forms of argument and contestation. *Khutaba²*, for example, not only provide a critical commentary on trends within society, actions taken by the state, and international events seen as important to Muslims but also commonly draw attention to erroneous positions put forward by other *khutaba²* or religious scholars. Likewise sermon listeners frequently disagree with arguments made by *khutaba²*, both in content and style. Many of my informants, for example, felt that Shaykh Kishk's style, at the time of the regime of Anwar Sadat (1970–1981), of criticizing public figures directly and openly was a violation of the ethics of public criticism within Islam. This points to another level of dialogue mediated by cassette sermons, namely, that tapes frequently serve as a catalyst for arguments between listeners, including arguments about the responsibility of the *khatib* in relation to the state.

The Virtues of Civic Debate

Within *da²wa* literature, and among the young men of my study, the performance of *da²wa* is understood to be predicated upon a prior cultivation of the virtues.[10] As I describe in this section, the virtues play more than an instrumental role in relation to the activity of *da'wa*: as with other practices that Muslims consider duties placed upon them in their status as Muslims—such as prayer, fasting, or alms giving—*da'wa* has conditions of enactment that include a particular set of virtues. In this sense it is both an activity that upholds the possibility for the virtuous performance of other Muslim practices and a virtuous act in itself.

As mentioned earlier, much of the Islamic print and audio media today concerns the qualities the *da'iya* must possess in order to perform the civic duty of *da'wa*. Such discourses fall within a long and continuing tradition of Islamic ethical and pedagogical writings on the virtues that uphold individual piety. Where they depart from this tradition is in addressing the virtues not simply from an ethical point of view but also from a rhetorical one, as conditions for the persuasiveness of speech and action within the public domain of *da'wa* practice. Virtuous conduct, in other words, is seen by the movement both as an end in itself and as a means internal to the dialogic process by which the reform of society is secured.

The virtues of the *da'iya* as cultivated and practiced within daily life tend to be understood behaviorally, as disciplined ways of being and acting, ways for which the body's performances and expressions constitute an integral part. They are cultivated gradually through disciplinary practices, such as prayer, Quranic recitation and memorization, *hadith* study, listening to sermons, as well as by undertaking the practice of *da'wa* itself.

Some of the virtues specific to the practice of *da'wa* are addressed within *da'wa* literature under the term *adab al-da'wa* (loosely, etiquette of *da'wa*) and include those qualities that ensure the orderliness and civility of public interaction. Much of *da'wa* print and cassette media focus on the task of developing these qualities. A tape by the popular *khatib* Wagdi Ghunim entitled "The Muslim as *Da'iya*" provides the listener with a list of thirteen requirements to which every individual in his or her capacity as *da'iya* must adhere. Among these he includes friendliness, gentleness of speech (*al-rifq wa al-lin*), temperateness, as well as neatness and cleanliness. Throughout the tape Ghunim provides numerous illustrations of how *da'wa* should be undertaken, as in the following:

> Say we are sitting and speaking with a fellow who then gets upset. I'll say to him, O' my brother, may God be generous with you; O' my brother, may God open your heart and mine [*yashrah sadrak wa sadri*]. Or say someone is sitting nearby smoking a cigarette, and then comes and offers you one. Take advantage of the opportunity. Don't try to take the pack of cigarettes away from him. No. *Da'wa* always entails politeness [*adab*]. Say to him: O' Brother, may God restore you to health. I ask God that you stop smoking. May God protect your chest [*sadrak*] from your act.

The prior cultivation of such virtues as friendliness, temperateness, and gentleness of speech ensures that *da'wa*, as a public act, be conducted in a calm, respectful manner, protected from the kind of passions that would vitiate the act and the social benefit it seeks to realize. The *adab* of *da'wa*, in other words, entails not a simple suppression of the passions but their moderation or attunement in accord with an authoritative model of the virtues. A speech devoid of passion —what Muhammed Hassan, referring to certain modern media style, calls "cold culture [al-thaqafa al-barida] addressing only the intellect [al-adhan]"—lacks the rhetorical force to move the moral self toward correct behavior—the central aim of daʿwa public discourse. The men I worked with sought to achieve this attunement through disciplinary techniques including listening to cassette sermons, Quranic recitation, mosque lessons, and the ongoing practice of daʿwa itself.

Also necessary for the practice of daʿwa is the virtue of courage (shajaʿa). Indeed, courage was one of the qualities most often cited by the men I knew in identifying the excellence of a particular daʿiya. The exemplary figures here are again the khutabaʾ. One of the most commonly mentioned attributes of a true daʿiya-khatib is his courage to speak the truth in the face of the very real danger of arrest and torture by the Egyptian state. Tales of Shaykh Kishk's feats of courage while in prison, including standing undaunted before attack dogs brought to his cell, are widely known and frequently recited by daʿwa participants. In addition, many of the young men I knew in Cairo cited a lack of courage as largely responsible for the failure of people to enact daʿwa, and they worried that Egypt would become like the U.S. where (as they had heard) no one dares speak or take action in public on the behalf of others out of fear.

The virtues of sincerity (ikhlas), humility (khushuʿ), and fear of God (taqwa or khauf) are also frequently associated with the performance of daʿwa and are given great emphasis in sermons and manuals on the practice. As elaborated within classical Islamic moral doctrine, these dispositions endow a believer's heart with the capacities of discrimination necessary for proper moral conduct and reasoning. In the rhetorical context of public deliberation discussed here, this understanding has implications for both speaker and listener. For the speaker's discourse to result not merely in abstract understanding but in the kind of practical knowledge that impacts on how one lives, the discourse must be imbued with those virtues that enable it to reach the heart of the listener. Alternatively, from the listener's perspective, without having first imbued the heart with the requisite emotional dispositions he or she will be incapable of actually grasping and digesting what is at stake in the discourse. The virtues, that is, are a condition for both the effectiveness of the daʿiya's utterance and the listener's audition. As affective-volitional dispositions sedimented in one's character, they form the evaluative background enabling one to act and speak reasonably and effectively within the public realm.

The kind of public arena that has been created by the daʿwa movement in Egypt is both normative and deliberative, a domain for both subjection to authority and the exercise of individual reasoning. As I have argued, it is less an empirical structure than a framework for a kind of action, one intertwining moments of learning, dialogue, and dispute, as practices necessary for the moral guidance of the collective. In this sense we can see that one does not undertake sermon audition and the associated practices of *da'wa* with a preformed or unchanging set of interests and goals. Rather, one comes to acquire an understanding of the good and the virtues that enable its realization in the course of participation in this domain. This learning is not simply a process of acculturation nor of ideological indoctrination insomuch as both these notions fail to capture the extent to which one's participation within this arena necessarily involves practices of argument, criticism, and debate. Although some shared orientations and languages are a prerequisite for this type of public engagement, and one participates with the assumption that there is a proper and divinely sanctioned form of life to which one aspires, this does not imply a uniformity of thought and action. Rather, the aim is to uphold those practices understood to be essential to an Islamic society, practices whose proper form, however, must be continuously determined by public acts of guidance, argument, and discussion by all members of the collective.

My argument is that we should not view *da'wa* as simply an Islamic rendition of the normative structure of the public sphere, one enabled and produced through an incorporation of Islamic symbols and culturally grounded frames of reference. To focus solely on the process through which the concepts and modular institutions of modern liberal-democracy have been inflected by non-Western traditions is to fail to explore the often parallel projects of renewal and reform launched from within the conceptual and practical horizons of those traditions. This is not to reinstate the binary of tradition and modernity but, on the contrary, to point to processes that cannot be adequately analyzed via this opposition. It is for this reason that I find unhelpful discussions of contemporary Islamic movements in terms of the notion of an "invented tradition," a modern institution in the guise of an ancient one. An approach adequate to the historical form I have described here will necessarily understand tradition as a set of discourses and practices that, while enabled by modern power, nonetheless articulate a politics and a set of sensibilities incommensurate with many of the secular-liberal assumptions that attend that power. Of course, the Islamic tradition is not the only framework within which the actions of the participants of the *da'wa* movement are meaningful, nor is it by any means the most powerful.

Lastly, note that while debate and argumentation are ascribed a salient role within the Islamic counterpublic examined here, this does not imply a move toward liberalism. Indeed, many of the social norms which the practice of *da'wa* has helped to strengthen in Egypt would not be acceptable for most liberals. *Da'wa* is not geared toward securing the freedom of individuals to pursue their own interests but rather their conformity with a divine model of moral conduct. This model is not static, a labor of timeless repetition, but instead involves a historical dynamism derived precisely from the sort of practices of reasoning and argument foregrounded by the *da'wa* movement, practices that depart from the assumption of an authoritative corpus by which the status of current practices may be assessed. Thus, while liberals may wish to take strong issue with this tradition of public reasoning, those concerned with democracy and its cultural conditions and possibilities in the contemporary world will want to pay close attention to religious movements of this kind.

Notes

This essay is based on fieldwork carried out in Egypt between 1994 and 1996 with the support of dissertation grants from the Wenner Gren Foundation for Anthropological Research and the Social Science Research Council. An earlier version of the article appeared in *Cultural Anthropology* 16, no. 1 (2001): 3–34.

1. On the history of the concept and practice of *da'wa* and its classical origins, see al-Faruqi 1976; Mendel 1995; and Waardenburg 1995.

2. The most comprehensive discussion of the history of the Muslim Brotherhood remains that of Mitchell 1993 [1969].

3. Al-Banna understood the nation-state as a legitimate object of political loyalty and identity but one secondary to and subsumed within a broader community based on adherence to Islamic practice: "The bone of contention between us [the Muslim Brotherhood] and them [Egyptian nationalists] is that we define patriotism according to the standard of credal belief, while they define it according to territorial borders and geographical boundaries" (al-Banna 1978, 50).

4. The *sunna* refers to the prophet's exemplary behavior as witnessed by a contemporary of the prophet and passed down by means of an authoritative chain of transmitters.

5. I am not suggesting here, of course, that the *da'wa* movement is founded upon a notion of gender equality. On the contrary, participants in the movement and the *khutaba'* who are its most prominent exponents generally emphasize a certain patriarchal order as essential for the organization of social and individual conduct in a Muslim society. That said, the actual practice of *da'wa* has been one area where women's subordinate status has been relatively attenuated, and where many of the arguments commonly used to disqualify women from domains of political and religious authority are seen not to apply. As Saba Mahmood (2005) has noted in her rich study of pious women in Egypt, one of the apparent contradictions of the *da'wa* movement lies in the fact that while its participants generally insist on the subordinate status of women within social life, the movement itself has been more open to women's participation than have other currents of the broader Islamic revival.

6. My own discussion of the Islamic public sphere overlaps with Armando Salvatore's (1998) at numerous points, especially in his exploration of the interlinkages between the ethical and deliberative aspects of this sphere. Where our analyses differ lies in Salvatore's greater emphasis on the techniques and practices of mass publicity, and particularly styles of media commoditization and consumption, as enabling conditions for the emergence of this sphere. Also, for an insightful analysis of the market in Islamic commodities in Cairo, see Starrett 1995.

7. A comparison can be drawn here to the Turkish government's decision to forbid the reading of the Quran in schools: the worry is that such training will orient schoolchildren favorably to projects that would challenge the secular basis of the state and its goals of Europeanization.

8. The Egyptian state, it should be mentioned, has established its own institutions

of *daʿwa* as part of its attempt to purge this field of currents not supportive of its modernizing policies. Numerous governmental associations operate under the rubric of *daʿwa*, including a college at al-Azhar University (*Kulliyat al-daʿwa*), which was set up in 1977 to train *khutabaʾ*, as well as more than a dozen state-affiliated institutes of *daʿwa* (*maʿahud al-daʿwa*) aimed at nonspecialists (i.e., people who are not *khutabaʾ* by profession but wish to study Islam in order to serve the community). These efforts, however, have failed to dislodge the popular perception that the activity of *daʿwa* is incompatible with the directives and policies of the state. This judgment is evident in the contrasting appellations popularly used to distinguish preachers who categorically support government positions from those willing to question state policy: while the former are referred to by the more neutral designations *khatib* or *imam*, the latter are generally granted the more commendatory status of *daʿiya*.

9. The most thorough and interesting anthropological work on Islamic sermons are those of Patrick Gaffney (1994) and Richard Antoun (1989).

10. For an extensive discussion of the use of cassette sermons within practices of ethical discipline, see Hirschkind 2001, 1999.

References

Antoun, Richard. 1989. *Muslim Preacher in the Modern World: A Jordanian Case Study in Contemporary Perspective.* Princeton, N.J.: Princeton University Press.

al-Banna, Hassan. 1978. *Five Tracts of Hassan al-Banna (1906–1949).* Translated by Charles Wendell. Berkeley: University of California Press.

Eickelman, Dale. 1999. Communication and Control in the Middle East: Publication and its Discontents. In *New Media in the Muslim World: The Emerging Public Sphere,* ed. Dale F. Eickelman and Jon W. Anderson, 29–40. Bloomington and Indianapolis: Indiana University Press.

———. 1992. Mass Higher Education and the Religious Imagination in Contemporary Arab Societies. *American Ethnologist* 19 (4): 643–655.

al-Faruqi, Isma'il. 1976. On the Nature of the Islamic Daʾwah. *International Review of Missions* 65:391–409.

Gaffney, Patrick. 1994. *The Prophet's Pulpit: Islamic Preaching in Contemporary Egypt.* Berkeley: University of California Press.

Hirschkind, Charles. 2001. The Ethics of Listening: Cassette-Sermon Audition in Contemporary Cairo. *American Ethnologist* 28 (3): 623–649.

———. 1999. Technologies of Islamic Piety: Cassette-Sermons and the Ethics of Listening. Ph.D. dissertation, Johns Hopkins University.

Mahmood, Saba. 2005. *Politics of Piety: The Islamic Revival and the Feminist Subject.* Princeton, N.J.: Princeton University Press.

Mendel, Miloš. 1995. The Concept of "ad-Daʿwa al-Islamiyya": Towards a Discussion of the Islamic Reformist Religio-Political Terminology. *Archiv Orientalni* 63:286–304.

Mitchell, Richard. 1993 [1969]. *The Society of the Muslim Brothers.* Oxford: Oxford University Press.

Salvatore, Armando. 1998. Staging Virtue: The Disembodiment of Self-Correctness and the Making of Islam as Public Norm. In *Islam-Motor or Challenge of Modernity.* Vol. 1,

Yearbook of the Sociology of Islam, ed. Georg Stauth, 87–120. Hamburg: Transaction Books.

Starrett, Gregory. 1995. The Political Economy of Religious Commodities in Cairo. *American Anthropologist* 97 (1): 51–68.

Waardenburg, Jacques. 1995. The Daʿwa of Islamic Movements. Actas, XVI Congreso Union Europeenne d'Arabisants et d'Islamisants, 539–549.

2   Future in the Mirror: Media, Evangelicals, and Politics in Rio de Janeiro

Patricia Birman

When the world's biggest football stadium, Rio de Janeiro's Maracanã, hosted a non-Catholic religious event in the mid-1980s it was clear that something in the city's traditional religious patterns was changing. Even so, it had taken several years for the stadium to be used in this way by what was then still a low-profile religious group, the Universal Church of the Kingdom of God (UCKG), but was to become a regular feature of the city's religious and political calendar, closely connected with the incursions of the church into the media. The first "evangelical" television channel was launched in 1990, operated by the same Universal Church, and today religious mega-shows in football stadiums have become routine events throughout Brazil. The TV channel of the Universal Church regularly broadcasts coverage of gatherings around the world, placing heavy emphasis on the lavish extravagance that accompanies them. The Pentecostalist UCKG revealed an early attraction toward the spectacular in its religious, social, and political enterprises, and has never denied its penchant for turning disused cinemas, theaters, and nightclubs into religious spaces. This tendency has been intensified by its keen pursuit of the triple formula of stage, pulpit, and virtual space.

A decade later the sheer number of religious rituals presented as public shows is a clear sign of the social, religious, and political importance that Pentecostal churches have now attained in Brazil, clearly demonstrating the new religious face of what was once the "largest Catholic country in the world." Along with an increasingly diverse range of religious actors, it appears that public acknowledgment of one's evangelical affiliation is becoming ever more frequent. Thus evangelicals are not just growing in number but are also growing in visibility through the adoption of new ways of displaying their faith. Their presence is felt in performative settings in politics, musical events, religious spectacles, on television, and in both the secular and the religious press. In turn, this visibility is translated into a close connection between personalities linked to the Universal Church, public shows, and the media.

Between the 1980s and 1990s Brazil's identity as an essentially Catholic coun-

Fig. 2.1. Interior of the Cathedral in Rio. Postcard sold in the cathedral's shop.

try underwent significant upheaval. The continuous expansion of evangelical religiosity in the media has given rise to new perceptions among much of the populace concerning "who we Brazilians are"—a "we" that historically took pride in its status as a Catholic nation. The country's religious self-awareness has been transformed by the gradual inclusion of this large group of believers who project an image of themselves largely alien to the nation's dominant self-image. Focusing, in particular, on the Pentecostal media, this chapter provides an account of some of the religious strategies that have wrought this turnabout in the position of these churches in Brazilian society, as well as changes in what it means to be an "evangelical" or indeed a "Brazilian" in contemporary society.

I shall describe how the Universal Church of the Kingdom of God has worked to integrate the secular and religious media into its ritual and symbolic activities inside and outside the church. I intend to show that its ritual activities only take on their full meaning when they start to appear in TV shows as well as the secular and religious press. Exploiting the media's resources seems to be an essential aspect of the church's religious activities, including exorcism. This is part and parcel of the symbolic transformation of its followers from poor individuals to shareholders in a stock of social and religious capital that affords them effective means of claiming greater recognition and rights in society.[1]

These media incursions become even more interesting when we recall that one of today's key issues concerning the religious in public space is the contested nature of its frontiers with other domains such as politics and economics.[2] These frontiers provoke tension and conflict and also form the subject of academic discussion insofar as a relatively natural cross-section of social phenomena and their forms of comprehension have been thrown into doubt, questioning the possibility of any stable or universal definition of where religion starts and where, for example, politics or economics ends. The boundary blurring produced by contemporary phenomena provides us with a rich field for debate.[3] These spectacular events can be seen to threaten a world order conceived in terms of a normative European ideal, upsetting the balance between reason and emotion, the religious and the secular, the public and the private.

By generating new meanings for religion and politics, while simultaneously mixing the religious with business and finance, the Universal Church creates spectacular events and media personalities out of the ways in which various distinct levels and spheres are associated, hierarchized, altered, and extended. Despite its quasi-official standing and its enduring links with the Brazilian state, the Catholic Church has so far failed to match the success of the Universal Church in projecting a close association between stage, pulpit, and the virtual domain on such a grandiose scale, a success that indeed now threatens the Catholic hegemony.

A Holy War or an Industry of Miracles?

References to religion in the public sphere have acquired an ever higher profile in Rio de Janeiro, as well as in other Brazilian states. The reasons for this are many and complex. New religious cults and movements appear to be linked to a weakening in the unifying and collective value of Catholic beliefs within national society.

Catholicism remained the country's official religion until the last decade of the nineteenth century, when a republican constitution was promulgated. But despite its official status, the Catholicism that developed in Brazil always paid limited attention to the dissemination of Christian values. From the early colonial period on, it adapted itself to the beliefs and practices of a local population made up of Amerindians, African slaves, Portuguese heretics, and exiled criminals who inhabited what many contemporary observers—especially Jesuits—labeled the "Tropics of Sin" (Vainfas 1998). This adaptation resulted in one of the most persistent features of the colonial church in Brazil, namely, the difficulty it faced in achieving any effective and exclusive conversion to its doctrine. Despite enjoying its status as the official state religion, the Catholic Church was unable to eradicate non-Christian values and practices (Birman and Leite 2000).

Given this situation, the Eurocentric hierarchy of the church sought to maintain its place within the local power structures by turning something of a blind eye to the non-Christian practices of landowners and the populace in general. Thus, as Gilberto Freyre (1963 [1938]) argued, the church long remained subordinate to the representatives of the Portuguese crown[4] and to the dominant order in the slave enclaves, particularly the sugar cane plantations of the Northeast. From the viewpoint of most of those taking part in Church rites, the

Catholic God seemed quite at ease with the innumerable syncretic gods (or *santos*) and the myriad other supernatural beings attributed with the power to intervene in their lives. The relative unimportance attached to theological rigor underlay an ethical order in which good and evil were far from clearly defined. Saints and demons lived cheek to cheek, and the capacity of these spirits to resolve daily problems was a crucial aspect of people's lives (Birman and Leite 2000). Until quite recently, to be Brazilian naturally meant to be Catholic but with the leeway to participate in other beliefs, such as spiritualism, umbanda, or candomblé—the so-called Afro-Brazilian cults. This theme of syncretism and its deep ties to the myth of nation building was enhanced by the idea that Catholicism—like an enormous nationwide umbrella—provided shelter for other minority religious beliefs.

However, the Pentecostalists and above all the Assembly of God, a frankly minority group, did not try to assume the universal and all-embracing position of the Catholic Church. For decades they grew *hidden from the world*, challenging the Catholic environment as numerous small-scale "communities of believers" set apart by their different lifestyle. The UCKG, however, contrary to these groups of believers (*crentes:* a term used in Brazil in a slightly disparaging sense), has entertained more universalist pretensions: it therefore tends to clash head-on with the Catholic Church as a national and international hegemonic force. The lifestyle of the new believers far more closely approximated that of Catholics.

By confronting the possession cults through its routine practice of exorcism and the identification of cult divinities with demons, the Universal Church opposes the syncretic bonds that made the Afro-Brazilian cults Catholic, albeit nonpracticing. It vigorously denounces Catholicism for its idolatry and complacency in the face of the many forms of evil, and it has launched a *holy war,* as the Universal Church calls it, against the umbanda and candomblé cults, encouraging the destruction of images and performing exorcisms to *cast out* the demons possessing individuals who attend their meetings.

This war against the demonic forces of evil pursued by churches rooted in the popular sectors has shaken a range of assumptions embedded in the everyday life of a once stable and harmonious Catholic country. In an oblique way the use of exorcism in the war against syncretic gods has constituted a broader attack against the general premise of tolerance which survived under the protective mantle of Catholicism, a tolerance based on the popular sectors—or those among them who profess a religious affiliation—accepting a relationship of dependency on a superior and all-encompassing Church.[5] This association between tolerance and syncretism was a core element in imagining the nation as a hierarchical but harmonious whole. As a result, there have been strong reactions from various sectors of Brazilian society against the Universal Church, whose propagation of a theology of prosperity and a belief in social mobility challenges the idea of poverty as natural and ineradicable and thus threatens the stability of the social hierarchy.

Reaction came initially from the communications media because of the competition from the church (it bought a concession for a TV channel) as well as from the country's elite, whose ethos has long been predominantly Catholic. An intense campaign was waged against the Universal Church by the nominally secular media, implicitly reflecting a Catholic sensibility wounded by the methods of this emerging cult, that is, its combining of televised shows of exorcism with successful business through an "industry" of miracles and the payment of a tithe by its followers. Bishop Macedo, the church's religious leader, was depicted on TV as someone who cheated the poor by promising wealth and happiness. Dishonesty and charlatanism were associated with the economic exploitation of the poor through false promises.[6]

Fight the Devil, Fight Poverty, Fight the (Sources of) Disorder

One of the ways in which the campaign against the Universal Church was waged was through the systematic exploitation of a supposed similarity between religious intolerance and the violence of the poor, associated territorially with *favelas* (squatter settlements) and the outskirts of Rio, regions held to be dominated by drug trafficking. The 1990s saw the media giving ever more prominence to the theme of violence in society, primarily linked to what was once called the dangerous classes, a group that for a time included the Pentecostals, identified on the whole with the poor and especially with followers of the UCKG. The most powerful media companies sustained a discussion on violence between 1993 and 1994 that placed heavy blame on the Pentecostals (among other people) for causing a historically unparalleled internal split among the poor. By conducting a holy war against traditional and popular religiosity, they were accused of producing intolerance and religious conflict where before there had only been peace.[7] The media at this time treated the two social factions shown to be the sources of disturbance and conflict—the poor and the fanatical Pentecostals from the UCKG—as one and the same. Coincidentally these two groups came from the same urban regions. In Rio de Janeiro the denunciation of religious violence combined with virulent attacks on another faction widely accused as a source of danger and violence in the city, namely, the young funkies, blacks who came from *favelas* and urban outskirts and invaded the more upper-class areas of the city.

In Rio de Janeiro the media has played a key role in building up an image of a violent city, producing highly emotive imagery in which blacks and youths are shown to be the most dangerous source of social upheaval. Identifying these youth groups with drugs has consolidated a terrifying profile of the poor zones in the imaginations of the city's respectable and conservative classes. The criminalization of poverty among youths, especially the young funkies, which initiated in 1992 and 1993,[8] reveals a profound shift in the city's social imagination. In the case of Rio de Janeiro these polemics also frequently reinforce a projection of social polarization in terms of urban geography. In other words, the public image of poverty has strong territorial implications. The impact of this endless stream of TV imagery contributes to a strong and widely held belief that we are in a state of war fought between the police and so-called heavily armed bandits and drug dealers—and this is accepted as legitimate (cf. Leite 1997).

However, the association cultivated in the public imagination between a holy war waged by Pentecostals from the UCKG against other cults and the drug war or the general image of a city at war failed to last very long. Not only were the violence and social conflicts disassociated from the churches but the churches became—with the willing complicity of the media—a new instrument for pacification.[9]

In recent years, then, the image of a peaceful society, which historically coincides with the predominance of a Catholic ideology espousing the unity of the Brazilian people, has lost ground to a disruptive and conflict-ridden image. This in turn has been absorbed into Pentecostalist discourses concerning the paths to salvation, which proclaim Pentecostalism as one of the sources of peace in the world. New entrants are transformed into people capable of combating evil with the Word and through Exorcism. Those who have taken Jesus into their hearts are the new messengers of Good, Peace, and Prosperity.

Faith Is the Star

One of the clearest signs of the religious transformation in society—and of its impact in the communications media—is the importance given to the religious affiliations of public figures. Mention of the religious beliefs (or virtues) of media personalities has increased both in frequency and importance. This has become a form of identification demanded by the faithful themselves as part of their religious practice, a tendency reinforced by the media, which consequently reifies identity-based categories in its reporting and analysis of conflicts. The media also ensures that, in addition to declaring their religious affiliation, these personalities openly display their emotional responses to the events in which they participate. Hence the value produced by insistent reference to evangelicals as social actors in religious/political interactions is not entirely innocuous. The media, in fact, creates ways of identifying attributes that guide, institute, or simply reinforce certain modes of religious intervention in society.

A wealth of reading matter has been published by the media on the significance of being evangelical in today's Brazil. During the initial stages of the Pentecostal explosion in the media, led by the UCKG, the Pentecostals were branded as a disruptive presence, provoking conflict and disorder. As this image was transformed, so was their name, and from "Pentecostals" or "believers" they became "evangelicals." This originally more restricted term, used to refer to denominational groups, is used indiscriminately today by all groups.[10] The Universal Church of the Kingdom of God, formerly designated as "Pentecostal," also began to call itself "evangelical," thereby aligning itself with the broad spectrum of Pentecostal or Protestant-leaning groups now existing in Brazil.

As a direct result of this overall process, images of Pentecostalism are negotiated with the media as a function of the social, economic, and political power
these religious groups have acquired. To understand how this new political-
religious role was created, we need to recognize—aside from the work of the
media—how the "evangelicals" have continually presented themselves as those
who bring Good in contrast to other social groups that operate diabolically
through the use of violence. The association of Good and Peace against Violence was exploited to an extreme in media terms by an evangelical segment
that opposed the Universal Church and joined the "civil religion" movement
organized by nongovernmental organizations (NGOs) against violence in the
city.[11]

The inclusion of prayers has become a standard and expected feature of public events, such as meetings or political manifestations. What these contexts
have in common is the assertion of religious language as a means of expression
and interaction in public encounters. Catholicism's loss of status as the natural
expression of religion in Brazil, and the concomitant loss of a widely shared
sense of religious belonging, has therefore had the effect, among other things,
of proliferating identity-based demands for a space to be seen and heard in the
public sphere. The Word, testimony, and exorcism transform individuals and
the interactions between them: religious language is being disseminated as a
form of changing the world by acting positively within social circles. This explains a sharp increase in the number of religiously inclined individuals and
organizations that, based on an evangelical identity, appear in public to propagate their faith. Athletes of Christ, one of the oldest, is an association of soc-
cer players, while other groups have been formed by prisoners, congressmen,
businessmen, women, union members, youth groups, and various sporting
groups who turn faith and its propagation into a means of raising their profile
in society.

A recent example of the importance of media impact involved the kidnapping of the daughter of a television mogul. An enormous spectacle was created
around an event broadcast live on national TV—indeed, the moment the young
woman was freed by her captors and returned to the family home achieved in-
credible audience ratings. The importance this spectacle attained was not only
owing to the emotional moment when she was reunited with her family and its
sentimental exploitation by the TV cameras. Another important aspect was the
young woman's declaration that the happy ending to this violent episode was
entirely owing to her faith in God: the Holy Spirit had given her the means to
communicate with the bandits and alter their behavior. Her faith had modified
their interaction to such an extent that they treated her well and called her
"princess." In her later interviews she not only spoke about the importance of
her love of Christ, she also blamed her kidnapping on an unjust social system.
Thus her liberation was presented live as testimony of the moral and pragmatic
value of faith, capable of interfering in social affairs, altering the course of a
violent situation by moving even the most hardened criminal, a product of both
a lack of faith and an unfair social system. Quoted below is a front-page report

from one of Rio's newspapers, *Jornal do Brasil*, printed under the headline "A Star Is Born":

> The scene was worthy of the last episode of a soap on the SBT channel, fully in keeping with the style of its Mexican melodramas: the rich girl at the door of the mansion, with a crowd to witness the happy ending. The heroine manages to escape unhurt, declares that she forgives her kidnappers and blames their act on an unjust and corrupt economic system, claims that her drama ended because of divine intervention and rebukes her millionaire father for not having the faith of God in his heart. It was phenomenal: in São Paulo alone, 37 million viewers followed, mesmerized, yesterday afternoon's TV broadcast of the happy ending to the kidnapping of Patricia Abravanel, 23 years old, daughter of TV presenter Silvio Santos. (*Jornal do Brasil*, August 29, 2001)[12]

The article continues with the girl's declaration: "My father needs God. He who has God suffers not."

The evangelical groups—which include the more populist Pentecostal churches and others in which the middle classes predominates—have claimed to be the builders of social well-being and peace in the midst of a society riddled by conflict and violence. Expanding images of testimony and the production of political/religious events that enhance the evangelical presence as a social actor in public spaces are held to offer new ways of enabling the moral and social management of society. The testimony of faith reinforces the evangelicals' claim to represent the only social and political alternative capable of achieving the moral reunification of the nation, together with the still possible and desirable approximation of Brazil's rich and poor. The evangelical groups appear in public as the social actors most clearly qualified to mediate through *good* and the exorcism of *evil* in the zone of conflict, violence, and poverty in which the urban areas of the major Brazilian cities have become submerged.

Chains of Faith and Transnationalization

The UCKG is one of the most impressive examples of the growth in religious media in Brazil. It has run its own TV channel since 1990, plus a weekly newspaper, which imitates the formulas used by the national press with a print run of 1.18 million copies, a website on the Internet, and a monthly magazine of high journalistic quality.[13] In addition, it has created a new style of presenting itself, revealed in the behavior of its pastors as well as the events it produces.

As a part of this evangelical movement, the UCKG has been developing its own concept of integration in society. Today it attracts followers by offering them a vision of the world and a political religious practice presented both as an individual solution to their problems and as a model of social integration. The new evangelicals acquire the chance of frequenting a wider world with fewer barriers and more paths to prosperity. Alternative scenes are shown, accentuating the church's links to other continents, with centers of power and wealth in national and international contexts.[14]

The first entry to this new world is provided by rituals delivering the incomer from evil forces. Emphasis is given to the follower's potential to transform his or her social and economic life by exorcising his or her demons.[15] In a report from the UCKG newspaper entitled "Unburden: Against the Threats of Demons," we read:

> Bishop Romualdo reminds us that people must struggle not against the flesh but against the evil spirits that relentlessly use people to transform life into a living hell.
> —Your struggle is not against your boss who refuses to give you a raise, against your husband's mistress, or against your neighbor, it is against the demons who take possession of people's bodies and make everything in life turn bad. . . . The demon takes possession of body and mind, bringing illness, fear, doubts, anxiety and much pain. Then there are also external problems, which include financial difficulties, for example. . . . Thus, either the person rids him or herself of the demon, expelling it from his/her life, or he/she will be defeated by it. (*Folha Universal,* September 15–21, 2002)

However, the exorcism activities of the church are not the monopoly of its pastors. The latter share this task with church lay members who, by offering a ritual service to their neighbors and families, connect them to the evangelicals' benefits. These connections produced by local mediation to some extent recover traditional religious repertoires and transform them within a process extending from the small mediator to the church to large-scale media events. Exorcism thereby attains different meanings as it progresses from the local scene, associated with violence and poverty, to a broader public space, where the UCKG follower is endowed with an image that associates him or her with symbolic capital and prosperity.

The ritual activities of the UCKG establish a certain continuity with possession cults. Its followers can appropriate its rituals as a form of interlocution with *santos* and *orixás* (Afro-Brazilian deities) from the Afro-Brazilian cults. The intense circulation of objects and images within its rites enables its followers to recognize within them a power of agency and intervention in social life that was previously attributed to possession cults alone. The ritual practices of the Universal Church are especially suited to the interests of women, many older women having been sacerdotes in possession cults in the past. As evangelicals, these women are able to retain their powers of religious mediation among their family and friends, protecting them through the rituals of the church and integrating them within the latter's campaigns as benefactors of its circuits of donations and miracles. Acting in this way, they succeed in attracting their relatives into the church. In turn they are able to join other social networks, participating, as we shall see, in their rituals, "chains," and "campaigns" (Birman 1998).

The followers are invited to become part of a national and transnational religious community. The most recurrent image of this religious community is provided by photos of multitudes packing stadiums in different capitals around the world. Here it is worth noting that in the 1990s the UCKG started to construct *cathedrals of faith*—spaces capable of holding gigantic crowds.[16] By showing these enormous spaces and the expression of faith by the multitudes that fill them, the UCKG associates the image of a community of believers with the religious conquest of the world:

> "The UCKG helps Christianity grow in Japan," "The UCKG packs a stadium in Cape Verde," "Worship of the Holy Spirit gathers multitudes," "The Holy Spirit attracts a multitude," "More than 40,000 people gather in the Amazon for an Afternoon of Songs."

These reports are accompanied by images of endless public spaces being occupied by enormous crowds of people from all over the world: scene after scene of rituals where the principal performer is, according to a common expression, "a multitude united in one faith," wherever it may be—in Africa, Bahia, or Portugal, to cite some recent examples.

In Brazil, especially in the various state capitals, the use of stadiums in the organization of events is relatively frequent and always a subject of press interest. Occasionally the Universal and the Catholic churches are shown to wage a public battle for attendance numbers and a more successful spectacle in terms of public and social impact. The following example comes from the Rio newspaper *O Globo:*

> "Universal Church cult packs Maracanã." The Universal Church's "Night of Abraham" vigil filled the Maracanã and Maracanãzinho stadiums with around 175,000 people according to the Rio Department of Sports (Suderj). The celebration lasted 20 hours, with no set time for ending, and attracted convoys of buses from as far away as Chile. The meeting of singing priests from the Catholic Church on the October 12th holiday, the day of the Madonna of Aparecida, was attended by 161,722 people. (October 30, 1999)

Part of the strategy of both churches is to turn these spectacles into events that can be consumed by both the secular and religious media, as proof of the church's importance in society. As in the above case, this does not involve the different media controlled by the church simply "broadcasting" material of purely news interest. The church's media are themselves involved in the production of these events, and there is a constant effort to create rituals that reveal the church to the world in a spectacular way. Likewise there is an emphasis on reports, such as those quoted from the *Folha Universal,* that enhance the spectacular dimension of its rituals:[17] "The UCKG gathers together more than 60,000 people in Lisbon" reads the front page headline in the July 29 edition of the *Folha Universal,* showing photos of a football stadium packed with followers. The article continues:

> The Belenense football stadium in Lisbon, capital of Portugal, wasn't big enough to accommodate all who wanted to participate in "The family at the foot of the cross," the faith meeting held by the Universal Church of the Kingdom of God.

More than 60,000 people filled the stands, and, in the words of the local press, the UCKG won the hearts of the Portuguese people.

Another set of rituals is developed through the creation of benefits, which are derived from transnational circuits. The members of the religious community are constantly invited to take part in *chains* and *campaigns* to obtain access to spiritual, social, and economic resources on a national and international level.

For many years the Universal Church promoted ceremonies and spectacles projecting the image of a large-scale community linked to a world of well-being and power. One of the objectives was to obtain miracles by means of a "Fire of Israel" in Jerusalem. This ritual was realized through the progressive and continuous uniting of permanent and occasional church followers in a chain. The campaign theme and the encouragement to participate were announced in the church over a period of months. To participate, a cash donation had to be made in an envelope containing requests for miracles. These offerings and requests were to be taken on a pilgrimage by the church's bishops to the Holy Land, there finally to be "burned" in a ritual ceremony conducted by church dignitaries. This immense bonfire—the result of the efforts of thousands of followers, and the everyday bricolage of biblical images registering different stages of the journey—sent thousands of envelopes (containing money at the beginning of the trip) and requests for miracles up into flames. Held by the church in a world center of pilgrimage, the ceremony was made possible by the donations of its loyal followers. As a ritual, the Fire of Israel can be compared to a kind of *potlatch* with its redistributive network of miracles. Images of the Fire of Israel were subsequently broadcast on the church's network (TV Record).[18]

With the media's help, an image was projected enabling all the participants in the "chain" to be present anywhere the chain went, through the donations they had made, accumulated, and displayed at the bonfire held in the presence of the bishops. By becoming the world focus of all biblical religions through its followers' petitions and the meeting of its bishops, the Universal Church once more produced a spectacular and iconic event that unified followers around the world. The spectacle demonstrates the grandiose scale of the offering—its opulence and its transnational character. The total audience was much larger than the number of people actually present. Presence was both real and virtual, in the same way that the church worked to ensure that the benefits would reach all types of participant.

The Fire of Israel highlighted the link between the church and the Christian Holy Land, as well as bringing together the church's followers from a number of different countries via the pilgrimages. Hence their TV network broadcast an image of the Universal Church "occupying" the sacred center of the whole Christian world. One headline describing these pilgrimages announced, "The Universal Church occupies Israel." According to Edlaine de Campos Gomes,

This report covered a pilgrimage of some 1,300 followers of the UCKG from various countries (Brazil, Portugal, Argentina, Paraguay, Mexico, Belgium, France, Africa and England) to the Holy Land, emphasizing that the dream of every Chris-

Fig. 2.2. Reproduction inside the Cathedral of "The Fire of Israel." Photograph by
Edlaine Gomes. Used by permission.

tian is to travel to the Holy Land. . . . On this occasion, Bishop Macedo was received by Israel's Minister of Tourism, demonstrating his intention to bring "tens
of thousands of people" to Israel every year. . . . On its twentieth anniversary, the
UCKG took 2,300 followers from all over the world to Jerusalem. (Campos Gomes
2001, 23)

The production of this kind of chain is part of the routine activities developed
by the church in all its branches. Even if these productions do not all achieve
grandiose moments equal to the ceremonial burning of the petitions in Israel,
most are structured around some sort of spectacle involving the church's followers, or at least their donations, achieving what could be termed a politico-
religious appropriation of the world. As a consequence, the world is visually depicted as a huge area of circulation, connected to important social circles on a
global scale. The image of the church occupying an ever larger public space is
complemented with another image of its followers as people possessing reli
gious attributes that enable them to take part in this expanded world. Embodying the image of an exemplary follower, the pastors are people who act on a map
extending far beyond the local or even the national. The world in which they
live is offered to them through territories in the process of being conquered by
new branches of the church. In a UCKG report entitled "Brazil exports pastors,"
we read:

Can anyone imagine a Brazilian evangelizing in Russian, Afrikaans, Japanese or
any of the many other dialects existing on the planet, like Zulu for example? Liv-

Fig. 2.3. Close up Fire of Israel. Photograph by Edlaine Gomes. Used by permission.

ing among people with completely different customs, with almost prehistoric hygiene? Confronting racial segregation or totalitarian regimes?

A pastor's wife gives her opinion in the same report:

> I thought we were going to the interior of Brazil, but when he told me we were going to Africa, I didn't know what sort of culture we would find. My children were small, 6 and 8 years old. I was aghast. How could we go to an unknown land, far from family and friends? But then something spoke in my heart: Leave your family and go to this land you don't know, and I will make of you a conqueror. (*Plenitude* 2000, 33)

The Perfect Pastor

In October 2002 Rio de Janeiro, for the first time, elected a senator of the Republic who belonged to the Universal Church: Bishop Marcelo Crivela, nephew of the church's supreme mandatory bishop Macedo. Bishop Crivela's public image focuses on the way he gave direction to his life as a faithful executive of the UCKG's projects. His obedience to the plans of the church transformed him personally, while enabling his church to grow. At the same time his work picked him out as someone capable of bringing the country's poverty to an end. His biography, published in *Folha Universal* and partly reproduced in the electoral propaganda broadcast on radio and television, tells us:

> Bishop Marcelo Crivela has possessed the wish to evangelize since the age of seven, when he first became acquainted with the Bible. Trained in civil engineering and a member of the UCKG from the outset, he coordinated public works undertaken

by the Church in Brazil and in foreign countries, including the Catedral Mundial da Fé in Rio de Janeiro, involving more than 55,000 square meters of construction.

As a pastor, he presented the program "Vigésima Quinta Hora" on the television network Record for more than three years. When the work of the Universal Church started in Africa seven years ago, Pastor Marcelo Crivela was sent there with his wife, Silvia Jane and their three kids. Africa is made up of countries with tribal practices, where parents can legally sell their daughters and men can have several wives. There are 34 million people infected with the HIV virus (figures from the WHO [World Health Organization]) and the influence of sorcerers, witches, sects and even black magic is huge. It was here in this hostile environment, filled with prejudice, wars and poverty, that Bishop Marcelo lived, preaching the equality of all men, opening churches for black people, bringing the word of God to places where white people did not go, like the Soweto township in Johannesburg, South-Africa. The Universal Church grew and spread all over the African continent, establishing hundreds of support centers for the poor, supplying meals, medical and hygiene services, as well as spiritual guidance. Today there are 700 UCKGs in 23 countries. (*Folha Universal*, August 19, 2001, 7[A])

The missionary work described here is pursued in a continent, Africa, which has always haunted the Brazilian cultural and religious imaginary. As a sacred place for the possession cults, Africa constituted one of the mystical sources of Brazilian nationality. In this way it supposedly contributed to the "formation of Brazilian culture" in its origins in relation to Europe. Africa is presented as historically related to a large number of national symbols, like *feijoada, candomblé,* and *carnaval* (Fry 1982).

From the Pentecostal perspective, this African heritage—a much-desired object in the dispute between religious movements in Brazil, Latin America, and the United States—becomes synonymous with a backward civilization. From being the object of missions sent out by European and American Christian churches, religious Brazilians for the first time assign themselves the role of missionaries. The flow between donors and receivers of spiritual gifts is redirected through the UCKG's mediation. The country's change of image disseminates beyond the Pentecostal environment: instead of being the contributor to African tradition in the positive elaboration of its image, Brazil becomes the source of the moral and material progress of a "backward" continent.

This investment in Africa is largely made by Brazilian pastors, coming from subaltern social groups, many of them practically illiterate or often from a low social and cultural level, former habitants of the periphery or the suburban zones (Freston 2001). A barely hidden pride among persons of different social origins can be perceived when they comment on the fact that this religious "conquest" of other continents has been carried out by a national church. "Although Bishop Crivela was adapted and devoted to the work he went to do in the African continent," continues his biography,

in 1999, Bishop Macedo sent for him as he had an important mission for him to undertake: to coordinate an agro-industrial kibbutz in Irecê, in inland Bahia, which would help improve the *nordestino*'s quality of life. In this region of the country, poverty has destroyed families and children starve on a daily basis, as a consequence of the climate and the lack of any policy to overcome the problems brought by the drought. The *Projeto Nordeste* [Northeast Project] was launched, a revolutionary idea, whose first pole, the *Fazenda Nova Canaã* [New Canaan Farm], is proving that if subsoil water is used, the rough land of the *sertão* becomes very fertile.

Bishop Crivela is presented in both the religious and secular media as the person responsible for creating and running a project claimed to be one of the best prospects for the country: the New Canaan Farm, part of the Northeast Project.[19] According to the information in the media and the accompanying video (for sale in the church), the Northeast Project realizes the greatest dream, historically associated with peasant land reform movements: the transformation of land devastated by drought and poverty into a prosperous estate, with verdant fields, modern machinery, and high-tech irrigation-systems. The video depicts people in a condition of absolute poverty in melodramatic scenes, portrayed in black and white—the popular aesthetics of starvation—who are subsequently depicted in a state of bliss, belonging to a prosperous community, living and working at the New Canaan Farm.

To turn this dream into reality, Bishop Crivela brought the necessary social and economic knowledge from Israel—how to organize a kibbutz—along with irrigation technology. The communitarian and religious resonance of these images acquires even more force when applied to the clearest symbol of poverty in the country: the *Nordeste*, a region of drought and starvation, with Brazil's highest rates of illiteracy and infant mortality.

The dream of "giving land to those who work," deeply anchored in the political and religious imaginary of the peasant movements, is thus rechanneled. When supported in the past by the Church of Liberation, this dream was little more than a messianic vision for the popular movements; it was the struggle against the agrarian oligarchies and an unjust social structure,[20] to realize one of God's wishes, disrespected by the greed of men. But from now on, the triumph of the "oppressed people" had to be accomplished through other means. The biblical image of the right to the land would be attained through a concrete development project: the practical and financial mobilization of the community directed by the UCKG was to be the new route to social integration.

The video tells us it was Bishop Crivela's initiative to create the New Canaan Farm; likewise it was he who left Brazil to learn about the Israeli technology in order to organize a kibbutz and construct an irrigation system. Israel, the nation built in a desert, prospered in the hands of a "chosen people, the people of Israel," and can now offer Brazil—to those who belong to the same biblical community—a model of work, sociability, and technology.

According to the video, Bishop Crivela was able to raise the means to buy the hectares in this wretched desert by becoming an *evangelical singer:* he made a CD and sold millions of copies.[21] Buying the CD, *a romantic gospel,* is also advertised as a way of participating in the project's development. Followers interested in collaborating can become part of this campaign by donating money in a curious way: by presenting a special "project associate" card in those super-markets indicated by the church, members of the UCKG can donate a percent-age (which is not shown) of the costs of their monthly supermarket shopping to the New Canaan Farm and the Northeast Project. This act of participating is thus a way of becoming part of a community, which strives to achieve its income redistribution project on a national level. The image projected by the New Canaan Farm, associated with the bishop, is also that of a prosperous coun-try without poverty, constructed by the church and above all by those followers possessing a sense of business, evangelical initiative, and practical solidarity.

Bishop Crivela's biography also depicts, therefore, the image of a successful entrepreneur. The Universal Church offers this particular ideal-type "business-man" to all those who liberate themselves and gain the chance to win prosperity through active participation in its rituals. These converts, men of God, aim to-ward a social position whose supreme value is given by the three positions of entrepreneur, pastor, and benefactor of the nation.

In effect, the success of the UCKG and its public image is associated with innumerable symbols that belong to the world of business and global values. It has broken into public space through a type of religious participation that raises the church's pastors and followers to another social level: having once been the poor hidden away in the parish, they now become people perfectly adapted to a world hitherto reserved only for the rich and the well-off. Through its mega-shows, the church has created nontraditionalist images of a religion practiced by the urban poor and its followers (seen until then as common people), defini-tively disassociated from the stereotypes associated with the "Brazilian people," a suffering population according to the long cultivated paternalistic view of the Catholic Church. It has thus created, on the one hand, a new image of the religion of the poor and, on the other, a new image of the poor as religious, belonging to the church. The way pastors and *obreiros* (church attendants or workers) are dressed is highly significant: they wear uniforms designed to make them look just like "executives" belonging to the international business world, or like politicians in Brasilia: white shirts, black ties, costumes, and the like.

The ideal UCKG member is someone who belongs to the world in another way. Through the church the person's presence gains forms that contrast with the marks of poverty, above all the territorial marks, which possess an enormous power of provocation. The UCKG follower tries to move in social circles formerly considered the monopoly of the rich. Removed from their traditional circle, and therefore from a ghetto image of the poor, its members are invited to broaden their horizons and participate in other national and international circles, asso-ciated with the world of the rich. To achieve this opening, the church's rituals and the media have been mobilized. The UCKG started to frequent transnational circles and public spaces of high social and political visibility, such as television and newspapers, which have become increasingly amenable to showing scenes of the UCKG Pentecostals.[22]

The production of spectacular events by the Universal Church has been fundamental to the creation of this new religiosity, based on the transformation of the image of the poor into individuals who possess the same social and symbolic resources as any other citizen belonging to more favored social groups. The image of the church as a rich and prosperous institution is built with the images seen of its followers in the media, principally its pastors. The church has created a space in the media enabling religious ways of connecting with secular space, seen as a source of power and prestige. In this context, the media exploit religion as a pragmatic means of elaborating plans for the future and insertion into the world. Above all, the Pentecostals appear as being well connected in society and politics, so that, by reflection, the followers of this religion move up the social ladder.[23]

This accumulation of social capital is offered through the media as an asset held by the followers of the UCKG. To be evangelical means to have the right to join social life in a dignified manner, to participate in a redistributive network of miracles in the social and political spheres. To be an evangelical from the UCKG therefore implies permanent witnessing of spectacular events and testimonies. Finally, to be an evangelical in the Universal Church is also to be a mediator who restores the social links between the poor and the global world of power and business.

Notes

I am grateful to Birgit Meyer and Annelies Moors for their invitation to take part in the seminar "Religion, Media, and the Public Sphere," which gave me the opportunity to write this paper. Their questions were decisive for improving it. My thanks also to Marc Piault, David Lehmann, and Martijd Maaden, whose combined efforts toward a better translation were also enlightening and helpful.

1. The UCKG explores the possibilities enabled by electronic media in order to achieve what Appadurai (1996) calls a "work of imagination," involving the opening of new possibilities and new fields where the "self" and its imaginary worlds can be built.

2. There is a reason why Pierre Brechon (2000), analyzing the huge spectacles promoted by the Vatican, such as the "World Youth Meeting," or the "Pope's Visit" to Russia, Kazakhstan, Africa, and so on, refers to these as political-religious events. They cannot be characterized as "religious" within a "secular" space; rather, they are both simultaneously. This double dimension makes it difficult to conceive such events according to any single interpretative key, whether as "religious" or "political," or even as local or global, public or private. And certainly the spectators employ various keys simultaneously to classify these spectacular events. The multiplicity of feelings and the fluidity of their boundaries must be recognized in order to understand them.

3. Talal Asad (1999, 192) suggests: "The categories of politics and religion turn out to implicate each other more profoundly than we thought, a discovery that has accompanied our growing understanding of the powers of the modern nation-state. The concept of secular cannot do without the idea of religion. True, 'the proper domain of reli-

gion' is distinguished from and separated by the state in modern secular constitutions. But formal constitutions never give the whole story. On one hand, objects, sites, practices, words, representations—even the minds and bodies of worshipers—cannot be confined within the exclusive space of what secularists name religion. . . . On the other hand, the nation-state requires clearly demarcated spaces that it can classify and regulate: religion, education, health, leisure, work, income, justice and war."

4. This was because of an arrangement that granted the Crown unusually autonomous control of the Church.

5. As Luis Eduardo Soares (1992) points out, the Universal Church, in conducting its war against the possession cults, introduces a more egalitarian dimension into religious disagreement among the popular sectors: through their "holy war," the attacks are substituting a contest among equals in place of the hierarchical relationships associated with allegiance to the Catholic Church.

6. The clashes between the UCKG and the media, and the accusations that developed in 1994 and 1995, have been examined in an article by Birman and Lehmann (1999), and by other authors such as Giumbelli (2002) and Mariz (1999). See also Eric Kramer's (2000, 58) analysis of "religious freedom" in Brazil, which interprets these same events from the juridical and political viewpoint. According to Kramer, "Harmony among religious groups is taken to be a normative part of the public order guaranteed by the Brazilian Constitution, not something that is negotiated through public discourse. Religious conflict at the level of ideological and vocal opposition is unacceptable" (ibid.).

7. There are various interesting articles about the so-called holy war during this period, some of which align themselves with those who "combat" Pentecostalism by adopting a sociological slant that fails to disguise the militant position of the authors. Others seek to respond to the social controversy created by critically analyzing it and putting the "holy war" into the context of current social processes. For this kind of approach, see, among others, Soares 1992; Sanchis 1994; Giumbelli 2002; and Birman and Lehmann 1999.

8. For an analysis of discourse relating to violence in the city, see Leite 1997; on the relations between narratives about violence and youth manifestations, see Novaes 2000 and Herschmann 2000.

9. Recent research supplies us with the following data concerning the evangelical share of television airtime: "In the first semester of 2000, the evangelical TV programs in the city of Rio represented around 105 hours weekly of TV time—in 1992 this number was less than 50. . . . Every day, churches lease airtime, buy radio stations and seek more and more space on the media. . . . Currently around 10 percent of the content transmitted weekly by Brazilian TV is produced by churches and evangelical organizations. In this way the 'evangelicals' not only guarantee for themselves 10 percent of Brazilian television programming, their participation as social actors in the rest of the media is also growing" (Fonseca 2003).

10. Cecilia Mariz called my attention to the indiscriminate use, including by researchers, of the term "evangelical" for groups that had previously been referred to as "Pentecostals," distinguishing them from the denominational Protestants such as the Baptists or Presbyterians.

11. The start of the 1990s saw the emergence of a Presbyterian pastor, Caio Fabio, in Rio de Janeiro who presented himself as a religious leader disposed to interfere pragmatically in situations of conflict with drug traffickers in the city, as well as having allied himself with NGOs involved in voluntary work in the *favelas* and in antiviolence campaigns. At that very time the UCKG set up its own charitable organization which com-

peted within the evangelical movement, on the one hand, while at the same time helping to dissipate the image of a religion that "exploits" the poor (cf. Birman and Leite 2000).

12. All original Portuguese sources have been translated by the author.

13. Among the evangelical churches, the UCKG, together with the Assemblies of God, has the highest number of readers, even though its followers have the lowest level of education (Fonseca 2003).

14. See Corten and Marshall-Fratani's (2001) analysis of the media and the processes involved in creating "new imagined communities" linked to Pentecostalism in Latin America and Nigeria.

15. Possession cults are an even more popular topic on radio programs, and references to the person being *occupied* by demons are more frequent than in the church's newspaper, *A Folha Universal*. In the latter we find an effort to introduce a psychological mediation between one's mind and the devil. As a consequence, an increasing importance is attached to a closed inner self. As Birgit Meyer (2002) points out in reference to Pentecostalism in Ghana: "The notion of personal choice and responsibility is increasingly popularized, without however neutralizing the notion of possession. What is emphasized here is the ideal of a closed inner self which is not vulnerable to any intruding, evil forces from outside (from witchcraft to local village—or family-based gods, from Mami Water to Indian spirits, from ancestors to black magic) and able to act in a morally sound way on the basis of inner reflection."

16. André Corten (1997) describes the elaboration of these new spaces as the emergence of a new religious imagination that creates an equivalence between the temple and the stadium as a consequence of the proximity of the religious activities to a "show."

17. See the Folha Universal's headlines from August 19, 2001, and the photos that invariably accompany the reports.

18. According to Daniel Dayan (2000), what we have here is the broadcasting of an event produced by using certain procedures similar to those found in "rituals," as formulated by Victor Turner: one builds a moment of suspense, a "suspension" of commonplace time, during which the very matrix of the programs is altered, a collective participation of the spectators who generally attend these events, a constructed image that is produced in real time, binding the event together with a narrative that accompanies things as they happen. Events/spectacles produced in this way cross territorial frontiers but at the same time reinforce social links on a local scale: they involve various small gatherings that watch the same event together. The "community" used as a reference for the ritual are all these combined, participating simultaneously on various planes.

19. During a period of electoral campaigning, the propaganda of Bishop Crivela as candidate to the Senate was based primarily on presenting the Projeto Nordeste and the images of the Fazenda Nova Canaã.

20. I am indebted to Regina Novaes for pointing out the powerful mythical dimension of the theme of land possession appropriated by the Universal Church. In her work Regina Novaes (1997) analyzes the religious foundations of the claims for social "rights" in peasant movements. Pursuing the same topic, Otávio Velho has pointed to the importance of biblical culture in the peasant movements, in which the notions of *cativeiro* (servitude) and "The Beast" are found in continual transformation. Liberation from the lands of servitude is thus a classic theme with a powerful religious and political evocation. See, too, Lehmann 1996, on religious transformation in Brazilian popular culture.

21. This CD, entitled *The Messenger of Solidarity*, has sold more than one million copies and was awarded with a "diamond record." As a follow-up, Bishop Crivela launched two other CDs: *Vamos irrigar o sertão* (Let's irrigate the backlands) and *Irmão do Sertão*

(Brother from the Backland), produced by Line Records, owned by the UCKG (see Pinheiro 2002).

22. I refer especially to the strong reaction of the traditionally Catholic elite to the eruption of the Universal Church on the national scene and in the media, emphasizing how much this is against the Catholic hegemonic ethos (see Birman and Lehmann 1999). The media's "good-will" seems to be more akin to a "surrender," deriving from the fact that it is unable to ignore the political events in which social actors claiming to be "evangelicals" participate.

23. Although I have no data to support my conjecture, I believe that the expansion of the Universal Church has created a small labor market for its followers, above all for pastors, preachers, and church attendants. Connections with a wide range of social welfare projects, as well as association with the state and business enterprises, have produced job opportunities for its members. The spread of the evangelical gospel was also based on offering new opportunities for joining the labor market.

References

Agier, Michel. 2000. *Anthropologie du carnaval: La ville, la fête et l'Afrique à Bahia.* Paris: Edition Parenthèses.

Appadurai, Arjun. 1996. *Modernity at Large. Cultural Dimensions of Globalization.* Minneapolis: University of Minnesota Press.

Asad, Talal. 1999. Religion, Nation-State and Secularism. In *Nation and Religion: Perspectives on Europe and Asia,* ed. Peter van der Veer and Hartmut Lehman, 178–196. Princeton, N.J.: Princeton University Press.

Birman, Patricia. 1998. Les cultes de possession et le pentecôtisme au Brésil: Passages. *Cahiers du Brésil Contemporain,* no. 35/36: 185–208.

———. 2002. Nasce uma estrela: Estratégias de reconhecimento espetacularização da violência. *Cadernos de Antropologia e Imagem* 14 (1): 57–69.

Birman, Patricia, and David Lehmann. 1999. Religion and the Media in a Battle for Ideological Hegemony: The Universal Church of the Kingdom of God and the TV Globo in Brazil. *Bulletin of Latin American Research* 18 (2) (April): 145–164.

Birman, Patricia, and Marcia Leite. 2000. Whatever Happened to What Used to Be the Largest Catholic Country in the World? *Daedalus: Journal of the American Academy of Arts and Sciences* 129 (2): 271–290.

Bréchon, Pierre. 2000. Médias et religions: Une question trop occultée, des problématiques en débat. In *Médias et religions en miroir,* ed. Pierre Bréchon and Jean-Paul Willaime. Paris: Press Universitaire de France.

Campos Gomes, Edlaine de. 2001. *Catedrais e as representaçoes da memória na Igreja Universal do Reino de Deus.* Rio de Janeiro, Programa de Pós-Graduação em Ciências Sociais da Universidade do Estado do Rio de Janeiro (PCIS/UERJ), mimeo.

Corten, André. 1997. Pentecôtisme et politique en Amérique Latine. *Problèmes d'Amérique Latine* 24 (January–March): 17–31.

Corten, André, and Ruth Marshall Fratani, eds. 2001. *Between Babel and Pentecost: Transnational Pentecostalism in Africa and Latin America.* Bloomington and Indianapolis: Indiana University Press.

Crivella, Marcelo. 2000. Golpe Baixo. *Plenitude* 75 (21): 17–20.

Dayan, Daniel. 2000. Les grands événements médiatiques au miroir du rituel. In *Médias et religions en miroir*, ed. Pierre Bréchon and Jean-Paul Willaime, 245–264. Paris: Press Universitaire de France.

Fonseca, Alexandre. 2003. *Evangélicos e mídia no Brasil*. Rio de Janeiro: Bragança Paulista, EDUSF.

Freston, Paul. 2001. The Transnationalisation of Brazilian Pentecostalism: The Universal Church of the Kingdom of God. In *Between Babel and Pentecost: Transnational Pentecostalism in Africa and Latin America*, ed. André Corten and Ruth Marshall-Fratani, 196–213. Bloomington and Indianapolis: Indiana University Press.

Freyre, Gilberto. 1963 [1938]. *The Masters and the Slaves. 2nd English ed.* New York: Knopf.

Fry, Peter. 1982. *Para inglês ver: Identidade e política na cultura brasileira*. Rio de Janeiro: Ed. Zakar.

Giumbelli, Emerson. 2002. *O fim da Religião: Dilemas da liberdade religiosa no Brasil e na França*. São Paulo: Attar.

Herschmann, Micael. 2000. As imagens da galera funk na imprensa. In *Linguagens da Violência*, ed. Messeder Pereira et allii, 163–196. Rio: Rocco.

Kramer, Eric W. 2001. Law and the Image of Nation: Religious Conflict and Religious Freedom in a Brazilian Criminal Case. *Law & Social Inquiry: Journal of the American Bar Foundation* 26 (1): 35–62.

Lehmann, David. 1996. *Struggle for the Spirit: Religious Transformation and Popular Culture in Brazil and Latin America*. Oxford: Polity.

Leite, Marcia. 1997. Da metáfora da guerra à mobilização pela paz: Temas e imagens do Reage Rio. *Cadernos de Antropologia e Imagem* 4 (1): 121–146.

Mariz, Cecília. 1999. A Teologia da Batalha Espiritual: Uma Revisão da Bibliografia. *Revista Brasileira de Informação Bibiográfica em Ciências Sociais* 47 (1): 33–48.

———. 1998. Rede Vida: O catolicismo na TV. *Cadernos de Antropologia e Imagem* 7 (2): 41–55.

Meyer, Birgit. 2002. Pentecostalism, Prosperity and Popular Cinema in Ghana. *Culture and Religion* 3 (1): 67–87.

Novaes, Regina. 2000. Encontros e desencontros entre religião e mídia. *Revista Democracia Viva* 8:3–10.

———. 1997. As metamorfoses da Besta Fera: o mal, a religião e a política entre Trabalhadores rurais. In *O mal à brasileira*, ed. Patricia Birman, Regina Novaes, and Samira Crespo, 81–106. Rio de Janeiro: Eduerj.

Pinheiro, Marcia. 2002. Música religiosa: Circuito de produção e consumo. Instituto de Filosofia e Ciências Sociais, Universidade Federal do Rio de Janeiro. Unpublished.

Sanchis, Pierre. 1994. O repto pentecostal à cultura católica brasileira. In *Nem anjos nem demônios: Interpretaçoes sociologicas do pentecostalismo*, 34–63. Petrópolis: Vozes.

Soares, Luiz Eduardo. 1992. *A guerra dos pentecostais contra o afro-brasileiro: Dimensoes democráticas do conflito religiioso no Brasil*. Rio: Cadernos do Iser.

Vainfas, Ronaldo. 1998. *Trópico dos pecados: Moral, sexualidade e Inquisição do Brasil*. Rio: Nova Fronteira.

Velho, Otavio. 1987. O cativeiro da Besta Fera. *Religião e Sociedade* 14 (1): 4–27.

3 Communicating Authority, Consuming Tradition: Jewish Orthodox Outreach Literature and Its Reading Public

Jeremy Stolow

What has happened to religious authority in the information age? In our current communications geography of electronic flow, expanding participation, and deregulated markets it is becoming increasingly difficult to locate the institutional and symbolic boundaries demarcating not only the private and the public but also the secular and the sacred dimensions of communities and nation-states. For some, these shifts are responsible for the emergence of new classes of interpreters empowered to appropriate religious systems of signification to their own, autonomous ends. From another vantage point, claims about the democratization of religious communication, the display of popular self-determination, and the exercise of "consumer sovereignty" are overshadowed by the image of religious elites entrenching their authority in new ways, as they extend their presence across the horizon set by advanced communications technologies and as they draw new populations into their orbit. However, in order to determine whether religious authority is waxing or waning, diversifying or centralizing, we must first decide what are the signs of religious authority and how they are made visible. How, we should ask, are these signs produced and reproduced, put to use, naturalized or fought over within specific locales and among particular social groups? And to what, exactly, does the term "religious authority" refer in the context of the mediated channels of communication shaping our present?

I pose these questions from the vantage point of my engagement with a cultural field encompassing an English-language Judaica publishing house, ArtScroll Publications, its constellation of authors and editors, and some of its local sites of textual consumption. Since the early 1980s ArtScroll has sprouted from its roots in Brooklyn, New York, to become one of the leading Judaica publishers in the English-speaking Jewish world—in the U.S., Canada, the U.K., Australia, South Africa, and the anglophone community in Israel. ArtScroll furnishes this international market with a broad range of materials of interest to Jewish readers, including bilingual Bibles, liturgical and Talmudic texts, translations of rabbinic literature, and, increasingly, nonreligious texts such as popular history books, biographies and memoirs, youth literature, novels, pop-psychology and self-help books, and curriculum materials for primary Jewish education.[1] This press merits our attention not simply as a successful publisher of Jewish literature but also for its close links with *Agudat Israel,* one of the preeminent *haredi* (or so-called ultra-Orthodox) political and cultural movements of the past century.[2]

Haredism is a relatively recent tendency within Jewish society, stressing punctiliousness and stringency in the observance of Jewish law, intensive study, and obeisance to the authority of an exclusive rabbinic elite.[3] Among the various, often competing communal associations, schools, and political organizations that make up *haredi* society, *Agudat Israel* represents a leading voice in the defense and cultivation of *haredi* social spaces, cultural practices, orientations, and values. As a loose coalition of rabbis, politicians, and community activists, *Agudat Israel* situates itself at the vanguard of a global effort to secure a place for "Jewish authenticity" in a fragmented and hostile modernity, addressing the community of God's Chosen People, who apparently have failed to recognize themselves as such.[4] In key respects, the cadre of authors and editors associated with ArtScroll has defined its work as an extension of this dialogue with fellow Jews. These cultural workers are not distinguished for having produced major theological statements or new interpretations of canonical Jewish texts. Rather, within the specific context of English-speaking Jewry, their avowed aim is to extend and to legitimate the interpretive and moral framework of the *haredi* world by supplanting what they regard as illegitimate representations of Jewish knowledge, ritual practice, and historical imagination with new translations and representations of Jewish tradition and the Jewish canon in the form of accessible popular texts, authorized and approved by the governing bodies of *Agudat Israel.* In this way ArtScroll can be understood as a vehicle for transmitting the voice of *haredi* authority, for bringing it into the presence of both committed adherents and various categories of outsiders, and for lodging this authority within new spaces of Jewish public culture made available through the medium of popular print.

Unlike other *haredi* presses—of which there are many, and which typically cater to small if loyal clienteles of *haredi* readers—ArtScroll addresses a diversity of audiences within the Jewish world. It has capitalized on a fortuitous opportunity to communicate with broad sectors of the non-*haredi* Jewish population by directing a seemingly unquenchable thirst for "Jewish content" toward *haredi*-oriented print commodities. But how successful is this attempt to constitute a community subject to *haredi* authority through a textual mode of communication? And by what standard should we measure its success? Does the growing popularity of ArtScroll books suggest that *haredi* authors are indeed advancing their hegemony over the English-speaking Jewish reading public? Or might this spread indicate a crisis of legitimacy and control for *haredi* authors, as their books circulate beyond their reach and are put to diverse uses in local contexts?

To answer these questions it is necessary to situate ArtScroll's position in a larger field of cultural production encompassing a range of competing presses and institutions, merchants and customers, and local brokers. A study of this field shows that the ArtScroll authors address non-*haredi* readers without recourse to any of the mechanisms of coercion that sustain the *haredi* society in which they themselves are located (and to which they are beholden), such as courts of religious law or the disciplining presence of *haredi* rabbinic elites as neighbors, teachers, or counselors. Instead, these *haredi* authors are obliged to compete with various contenders for the loyalty and attention of Jewish constituencies, representing the distinct strands of institutionalized Jewish expression, from "modern" Orthodoxy to the *Masorti* (Conservative) movement, Reform, Reconstructionism, secular Zionism, and so on. This competition over access to audiences, and the authority to represent their needs and desires, is most palpably registered in the local contexts where ArtScroll books make an appearance—such as bookstores, synagogues, schools, and libraries—and where the activity of textual consumption is managed by intermediary figures—booksellers, rabbis, teachers, and librarians—who often do not represent *Agudat Israel* and who do not necessarily subscribe to its *haredi* ideology; some, in fact, are quite hostile to it. Lastly, it is evident that within this field the authority of the ArtScroll cadre is attenuated by its very reliance upon the principles of commodity exchange. By addressing non-*haredi* Jews through the medium of the market, they must accept its constraints of competition and financial viability, which among other things grant to consumers/readers a certain degree of sovereignty over the terms of reception and use of ArtScroll texts.

Nevertheless, ArtScroll's success as a producer of popular Judaica literature represents a significant incursion into the non-*haredi* Jewish imaginary. This can be inferred from the practices of consumers, readers, and users who incorporate ArtScroll's print commodities into the habitus of their everyday lives, such as in their performance of liturgical practices or kosher observance. Through the seemingly uncoerced activity of consumption, readers and users succeed in naturalizing ArtScroll texts, among other things, as sources of reliable information and aesthetic pleasure, and as repositories of Jewish tradition. This process of naturalization offers the ArtScroll cadre the opportunity to forge a path, as it were, beneath the surface of Jewish society, and beneath the gaze of many of its more "official" local authority figures. At an even deeper level, ArtScroll's achievements in the market are coextensive with their success in having enshrouded their texts in an aura of "authenticity"—even from the vantage point of those who appear to have little interest in embracing it. To the extent that they are anchored by the authority of *haredi* scholarship and its mechanisms of consecration, ArtScroll books invoke the presence of *haredism* as the sole legitimate expression of Jewish tradition, promulgated by those who have taken the hard road of noncompromise with modernity. And by ceding this ground of authenticity and tradition to *haredi* elites, Jewish constituencies make them-selves available for articulation with distinct political claims within the sphere of *haredi* polemics, and with a cultural politics of authenticity that extends far beyond the *haredi* community.

In the following pages I elaborate this thesis by offering some general reflec-tions on the constitution of modern Jewish public culture, and by considering one local context in which ArtScroll has made its presence felt: in the Jewish community of London, England.

The People of the Book: The Modern Jewish Reading Public

It is common to describe Jewish society and culture as text-centric, and to suggest that Judaism is a "religion of the book," defined by a shared commit-ment to a canon of sacred texts and a privileging of study, textual mastery, and interpretive expertise (see, e.g., Halbertal 1997). This text centrism has for cen-turies been key to the production of knowledge, the consolidation of authority, and the social organization of local Jewish communities.[5] Long before the ad-vent of modern mass communications, mediaeval Jewish society relied heavily on the written word and on the technology of the book for regulating everyday practices, codifying communal norms, and communicating across great dis-tances in the Jewish diaspora. Nevertheless, we must not assume simple conti-nuities between "traditional" society and contemporary renditions of Jewish public culture, which owe their existence to radical transformations in the ar-rangement of markets and modes of participation in communicative practice.

One can, of course, distinguish modern Jewish reading publics in terms of the development of new markets and the willingness and ability of expanding sectors of the nonelite Jewish population to make their demand felt for print commodities. In the aftermath of nineteenth-century revolutions in paper-making and production techniques, the printed word was brought within reach of even those with very modest incomes, and a growing number of Jews were thereby inculcated into new consumption habits of daily newspapers, pulp fic-tion, and other works. This one might surmise from the rapid proliferation of Jewish presses and publishing houses across Europe and in North America in the late nineteenth and early twentieth centuries. But what makes this a distinc-tively "Jewish" imagined community cannot be explained simply by the expan-sion of the book market; nor is it fruitful to interpret the history of these inter-actions through the lens of nation-state-centric narratives of the rise of modern public spheres. Rather, we must attend to its distinct ordering and distribution of the categories of language, literacy, territory, communicational media, ideo-logical formation, and sentiments of collective belonging.

"Traditional" European Jewish society, as it existed for several centuries, was defined by obligatory membership in geographically and legally constricted cor-porate communities, *kehilot*, which sustained a complex web of local traditions and broad, international links of commerce and the exchange of letters (see Katz 1993 [1957], 63–179; Manache 1996). In the context of the *kehila,* Jewish public life was ordered into "a multifaceted and multilingual literary system" (Parush 1994, 6) that anchored cultural practice, political power, and the formation of Jewish subjects in relatively stable institutions of governance. This authority was also recognizable in the hierarchical distinction between the use of *leshon ha-kodesh* (the holy tongue)—the (overtly masculinized) language of liturgy, scholarship, jurisprudence, correspondence, and "official" documents—and Jewish vernaculars (Yiddish, Judeo-Arabic, Ladino, etc.) which were reserved for everyday spheres of oral discourse and popular writing, and which were available to the broad masses of unlearned people (*'am ha-aretz*) and women.[6]

Over the course of the nineteenth century, the great age of European imperial expansion and nation-building, corporate Jewish society became exposed to an evolving set of promises and demands from the project of so-called Emancipation, which aimed to integrate Jewish subjects into the emerging European civil order and to redefine collective Jewish identity on the basis of principles of private confession and voluntary association. A well-known example of the new arrangements that defined Jewish public culture in the wake of these shifts is that of the *Haskalah* (Jewish Enlightenment), an intellectual and cultural movement that first appeared in Germany at the close of the eighteenth century and quickly spread across Europe. In an effort to "rescue" fellow Jews from the privations of corporate life and to bring them into conformity with the exigencies and sensibilities of modern civil society, *maskilim* (adherents of the Enlightenment) enacted a series of revisions to liturgical practice (out of which the Reform movement was born) and amendments to Talmudic scholarship and legal reasoning, based on approaches to the Bible that incorporated the emerging academic discourses of Orientalist historiography and philology. *Maskilim* also waged war on the patterns of diglossia that shaped traditional Jewish society, by promoting the replacement of Jewish vernaculars with European languages-of-state (German, Russian, French), and *leshon ha-kodesh* with a reconstructed, "purified" Hebrew that could be extended into hitherto unfamiliar literary terrains, such as with the translation of European belles lettres and leading scientific and philosophical works of the period (see Bartal 1993; Parush 1994, 1995).

We must be careful, however, not to presume that this public sphere of *maskilim,* schooled in the liberal sensibilities of cosmopolitanism, tolerance, and rational argument, defined a single, centripetal force leading European Jews from communal medievalism to modernity. Nineteenth-century Jewish modernization was, in fact, shaped by considerable differences between national and regional contexts, competing political programs of assimilation and dissimilation (such as Bundism and Zionism), and class- and cohort-specific experiences, a full accounting of which is far beyond the means of this essay. Suffice it to suggest that modern Jewish public culture, in all its variety, shares a common location after the dismantling of the *kehila,* and the circulation of promises, whether near or distant, of a new life in the form of new ideas, new political formations, new commodities, and new relationships with the institutions and technologies of mediated communication. It is only against this broad transnational backdrop of the modern Jewish imaginary that we can discern the significance of the major events that reconfigured Jewish society over the course of the twentieth century, most notably the waves of trans- and intercontinental migration from Eastern Europe, the Holocaust, and the founding of the modern Israeli state.

These cataclysmic events decisively redefined the conditions of possibility for participation in public communication across the Jewish transnation. The adoption of Hebrew as Israel's official language of state, national literature, science, diplomacy, law, and commerce not only materialized the vision of an autochthonous Jewish culture as promulgated by earlier generations of Zionist intellectuals; it also effected a radical displacement of the diglossic hierarchy between uniquely Jewish vernaculars and the traditional language of sacred and scholarly discourse, *leshon ha-kodesh*. The centripetal force of a newly indigenized, Hebrew-speaking public sphere was further entrenched by the decline of other Jewish vernaculars, such as Yiddish, especially in the wake of the destruction of European Jewish communities in the Holocaust. The rising cultural force of Hebrew is aptly illustrated in the case of Jews who emigrated from Eastern Europe to the English-speaking world, and who in successive generations embraced English as their new vernacular.[7] For in order to retain their right of access to public Jewish life, English-speaking Jews have been obliged to acknowledge Hebrew both as the Israeli language-of-state and as the time-honored idiom of scholarly discourse and religious ritual (even if, for many, this recognition does not amount to much more than a symbolic mark of their membership in the Jewish imaginary).

It is within the context of these shifts in Jewish languages and hierarchies of cultural literacy that one can best understand the flourishing of English-language Judaica presses in the twentieth century. Most readily familiar to broad sectors of this reading public, no doubt, are the "mainstream" Jewish presses dominated by a Reform- and Conservative-affiliated intellectual elite. But we must also include here *haredi* publishers such as ArtScroll. This field is constituted through social structures of address commensurate with a reading public that is simultaneously transnational and parochial, diglossic and monolingual. It partakes of a global—and in many respects Israeli-centric—Jewish imaginary, but at the same time it is restricted to the geographic spread of English (and for much periodical publishing, further restricted to specific regional contexts). It is oriented to Hebrew, but principally as a mark of Jewish identity or as a basis for participation in liturgy and ritual practice, and much less as a means of access to works of scholarship, literature, news, or debate. For beneath the diglossic surface of this public one finds a predominantly monolingual readership, as can be surmised from the high demand for Hebrew texts translated into English, or for texts that assist the reader's encounter with the Hebrew original by providing an accompanying English translation, as is the case with much of the ArtScroll corpus.

Reaching the People: The *Haredi* Rescue Operation

If the dispersal of the traditional Jewish corporation and the rise of modern technologies of rapid communication were able to make visible new imagined communities, they also redefined the means of legitimating authority and securing popular support within Jewish society at large. This certainly applies to the case of *Agudat Israel,* a movement that presents itself as a direct legatee of God's covenant at Sinai, and as the bearer of authentic Jewish practice, materialized in standards of observance proposed by the organization's supreme governing body, the *Moetzet Gedolei ha-Torah* (Council of Torah Sages). Nevertheless, it is striking how little this movement shares with the rabbinic elite of the "traditional" *kehila,* which the *Agudah* claims simply to have restored. Instead, like all modern Jewish institutions, *Agudat Israel* encompasses a range of voluntary associations and cultural practices unique to the post-Emancipation period and, more specifically, that were formed as consequences of the Holocaust and the destruction of European Jewish society (see Stolow 2004).

Although one can trace the intellectual roots of Jewish Orthodoxy back to the nineteenth century (if not further), *haredism* really came to prominence in the post–World War II context, which, I have suggested, is defined by the emergence of the new geography of Jewish diaspora inclined toward the English-speaking world, and a secular state organized both ideologically and institutionally as a "Jewish homeland," and heralded as a reversal of the centuries-old condition of exile. Among other things, this new transnational space afforded *haredim* opportunities to form organizational structures to which degree of affiliation would be determined by individuals, and for which distinct rules and directives could be formulated that would be binding upon those committed members alone.[8] On this basis, cadres of *haredi* intellectuals, including those associated with *Agudat Israel,* have sought to reconstitute Jewish knowledge, practice, and belief, as exemplified by their innovation of "unchallengeable" *ex cathedra* pronouncements within the realm of *halakhic* (Jewish-legal) decision making. Thus have the *haredim* secured a formidable presence in the post–World War II Jewish scene, as registered in their scholarship, and also their intensive involvements in Jewish education and welfare provision, kosher certification, and electoral politics, both within and outside Israel.

Such influence can also be measured by the growing participation of *haredi* intellectuals and cultural workers in institutions and practices of mass-mediated communication. In this respect, one must acknowledge the distance of contemporary *haredi* elites from their "traditional" forebears, whose attitude toward mechanical reproducibility was one of guarded suspicion. Of course, despite the repeated complaints registered by rabbinic elites about the dangers of modern media, it is possible to trace a fairly long history of Orthodox involvement in its institutions and technologies. Throughout the nineteenth century an expanding market for print commodities presented Orthodox intellectuals with new opportunities, and new obligations, to rescue "traditional" Judaism from the obloquy heaped upon it by its detractors, and to communicate with followers spread across the transnational landscape of Jewish society. By the early twentieth century Orthodox Jews had become routine producers of daily presses aimed at large sectors of the Jewish population in Central and East Europe. And by the post–World War II period such involvements in the daily press, periodical publications, and other forms of popular literature had increased exponentially, especially in Israel and the United States, the two most important sites of production for Orthodox literature. This growth in production delineates the contours of an expanding *haredi* reading public able to express demand not just for canonical texts but also for newspapers, journals, and popular literature.

But as I have also suggested, these expanding circuits of textually mediated communication cannot be understood without reference to the dissolution of the *kehila* and its customary mechanisms for regulating routine practices and enforcing Jewish law. For post-Emancipation rabbinic elites, therefore, mass communication technologies delineated a new horizon for the exercise of authority, according to which "success" increasingly becomes equated with one's ability to reach out to others and to win their assent. In more recent years, and especially over the past three decades, this principle has been deeply entrenched within *haredi* circles and expressed as a growing concern to proselytize to Jews who are "not yet" *haredim,* known in Orthodox parlance as *tinookot shenishbu* ("children raised in [gentile] captivity"). This preoccupation consists of bringing into the *haredi* fold nonaffiliated or marginally affiliated Jews by inducing them to become *ba'alei teshuva* ("masters of return or repentance"), that is, Jews who will voluntarily affiliate with the *haredi* community, its prescriptions, its discourses, and its cultural practices.

The urge to rescue lost Jews has been institutionalized through sustained efforts at recruitment or outreach or, to use the *haredi* term, *kiruv r'hokim* ("bringing closer those who are far away"). This *kiruv* movement consists of a loose articulation of activists and institutions, encompassing an extensive international network of *yeshivot* (religious academies) catering specifically to *ba'alei teshuva* (most notably, *Aish HaTorah* and *Ohr Somayach,* which both run schools in Israel and in many countries in the diaspora), as well as outreach organizations such as the Central Forum for Worldwide Jewish Outreach, the Association of Jewish Outreach Professionals, or the National Jewish Outreach Program.[9] Within this framework, *kiruv* activists orchestrate a variety of encounters with non-*haredi* Jews through such diverse offerings as Hebrew lessons, public lectures, invitations to Shabbat dinners in *haredi* homes, crash courses in Jewish history, or revival meetings in sports arenas. Unsurprisingly *kiruv* efforts have also been manifested through such channels as radio, audiocassettes, the Internet, and print matter. Although they do not explicitly define themselves as a *kiruv* organization, ArtScroll devotes considerable energy to addressing, and thereby rescuing, lost Jews through the medium of liturgical texts, rabbinic commentaries, and popular literature. To those extents, ArtScroll is a notable example of a textually mediated *kiruv* strategy.

To Capture a Market: ArtScroll in the London Jewish Community

The position ArtScroll commands within the market of English Judaica literature is defined by its success in catering to diverse constituencies of consumers.[10] These groups are distinguishable through their relation to different genres within the ArtScroll corpus. For some, ArtScroll is known as a producer of attractive and well-organized bilingual liturgical texts, most notably the *Siddur* (daily prayer book) and *Chumash* (Pentateuch plus commentaries) (Scherman 1984, 1993). For others, ArtScroll is favored for its growing body of commentaries and rabbinic works, starting with its ongoing project to translate the entire *Talmud*. For others still, the press is associated with a range of ethical works, novels, self-help books, children's literature, histories, and biographies and memoirs (mostly of key figures within the history of *Agudat Israel*), all of which are authorized by established *haredi* rabbinic elites as "Torah-true," as one can note from the frequent presence of *haskamot* (official letters of approbation) in book prefaces, authenticating the texts in question and consecrating them as works with which the devout are permitted to engage. But how successful is ArtScroll in capturing, cultivating, and expanding these distinct market niches? And to what extent does their exploitation translate into success for the ArtScroll cadre in its larger mission of *kiruv*?

It is one thing to suggest that an author is able to craft texts within the constraints of specific genres of writing, and at the same time win the loyalty of consumers. It is quite another to propose that such accomplishments indicate the assent of readers to the author's address and its intentions. Because authors and readers do not normally meet except through the medium of the market and the local institutions that provide for the occasion to consume, notions of authorial intent and reader response are only instructive when they attend to the precariousness of negotiations over textual meaning and authority. This is especially the case for modern Jewish public culture, where such negotiations proceed outside the framework of power and privilege once enjoyed by the rabbinic elites of "traditional" corporate society. The workings of this modern regime of voluntarism are most clearly discerned at the local level, where ArtScroll books make their appearance before consumers within specific institutional settings, and where consumers exercise their demand not simply in relation to authors and their products but, more precisely, in the context of their ongoing relationships with individual mediating figures such as booksellers, librarians, rabbis, synagogue administrators, or educational professionals, as well as fellow consumers.

One such constellation of local relations is the Jewish community of London, where ArtScroll has established a presence in synagogues, libraries, and the retail Judaica book market, most prominently as purveyor of liturgical texts that aim to replace the standard works authorized for use within the United Hebrew Congregations of the British Commonwealth, which have dominated the "mainstream" of Anglo-Jewish Orthodoxy for the past century.[11] Although it is impossible to indicate the precise degree of penetration of ArtScroll books in the London community (such as total sales per annum or frequency of use in libraries), there is a striking pattern of a growing acceptance of the press as a legitimate alternative to the existing English-Judaica literature, despite the presence of a vocal minority who disparage ArtScroll's ideologically motivated translations. Among enthusiasts, ArtScroll's arrival on the scene is understood to have offered a compelling opportunity to counterbalance trends toward liberalism and assimilation, against which the turgid prose of the standard English texts, they claim, offers no compelling remedy. One Orthodox Rabbi, responsible for the incorporation of the ArtScroll *Siddur* into his congregation, explained the importance of ArtScroll in revitalizing the London community in this way:

> The *Masorti* [Conservative] and the Reform movements don't seem to have the confidence or conviction to produce books like ArtScroll. They're always too diffident: "*x* says this and *y* says that." ArtScroll, on the other hand, claim to have produced a *definitive* version. What's better? People won't observe *Pesach* [Passover] if they are presented with twenty opportunities not to observe it. People don't seem to get this message so clearly from Hertz or Singer [the "standard" Orthodox texts].[12]

This claim of definitiveness merits further attention. But first it is necessary to point out that ArtScroll's penetration in the London community has been neither total nor indiscriminate. Rather, it has proceeded along culturally and ideologically circumscribed routes, defined by differences within the community based on religious affiliation, and also by differences of generation, gender, and degree of command of Jewish canonical texts and of the Hebrew language in general. In this respect, significant distinctions may be drawn within the ArtScroll corpus between the demand for liturgical works and for the "nonreligious" texts. For instance, a survey of the spectrum of differently affiliated synagogues in the London area—Liberal, Reform, *Masorti* (Conservative), United Synagogue (mainstream Orthodox), Federation of Synagogues (mainstream but "slightly more Orthodox" than United), Union of Orthodox (*Haredi*), and "Independent" Orthodox—reveals that ArtScroll's liturgical works are most popular among the "mainstream" Orthodox congregations, whereas other non-*haredi* communities (Liberal, Reform, and *Masorti*) show much less interest in acquiring or using them.[13] In fact, beyond the *Chumash*, the *Siddur*, and the *Talmud*, the ArtScroll corpus does not appear to have secured a very strong place in the "mainstream" institutions of the London community. Their various series of popular history, self-help, youth and children's stories, and so on, are less widely known, are not systematically acquired by Jewish libraries (although a scattering of their volumes can always be found), and only rarely are incorporated into formal curricula in Jewish schools.

But no picture of ArtScroll's presence in the London community is complete if restricted to an examination of the established institutions, since it is through the retail book market that the press appears to have made the greatest impact. This is evident from a survey of Judaica bookstores in the London area, which reveals the press's prominence in terms of percentage of total shelf space, the positioning of texts in window and in-store displays, and promotional offerings—most significant, an annual sale organized by the publisher. Although retail booksellers are generally unwilling to divulge specific data about profits, the heavy presence of ArtScroll books in their stores (in several cases, they represented as much as 50 percent of the total stock) is a clear indication of steady demand. Nevertheless here, too, significant distinctions must be drawn within the ArtScroll corpus. Several London-area Judaica booksellers reported only a limited interest in non-liturgical titles among non-*haredi* customers, with the exception of of a few "best-sellers," such as Rabbi Berel Wein's three-volume Jewish history. As for the rest of the booklist, dominated by biographies and self-help titles, its principal customers are characterized by booksellers as either existing members of the *haredi* community or as *ba'alei teshuva* "looking for background information" or "impulse shopping," as one merchant put it.

These observations suggest that ArtScroll has won the loyalty of certain categories of consumers and users, but the ability of the press to dominate this market is restricted by the institutional affiliations of Jewish groups within the London community, and by the attitudes of local authorities toward the press and its various genres of writing. In this regard, it is noteworthy that rabbis, librarians, booksellers, and educational professionals play a key role in enforcing the distinction between the "religious" texts, which they often praise as "valuable additions," and the other works on the ArtScroll booklist. Many of these non-*haredi* local brokers speak quite disparagingly of the history and self-help books in particular. One librarian, responsible for stocking and maintaining libraries at two Orthodox synagogues in London (both of which happen to use the ArtScroll *Siddur*) put it this way:

Any thinking, modern, educated Jew finds the whole ArtScroll ethos extraordinarily banal and sanitized. I think most people are aware of that. But again, they accept that because of the parallel benefits of information that the books contain, and that they're generally well presented and well argued, and have a lot of useful material in them. So for example, the ArtScroll books on particular topics, like *kashrut* [kosher laws], or even explanations of parts of the service, stuff like that—all these specific books which give information about *halakhic* matters or liturgical matters—generally speaking, they're quite reasonably received as being informative. The stuff on history is what people find the least interesting. I mean, I find it all amazingly bland and repetitive. Rabbis are seen in a uniformly pink glow; their human complexities are just not addressed in the ArtScroll texts. You can substitute one rabbi for another, and you could almost say the same about all of them.

And the stuff for young couples—the relationship books—that's amazingly banal. It's obviously written mainly for *yeshiva bochurim* [religious students], who don't know anything about girls. That comes through very clearly.[14]

A partial opinion, no doubt. But one must not underestimate the influence librarians, booksellers, rabbis, and other intermediaries enjoy over "common" readers. Through policies of acquisition and distribution, whether formal or informal, they consecrate texts and legitimate their use. This is indicative of the difficulty the ArtScroll cadre faces when trying to speak directly to its target audience, over the heads of local intermediary figures.[15]

In sum, although ArtScroll claims to be engaged in a process of reaching beyond the *haredi* community, addressing and thereby reclaiming a universal class of Jews in search of authentic meaning, in practice the press succeeds only in colonizing particular segments of the Jewish reading public, and wins a foothold only within the local institutions that are receptive to the specific advantages which ownership of ArtScroll texts appears to entail.

Commodity Exchange and the Rhetoric of Authenticity

ArtScroll's precarious influence among locally situated communities of readers and users is aptly illustrated in the case of London's *Saatchi Synagogue*, an Independent Orthodox congregation founded in 1998 by the advertising moguls Charles and Maurice Saatchi. Nicknamed "coolshul"[16] and inaugurated with a controversial campaign vowing to "ban boring services," the Saatchi Synagogue has defined itself as "London's leading venue for everything Jewish for 25–45-year-olds," "the missing generation." Its rabbi, Pini Dunner, a *yeshiva* graduate and former radio DJ, "London's funkiest young rabbi," has branded the synagogue as "a young, hip place to be." It incorporates, in one institution, an Orthodox service using *hasidic niggunim* (melodies), suppers and social evenings, an introduction service (which has led, apparently, to more than four hundred marriages in less than three years), and a very popular public lecture series featuring leading figures in the Jewish world, as well as other politicians and celebrities. In the course of its short life, the Saatchi Synagogue has generated a considerable response, boasting a committed membership of more than two hundred, a mailing list of three thousand, and roughly ten thousand attendees of events per year. There are two collections of *Siddurim* at "coolshul": ArtScroll's basic bilingual *Siddur* and their new bilingual edition with an added transliteration of the Hebrew text, designed specifically for those without sufficient knowledge to recite from the Hebrew script.

What are we to make of the presence of ArtScroll texts in this local community? To answer this question, we must understand that the Saatchi congregation is engaged in a process of claiming for itself a class- and cohort-specific Jewish identity. This is an institutional haven for the current generation of young professionals in the London area, who either have disaffiliated from the Jewish attachments of their parents or who grew up in unaffiliated homes. They represent the category of "lost Jews" which has so preoccupied *kiruv* activists. But their "return" to Jewish practice has not been carried out under the watchful eye of *haredi* organizations like *Agudat Israel*. Theirs is an independently driven project, underscored by their rabbi's idiosyncratic conception of *kiruv* as the assertion of Orthodox standards of observance, combined with the deployment of a variety of aesthetic signifiers of youthfulness, cosmopolitanism, and civic activism within the London Jewish community. Although this exercise is mediated in part through the use of ArtScroll texts, it does not entail any specific ideological commitments to *Agudat Israel*, the movement to which the ArtScroll cadre claims loyalty. Instead, ArtScroll serves as a vehicle for bringing this local community into contact with the sources they seek to reclaim; the *Siddur* in particular appears to function as a screen upon which members of the Saatchi congregation can project their own representations of authentic Jewish practice and meaning. Rabbi Dunner puts the issue this way:

> For me, ArtScroll is an extremely valuable resource, whether or not I subscribe to their ideology. I don't know why people are so resistant to ArtScroll publications just because they emerge from an agenda-driven source. Why should people care? I think they [ArtScroll] have done an absolutely sterling job of opening up Jewish texts and Judaism to a wide audience. People can read it, not agree with it, and not have to worry about it. They take what they want to take. The publisher's agenda and the reader's agenda don't have to be the same. Readers aren't unintelligent, so let's not insult them.[17]

Rabbi Dunner's caution is well taken. But selective use does not necessarily imply a rejection of authority per se. Here we must guard against a naive populism that exaggerates the significance of the fact that "the masses" always engage in processes of reinterpretation and creative reconstruction, extending the meaning of the products they consume into fields of semiotic productivity beyond the reach, let alone the original intentions, of the producer. It does not follow, however, that such reconstructions are entirely without design or constraint. Nor is it the case that producers are denied the possibility of accruing other sorts of dividends from the apparently uncoerced expressions of demand by consumers: profits that may exceed the restricted economy of exchanging money for books.

I suggest that the ArtScroll cadre succeeds in establishing a sort of hegemony over its readership in at least two ways. The first is evident in the very incorporation of ArtScroll texts into the liturgy of constituencies of non-*haredi* Jews such as members of the Saatchi congregation. Despite the proclamations of nonaffiliation with *haredism*, it is through their routine use that ArtScroll texts are naturalized as reliable companions in the effort to recuperate authentic Jewish meaning, thereby exposing local communities to the colonizing mission of the ArtScroll cadre. ArtScroll liturgical works seem to enjoy this status because they offer manifold instructions at a level of detail unrivaled by other prayer books: how to inspect a *tallis* (prayer shawl) to determine its validity, the correct order of prayers to be recited while donning *tefillin* (phylacteries), the correct *b'racha* (blessing) to recite while building a protective railing around one's roof or upon seeing a rainbow, when to bow to the right and when to the left while reciting the *Kaddish* (mourner's prayer), and so on. Such minutiae help to secure the hegemony of ArtScroll books as "better products." Among groups of non-*haredim* in the London community, such as congregants at Saatchi, the *Siddur* in particular has won favor as a text which, in their words, is "better organized," "more readable," "well indexed," "extremely well presented," "more complete," "more easy to use"; it offers "better commentaries," "clear instructions"; "it gives you all the choreography"; in short, it is "up-to-date," "modern"; "I wouldn't leave home without it."

We might conclude from these paeans that the ArtScroll cadre consolidates its grip on fellow Jews not by fiat or through polemical victories but rather through a molecular transformation of standards of observance, materialized in the extensive codification of practice and in the plethora of detail concerning its execution. Of course, this is a far cry from the sort of legitimate authority sought by the ArtScroll cadre; there is no doubt something deeply unsettling about being forced to obey the laws of commodity exchange, in competition with a spectrum of intellectual producers seeking the attention and loyalty of consumers. Nevertheless, even though local communities are not directly subject to the disciplining presence of *haredi* authorities, their appropriation of *haredi* texts sets the stage for an assimilation of a different kind of authority, one that is displaced onto codes of conduct and images of tradition, anchored in the "accessible" prose of their texts. The pleasure evinced by users of ArtScroll is thus directly related not only to the handsome format of the texts but also to their fidelity as vehicles for coming into the presence of the divine, a certainty secured by the scholarly prestige and communicative competence of the ArtScroll cadre.

This mediated presence of *haredi* authority in the form of ArtScroll books points to a second sort of hegemony, one that extends beyond questions of how successfully the ArtScroll cadre manages to shape the everyday practices of specific local communities through the codification of ritual or the dissemination of *haredi* standards of observance. Hegemony can also be secured by orchestrating the desire for authenticity and shaping the means of its attainment. Because modern Jewish public culture defines the search for Jewish meaning in no small measure through the consumption of what are taken to be the "most reliable" signs of Jewishness and Jewish tradition, consumerism becomes a terrain for the strategic mobilization of *haredi* authority, now transmuted into a bid for a monopoly in the economy of the authentic. Accordingly, through their textual products, *haredi* authorities are able to present themselves as metonyms of an authentic Jewish life, which is said to have existed before the destruction of traditional society, and which, they propose, can only be recaptured through the adoption of *haredi* practices and habits, and the submission to its structures of authority. In this way the past that is reclaimed for the lost Jew is intimately linked with the possibilities of belonging in the present, within which the *haredim* are figured as the most legitimate bearers of tradition, and purveyors of the greatest knowledge of "correct practice," even among those who have little interest in accruing such capital.

In conclusion, the ArtScroll phenomenon is instructive as an instance where new conditions of mediated communication have transformed, not dissipated, religious authority according to the evolution of a logic of commodity exchange. The market principles which, from one vantage point, appear to circumscribe ArtScroll's influence from another view allow for the extraction, accumulation, and reinvestment of surpluses of symbolic value, so to speak, derived from the activity of consumption itself. And as some local variants of this story suggest, there is no reason to assume that the mantle of authority which the ArtScroll cadre has won for itself within this field is about to slip.

Notes

Among the readers who have helped me to clarify this text, I especially thank Victoria Heftler, David Lehmann, Birgit Meyer, Annelies Moors, Arvind Rajagopal, and Nurit Stadler. I bear sole responsibility for failing to heed some of their best advice. Financial support for this research was provided by the Social Sciences and Humanities Research Council of Canada.

1. For a full booklist, see the ArtScroll catalogue on its website, http://www.artscroll.com.

2. To date, there has been no serious study of this cultural field. This is most evident from the several disparaging critiques that have been advanced with regard to ArtScroll texts as the product of careless scholarship and questionable ideological investment (see, e.g., Levy 1983). Such indictments, however, tell us next to nothing about the degree of resonance of ArtScroll with the popular Jewish imaginary, which is the focus of my discussion.

3. The term *haredim* translates literally as "those who tremble," a scriptural reference to the righteous ones who fear the word of God (as in Isaiah 66.5). Vexing problems of historical periodization and provenance, ideological ambiguity, and cultural specificity have plagued scholars in their efforts to produce a consistent definition of *haredism*. Given this ambiguity, the terms *haredism, haredi,* and the *haredim* are used here to refer figuratively to a loosely defined cultural formation. For key studies, see, inter alia, El-Or 1994; Friedman 1986, 1987; Heilman and Friedman 1991; Silberstein 1993; and Soloveitchik 1994.

4. On the rise of *Agudat Israel,* see Bacon 1996; Mittelman 1996; and Stolow 2004.

5. The ensuing discussion assumes an *Ashkenazi*-centric (i.e., a central and east European) perspective on modern Jewish culture and history, and thus ignores developments within *sephardi* (Mediterranean) and *mizrahi* (Middle Eastern and Asian) communities. This choice of focus is legitimate only in so far as the key forces which have made *haredism* in general, and *Agudat Israel* in particular, ideologically and institutionally effective appear to be of distinctly *ashkenazic* provenance (cf. Friedman 1987, 252 n. 12). It is also of significance for this discussion that the majority of English-speaking Jews are ethnically *ashkenazim*.

6. See Bartal 1993, 142–143. *Leshon ha-kodesh* must not be confused with either

classical or modern Hebrew. It consists of a distinctively post-biblical form of Hebrew, infused with Aramaic, and ordered by specific traditions of composition, as found in *Talmudic* and other rabbinic writings.

7. English-speaking Jewry is not, of course, simply a product of migratory flows from East Europe in the nineteenth century. The British Jewish community, for instance, can be traced back much further, and is based on political and cultural experiences quite distinct from its counterparts on the European continent. For a useful history, see Endelman 1979.

8. See Silberstein 1993, 206–213. Cf. Friedman 1986, 77; 1987, 250; and Heilman and Friedman 1991, 206–211.

9. See, for example, http://www.njop.org. The largest *kiruv* network is probably the one managed by *Habad-Lubavitcher* Hasidim, who have launched a succession of outreach campaigns in keeping with their messianic mission to heal the Jewish nation and hasten the Redemption. See http://www.chabad.org. Cf. Friedman 1994.

10. The following analysis is based on field research conducted in the London Jewish community in 2001. This included a survey of twenty-seven synagogues and eleven Judaica bookstores in the Greater London area, as well as extensive, open-ended interviews. For useful overviews of the contemporary Jewish community in the United Kingdom, see Schmool 1998; Becher et al. 2002; and Graham 2003.

11. The most common *Siddurim* and *Chumashim* found in modern Orthodox and conservative synagogues in the United Kingdom are Hertz 1929–36, 1947; Singer 1992; Birnbaum 1977 [1949]; and Cohen 1983 [1960].

12. Personal communication, June 2001.

13. *Haredi* congregations, on the other hand, tend to have little interest in ArtScroll's *Siddur* or *Chumash,* not for ideological reasons but more simply because their command of Hebrew precludes the need for a bilingual text.

14. Personal communication, July 2001.

15. One strategy ArtScroll has recently initiated to shift this balance of power is direct marketing through the Internet. It will be interesting to see how successful this venture is in terms of generating sales from customers who would not have the opportunity to come into contact with specific ArtScroll titles by other means.

16. See the synagogue's website, http://www.coolshul.org.

17. Personal communication, July 2001. Revised version by Rabbi Dunner in February 2002.

References

Bacon, Gershon. 1996. *The Politics of Tradition: Agudat Yisrael in Poland, 1916–1939.* Jerusalem: Magnes.

Bartal, Israel. 1993. From Traditional Bilingualism to National Monolingualism. In *Hebrew in Ashkenaz: A Language in Exile,* ed. Lewis Glinert, 141–150. Oxford: Oxford University Press.

Becher, Harriet, Stanley Waterman, Barry Kosmin, and Katarina Thompson. 2002. *A Portrait of Jews in London and the South-East: A Community Study.* JPR Report No. 4. London: Institute for Jewish Policy Research.

Birnbaum, Philip. 1977 [1949]. *Daily Prayer Book.* New York: Hebrew Publishing.

Cohen, Abraham. 1983 [1960]. *The Pentateuch and Haphtarot: Hebrew Text and English Translation with an Exposition Based on the Classical Jewish Commentaries.* Rev. ed. London: Soncino.

El-Or, Tamar. 1994. *Educated and Ignorant: Ultraorthodox Jewish Women and Their World.* Boulder, Colo.: Lynne Rienner.

Endelman, Todd. 1979. *The Jews of Georgian England: Tradition and Change in a Liberal Society.* Philadelphia: Jewish Publication Society.

Friedman, Menachem. 1994. Habad as Messianic Fundamentalism: From Local Particularism to Universal Jewish Mission. In *Accounting for Fundamentalisms*, ed. Martin Marty and R. Scott Appleby, 328–357. Chicago: University of Chicago Press.

Friedman, Menachem. 1986. Haredim Confront the Modern City. *Studies in Contemporary Jewry* 2:74–96.

———. 1987. Life Tradition and Book Tradition in the Development of Ultraorthodox Judaism. In *Judaism Viewed from Within and from Without: Anthropological Studies*, ed. Harvey Goldberg, 235–255. Albany: State University of New York Press.

Graham, David. 2003. *Secular or Religious? The Outlook of London's Jews.* Planning for Jewish Communities Report No. 3. London: Institute for Jewish Policy Research.

Halbertal, Moshe. 1997. *People of the Book: Canon, Meaning, and Authority.* Cambridge, Mass.: Harvard University Press.

Heilman, Samuel, and Menachem Friedman. 1991. Religious Fundamentalism and Religious Jews: The Case of the Haredim. In *Fundamentalisms Observed*, ed. Martin Marty and R. Scott Appleby, 197–264. Chicago: University of Chicago Press.

Hertz, Joseph H. 1929–36. *The Pentateuch and Haftorahs: Hebrew Text, English Translation and Commentary.* 5 vols. Oxford: Oxford University Press.

———. 1947. *The Authorised Daily Prayer Book of the United Hebrew Congregations of the British Empire: Revised Edition with Commentary.* London: Shapiro Vallentine.

Katz, Jacob. 1993 [1957]. *Tradition and Crisis: Jewish Society at the End of the Middle Ages.* New York: Schocken Books.

Levy, Barry. 1983. Our Torah, Your Torah, and Their Torah: An Evaluation of the Artscroll Phenomenon. In *Truth and Compassion: Essays on Judaism and Religion in Memory of Rabbi Dr. Solomon Frank*, ed. Howard Joseph, Jack N. Lightstone, and Michael D. Oppenheim, 137–189. Waterloo, Ontario: Wilfred Laurier University Press.

Manache, Sophia, ed. 1996. *Communication in the Jewish Diaspora: The Pre-Modern World.* Leiden: E. J. Brill.

Mittelman, Alan L. 1996. *The Politics of Torah: The Jewish Political Tradition and the Founding of Agudat Israel.* Albany: State University of New York Press.

Parush, Iris. 1994. Readers in Cameo: Women Readers in Jewish Society of Nineteenth-Century Eastern Europe. *Prooftexts: A Journal of Jewish Literary History* 14 (1): 1–23.

———. 1995. The Politics of Literacy: Women and Foreign Languages in Jewish Society of 19th-Century Eastern Europe. *Modern Judaism* 15 (2): 183–206.

Scherman, Nosson. 1984. *The Complete ArtScroll Siddur: Weekday/Sabbath/Festival—A New Translation and Anthologized Commentary.* Brooklyn, N.Y.: ArtScroll/Mesorah.

———. 1993. *Stone Edition of the Chumash: The Torah, Haftoras and Five Megillos, with a Commentary Anthologized from the Rabbinic Writings.* Brooklyn, N.Y.: ArtScroll/Mesorah.

Schmool, Marlena. 1998. British Jewry: Prospects and Problems. In *Jewish Centers and Peripheries: Europe between America and Israel Fifty Years after WW II*, ed. Ilan Troen, 227–252. New Brunswick, N.J.: Transaction.

Silberstein, Lawrence J., ed. 1993. *Jewish Fundamentalism in Comparative Perspective: Religion, Ideology, and the Crisis of Modernity.* New York: New York University Press.

Singer, S. 1992. *The Authorised Daily Prayer Book of the United Hebrew Congregations of the Commonwealth.* Centenary edition, with a new translation and introductions. Cambridge: Cambridge University Press.

Soloveitchik, Haym. 1994. Rupture and Reconstruction: The Transformation of Contemporary Orthodoxy. *Tradition* 28 (4): 64–130.

Stolow, Jeremy. 2004. Transnationalism and the New Religio-Politics: Reflections on a Jewish Orthodox Case. *Theory, Culture and Society* 21 (2): 109–137.

4   Holy Pirates: Media, Ethnicity, and Religious Renewal in Israel

David Lehmann and Batia Siebzehner

A Society of Enclaves

Israel is a society of enclaves, and of profound cultural divisions. The enclaves emerged in the way the country was settled, first in the quasi-legal status of early Zionist settlement, and in the leading role played in that settlement by highly centralized political parties parceling out power and space among themselves, and later in the peculiar relationship (for a modern democracy) between religion and the state. The pattern is graphically described by Swirski (1999), who uses the term "micro-societies"[1] and by Horowitz and Lissak (1987) in their discussion of social enclaves.

The notion of enclaves is both territorial and analytical: it describes distinct de facto enclaves inhabited, for example, by the highly observant ultra-Orthodox Jews, by the secular, even by the fairly observant Arab population—and the settlements in occupied territories are an extension of the same principle; it also describes the parceling out of state bureaucracies or departments as fiefdoms to particular parties or factions. It can even be seen in the way governing coalitions are formed: once a party has a minister in place, that minister is in effect the owner of his or her ministry and does not seem to be bound by collective Cabinet responsibility.[2] Beyond these tangible enclaves are the less tangible ones: people signal their religious or political allegiance in how they dress, in whether they speak Yiddish, in what they eat and where they shop, even in how they walk on the street. Given that religious life is deeply marked by concepts of pollution and the proliferating taboos arising therefrom, it is hardly surprising that the social and territorial space of the country is criss-crossed by an infinite number of additional boundaries.

Institutional enclaves are seen in rabbinical control over family law,[3] and therefore over nationality law, but also in the influence of rabbinic authorities over vast areas of public life, from the El-Al flight timetable to the subsidies accorded to hundreds of thousands of full-time young and adult Torah students (who neither work nor serve in the army) and their vast families (average fertility of eight), and to the institutions in which they study. Enclaves mean muscle, and the ultra-Orthodox exercise their muscle in issues of Sabbath observance just as West Bank settlers exercise theirs territorially and politically. Likewise state-funded education is divided, for the Jewish population, into a mainstream secular system, a "national religious" system, both directly funded and operated by the state, and an ultra-Orthodox system, as well as a separate state-run system for the Arab population. The ultra-Orthodox educational system is in turn divided into two separate systems, one controlled by the Ashkenazi authorities of the Eastern European tradition and the other, recently created and predominantly Sephardi, controlled by the leadership of Shas, the party of religious renewal and Sephardi identity, founded in 1982.

The discourse and actions of the Shas leadership and the most active followers have tended toward the superimposition of disagreement and conflict across several different fault-lines at once: the secular-religious conflict, the ethnic divisions between Ashkenazim—people of European descent—and Sephardim—migrants from North Africa and the Middle East and their descendants—and the division between elite and popular culture. Shas is different from the Ashkenazi ultra-Orthodox parties because of its emphasis on *t'shuva*—the process whereby large numbers of people are brought "back" to religious observance.[4] Shas attracts people who are either "traditional" (*masorati*), in that they preserve some customs but are not punctiliously observant, or who are from a highly secularized lifestyle. Shas is also recognized as the party of the Sephardim. The word *Sephardi* refers, strictly speaking, to the Judeo-Spanish (or *Ladino*)–speaking people of the northern Mediterranean and northern Morocco, but in recent decades it has come to refer to all Jews of North African, Middle Eastern, and Persian descent, most of whom are by now second and third generation immigrants, and many of whom are married to non-Sephardim. Taking into account the resulting impossibility of giving precise numbers, it is generally accepted that they constitute slightly less than half of Israel's Jewish population. In political campaigns the party capitalizes deftly on the symbols and accoutrements of Sephardi identity—accent, popular language and culture, Oriental music, popular religion such as healing and the veneration of saints—but, in more formal statements of policy, the leadership emphasizes *t'shuva* above everything else. That different authors emphasize in different ways the ethnic and religious elements in Shas's appeal demonstrates the impossibility of separating the two (Herzog 1995; Willis 1995; and Shafir and Peled 2002). In the long run, as some have also said (Zohar 2001), Shas is transcending these alternatives and forging an Orthodox Israeli Judaism which, if its influence continues to grow, will become the dominant form, replacing the Ashkenazi-Sephardi divide inherited from Jewish history and deepening the divide between Israeli religious culture and the diaspora. Like the Pentecostals in Latin America, Shas and the *t'shuva* movement in which it is the leading force can be understood as a revolt against the hegemony of a cultural elite, and also as a project of reshaping the religious sphere (Lehmann 1996; Lehmann 1998; Birman and Lehmann 1999).

What Kind of Social Movement?

The genius or good fortune of the founders of Shah was to link ethnic and religious renewal so that now it is hard to choose between a description of Shas as embedded within a broader *t'shuva* movement or of *t'shuva* as embedded within the ethnic renewal, which Shas has led. In common with social movements generally, the *t'shuva* movement uses multifarious means of communication and organization—adopting a capillary approach to social mobilization as opposed to the hierarchical methods used by conventional political parties or trade unions, or the Ashkenazi *haredim*—whose communal activity is much more subject to rabbinical control and therefore leaves less space for initiative and entrepreneurship (El-Or 1994).[5] This *t'shuva* movement lives by trusting its emissaries, and by drawing them from its "target population." A movement spreads by capitalizing on points of commonality with a range of constituencies as much as by broadcasting a message. Thus the emissaries or activists of Shas have a language in common with the second- and third-generation Sephardim, but they also have a common taste in Oriental popular music with some, and a common taste in Oriental liturgical music with others; with some they may share a hostility to the secular establishment, with others to the *haredi* (ultra-Orthodox) establishment; they develop characteristic ways of dressing, characteristic headgear (black velvet skull caps), and, as Nissim Leon (1999, 2000, 2001) explains, a characteristic language so that gradually people find multiple ways of joining, of being part of the flow. In all these niches of social life the movement's activists introduce an unfamiliar innovative set of signs, symbols, emblems, and markers, by joining a *haredi* motif with elements of secular Israeli culture which have been kept at arm's length by the Ashkenazi *haredim:* they bring in army slang; they bring in the jargon of *t'shuva* (with, for example, special terms to describe newcomers, the ones who "need strengthening," the ones whose strength "is confirmed"); they adopt slight but significant variations in speech, accentuating Sephardi, or conceivably pseudo-Sephardi, pronunciation (Leon 2000).

The pattern can be described as the conformation of a movement's identity by the creation of unaccustomed, innovative symbolic and behavioral allusions across previously or otherwise watertight boundaries, and this is facilitated by the recourse to the media. The role of the broadcast media in promoting the movement arises not only, perhaps not principally, from the size of their audience, especially in this case where television is excluded for reasons of religious principle, and where the radios are mostly shoestring operations that rely heavily on phone-in programs and have a limited range. Rather, the media provide more markers for the movement and its followers: the regularity of programs, the consistent tone or content of programs broadcast at certain times of the day on certain frequencies, the differentiation of the audience into *t'shuva*-defined segments, and, perhaps above all, the bridge provided by these media between public and private spheres, all contribute in making radio stations and cassettes integral parts of the movement of ethnic and religious renewal.

Stated more simply, the use of media characteristic of popular culture, namely, radio and cassette tapes, of itself provides an interface between religion and the ethnic group most identified with "the popular" in Israel. In appealing to Sephardim, and among them often to young people whom they regard as mired in the frivolities—or worse—of consumer culture, the broadcasters could not but adopt a language and a style unfamiliar to traditional Ashkenazi ultra-Orthodoxy, more streetwise, less hidebound, less weighed down by the somniferous tones of traditional yeshivas (Torah study seminaries and centers), a trend reinforced by the intervention of free-booting social and religious entrepreneurs in media previously unused by ultra-Orthodoxy.

All this does not mean that the core of the *t'shuva* movement is not deeply rooted in yeshiva life. But social movements are like concentric circles, with a hard center (the "cadres") and ever softer peripheries, and they conform social spaces linked not by organizational structures but by inferential symbols embodied as we have indicated, in language, posters, iconic figures, and much more besides.

Pirate Radios in the Broadcasting System

Until 1999 the Israeli state had direct legal control of all nationwide radio and TV stations through the Israel Broadcasting Authority. Only in 1995 were private commercial radio stations permitted, and operated exclusively at the local[6] level under a franchise arrangement with the Israel Broadcasting Authority. The state monopoly had been challenged long before, though more for political reasons, by unofficial "pirate" broadcasting, which began in 1973 when dissident political groups, first those who opposed the country's occupation of the West Bank and later those who opposed settlers in the selfsame West Bank, began transmitting from ships offshore. By 1995 "more than 50" active pirate stations were identified, and in the late 1990s they were no longer particularly political, broadcasting mainly music and entertainment (Caspi and Limor 1999). After some resistance from their senior leader, Rav Schach,[7] the Ashkenazi *haredi* community began to use radio stations, although they remain controversial in this prickly constituency, and today there seems to be only one pirate station broadcasting specifically in the idiom of the Ashkenazi *haredim*— Kol Simcha (The Voice of Celebration). However, radio transmission enables people to cross boundaries without doing so too publicly, and there is no reason to believe that Ashkenazim do not listen to other stations of a more Sephardi complexion. The stations' broadcasts, despite their Sephardi tinge reflected in accent, style, and music, do not give any space to material expressing some of the resentment against Ashkenazim, which we have heard in interviews.

Although the Sephardi tinge is not explicitly promoted, it is a very important feature of these radios' broadcasting and of their appeal, expressed in broadcasters' accents, in much accompanying music, even in the streetwise language they use. This appeal is most straightforwardly explained by the limited presence of Oriental music and culture in the official stations. Those stations only broadcast one hour of Oriental content until a few years ago, but even now, though the amount has increased, the content is not in tune with Israeli popular taste, let alone with the religious tastes of the *t'shuva* movement or of Shas followers. Official radio in Israel is heavily oriented to high culture and educational themes, plus an endless diet of news, and this narrowness opens a space for more popular—and therefore more Sephardi—modes of communication and entertainment. The entertainment stations on official radio certainly lack any appeal to a public at once popular and interested in religious themes and traditions.

From another point of view, it could be said that by their use of Oriental-style music the stations are joining the Israeli mainstream, just as by promoting a Sephardi religiosity Shas is trying to create an Israeli mainstream Orthodoxy in the religious field. Israeli popular music is distinguished by continual mixing of styles, combining either the "indigenous" tradition originating with the formative period of Israeli Jewish culture with rock and other cosmopolitan forms, or the Oriental style with those forms and with the indigenous ones (Regev 1996). Although there was for a time a prejudice against both cosmopolitan and quasi-Arab music, this has now given way to postmodern syncretism, but both kinds of music are acceptable if they catch on. The pirate radios, then, which to some might appear as beyond the mainstream, may be fitting very nicely into this nonelite mainstream.

Today, at least in the Jerusalem area, many, if not most, of the pirate stations are religious, and although they sometimes like to call themselves "Holiness channels" (*arutsei kodesh*), they are happy to be known as *piratim*. There are also pirate stations devoted to popular music, and serving the West Bank settlers and the million-strong Arab population. But the religious stations, whose central theme is *t'shuva*, are now so numerous that people find themselves listening almost by accident as they turn the knobs on their car radios or in their kitchens, and as a welcome alternative to the official stations.[8] During 2002 it has been noticeable that they are going beyond their core audience and penetrating the secular world, and they are also becoming the subject of debates on the mainstream channels' chat shows and political discussions. Their number and proportion are matters for speculation. In a Knesset debate on October 20, 1999, a Shas member (MK) stated that there were 150 between 1996 and 1999 of which only 14 were religious. Yet he also said that in 1999 the authorities closed down 90 stations, of which 48 were religious, and that, in the two months prior to the debate, 21 out of the 28 stations that closed down were religious. Any conclusions drawn from these numbers should keep in mind that stations routinely reopen after being "closed down"—a blatantly illegal procedure that has never been followed by a prosecution or conviction (leading in theory to a sentence of three years' imprisonment or a fine of up to U.S.$330,000).

The pirate stations play a game of cat-and-mouse with the government, operating under the constant threat of having their equipment confiscated. They do not like to give out their address, and they say that not infrequently they have to bundle their equipment out of a location in the face of a possible police raid. Although insiders mention links between particular stations and religious organizations or prominent rabbis, they do not publicize these links. The degree of indulgence or repression by the authorities varies with the color of the government of the day—the more right wing, the more tolerant. But the received wisdom among the *haredim* is that they suffer relentless persecution, and they make the point with the customary hyperbole of Israeli political debate. The Shas MK quoted above declared that the persecution of the pirate radios reminded him of when the authorities in his native Georgia sent tractors to steamroller their synagogues in 1953 and the people lay down on the ground to stop them. The unwillingness of successive governments and parliaments to legalize their radio stations is also taken as proof of the discrimination they suffer at the hands of what they see as a secular dictatorship: the same MK, referring unashamedly to the pirate stations' support for his party, said that it was clear that "they" want to "silence millions who have no other station," and that the prime minister (Ehud Barak) "wants to destroy Shas" (which was a member of his coalition). A broadcaster in the city of Natanya spoke to us bitterly of their treatment by the Rabin government. *Haredim,* of course, would never accept space in what they regard as a godless state broadcasting station, but this does not stand in the way of routine point scoring: thus the Shas MK did not miss the opportunity to make the further point that, although the religious population comprised 20 percent of the population, religious broadcasting accounted only for 0.5 percent of broadcasting time on legal channels.

In recent years debates on this subject have been held on March 12 and May 28, 1997, February 18, 1998, October 20, 1999, June 20 and July 23, 2001, and they convey both the tenor of debate in Israel on and with *haredim,* as well as the unwillingness of the political class to regularize the situation. All have a vested interest in the status quo whereby the pirate radios—mostly religious as far as the MKs are concerned—are de facto tolerated. Caspi and Limor (1999, 144) confirm the same point, although writing at a time when the religious stations had not become major players in pirate broadcasting, saying that they preserve an "illusion of media pluralism," and are "not perceived as threatening." Today they are perceived as a threat, along with the *t'shuva* movement as a whole, by secular Israel, but in practice almost the entire political class has a vested interest in turning a blind eye. All the Knesset debates have a tone of polemical banter, and end inconclusively as the participants disingenuously fail to decide to which committee the issue should be referred. On one occasion the chair asks how many pirate radios there are in Jerusalem, and a Shas MK responds "one—the state radio!" In March 1997 the Shas minister of transport said that when the only pirate radios were those of the Peace Movement (Kol Hashalom) and the settlers (Channel 7) they were left alone, but as soon as religious groups started to broadcast they were persecuted. In May of that year a Shas MK said that the stations might not be "very legal," but they do express the views of a "hated and persecuted" section of the population. On another occasion a member complained that the police leave undisturbed the Christian evangelical radios, "which propagate a mistaken interpretation of the sources," leading gullible Jewish listeners to fall into a trap, while harassing the religious radios that broadcast "love for Israel and the truth." Secular parties, namely Meretz and Labour, intervene little, and when they do it is to complain that the law is not being implemented—a complaint that cuts little ice with Shas, or with any government in this connection.[9]

The views of the Shas MKs quoted above are echoed by the pirate station operators. The director of the Micol Halev (Giving with All Your Heart) station also says that there are hundreds of pirate stations in the country but that only the religious ones are troubled by the police. Asked whether there might be advantages to illegality, he responds guardedly: he does not see benefits from legalization "in all situations," especially because legal stations are watched by the authorities and he does not want any authority looking over his shoulder or, as he put it, "telling him what to say." (This may reflect anxiety over a law against incitement that was passed in the wake of the Rabin assassination in 1995, described by some, again with customary hyperbole, as a device for muzzling right-wing voices.) A newspaper journalist explained to us that becoming legal also involves bidding for a wave band, which would be far beyond the means of any of these stations because of the heavy competition for the few legally available bands. Legality would also impose all sorts of time-consuming paperwork. On the other hand, legal status would allow the stations to earn revenues from advertising. In short, while authorities tolerate radio "piracy," the attitude of the radios themselves is neatly summed up in a broadcaster's comment that "no revolution is ever made in legality."

Outside the officially recognized media sector cash is scarce. It can be raised from donors, and collections for the radios are often made at open-air public meetings in support of the *t'shuva* movement. At Micol Halev the broadcasters and workers, even the website designer, are volunteers, yeshiva students or people who have returned to religion full time. The station receives many offers—or approaches—from people who want to broadcast, but the director only accepts those recommended by trusted individuals. For someone who wants to build a reputation as a preacher the radio is a good opportunity, as in the case of Rav Shalom Arush who heads a network of several yeshivas and broadcasts on Kol HaChesed (The Voice of Charity). There are also degrees of professionalization, exemplified by Rav Gilles, an experienced broadcaster in several different idioms on several stations, sometimes answering phone-ins, sometimes delivering learned commentaries, sometimes interviewing a guest— always adept at switching his accent and style of speech for different audiences. Stations are now taking to recruiting media professionals who have made *t'shuva* or are at least sympathetic to its cause. Rav Gilles's ethnic/community identity is of no concern to the stations, which are eager to put this well-known and experienced voice on their own wavelengths.

The radios do not stand still. Micol Halev, which looks and sounds like a shoestring operation, has a website that permits listeners to hear native-speaking rabbis expounding in Hebrew, Spanish, French, and English. The size of their audience is of course impossible to judge, and many wavering listeners, responding to an audience survey, might not admit they do listen until "they have crossed a certain line." Rav Gilles reckons he can tell by the number of callers— on some stations he has long queues of callers while on others there are very few. All arrange for a few callers in advance to get the show going. On this basis he surmises that Micol Halev is a small station, whereas its director claims it is one of the biggest.

Pirate Radios and the *T'shuva* Movement

The pirate religious stations are linked with a range of grassroots and street-level activities. We have seen the links with evangelists, but the case of Kol HaChesed shows that these links can spread much further, and that their multimedia capacity has the effect of shifting established social boundaries. This is a nationwide broadcaster run out of Natanya by a group who resemble a social rescue brigade. Asked about their mission the first word they say is "family"—their vocation is to spread a message of love, of reconciliation within families, and to do so in a language that is readily understandable to people unfamiliar with Judaism. Their radio is at the hub of a range of activities: they distribute didactic cassettes by giving a person one hundred of them to sell as a good deed (*mitzvah*), they respond to requests for help and advice, on family and education matters especially; they provide a marriage guidance service whereby listeners can consult a rabbi personally or by telephone, off the air. And every so often there are miracles: when a lady rang in saying she was having difficulty finding a husband, the rabbi on the air told her she should sell one hundred cassettes—three weeks later she was married!

The station operates within the framework of a nongovernmental organization (NGO) that is itself involved in many other activities—indeed, our interlocutors say that they could not operate without that framework. The NGO is in the early stages of setting up a school for yeshiva dropouts who, having never served in the army, fall between these two poles of Israeli society and find themselves unequipped for making their own lives. Volunteers provide their services as teachers, and the students serve a type of apprenticeship, but there is an important condition for their participation: they must study Torah for two hours each day. Another project takes in 120 school dropouts—in premises that are rented out for private gatherings to fund the operation. Together with other organizations they provide food boxes to one thousand needy families, train orphans for their bar mitzvah, and help young women who might be thinking of having an abortion—if necessary and possible, by arranging marriages for them. Through the organization fifteen doctors provide weekly free medical attention—and although this service is not paid for they benefit from the advertising of their work on the radio station. Their radio also advertises seminars—often residential and sometimes at no cost—run by Arachim (Values) an organization devoted to the cause of *t'shuva* and also to training activists and professionals in propagating the message.

Thus we can see how radios are linked with other activities and organizations, crossing boundaries that in the routine of everyday life would be much thicker. The nonsectarian quality of the Kol HaChesed operation is seen in the lack of interest in emphasizing Sephardi or Ashkenazi traditions and in the use of rabbis from different traditions and tendencies. The wider impact of such an approach should not, however, be exaggerated. Sectarian attitudes to secular Jews are definitely not softened, as witness the barely concealed fury at the persecution the Natanya radio activists say they suffered from the Rabin government.

Partly because of its doubtful legal status, pirate broadcasting creates an intimacy with its audience: callers are not all that numerous, so they have time to chat, they are invited to make their needs known, and the speakers follow up through their religious or political networks to satisfy urgent personal needs. Most programming consists of homilies or phone-ins, with musical interludes of varying length. Micol Halev is hosted every morning by a former ice-cream seller known as Ovadia Mehaglida (Ovadia Ice-Cream), for whom nothing is too much trouble. While we were there, someone rang in with a request for thirty items of religious apparel for a group of students who want to begin adopting religious dress. They sounded like candidates for *t'shuva*, and the radio's prompt call brought immediate offers of money or donations in kind. Once a week there is a program to match buyers and sellers of anything from household goods to real estate. Many stations reserve extensive airtime for requests from individuals for help in emergencies. They also broadcast on health issues and (not surprisingly in this connection) alternative medicine.[10] Whereas previously the stations tended to shy away from explicit political statements, in the increasingly polarized context of the second Intifada (from late 2000) some stations have become more vociferous and partisan on the subject of Jewish relations with Arabs and Palestinians. Sephardim may express occasional nostalgia for the North Africa of their ancestors where Jews and Arabs coexisted in peace, and "everyone was religious," but they do not transpose that into the context of contemporary Israel.

The radios, therefore, fit into the dense undergrowth of the *t'shuva* movement. The Sephardi element is not explicitly played up but is an implicit presence through references to Shas or to Ovadia Yosef, through the accent of broadcasters and their chatty style which stands in contrast to the formalism of the state channels, characteristic of the Ashkenazi (secular) elite. Boundaries are redrawn by bringing listeners into new networks, which at first may be only virtual; but, if the radios achieve their aims, they eventually will reshape social lives as people enroll children into religious school, start attending synagogue, and become ever more involved in religious life. The content of the broadcasts, like the videos and tapes directed to the popular, less-educated sectors, could be described as "folksy." They make a point of using images, proverbs, and examples from everyday life, and these produce conclusions in the manner of folk wisdom. There is a similarity with Pentecostal preaching, and a contrast with the heavily text-centered disquisitions of fundamentalist Christians and of the more erudite, especially Ashkenazi, *haredim*. Indeed, it is a trademark of Ovadia Yosef himself that he peppers his addresses—though not his writings—with popular language and anecdotes.

It is clear that women are an important section of the audience, and that stations pay a great deal of attention to their needs and problems. Although managers are uneasy about allowing them to speak on air when they phone in, the emphasis given to family problems—and family solutions—reflects women's presence in the audience. Some speakers allow women on the air (but only "so long as they keep to the point") while others only allow them to leave messages—questions that are read out and answered, and that listeners can then follow up with requests for further clarification. In response to frequent requests for advice in overcoming family conflicts, speakers tend to recommend patience, long-term commitment, and love in the family. For these broadcasters, even major political problems have their solution in the rebuilding of the family, helped by a more observant lifestyle. This reflects the much-discussed collapse of family values and parental authority among Israel's Sephardi population. A man wants more children but cannot convince his wife; a woman wants to convince her household to adopt stricter observance but encounters resistance among her menfolk; men and women call to ask advice in resolving family conflicts. The responses tend to focus on "peace-building" in the home, especially by advising women not to respond to their husbands' inconsiderate or offensive behavior. Thus a woman calls to complain that her husband shouts at her constantly. In response, the speaker (somewhat counterintuitively) tells a story about a rabbi who gave a woman an amulet to put in her mouth and keep it there. As a result she could not speak, of course, but each day her husband came with more and more generous presents—flowers, a diamond ring, and so on. Eventually the rabbi tells her that the "amulet" is nothing but an empty card. Independent of the content of such advice, the allusion to an amulet provides a ready referent to the world of Israeli Sephardim.

Listeners identify quite readily with "their" station, to the point that, when asked to place themselves on a religious spectrum, they may use the name of their preferred radio station as a shorthand response. The format makes the station an extension of the home, helped in this by the unofficial status of the station, and the friendly, helpful, "can-do" responses of the speakers. Some daytime programs are for children, often using cautionary tales to convey a message.

Thus we see a range of mechanisms whereby the activities of radios, when combined with other organizations and, of course, with politics, are redrawing some of the boundaries which separate—although, by emphasizing religious belonging and encouraging religious and political activism, also integrate—the multiple ethnic, religious, and cultural enclaves of Israeli society. Listeners can find a radio that uses a particular style of speech, plays a certain type of music, emphasizes certain themes, and enables them to combine religious observance with an engagement with the media—something quite uncommon in the *haredi* world until the *t'shuva* movement took hold. The intimacy of radio—both in the sense that it can be heard in private and in the home, and also that its style is designed to make listeners feel at home among an audience with whom they have a strong social and implicitly ethnic affinity—redraws boundaries in a society where these are unusually important in daily life. The airwaves are used to form networks of solidarity that feed into Israel's enclave system. Politically the organizations that radio promotes rely directly or indirectly on government funding, and thus, when the party is in power, Shas's strongholds in the apparatuses of the ministries of social affairs, labour, the interior, and religious affairs are strengthened. This fits in with the pattern of Shas activism, and indeed of nationalist and religious activism in Israel generally, which advances by creating "facts on the ground," enclaves that begin as territorial entities—settlements, ultra-Orthodox neighborhoods—and then become institutionalized in political parties or factions, and may eventually gain control of ministries or ministerial departments.[11]

T'shuva and the Tension between High and Low Culture

For those whose knowledge or experience of Judaism is limited to the diaspora, it is hard to imagine the adoption of strict religious observance as a dissidence directed against high culture, or that the propagation of an observant lifestyle might be wrapped in symbols and motifs drawn from the sphere of popular culture. Ultra-Orthodoxy, after all, seems so austere, so bound up with the written word and canonical texts, that it is hard to think of it as anything but high culture. In Israel the ultra-Orthodox communities could long be regarded as erudite, austere, and self-isolated, relating to the rest of society only through their leaders' indefatigable political pressure and occasional direct action against violations of their bodily inhibitions and Sabbath observance. Drawing the line between high and popular culture turns out to be a complex matter, requiring that account be taken of the diversity of the ultra-Orthodox world itself and the difficulties of setting the secular-religious contrast against that between high culture and its popular counterpart. For the time being, therefore, it is enough to say that the powerful Chassidic strand in ultra-Orthodoxy, with its elements of mysticism and physical expressions of devotion and identity (through chanting and dance), is clearly self-identified as popular culture; that the text-centered character of the life of ultra-Orthodox men (including the Chassidim, for they too study Torah) does not in itself detach them from the popular; and, finally, that even in nineteenth-century Eastern Europe, ultra-Orthodox identity developed as a reaction against the sophistication of secularized and modernized Jews who wanted to join an overwhelmingly non-Jewish elite (Katz 1973), and was also powerfully enhanced by the struggles over intellectualism within highly observant circles that witnessed ferocious denunciations of the Chassidim by extremely learned rabbis for their corporal effusion and messianism.

To understand the popular cultural dimension of today's movement of return to religion, it must first be recalled how radically different circumstances are in Israel from those in pre-Holocaust Europe or indeed in today's diaspora, if only because, as a state, Israel constitutes a space in which the interaction of high and low culture is bound up with relations of power. In Israel, also, high culture is not a matter of religion; rather, it is the culture of the secular elite, English-speaking, sophisticated, cosmopolitan and enamored of the canon of Western civilization, and many indications tell us that the *t'shuva* movement is a cultural dissidence against that culture and its secularism. The rabbinic erudition of the *haredi* communities stands in sharp contrast to the secular erudition of the university: where academics bring modern sciences such as archaeology and linguistics to bear on canonic texts, and place them in a historical context, while in the yeshivas the rabbis do not accept the treatment of those texts as historical documents. Although they cultivate an extraordinary command of the texts, as far as they are concerned, Rashi (1040–1105) in France, Maimonides (1135–1204) in Cordoba and Cairo, and the authors and editors of the Talmud (300 B.C.–A.D. 400) in Babylon and Jerusalem, might as well all have lived at the same time in the same place.

The Ashkenazi rabbinical world has imparted to its Sephardi pupils its hostility to the secular elite. The broader Sephardi population, for their part, are themselves marked out from the secular elite by a range of linguistic, educational, and socioeconomic markers, and they repeatedly charge that elite with making them feel inferior in culture and social status. So the *t'shuva* movement has been able to mobilize popular culture and strict religion against the secular elite and its cosmopolitan (European-Ashkenazi) practices, building on the affinity of the ethnic Sephardi theme with return to religion. The streetwise tinge to the movement—evidenced in Ovadia Yosef's asides, the chatty style of some cassette tapes, the religious music on tape, and, as we shall see, the fabulous imagery (mixed with an abundance of wit) of the evangelist Amnon Yitzchak's apocalyptic discourses—is the vehicle for its openness to the broader society, and demarcates *t'shuva* from the *haredi* obsession with practices denoting taboo, pollution and thus closure, introspection, and exclusion. The circle of dissidence is finally closed by the identification in Israel of the popular sectors with the Judeo-Arab heritage rather than with the Yiddish-speaking Eastern European culture, because the Sephardim are disadvantaged since theirs is the language of the street, of the criminal underworld, and even because the pronunciation of modern Hebrew itself derives from the Hebrew of the Northern and Southern Mediterranean shores and of historic Palestine itself and not from Russia, Poland, Lithuania, or Germany. Similarly Israeli popular music also derives from the North African and Middle Eastern musical modes, not from those of Eastern Europe.

Some might remind us that outside Israel other *t'shuva* movements also use modern media and also conduct extensive *t'shuva* campaigns. This is true especially of Chabad, also known as the Lubavitch Chassidim, the one Ashkenazi sect that regards *t'shuva* as its primary commitment, that uses cassettes, co-opts popular music, and also brings New Age themes and motifs into its activities. Chabad has outreach programs in the Jewish community, on many university campuses especially in the United States, and is well known for its missionary activities in peripheral Jewish communities, for example, in Madrid, Rio de Janeiro, São Paulo, Santiago, Caracas, and Buenos Aires. But these are directed inevitably at middle-class people, and operate in a parochial Jewish cultural field in the diaspora, not in a national cultural space as is possible in Israel. Indeed, it is striking that Chabad, though it has extensive operations in Israel, including an entire settlement known as Kfar Chabad, and although its methods have been borrowed by sections of the *t'shuva* movement (especially the Or HaChayyim educational network which is closely identified with Shas), does not have a high profile there—for example, in radio or other media. The Israeli *t'shuva* movement, in contrast, has developed not just as a "conversion" (or "reversion") movement but also as a form of cultural dissidence vis-à-vis the Ashkenazi secular elite, and with Shas as its vanguard and political wing has been able to marshal an ethnically based electorate and large-scale state finance to fuel its advance.

The confluence of popular culture, religious renewal, and multimedia intervention is well represented in the figure of Amnon Yitzchak. Yitzchak is a one-man road show: his cassettes are distributed for free at street intersections; he makes CDs of his appearances in Israel, England, and the U.S.; and his personal appearances in Israel seem calculated to challenge or offend the country's cultural elite. Like evangelists in other religious traditions and other places (Birman and Lehmann 1999), he uses shock tactics in a symbolic anti-elitist crusade, for example, by hiring venues usually occupied by symphony orchestras and international theater groups. When he hired Tel-Aviv's Hichal Hatarbut (Temple of Culture) legal challenges were (unsuccessfully) taken right up to the Supreme Court to stop his appearance there, and the audience at his— by now unchallenged—appearance in the equally highbrow Jerusalem Theater auditorium in November 2001 were gleefully treated to a video of those very protests. To support his campaign against television, another symbol of Israeli secular culture, Yitzchak promises that anyone who throws out his or her TV will receive a free copy of the Babylonian Talmud (Talmud Babli), and to demonstrate the success of his evangelizing campaign, he exhibits a box of earrings and ponytails discarded by women and men (respectively) who have converted at his public meetings. ("Throwing the television out" is a metaphor, or at least a rhetorical device: ultra-Orthodox people still watch approved videos, for example, in community centers. Yitzchak's target audience, however, are people who still have a long way to go before their "conversion" has reached the point of literally throwing out the television.)

Yitzchak's Yemeni origin is central to his mediatic persona: his accent identifies him with that underprivileged and Oriental sector of society, and he wears a *djellaba* with unique accoutrements, including a skull cap which he jokingly refers to as his "antenna." He litters his addresses with wordplay, talking of the "temblevisia" instead of the "televisia"—an allusion to the mind-numbing effects of television[12]—and likening (George W.) Bush's name to the Hebrew word for embarrassment—*busha*. Yitzchak manages to soften stark choices and thick boundaries, presenting *t'shuva* as a gradual purification of social relations, with an emphasis on joining a new community rather than on breaking bonds with the old, as a solution to everyday problems of love, family, and finding a spouse, and as a gradual process rather than a painful radical break.

Yitzchak's road show is also a business operation with some characteristics of an NGO, relying heavily on the cooperation of volunteers and on donations. His Shofar organization claims to have distributed one million videos for free in its first year, and to have sold a further million after 1996. The free distributions of videos and cassette tapes are made in the expectation that a certain number of the recipients will then become buyers and sellers. At meetings he invites his audience to "win" (i.e., buy) one thousand cassettes by making ten monthly payments of one hundred shekels. If, as in one instance, he persuades a mere twenty people out of five hundred at one neighborhood meeting to sign up, that means the sale of ten thousand tapes in a small area.

The Mischievous Millenarian: The Use of Parables and Myths to Subvert Official Discourse

Amnon Yitzchak claims to have distributed a million videos in one year for free, to have sold a million a year since 1996, and to have brought one hundred thousand returnees per year back to religion.[13] As illustrated in the previous paragraph, blanket coverage trawls a small number of committed activists, who then become collectors and distributors of cassettes and propagandists for the cause. His Hayyim Keflayim (Living Twice—and therefore being "born again") program follows up people who give their names at meetings, and gives them cassettes. Thus the organization builds up a database of people with whom it comes into contact, who might become more involved or donate funds. Like the radio stations, it encourages people to put their children into religious schools and encourages returnees on their road back to religious observance, but Yitzchak and his people have gone much further than the radio stations in creating a public of their own, in the application of business principles, and in adopting the content of American millenarian fundamentalism (Ammerman 1987). His rhetoric also goes further than (almost) any Israeli politician would dare.

At the Jerusalem Theater Yitzchak made constant reference to his cassettes: "I am saying this now that we are on cassette 200, but I already predicted it in cassette 35"; in responses to the public he would say: "but have you not listened to the last cassette"; the promotional warm-up videos already had shown his supporters distributing cassettes for free at road junctions. The cassettes seem to be the emblem of his operation, to own and listen to them is to belong, and to distribute them among one's friends and relations is to draw even closer to his campaign of t'shuva.

Dressed in his distinctive attire, Yitzchak is his own trademark. The format of his meetings includes an address by Yitzchak followed by questions from the floor. Many people want their personal problems resolved—one needs a husband, the other a wife, a young boy wants to attend religious school but his mother will not let him, and so on. Almost all the questioners—some of whom may be "planted"—speak with ease and eloquence, and Yitzchak responds in a down-to-earth sort of way. Those who have specific needs are asked to hand in a piece of paper and he blesses them all at the end of the meeting.

Antiestablishment rhetoric is fueled by wordplay and by judicious use of accent and turns of phrase. In one videocassette, filmed live, he defends the privileges, or exemptions, enjoyed by *haredim* in Israel, on the analogy of a watermelon. This is a reference to a remark by Ezer Weizman, Israel's recent head of state and, for the preacher's audience, an archetypal representative of the European, educated, secular elite, who had picked out the development of the seedless watermelon as a source of great national pride. For religious people, to whom Israel is above all the Promised Land, the notion that the country should take pride in such mundane achievements is itself laughable. But Yitzchak builds his retort around the metaphor of "black" as the color of strict religious observance. For him, Weizman, like all secular Israelis, wants an Israel without the black seeds, without the *haredim*. For Yitzchak, in contrast, the *haredim* are not only black seeds, they are also the seeds of continuity of Judaism, while the red flesh represents communism and dictatorship, that is, the godless Zionist secular regime—and the green outer skin represents fertile pasture, an image of a fertile Israel. The kibbutz, secular and emblematically Zionist, took the juice of state subsidies first, and so the *haredim* then had to come and extort their due: if the *haredim* had staked their claim first, they would not have had to exercise so much pressure later on. He then attacks a towering icon of Zionism, namely, David Ben-Gurion. Ben-Gurion, he claims, had said that Israel had to make the Jews into a "people with a culture"—thus ignoring fifty-three hundred years of Jewish culture—and introduced a German culture—that is, anti-Semitism. What, Yitzchak asks, of charity, of Sabbath observance, of respect for the sages—are these not also representative of culture?

We had occasion to appreciate the effectiveness of Yitchak's use of these devices in his address, entitled "Before the End," more or less the same, word for word, as a cassette he issued the day after the September 11 attacks which offered a golden opportunity to merchants of biblical millenarianism. He recalled his prediction at the time of the 1993 Oslo agreements that "there is no peace with terrorists" (Cassette no. 35, noted above). Two years earlier he had predicted that "the great America would shrink: no one would have predicted it, not even in their worst nightmares . . . a million Interpol agents . . . millions of recorded telephone conversations . . . all these 'sources' are of no use because those without '*spiritual* sources' are unprotected. Only those who had the Jewish sources knew it would happen."

The discourse then discusses the biblical origins of claims to the land of Israel, and quotes the Zohar, a thirteenth-century Kabbalistic text (Jacobs 1995):[14] "There will come a time when their right to the Holy Land will expire. Then the sons of Ishmael will wage war on the whole world—on sea, on land and near Jerusalem, and other peoples will participate in the struggle, but there will be no victor there will be three months of war in a far-off place and in the end only Israel will remain and the whole world will recognize the one God and his name is One. . . . No one believed these or other prophecies, yet 'the sons of Ishmael'[15] have made us the sixth power in the world and the Americans look like circus performers, like dwarfs: they took away the King's crown and slapped him in the face." Yitzchak ridicules the Americans branded by implication as the global champions of the consumer society—and, indeed, of the Israeli state itself, which trusts too much in military prowess. He predicts that two-thirds of the world will perish in the war of Gog and Magog:[16] "In 9 months of catastrophe, there will be epidemics, and limbs will be cut from bodies. Two thirds of the world will die. It is all written down—there is nothing to be done. The American attempt to impose globalization, democracy and liberalism, ignoring all religions, has come to this."

But there is a chance of salvation for Israel if the people make *t'shuva* and return to God. The history of the Jewish people is an endless alternation between abandonment of God and *t'shuva*—but "maybe this is the last *t'shuva*, maybe we can be saved as in the Exodus from Egypt. Maybe now we have finally understood and the Messiah will return in our times." (The last phrase is a frequent feature of the daily liturgy.)

Apart from the violence of the language and the message, it is worth remarking on the constant inversion of language in the discourse, with the use of word-play and caricature: the Twin Towers and the Tower of Babel, Bush juxtaposed with the Hebrew word *busha*, "intelligence sources" juxtaposed with "spiritual sources," and the ridiculing of a great power humiliated, an image of the "world upside down."

Written black on white, the speech seems extremely threatening, but in the auditorium, delivered in a low-key measured tone, mischievously peppered with jokes and ridicule of the great and powerful, including all Israeli political factions— save Shas—the audience did not respond with abnormal emotion or enthusiasm, as they might have done to fiery political rhetoric in a less genteel location.

The *T'shuva* Movement in a Comparative Perspective

As occasional remarks have indicated, there is much in the *t'shuva* movement that we have already encountered in Latin American Pentecostalism, and, although there are differences, of course, it is the similarities that deserve close attention, simply because similarities across the boundaries established by religious tradition—and certainly by the interests of religious bureaucracies—are more counterintuitive, as are differences within the boundaries.

Both Pentecostals and the *t'shuva* movement propagate a change of life, a strengthening of the family by infusing their discourse on family relationships with a halo of happiness and positive feelings, together with a strengthening of parental control over children and of husbands' authority over their wives. There are variations within as much as between: some churches insist more than others on the authority of husbands, as do some rabbis; some rabbis and preachers direct a message toward women and focus on the misfortunes of family life—unruly children, cruel husbands, lack of self-esteem—and both movements have in common a focus on changing one's life by changing one's attitudes or outlook, through return to Christ or trust in God. Occasionally a New Age tinge is added, as when people are called upon to "listen" to one another, to stay calm, to find an inner peace, but for the most part the solution offered is, in one case, a return to strict observance and, in the other, "accepting Jesus."

In both instances we observe much attention to fund-raising from the public, fronted by mediatic entrepreneurs. These entrepreneurs/preachers who combine proselytizing, managerial, and communications skills have become a standard feature of religious campaigning worldwide. The example of the Brazilian—but now international—Universal Church of the Kingdom of God (Birman and Lehmann 1999; Campos 1997; Freston 2001), which has developed a vast centralized bureaucratic and commercial apparatus out of this combination, is exceptional but emblematic: for the most part such ventures are one-man shows that operate in conjunction with other religious organizations on the ground, as Amnon Yitzchak does.

There is a straightforward explanation for the preference for radio over television, and for local stations over national networks.[17] Radio is cheaper and allows the broadcaster to target a niche audience. Local stations have technical and commercial advantages: their phone-in programs have low start-up costs, they probably avoid liability for copyright fees, operate with volunteers, and do not need to sustain uninterrupted programming—their audience quickly becomes accustomed to tuning in, so long as broadcasts keep to a regular timetable.

In Latin America, Pentecostalism has evolved a subtle and complex relationship with popular culture, and with the complex of relationships that bind the popular to the erudite in both religious and secular spheres (Lehmann 1996). Pentecostals attack the culture of Catholicism and its intertwined institutional and popular expressions, yet manage to do so while apparently deepening their penetration of popular culture. The institutional Catholic Church is depicted as luxurious and self-satisfied, cosseted in its finery and arrogant in its elaborate architecture. As in Israel, the intertwined secular cultures of the elite and the people are also targeted, using the media to present a counterculture against the rational secularism of the intellectual elite, and against the political elite (Birman and Lehmann 1999).

Popular culture exists in interdependence with the culture of the erudite and the elite—it is not a relationship of dependence, nor is the popular a mere artifact of elite manipulation. Rather, in these contexts the cultural struggle is not only for the control of popular culture but also for the power to state with authority what that culture consists of.

The paradox is that, despite their often dramatic rejection of the culture of the popular sectors, Pentecostals also successfully portray themselves as closer to the language and daily concerns of those same popular sectors. This is achieved by a refashioning of the imaginary of popular culture and by operating transformations in the popular-elite relationship. Pentecostals benefit from the contrast between the social distance separating highly trained Catholic priests, educated in seminaries and sometimes abroad, and the style of their own pastors who are close to "the people," speak a direct, jargon-free language, and confront the day-to-day problems of their followers. But the pastors retain a distance, although a different sort of distance: they do not adopt a humble persona of "men of the people." Instead, they present to their followers a role model of prosperity and bourgeois respectability.

If in Israel we have observed the affinity of *t'shuva* with the renaissance of the Sephardi ethnicity, in Latin America we find that Pentecostals are particularly successful among indigenous people, and that in Brazil Pentecostals have appropriated and refashioned the symbolic apparatus associated with the African heritage, even while claiming to discredit that heritage. The *t'shuva* movement's Sephardi leaders have inverted symbolic structures of exclusion and low status by invoking them as emblems of a grand tradition which, they say, remained unbroken while the Ashkenazi tradition was interrupted and weakened by the Enlightenment and the Holocaust. Like the Pentecostals, they have also mounted a two-pronged attack on the religious establishment of the Ashkenazi ultra-Orthodox—whose parties Shas outnumbered by seventeen to five Knesset seats in 2002—and on the secular elite. They have adapted the music of popular culture to their religious crusade by keeping the tunes but exchanging secular lyrics for liturgical verses; their radio broadcasts are a permanent thorn in the side of the regulators of broadcasting; they transform Talmudic debate by their use of street language and their evocation of the stresses and strains of daily life—sprinkled with abundant rabbinic allusions and stories.

T'shuva Israeli-style does not explicitly confront the religious establishment in the same way as Pentecostals confront Catholic hegemony. But in these matters content counts less than form—and by form is meant the rearrangement and appropriation of symbols and ethnic identifiers, and the concomitant redrawing of public spaces. In this chapter we have shown how, for all the use of modern communications media, the time-honored formal accoutrements of religion—ritual, taboo, the delineation of space, style, language, dress, and so forth—are more than equal to the challenge of reclaiming public space from a secular intelligentsia to whom these arms are quite foreign. The t'shuva movement is hardly likely to reclaim the whole of public space, as no doubt it would like, but it is certainly redrawing its boundaries.

Notes

The authors gratefully acknowledge the support received for this research from the Leverhulme Foundation. We wish to acknowledge the research assistance of Ari Engelberg, whose expertise has helped us avoid many mistakes. Remaining errors are ours alone. The essay does not take into account political developments after 2002.

1. "The major Zionist camps—the socialist camp, itself composed of several parties, the Zionist National Religious Party; the mainstream, liberal General Zionist Party; the right wing identified with Jabotinsky—all developed their own autonomous organizations in the various fields of Zionist activity: agricultural settlement, schooling, youth movements, banking, housing, employment, health, and defense" (Swirski 1999, 88).

2. Since Cabinet members vote and the votes are published, the Cabinet can be seen as Israel's de facto Upper House.

3. Technically this is on a par with Muslim and Christian control over family law as well, following the pattern established by the Ottoman Empire. On the Muslim side of the equation and the general framework, see R. Eisenman 1978 and G. Barzilai 2003.

4. T'shuva literally translated means "return" or "repentance." Estimates based on social surveys and the census show that the ultra-Orthodox population in 1995 numbered 280,000 and accounted for 5.2 percent of the total Israeli population (including Arabs); but their very high fertility plus t'shuva will bring those figures to 510,000 and 7.7 percent, respectively, and possibly higher by 2010 (Berman 2000).

5. Tamar El-Or (1994) describes how the leader of the Gur Chassidim (Chassidim being the more mystical wing of the Ashkenazi ultra-Orthodox community) decreed that in order to extend their influence in Israeli society young married couples should live away from their parents for at least five years. The result was that they created the same inward-looking communities, but as islands in a secular sea. The Chassidim, dependent as they are on very thick and impermeable boundaries to protect their ever more severe stringency, have not developed the method of concentric circles that serves Shas and the t'shuva movement, and many other social movements, so well.

6. The Israeli term is "regional," but it is better rendered as "local" given the small spaces involved.

7. Schach died in November 2001 at the age of 107 (or thereabouts).

8. There are seven official stations: two belong to the army, one of which is a news and current affairs channel and the other transmits mostly music—in both cases with an eye to a highly secular, youthful audience, especially soldiers; Programme 1 consists largely of high culture; Programme 2 is made up mostly of news and politics; and Programme 3 concentrates on Israeli music of all sorts; Network 88 broadcasts jazz and "world music," and Kol Hamusika (the Voice of Music) specializes in classical music. It is not hard to see that this leaves plenty of room for alternative stations.

9. An additional sub-controversy concerned air safety, since it is widely believed that the radios interfere, or could interfere, with air traffic control (hence the involvement of the minister of transport, who, however, seemed more concerned to make a political point than to ensure air safety!) On September 2, 2002, several flights had to be canceled because the pilots could not communicate with the control tower, apparently because of the pirate radios, and there was talk of a protest strike by air traffic control staff.

10. "Not surprisingly" because of the elective affinity between movements of religious renewal and the New Age culture, given their interest in healing, and in the case of Jewish ultra-Orthodoxy, an uneasy attitude to medical manipulation of the body—especially of women's bodies.

11. Even the history of television provides an example of this. The Second Television Channel started to function as an "experiment" in 1986 and continued to do so for seven years before the authorizing law was finally passed. This was partly because of the need to "seize" frequencies before other countries in the region did so, but also to meet public demand for an alternative to the only other channel available (Caspi and Limor 1999, 153). An article in Ha'aretz (Kim 2002) explains how West Bank settlers, despite the lack

of support for their cause in public opinion, have become an indispensable part of the Israeli economy and how they have also attracted a steady flow of people not for ideological reasons but because they provide cheap (subsidized) housing and social services, and even schools with smaller class sizes. These benefits are a result of unremitting political pressure creating, once again, "facts on the ground," not only physically but also politically.

12. *Tembel* is Hebrew for "foolish."

13. If that were true, the whole of Israel would soon be "black" (a standard usage referring to the black suits worn permanently by *haredi* men).

14. The legends and controversies are summarized by Louis Jacobs (1995, 628–630).

15. That is, the Arabs.

16. A periodic theme in Jewish and Christian eschatology, derived originally from the Book of the Prophet Ezekiel, 38,39.

17. Even the one apparent exception to this statement—Brazil's Universal Church of the Kingdom of God, which owns a nationwide television network (TV Record)—is deceptive, since TV Record only transmits religious content very late at night and very early in the morning: for the rest of the time its content is standard television—although a bit more restrained than its rivals. The church operates numerous local radios throughout Brazil.

References

Ammerman, N. T. 1987. *Bible Believers: Fundamentalists in the Modern World.* New Brunswick, N.J.: Rutgers University Press.

Barzilai, G. 2003. *Communities and Law: Politics and Cultures of Legal Identities.* Ann Arbor: University of Michigan Press.

Berman, Eli. 2000. Sect, Subsidy, and Sacrifice: An Economist's View of Ultra-Orthodox Jews. *Quarterly Journal of Economics* 115 (3): 905–953.

Birman, P., and D. Lehmann. 1999. Religion and the Media in a Battle for Ideological Hegemony. *Bulletin of Latin American Research* 18 (2): 145–164.

Campos, L. S. 1997. *Teatro, templo e mercado: Organizaçao e marketing de um empreendimento neopentecostal.* Petropolis, São Paulo, São Bernardo do Campo, UMESP, Vozes, Simposio.

Caspi, D., and Y. Limor. 1999. *The In/Outsiders: The Media in Israel.* Cresskill, N.J.: Hampton.

Eisenman, R. 1978. *Islamic Law in Palestine and Israel.* Leiden: E. J. Brill.

El-Or, T. 1994. *Educated and Ignorant: Ultra-Orthodox Jewish Women and Their World.* Boulder, Colo.: Lynne Rienner.

Freston, P. 2001. The Transnationalization of Brazilian Pentecostalism: The Universal Church of the Kingdom of God. In *Between Babel and Pentecost: Transnational Pentecostalism in Africa and Latin America,* ed. A. Corten and R. Marshall-Fratani. Bloomington: Indiana University Press.

Herzog, H. 1995. Penetrating the System: The Politics of Collective Identities. In *The Elections in Israel—1992,* ed. A. Arian and M. Shamir, 81–102. Albany: State University of New York Press.

Horowitz, D., and M. Lissak. 1987. *Trouble in Utopia: The Overburdened Polity in Israel.* Albany: State University of New York Press.

Jacobs, L. 1995. *The Jewish Religion: A Companion.* Oxford: Oxford University Press.

Katz, J. 1973. *Out of the Ghetto: The Social Background of Jewish Emancipation, 1770–1870.* Cambridge, Mass.: Harvard University Press.

Kim, Hannah. 2002. The Secret of the Settlers' Strength. *Ha'aretz,* July 2, 2002.

Lehmann, D. 1996. *Struggle for the Spirit: Religious Transformation and Popular Culture in Brazil and Latin America.* Oxford: Polity.

———. 1998. Fundamentalism and Globalism. *Third World Quarterly* 19 (4): 607–634.

Leon, N. 1999. Sephardim and *Haredim:* An Ethnographic Inquiry into the Meaning of the Influence of the Shas Movement on the Perception of Oriental Haredi Identity and Discourse Thereon. University of Tel-Aviv, Department of Sociology.

———. 2000. "The Generation Gap, the Persecuted, the Territory, and the 'Television Dupes': Research on the Language of the Shas Communities" (in Hebrew), *Panim* 14:15–24.

———. 2001. The Glory of a Generation: The Persecuted and the "Television Dupes" (in Hebrew). In *The Dividing Line,* ed. R. Rosenthal, 285–298. Tel Aviv: Hemed.

Regev, M. 1996. *Muzika mizrakhit:* Israeli Rock and National Culture in Israel. *Popular Music* 15 (3): 275–284.

Shafir, G., and Y. Peled. 2002. *Being Israeli: The Dynamics of Multiple Citizenship.* Cambridge: Cambridge University Press.

Swirski, S. 1999. *Politics and Education in Israel: Comparisons with the United States.* London: Falmer.

Willis, A. 1995. The Sephardic Torah Guardians: Religious "Movement" and Political Power. *The Elections in Israel—1992,* ed. A. Arian and M. Shamir. Albany: State University of New York Press.

Zohar, Z. 2001. *Restoring the Crown to Its Ancient Glory: Rabbi Ovadia Yossef's Vision of a Unified Israeli Judaism.* Bar Ilan University and Shalom Hartman Institute, Jerusalem.

Part Two | *Public Religion and the*
Politics of Difference

5 Representing Family Law Debates in Palestine: Gender and the Politics of Presence

Annelies Moors

In the 1990s family law was once more hotly contested throughout the Muslim world.[1] As a major means of regulating marriage, divorce, custody, and inheritance, family law is central to the organization of gender relations and to the reproduction of the social and cultural order in general. If this in itself makes reforming family law already a highly sensitive issue, it is more so in that family law, in many settings, is also the last stronghold of the religious establishment and the only field of law explicitly framed through Islamic notions of morality.[2] Debates about Palestinian family law, starting in the mid-1990s, bring such sensitivities to the fore. These debates have not only been a popular topic in the local news media but have also been addressed in academic writing and documentary filmmaking. A comparison of the work of a number of academic authors (such as Hammami and Johnson 1999; Jad, Johnson, and Giacaman 2000; Welchman 2003; and Hammami et al. 2004) with that of a prominent filmmaker (al-Zobaidi 1998) provides new insights into the ways in which particular media present and engage with public debates on family law. Whereas, as I argue in this chapter, the authors and the filmmaker analyze how gender and Islam are implicated in these debates in very similar ways, there are striking differences in the information that texts and film provide their audiences. Juxtaposing the verbal accounts of academic writing and the visual information presented in the documentary I point to these differences, but I also elaborate on issues that have been little theorized in current work on the modern public sphere, especially the importance of the styles of participating in the public and the various ways in which power is at stake, be it in terms of agency and discipline or as inclusion and exclusion.

In theoretical terms, if the neglect of gender has been a major flaw in earlier work on the modern public sphere, how religion is seen as impacting women—once recognized as a relevant category—also needs to be revisited.[3] The early Habermasian notion that secularization is a precondition for the development of a modern public sphere continues to be prominent in debates about women and Islam. More recently, however, the contribution of Islam to the emergence of a modern public sphere has been recognized.[4] It has been argued that a modern *Muslim* public sphere has come into being with an increasingly diverse set of actors and publics engaging in public debate about the common good (Eickelman and Anderson 1999; Salvatore and Eickelman 2004). Within this framework, the Islamization of the public sphere is no longer viewed as necessarily negative for women. Yet those arguing for the emancipatory effects of processes of secularization, as well as those pointing to the enabling effects of Islamization, make assumptions that need to be scrutinized. Employing a notion of agency that is equated with freedom and emancipation leaves out the forms of disciplining that are simultaneously at stake, while a focus on the greater variety of participants involved in public debate may result in overlooking the people and practices that have become marginalized. At the same time, conceptualizing the modern public sphere—be it "secular" or "Muslim"—as an arena of verbal debate easily leads to the neglect of other forms of communication, such as comportment, body language, and styles of dress. In short, public spheres are not simply sites of disembodied debate but are also arenas for the formation and enactment of embodied social identities, where group identities and interests are always at play (Fraser 1992; Warner 1992). The central question, then, is how certain groups are able to deny their particularities and present themselves as embodying the common good, as *the* public (Mah 2000), a notion that is always unstable and a site of struggle and contestation. An analysis of public debates about family law in Palestine highlights the need to address issues of both voice and authority as well as the politics of embodied presence.

Debating Family Law in Palestine: Verbal and Visual Accounts

Public debates about family law emerged soon after the establishment of the Palestinian Authority (PA) in parts of the West Bank and the Gaza Strip in 1994. Unifying the legal systems of both areas and deciding what sort of legal system to adopt was one of the most pressing issues confronting legislators. Prominent members of the shari'a judiciary took the initiative to ensure separate communal jurisdiction of the shari'a courts. Human rights groups and women's nongovernmental organizations (NGOs) developed projects to identify legal provisions that discriminated against women and to propose reforms. When they started a series of public discussions on family law, the Islamists also entered into the debate.[5]

What lines of argumentation did the various participants use to legitimize their positions?[6] To the religious functionaries it was self-evident that family law fell within their field of expertise. The women's NGO movement, on the other hand, with a long history of nationalist engagement and a tradition of secularist cultural politics, argued on the basis of an equality platform within the framework of human rights and UN conventions.[7] While they had expected that this would be acceptable to the Palestinian public, it turned out to be a bone of contention. The Islamists sharply criticized the women's groups for receiving financial support from international organizations, labeled the women involved as "Westernized," and accused them of conspiring to weaken Palestinian society by undermining its most central institution, the family. They denounced them in the mosques and argued that they were not even qualified to take part in such debates. The very fierceness of the public attacks by the Islamists provoked a counter-mobilization of those defending the legitimacy of holding such debates. Next to human rights organizations, women's groups, and political parties, the Palestinian Authority also defended the organizers of these debates, less because it was concerned about the Islamist vision of family relations than because it worried about the mobilizing power of the Islamist rhetoric. As a result, the focus shifted from the substance of family law to a debate about freedom of expression.

While the academic authors highlight the sensitivities involved in debating family law, focusing on the tensions between the secular women NGOs and the Islamists, they simultaneously underline that neither the positions of the "men of religion" nor those of the women's groups were unidimensional. It is true that both the Islamists and the religious establishment argued for limiting the right to participate in debates about Muslim family law to "those qualified" (i.e., religiously trained scholars), but the ways in which the religious establishment dealt with these issues differed considerably from that of the Islamists. Once it became clear that the Islamists were intent on politicizing the issue, the religious functionaries kept their distance; also, those who considered drafting proposals as the prerogative of the religious establishment were willing to address issues raised by women activists and to engage in debate with them. In a similar vein the authors underlined the variety of points of view held by women activists, paying attention both to those arguing for an optional civil law and to those arguing for substantial reforms of Muslim family law. They also pointed to activists' growing awareness of class differences. If those who were better off could afford to criticize the concept of the male breadwinner, lower-class women may well have a greater interest in the implementation of women's maintenance rights.

Still, the emphasis on the oppositional positions taken by the "Islamists" and the "women NGO activists" has left one particular category, the Islamist women, largely out of the picture. Little attention has been paid to the points of view of women associated with Islamist movements, many of whom were very critical of women NGO projects. The visual information provided by Subhi al-Zobaidi's documentary film, *Women in the Sun* (1998), is helpful here.[8] It is true that the messages al-Zobaidi intends to convey in his film about family law debates tally neatly with the lines of argumentation present in the academic texts mentioned above: the various participants to the debates and their arguments are well presented. But as a visual means of communication the film also includes layers of information concerning issues such as comportment, body language, and styles of dress that the articles do not provide. Authors of written texts may have a number of reasons to refrain from informing readers about appearances and styles of presentation. They may consider writing about issues such as dressing styles not only irrelevant but also distracting from matters of content, and hence of substance. Including such issues may be seen as an intrusion of their informants' privacy, especially in those cases where the latter themselves underline that dressing styles are a matter of individual choice and ought to be irrelevant for the issues at hand. The problem is, however, that others may hold a different point of view on this issue. They may well consider styles of dress as a matter of substance; rather than seeing it as a private issue, they may see it as a matter of public morality. Hence, although dressing styles do not have an inherent meaning outside those attributed to it by those involved, be it as wearers or spectators or both, the latter may well assume such fixity. The main point is that, whereas in a written analysis the author can choose whether to include information about styles of self-presentation, this is much less an option in presenting visual documentary material, even if allowing for the possibilities producers have to cut and frame their material.

Al-Zobaidi's film includes shots of a number of NGO women speakers as well as an extremely vocal male Islamist, who attempted not only to silence the former but also to control the large number of women in the audience wearing "covered dress" (*hijab*). One element immediately visible in the documentary is the differences in women's dressing styles and the apparent overlap, even if partial, between styles of dress and positions taken in the debate. For without positing a necessary link between wearing (or not wearing) *hijab* and taking a particular political stance, it is hard to avoid noticing that those wearing covered dress and those not seemed to be taking up different positions in these debates. Yet, although those addressing the audience and presenting longer statements were the NGO women activists, who were not wearing *hijab*, the large number of covered women were not simply passive. If their presence in itself can already be read as a statement of sorts, it is through more explicit forms of body language, such as nodding, applauding, facial expressions, and other forms of showing approval and disapproval of the speakers' points of view, that they engaged in the debate as an active audience. Hence, whereas political positions cannot be read from styles of dress, focusing on body language in a wider sense indicates that these women largely supported Islamist arguments.

Visual mediation also provides insight into the styles of argumentation and, more generally, the ways in which particular participants try to gain the upper hand not only through the exchange of arguments but also through their attempts to control and silence other participants. The film shows how the previously mentioned male Islamist openly attempted to control both the women NGO activists and the Islamist women. In the case of the former he placed himself simultaneously in the position of participant and of moderator, ordering the Islamist women to remain silent and to let his secular counterpart speak first. He then set the parameters for the ensuing debate, by allowing his opponent to make an argument and then immediately making a counterargument himself. His attempts to control the Islamist women were highlighted in a revealing scene where he publicly discarded a statement they had prepared, apparently because its wordings diverged from what he himself had proposed. Although clearly such visual imagery can also be described verbally while the aural (spoken texts as well as sound) is also important toward understanding what we see, the visualization that film allows is nevertheless crucial to gaining insight into the relations between the participants in public debates.

Figs. 5.1 and 5.2. Stills 1 and 2 from *Women in the Sun* (produced by Subhi al-Zobaidi, 1998).

Women Entering the Modern Public Sphere

The attention paid in *Women in the Sun* to the attempts of a leading male Islamist to silence women, activist women in particular, makes it easy to read this film as a critique of political Islam.[9] As such, it would fit in with the Habermasian line of thought that considers public religion as antithetical to the development of a modern public sphere, and sees participatory politics and emancipation as intrinsically linked to processes of secularization. Such a point of view is based on the construction of a dichotomy between, on the one hand, a secular public sphere of rational debate between free and autonomous individuals and, on the other, an authoritarian religious world subjecting the individual to uniform models of moral behavior (see also Hirschkind 2001a). Yet this contrast scheme of linking secularization with freedom and religion with constraint disregards the ways in which participation in public debate is always based on particular notions of personhood, embodying long-standing practices of (self-)disciplining.

In order to better understand these disciplinary aspects of the modern secular public sphere, especially regarding gender relations, the work of Najmabadi (1993) on early-twentieth-century Tehran provides important insights. She takes issue with the notion that modernity has transformed early-twentieth-century Tehrani women from being absent from the public sphere into becoming active participants. Her analysis turns this transformation from absence to presence into something far more complicated. Rather than conceptualizing women entering the public sphere as free and autonomous agents, she points out how modernity simultaneously entailed a particular style of disciplining women's words, bodies, and minds. To be deemed fit to enter the modern public sphere, premodern women, in hindsight seen as ignorant, uncivilized, and restricted to an all-female world, had to be turned into women who were well-behaved, polite, and quiet, who were good mothers, suitable partners for their husbands, and committed supporters of the nation. Only after being thus transformed could they claim a space in the public sphere without threatening the social order.[10]

Those who see the modern public sphere as secular have pointed to the importance of education and the growing market for print media for the development of such a public sphere. In the case of women, such arguments have often been brought to the fore with particular urgency. Reconsidering such notions, Najmabadi (1993), however, highlights how modern education and the print media not only enabled women to participate in the public sphere but were also pivotal in disciplining women's styles of speaking and writing in particular ways. While among the higher circles in Tehran there is a long history of women engaging in oral performances for all-female audiences (with some handwritten texts circulating among a limited female audience), the shift to the printed journal and the book meant that women's words could be read by anyone, including men. Women engaging in creating texts for print had to take into account that they were now addressing a hetero-social rather than an all-female homo-social public. This uncontrolled circulation of texts engendered a particular form of self-censorship, necessitating the development of a language with sexual markers modified or removed. In a similar vein, modern schools not only provided children with scientific education but also installed certain forms of discipline. Through the format and content of the educational project these schools were instrumental for the development of new moral behaviors. They produced women who had learned the new, modern ways of managing the household, their children, and their husband, and who would be able to participate in a male public sphere without being too much of a disturbing factor. Both institutions, schools and the print media, did not simply allow greater access to the public sphere but simultaneously functioned as mechanisms for disciplining participants and installing a new sense of self, one directed toward self-control even if employing the language of freedom.

The Habermasian notion of the modern public sphere is also limiting in its exclusive focus on rational debate as the only legitimate form of participating in the modern public sphere. Because individuals are seen as abstracted from all social characteristics when participating in the modern public sphere, the only suitable mode of communication is rational argumentation; other forms and styles of communication are seen a priori as ineffective and undesirable. If, however, the public sphere is recognized as an arena where group identities and interests are always at stake, then there is a need for a more all-encompassing "politics of presence" that allows for the inclusion of other forms of critical expression and nonverbal modes of communication. Such forms and styles of presentation may include, for instance, bodily comportment, appearance, styles of dress, and the nature of the language used rather than only its substance. In other words, a "politics of presence," as a broadened notion of engagement in the public sphere, allows for the inclusion of a greater variety of ways in which people "make a statement," as it were. Whereas this gains particular saliency when discussing contributions of subaltern groups that may be less well versed in effectively presenting their points of view in normalized and hence acceptable formats of "rational argumentation," such forms of "body politics" may also be state-driven.

In Turkey and Iran a cultural politics that encouraged or even obliged women to unveil became a central element of state policy from the 1920s on. Here the modern public sphere did not stand in opposition to, or even at a distance from, the state; on the contrary, issues of dress were part and parcel of official reform programs of modernization. In Turkey, where the Kemalist state attempted to make Islam subservient to the state, state institutions were heavily involved in removing all markers of Islam from the public sphere. This included policies and regulations that were instrumental in discouraging women from wearing Islamic dress; in particular settings, such as state schools, women were, in fact, forbidden to cover their heads (Göle 1996). In Iran, where Reza Shah also strongly advocated cultural modernization through dress codes, the regulations concerning women's dress culminated in a general ban for women to wear the *chador* that lasted from 1936 till 1941 (Baker 1997). As a result, whereas some would avoid engaging in a hetero-social public sphere altogether, others started to take part in the developing secularist culture where refraining from wearing *hijab* was not only rapidly becoming acceptable but, as the crucial marker of modernity, also turned into a hegemonic practice (see Navaro-Yashin 2002). Yet, also for the latter, this did not simply mean a widening of the field of possibilities, an entry into the world of freedom and emancipation. As Najmabadi (1993) points out, the physical movement of uncovered women into the public sphere was conditioned upon women developing a particular form of desexualized body language, that required new forms of self-discipline.[11]

The cultural politics of particular state institutions that have strongly propagated (if not obliged) women to unveil and to participate in a hetero-social public sphere raises not only the question regarding the conditions in which women were deemed suitable to participate. Also inherent in such a modern public sphere may be the exclusion of those whose normative notions are different, often women from the rural areas and the poorer sections of urban society. Whereas a modern public sphere may indeed include new participants, women's moves into the modern-secular public sphere not only brought about the sanitization of women's language and the disciplining of women's bodies but also the concomitant demise of a homo-social women's world (Najmabadi 1993; see also Abu-Lughod 1998). The point here is not to naively idealize systems of gender segregation but, first, to acknowledge the existence of such semi-autonomous female public spheres and, more specifically, to investigate these in relation to the development of a modern public sphere.[12] For forms of female homo-social interaction have often been overlooked in debates about the public sphere as the former have not readily been recognized as public. From a man's viewpoint, such female public spheres contain an element of secrecy; they remain largely invisible and inaccessible to men. That activities often take place at the houses of the women involved further encourages the conception that these so-called female public spheres are actually located in the field of the private. Yet when investigating women's interactions and debates in these settings, these forms are, at least in some sense, clearly public.[13] For in many settings with a tradition of gender segregation, women have been, and to some extent still are, engaged in well-organized and formalized all-female visiting circles that work as fora for discussions of matters of general interest and the common good, varying from marital politics to national politics.[14] Such women-only settings may be considered as subaltern parallel publics that function, depending on the content and the style of their interactions and their positioning in relation to the general public, as sub- or counterpublics. Yet, with the development of a modern hetero-social public sphere, such female homo-social semipublic spheres have often become devalued and turned into something "merely private." Celebratory notions about women's moves into a hetero-social public sphere have often failed to analyze the concomitant demise of semi-autonomous female public spheres.

Gendering the New Muslim Public Sphere

If one reading of *Women in the Sun* supports the notion that women's interests are best served by secularizing the public sphere, another interpretation is also possible, one that highlights the presence of Islamist women as an active public yet marginalized by the vocal presence of male Islamist and secular women activists. Such an understanding brings us to a strand of thought that has questioned the negative evaluation of the presence of religion in the public sphere. The contributions of religious associations, movements, and informal networks to the development of a modern public sphere both in Europe and elsewhere have become increasingly recognized (van der Veer 2002; Eickelman and Salvatore 2002). Not only has the linkage of secularization with freedom become the subject of debate but so, too, has the association of religion with structural constraints. Religiously inspired subjects are no longer seen as simply acting out scripts imposed by religious authorities; notions of collective morality may recognize individual responsibility while agency needs to be acknowledged also when this entails aiming at self-control (Asad 1986; Hirschkind 2001a).

One line of argument is that the development of a new Muslim public sphere has allowed for a more diverse field of participants and publics to engage in public debate (Eickelman and Anderson 1999). Also in this case, as a mirror image of the discussion on the "secular" public sphere, the impact of mass literacy and the mass media is highlighted.[15] The spread of literacy and the development of higher education have been crucial means to enable individuals to access and read the central Islamic texts themselves, bypassing traditional religious authorities. The field of those able to directly engage in debates about textual interpretations has not only increased substantially but the growth of mass education and the mass media has also contributed to the "objectification of religion," that is, the development of a greater awareness and self-consciousness of what it means to be a Muslim (Eickelman 1992; Eickelman and Piscatori 1996, 37–42). Yet, also in this case, as has been argued above, such technologies of self are not simply emancipatory but simultaneously entail particular forms of discipline. Schools are not only sites where children acquire literacy; they are also institutions where children are socialized in particular ways and where new forms of discipline are internalized. The development of the new media not only enables new forms of participatory politics but also demands new sorts of practical knowledge and engenders particular forms of discipline (cf. Hirschkind 2001b).

More generally, debates about the contribution of religion to the development of the modern public sphere have mainly focused on intellectual trends or religious movements, with the spotlight on the points of view propagated by the leadership. Such studies tally quite neatly with Habermas's focus on the exchange of ideas and opinions as central in the formation of the modern public sphere, leaving out entirely nonverbal, embodied forms of communication. If, from the 1920s on, wearing "secular dress" has been encouraged, even proscribed by state institutions in Turkey and Iran and gradually spreading among the population, as well as in the postcolonial Arab republics, by the 1970s a new trend became visible with increasing numbers of women starting to wear a new style of covered dress. This particular style of dress has often been referred to as the "new veiling" or "Islamic dress," because it was both a new style of dress, visibly different from the covered dressing styles of poorer urban and rural women, and because it was first worn by young, well-educated, urban women who consciously chose to do so.[16]

This movement toward wearing a new style of covered dress was not supported by state institutions but began as an oppositional move. Women who started to wear this new form of covered dress in the 1970s and early 1980s often did so as an expression of their affinity to the cultural politics of Islamist movements (for Egypt, see El-Guindi 1981; for Turkey, see Göle 1996). For many others, especially in the 1980s and 1990s, wearing covered dress no longer signified a particular political stance but was related to wider social and cultural-religious trends, intrinsic to forms of Islamization from below (Saktanber 2002; Göle 2002). This tied in with women's growing access to education and the labor market. Whereas in the first half of the twentieth century higher education had been restricted to the elite and the professional classes, starting in the 1950s (and in some areas considerably later) female literacy, higher education, and, in its wake, women's employment in a hetero-social public sphere started to gain momentum. The large numbers of women from the lower-middle classes entering the public sphere often felt more comfortable doing so if wearing a modern style of covered dress (MacLeod 1995). To complicate matters further, for some groups notions of religious virtue such as female modesty and piety were at stake as a motivating force. These women considered bodily acts, such as wearing covered dress, not so much a critical marker of identity but also a crucial means to train oneself to be pious. In this case, dressing styles are not so much a reflection of a particular state of inner being but rather help to produce particular dispositions, such as modesty (Mahmood 2001).[17] Hence, next to the "unveiled woman," another actor appeared on the public stage, namely, the woman involved in the "new veiling." Just as in the case of her unveiled counterpart, this new veiled woman was also often seen as a rupture with the traditionally veiled woman. Wearing forms of modern covered dress, the latter became engaged in Islamizing the public sphere while at the same time distancing herself from premodern veiled women who lacked discipline and self-consciousness.[18]

This raises the questions of the extent to which the development of a new Muslim public sphere has indeed drawn a greater variety of participants in public debates, and, in particular, whether the Islamization of the public sphere has also brought about certain forms of exclusion. One issue to be discussed would be the space available for expressing different points of view about notions of morality, people's well-being, and the common good. The new Muslim publics, as they have been called, tend to base their claims to legitimacy and authority on their direct engagements with the central texts. This emphasis on the importance of unmediated access to the central Islamic texts rather than relying on the accumulated knowledge of religious scholars may encourage interpretations that allow for openness, debate, and pluralism. However, it may also lead to interpretations that are considered normative for all, linking one's being a pious Muslim to particular public lifestyles and forms of state authority. For it is not only secularist state projects that have excluded "others" from the public sphere. In Iran, for instance, after the Islamic Revolution, wearing Islamic dress turned from an expression of opposition to the ruling Shah into a dress code imposed on all by the new Islamic Republic.[19] In the case of Palestine, Hamas waged a campaign in 1989—the second year of the first intifada—for women to wear Islamic dress. Not only did Hamas sympathizers paint slogans on the houses of those not adhering to the covered-dress code imploring them to "wear Islamic dress" but some women were also physically attacked (Hammami 1990). Moving from self-discipline to disciplining others, both ruling secularist regimes and Islamic governments or strong local Islamic movements may limit or condition women's moving into the public sphere. Furthermore, the new emphasis on the importance of engaging with central texts may also effect publics involved in more "practical" forms of Islam. In many settings new patterns of authority among women have emerged. Often younger, well-educated women, who have started to engage in reading and interpreting the central Islamic texts, have become critical of the everyday, ritualistic forms of Islam that are practiced by elderly women or by women from the more popular sections of the population. While the former have increasingly started to participate in public, the latter have become increasingly marginalized.[20]

The "Not-Yet Conscious"

The understandings proposed by *Women in the Sun* about debates on family law and the previously mentioned academic writings support each other in many ways. Both point to the wide variety of actors involved in these debates and zoom in on the ways in which women activists address family law reforms. Still, the visual nature of the documentary film takes us beyond the verbal statements of major protagonists to such issues as body language and styles of dress. If in these debates few Islamist women take the floor as speakers, they have a presence of their own as active audience. As a visual medium *Women in the Sun* enables not only a reading that highlights how Islamists may impede women's participation in the public sphere but also one that points to the exclusion of women who seem supportive of an Islamist stance. In the first instance these two readings appear to take off from opposite positions. Yet an analysis of the ways in which notions of agency and power are implicated points to major convergences. Both those who consider secularization as a precondition for the development of a modern public sphere, and those who acknowledge the opportunities a Muslim public sphere offers, consider education and the media crucial in enabling women to participate in the public sphere. The difference, of course, rests on which practices and participants are to be included and excluded in the public sphere.

Employing a discourse of emancipation and freedom, those arguing for a secular public sphere tend to overlook the fact that, also in that case, women had to develop certain forms of discipline in order to be allowed to participate "in public." Those stating that the development of a Muslim public sphere has meant the participation of a greater variety of women in the public, including "religious women," often fail to recognize that their cultural politics may simultaneously restrict the options of others. Still, more interesting than this inversion of exclusions is the ways in which *both* distance themselves from "traditional women," that is, women who have (not yet) reached the required level of self-reflexivity, knowledge, and consciousness to count in the modern public sphere. In doing so they reinvent, as it were, another contrast scheme, not one of religious versus secular but rather one of "traditional" versus "modern," with the former seen as habitually conforming to existing structures and the latter as self-conscious and reflexive agents. The opposition of "conscious Muslims" (or, for that matter, "conscious secularists") versus those simply living according to their traditions needs to be recognized for what it is, a modern construction that produces the past as the Other. If "the modern" tend to overstate their reflexivity and consciousness, they also far too easily construct the not-yet modern / not-yet conscious as engaging in "unthinking conformity" (Asad 1986, 16). This then raises the question of who represents the interests of the not-yet modern in family law debates.

Notes

1. See, for instance, the contributions on Yemen, Morocco, Palestine, and Mali in the special issue of *Islamic Law and Society* 10, no. 1 (2003), entitled "Public Debates on Family Law Reform: Participants, Positions, and Styles of Argumentation in the 1990s."

2. Gender relations and "the position of women" have been controversial topics in both colonial and postcolonial periods, with discussions often framed in terms of the desirability of Westernization versus the call for cultural authenticity (see Ahmed 1992).

3. If the early Habermasian notion of the public sphere was a bourgeois public sphere or, more to the point, a male bourgeois sphere, in his more recent work Habermas (1992) has elaborated on the contribution of subaltern groups to the production of a modern public sphere (and the pluralization of the public sphere). Recognizing that women are not simply denied equal participation in the public sphere like other subaltern groups, he points out (following Pateman 1983) that the relation between the public and the private sphere is itself gendered, with men's participation in the public sphere building upon women's domestication. This contribution expresses a different take on the gendered nature of the public sphere by dealing with locally and historically specific notions of publicness and the ways in which gender is implicated.

4. The literature on Iran is a paradigmatic case. In her bibliographic essay, Mir-Hosseini (1999) distinguishes between the first wave of literature published in the 1980s shortly after the Islamic revolution and the second wave emerging in the 1990s. Whereas the first wave argues strongly against any possibility of reconciling Islam and women's rights (as in Tabari and Yeganeh 1982; Azari 1983; Afshar 1982), the second wave explores these possibilities more openly. Also, some authors have shifted position, as evident when comparing references from the 1980s with Afshar 1998, Najmabadi 1998 (formerly writing under the name Tabari), and Paidar 1995, 1996 (formerly writing under the name Yeganeh). In contrast, Moghissi (1994) has remained a strong proponent of the need for secularization. In popular writings and the media, the thesis "Islam is bad for women" is still common.

5. The main project referred to in the articles and the film is the Palestinian Model Parliament: Women and Legislation. The aim of the Model Parliament, initiated by a nongovernmental women's organization, the Women's Center for Legal Aid and Counseling (WCLAC) in 1996, was to identify legal provisions that discriminated against women's rights and to debate and build consensus around proposals for legal change that were to be brought to the attention of the Palestinian Legislative Council.

6. The following account is largely based on Hammami and Johnson 1999; Jad, Johnson, and Giacaman 2000; Hammami et al. 2004; and Welchman 2003. For a description of the different positions the participants put forward, see, especially, Jad, Johnson, and Giacaman 2000, 147ff.; for the diversity of positions taken up by the religious establishment, see, especially, Welchman 2003. As I focus on the differences between written texts and visual information, this is a generalizing account that does not do justice to differences between these articles and their authors.

7. The women's NGO movement refers to women activists organized in women's committees as well as in women's research and resource NGOs, such as WCLAC (see note 5, above). For the erosion of women's mass-based activism and the shift toward "formal politics" after the establishment of the Palestinian Authority, see Johnson and Kuttab 2001, 26ff.

8. Whereas the main focus of *Women in the Sun* is violence against women, the film also includes a considerable number of scenes where proposals for a Palestinian family law are publicly debated. This chapter only deals with the sections concerning family law debates; I do not discuss the contribution of the film to public debate more generally. *Women in the Sun* opened at the Popular Arts Center in Ramallah in 1998, and has also been widely shown abroad (at events such as the Arab Film Festival in San Francisco in 1999, the Amnesty International Film Festival in Amsterdam in 2001, and at various other festivals in Jordan, Belgium, Poland, Switzerland, Germany, and elsewhere). In an interview al-Zobaidi stated: "This is really a film for local audiences. I don't care about foreign audiences, let me say that in capital letters. I wish I could afford to make 50,000 copies and send them out for five shekels each so that this film can reach every Palestinian household" (*Palestine Report* 1998). I am grateful to Subhi al-Zobaidi for providing me with a copy of the film and for allowing me to include stills from this film to illustrate this chapter.

9. In the interview mentioned in note 8 above, al-Zobaidi expressed his support for the Women Parliament and was critical of the Islamists. In fact, the NGO that was instrumental in organizing these debates was also one of the sponsors of his film.

10. For similar lines of argumentation, see also the various contributions to Abu-Lughod's edited volume 1998.

11. Some of this is visible in the new genres of writing that developed, such as books containing rules of etiquette to serve as a guide for women on how to interact properly with unrelated men, rules that were based on new notions of modern womanhood (Najmabadi 1993).

12. As Leila Ahmed (1982, 531) had already argued some twenty years ago: "to believe that segregated societies are by definition more oppressive to women, or that women secluded from the company of men are women deprived, is only to allow ourselves to be servilely obedient to the constructs of men, Western or Middle Eastern."

13. It is interesting to compare this to Habermas's account of the emergence of the modern public sphere with the salons of bourgeois homes as one of its loci, that is, the salon as a meeting place for male intellectuals. In a critique of Habermas, Landes (in Fraser 1992, 113) highlights how this new republican public sphere in France developed in opposition to an existing more woman-friendly salon culture.

14. In urban Yemen, women have a system of afternoon visits (at one another's houses) called *tafrita*, which are structurally similarly to male *qat* chews. Yet whereas the latter, even if they are held at home, are generally recognized as part of the public sphere, women's *tafritas* have hardly been recognized as such (Meneley 1996; Vom Bruck 1997). Also, in settings where gender segregation is less central to social organization, such as in the city of Nablus on the West Bank, in the 1980s forms of a semi-autonomous female public sphere still operated through the monthly *istiqbâl* (reception), organized visiting circles with each participant having one fixed date a month set aside to receive the others at her home.

15. The rapid growth of education (Eickelman 1992) and of a variety of media, such as popular fiction (Huq 1999), commercial television (Öncü 1995), cassette tapes

(Hirschkind 2001b), and the Internet (Mandaville 2001; Wheeler 2001) has been critical to this development.

16. Using the term "Islamic dress" is in line with the ways in which many of those involved describe covered dress. This is not unproblematic, however, as many Muslims who do not wear covered dress consider themselves observant Muslims as well. Describing covered dress as "Islamic dress" may then be seen as accepting one particular interpretation about how Muslim women ought to dress.

17. If women wearing the "new veil" may be seen as both influenced by and participating in the Islamization of the public sphere, some women have also become involved in the Muslim public sphere in another way. The rapid increase of female literacy has stimulated women's involvement in the field of Islamic learning and the production of Islamic knowledge. Such forms of knowledge may vary from claiming a space within mainstream Islam to attempts to develop new perspectives that are both grounded in Islamic traditions and in the discourse about women's rights (see, for example, Webb 2000).

18. For similarities in the projects of secularist and Islamist modernity, see Abu-Lughod 1998 and Hatem 1998.

19. Whereas before the Islamic revolution women of very different walks of life and political persuasions had started to wear the *chador* in protest against the dominance of the United States, after Ayatollah Khomeini came to power both secularist and (some) Islamist women took to the streets to protest the proscription of Islamic dress (Paidar 1995). After the 1997 victory of Mohammed Khatami in the presidential elections and the opening up of political space, the issue of the imposition of *hijab,* suppressed since the revolution, surfaced again, with those opposing forced *hijab* arguing that it is not a divine rule but rather the imposition of the lifestyle and values of a specific group (Mir-Hosseini 2002).

20. Such shifting patterns of authority are, for instance, evident in the ways in which women's involvement with popular sufism in Algeria has changed from the late nineteenth century on. Whereas in those days a substantial number of women were involved in sisterhoods, in the course of the twentieth century these sisterhoods lost considerable prestige and power, and, by the 1980s, the small number of women still active in these sisterhoods had become increasingly marginalized. Not only men but also better-educated women had distanced themselves from these more "popular" forms of Islam (Jansen 1987, 79ff.).

References

Abu-Lughod, Lila. 1998. The Marriage of Feminism and Islamism in Egypt: Selective Repudiation as a Dynamic of Postcolonial Cultural Politics. In *Remaking Women: Feminism and Modernity in the Middle East,* ed. Lila Abu-Lughod, 243–270. Princeton, N.J.: Princeton University Press.

Afshar, Haleh. 1982. Khomeini's Teachings and Their Implications for Iranian Women. In *In the Shadow of Islam,* ed. Azar Tabari and Nahid Yeganeh, 75–90. London: Zed.

———. 1998. *Islam and Feminism: An Iranian Case-Study.* London: Macmillan.

Ahmed, Leila. 1982. Western Ethnocentrism and Perceptions of the Harem. *Feminist Studies* 8 (3): 521–542.

————. 1992. *Women and Gender in Islam: Historical Roots of a Modern Debate*. New Haven, Conn.: Yale University Press.

Asad, Talal. 1986. *The Idea of an Anthropology of Islam*. Occasional Paper Series. Washington, D.C.: Georgetown University.

Azari, Farah. 1983. *Women of Iran: The Conflict with Fundamentalist Islam*. London: Ithaca.

Baker, Patricia. 1997. Politics of Dress: The Dress Reform Laws of 1920–1930s Iran. In *Languages of Dress in the Middle East*, ed. Nancy Lindisfarne-Tapper and Bruce Ingham, 178–193. Richmont, Surrey: Curzon.

Bruck, Gabriele vom. 1997. A House Turned Inside Out. Inhabiting Space in a Yemeni City. *Journal of Material Culture* 2 (2): 139–173.

Eickelman, Dale. 1992. Mass Higher Education and the Religious Imagination in Contemporary Arab Societies. *American Ethnologist* 19 (4): 643–655.

Eickelman, Dale, and Jon Anderson. 1999. Redefining Muslim Publics. In *New Media in the Muslim World*, ed. Dale Eickelman and Jon Anderson, 1–19. Bloomington and Indianapolis: Indiana University Press.

Eickelman, Dale, and Armando Salvatore. 2002. The Public Sphere and Muslim Identities. *European Journal of Sociology* 43:92–115.

El Guindi, Fadwa. 1981. Veiling Infitah with Muslim Ethic: Egypt's Contemporary Islamic Movement. *Social Problems* 8:465–485.

Fraser, Nancy. 1992. Rethinking the Public Sphere: A Contribution to the Critique of Actually Existing Democracy. In *Habermas and the Public Sphere*, ed. Craig Calhoun, 109–142. Cambridge, Mass.: MIT Press.

Göle, Nilüfer. 1996. *The Forbidden Modern: Civilization and Veiling*. Ann Arbor: University of Michigan Press.

————. 2002. Islam in Public: New Visibilities and New Imaginaries. *Public Culture* 14 (1): 173–190.

Habermas, Jürgen. 1992. Further Reflections on the Public Sphere. In *Habermas and the Public Sphere*, ed. Craig Calhoun, 421–462. Cambridge, Mass.: MIT Press.

Hammami, R. 1990. Women, the *Hijab* and the Intifada. *Middle East Report* 20 (3/4): 24–28.

Hammami, Rema, and Penny Johnson. 1999. Equality with a Difference. *Social Politics* 6 (3): 315–342.

Hammami, Rema, Penny Johnson, Fadwa Labadi, and Lynn Welchman. 2004. Islamic Family Law and the Transition to Palestinian Statehood: Constraints and Opportunities for Legal Reform. In *Women's Rights and Islamic Family Law*, ed. Lynn Welchman. London: Zed.

Hatem, Mervat. 1998. Secularist and Islamist Discourses on Modernity in Egypt and the Evolution of the Postcolonial Nation-State. In *Islam, Gender, and Social Change*, ed. Yvonne Haddad and John Esposito, 85–100. New York: Oxford University Press.

Hirschkind, Charles. 2001a. Civic Virtue and Religious Reason: An Islamic Counter-Public. *Cultural Anthropology* 16 (1): 3–34.

————. 2001b. Ethics of Listening: Cassette-Sermon Audition in Contemporary Egypt. *American Ethnologist* 28 (3): 623–649.

Huq, Maimuna. 1999. From Piety to Romance: Islam-Oriented Texts in Bangladesh. In *New Media in the Muslim World*, ed. Dale Eickelman and Jon Anderson, 133–162. Bloomington and Indianapolis: Indiana University Press.

Islamic Law and Society. 2003. Special issue (vol. 10, no. 1), Public Debates on Family Law Reform: Participants, Positions, and Styles of Argumentation in the 1990s.

Jad, Islah, Penny Johnson, and Rita Giacaman. 2000. Gender and Citizenship under the Palestinian Authority. In *Gender and Citizenship in the Middle East,* ed. Suad Joseph, 137–158. Syracuse, N.Y.: Syracuse University Press.

Jansen, Willy. 1987. *Women without Men: Gender and Marginality in an Algerian Town.* Leiden: Brill.

Johnson, Penny, and Eileen Kuttab. 2001. Where Have All the Women (and Men) Gone? Reflections on Gender and the Second Palestinian Intifada. *Feminist Review* 69 (1): 21–43.

MacLeod, Arlene. 1991. *Accommodating Protest: Working Women, the New Veiling, and Change in Cairo.* New York: Columbia University Press.

Mah, Harold. 2000. Phantasies of the Public Sphere: Rethinking the Habermas of Historians. *The Journal of Modern History* 72:153–182.

Mahmood, Saba. 2001a. Feminist Theory, Embodiment, and the Docile Agent: Some Reflections on the Egyptian Islamic Revival. *Cultural Anthropology* 16 (2): 202–236.

Mandaville, Peter. 2001. Reimagining Islam in Diaspora: The Politics of Mediated Community. *Gazette* 63 (2–3): 169–187.

Meneley, Anne. 1996. *Tournaments of Value: Sociability and Hierarchy in a Yemeni Town.* Toronto: University of Toronto Press.

Mir-Hosseini, Ziba. 1999. *Islam and Gender: The Religious Debate in Contemporary Iran.* Princeton, N.J.: Princeton University Press.

———. 2002. The Conservative-Reformist Conflict over Women's Rights in Islam. *International Journal of Politics, Culture, and Society* 16 (1): 37–53.

Moghissi, Haideh. 1994. *Populism and Feminism in Iran: Women's Struggles in a Male-Dominated Revolutionary Movement.* London: Macmillan.

Najmabadi, Afsaneh. 1993. Veiled Discourse—Unveiled Bodies. *Feminist Studies* 19 (3): 487–518.

———. 1998. Feminism in an Islamic Republic: Years of Hardship, Years of Growth. In *Islam, Gender, and Political Change,* ed. Yvonne Haddad and John Esposito, 50–84. Oxford: Oxford University Press.

Navaro-Yashin, Yael. 2002. *Faces of the State: Secularism and Public Life in Turkey.* Princeton, N.J.: Princeton University Press.

Öncü, Ayşe. 1995. Packaging Islam: Cultural Politics on the Landscape of Turkish Commercial Television. *Public Culture* 8 (1): 51–71.

Paidar, Parvin. 1995. *Women and the Political Process in Twentieth-Century Iran.* Cambridge: Cambridge University Press.

———. 1996. Feminism and Islam in Iran. In *Gendering the Middle East: Emerging Perspectives,* ed. Deniz Kandiyoti, 51–68. London: Tauris.

Palestine Report. 1998. Filming from the Dark Places: Interview with Subhi Zobaidi. *Palestine Report* 5 (10).

Saktanber, Ayse. 2002. *Living Islam: Women, Religion and the Politicization of Culture in Turkey.* London: Taurus.

Salvatore, Armando, and Dale Eickelman, eds. 2004. *Public Islam and the Common Good.* Leiden: Brill.

Tabari, Azar, and Nahid Yeganeh, eds. 1982. *In the Shadow of Islam.* London: Zed.

Veer, Peter van der. 2002. Religion in South Asia. *Annual Review of Anthropology* 31:173–187.

Warner, Michael. 1992. The Mass Public and the Mass Subject. In *Habermas and the Public Sphere,* ed. Craig Calhoun, 377–402. Cambridge, Mass.: MIT Press.

Webb, Gisela, ed. 2000. *Windows of Faith: Muslim Women Scholar-Activists in North America*. Syracuse, N.Y.: Syracuse University Press.

Wheeler, Deborah. 2001. The Internet and Public Culture in Kuwait. *Gazette* 63 (2–3): 187–203.

Welchman, Lynn. 2003. In the Interim: Civil Society, the *Shar'i* Judiciary and Palestinian Personal Status: Law in the Transitional Period. *Islamic Law and Society* 10 (1): 34–70.

al-Zobaidi, Subhi. 1998. *Women in the Sun*. Video documentary. Palestine: Refugee Camp Productions.

6 Morality, Community, Publicness: Shifting Terms of Public Debate in Mali

Dorothea E. Schulz

Reconsidering the Place of Religious Activism in a Secular Public

In Mali economic liberalization and the introduction of multiparty democracy in 1991 have created favorable conditions for the proliferation of private media and for the emergence of a broad spectrum of interest groups that frame their political aspirations in the rhetoric of an international civil society discourse.[1] Among them are a multitude of Muslim actors who employ the mass media to assert and display an explicit Islamic position in public debates. Most often they engage in controversies among themselves to address, as they claim, matters of common interest. These include religious or ritual issues as much as they touch on governmental policy. Many controversies involve ferocious and often personalized attacks on individual clerics and intellectuals. They are made public in printed matter or in sermons broadcast on audiotapes, local radio, and national television.

The recent upsurge of religious activism points to an expanding arena of public activity that is located mostly outside institutions of the state and the formal economy, and that is fueled by processes of commercialization and mass mediation. The existence of this arena of activism suggests that the relationship between state and society is currently being reassessed and partially reconfigured. It is an area in which novel forms of articulation between the state and society are initiated, forms that simultaneously draw on existing social institutions and on expressive registers. The notion of the public seems particularly useful to account for the structure of and changes in the institutional and discursive forms through which the re-articulation of state-society relations is effected. Of special relevance is Habermas's (1962) historicizing perspective on "the structural transformation of the public sphere" in eighteenth-century Europe. His focus on discursive action furthers an understanding of the specific quality of "publicness" (*Öffentlichkeit*) that electronic media create, and of the new forms of social interaction and of being together that they favor. But in contrast to Habermas, who oscillates between a normative and a descriptive use of the term "public," I propose to use it as a descriptive tool to explore the relationship between the institutional arrangements of public communication and their historically and culturally specific normative foundations.[2] Furthermore, instead of assuming the existence of a unitary and homogeneous public, I conceive of it as a plurality of interlocking discursive fields (see Calhoun 1992, 37).

In the current era of postcolonial state politics, the nation-state serves less than before as a frame of reference for constructions of community and belonging (e.g., Appadurai 1990; Meyer and Geschiere 1997). The diminishing capacity of the state to define the common good goes hand in hand with a loss of control over the flow of economic and cultural resources. The current upsurge of identity politics, whether couched in terms of ethnic or religious difference, reveals the growing awareness among state officials and citizens that difference is irreconcilable and has to be contained. It is a situation in which "culture" no longer serves as a register to appeal to a common national identity and political agenda; instead, "culture" becomes the idiom through which claims to local particularity in a multicultural nation-state are articulated and partisan interests are justified (Geschiere and Nyamnjoh 2001). Citizens *in* (rather than *of;* cf. Comaroff and Comaroff 2001) postcolonial nation-states address in various ways the state's incapacity to grant the rights and conditions on which liberal conceptions of citizenship and the legitimacy of the state are founded.[3]

A number of authors have recently suggested that the rise of "political Islam" might be understood in this light, that is, by reference to the weakening capacity of the nation-state to claim and create allegiance (e.g., Esposito 1984; Roy 1994; also see Zubaida 1989; Kepel 1991). Political actors couch their aspirations in terms of a return to the original teachings of Islam and evoke models of community that challenge the ideological foundations of the secular state. Other authors focus on broadcast-mediated realms of religious activism. Some argue that new, mostly small media, by broadening the access to religious interpretation, have a potential to democratize religious knowledge and create greater transparency in public debate (e.g., Eickelman and Anderson 1999). Other studies suggest a more ambivalent role of small media in making religious topics part of mainstream public debate (e.g., Manuel 1993; Sreberny-Mohammadi and Mohammadi 1994; Rajagopal 2001). Common to these approaches is a focus on technological innovation and an analytical framework that views religious activists as representatives of a civil society that owes its existence and vigor to new broadcast media. This raises the question of whether the new public prominence of Islam in Mali should be interpreted along these lines.

Malian "political Islam" is represented by the so-called *intégristes* most of whom are men with ties to the Arab-speaking world, Egypt and Saudi Arabia in particular. They belong to a broader field of Muslim actors, the *arabisants* (Otayek 1993), who often received an education in religious sciences abroad and who, starting in the late 1970s, capitalized on personal ties they had established to individual sponsors and governmental institutions in the Arab-speaking world (see the next section, "The Nation as Political Community or as Moral Void?").[4] The *intégristes* made their first spectacular public appearance in 1991, when they sought to participate as religious parties in the first democratic elections ever held in Mali. Although they were denied official recognition at that time, they continue to make a public appearance whenever they feel that the principles of Islam are threatened.[5] The *intégristes* base their political aspirations on a model of citizenship that stipulates individual Islamic ethics as binding for the realization of the common good. Arguing that all Malians are Muslim, they conflate Muslim with a national Malian identity.[6] In their model, the regulation of social interaction is indiscriminately relegated to the political authority, and the divide between private faith and public interest is blurred. State authority should exert its power of arbitration on the basis of Islamic principles, or, as the *intégristes* call it, the *shariᶜa*.

In spite of their occasionally vociferous public appearances, the *intégristes* play a comparatively minor role, both numerically and in their actual capacity to mobilize a following. In spite of their claim to challenge the normative foundations of the secular state, they operate significantly within the institutional and discursive parameters of civil society.

To focus on these representatives of political Islam risks excluding social networks that cannot easily be located within the realm of civil society. One example for the latter type of activism is the movement *Ansar Dine* (a Bamanized[7] version of the Arabic *Ansar al-Din*, "the supporters of the religion") which, in contrast to the *intégristes,* has won wide popular support. The magnetic leader of this movement, Sharif Ousmane Haidara, has managed, since his first public appearance in the mid-1980s, to disseminate his audio- and video-taped sermons to a rapidly growing constituency of "rightful believers" (*silame dina kanubagaw;* literally, "those who love/support the Islamic religion"). His followers from the urban and semi-urban lower middle classes hail him as their spiritual guide who "puts an end to politicking."[8] Many Western-oriented government officials and representatives of influential Muslim lineages, on the other hand, denounce him as a fundamentalist threat to the secular state.[9] In this chapter I argue that these critics are mistaken in interpreting Haidara's movement as an instance of political Islam. However, their perception that he has enormous influence is accurate. One way of understanding Haidara's success is to interpret his call for a moral renewal as an attempt not only to appeal to a different moral order but to evoke a community that appears as a compelling alternative to the political community of the nation. Haidara's movement mobilizes followers outside the political arena in which the government interacts with nongovernmental organizations (NGOs) funded by Western donor organizations and with influential Muslim figures who benefit from their affiliation with the government. Sharif Haidara's remarkable success sheds light on recent social transformations and on a political situation characterized by the failure of the state to capture the allegiance of its citizens to the nation. The uneasiness with which members of the current political elite comment on Haidara's popularity reflects their awareness that their governance rests on shaky foundations. It is this political context that made Haidara so popular among the urban and semi-urban lower classes.

Sharif Haidara's public proclamations, the fact that much of his criticism is directed at leading members of the religious establishment who entertain close relations with party and state officials, call for a closer analysis of his aspirations. This will shed light on the particular dynamics of the current public and its relationship to state politics. Moreover, by exploring Haidara's complex location in the field of Muslim activism, we might gain a better understanding of the internal structuring of the public and how it is constituted through strategies of exclusion. As a number of critics of Habermas's notion of a critical bourgeois public have pointed out, in contrast to his assumption of a free, open access to public and critical-rational argument, eighteenth-century public debate existed *because* of the exclusion of certain categories of actors (e.g., Fraser 1992). An analysis of the controversy between Sharif Haidara and his Muslim dissidents allows us to identify the strategies of exclusion and inclusion they employ and how, through these discourses of commonality and difference, access to the public arena is justified or denied. This perspective enables us to identify continuities with previous practices of exclusion within a Muslim public (Launay and Soares 1999; Brenner 2000), and to account for potentially novel institutions and discourses through which these struggles are played out. Another guiding concern of the discussion that follows is to understand how the rise of commercial, mass-mediated culture plays into the controversy among Muslim contestants. Do mass media provide a new and neutral platform for the debate of religious issues and matters of common interest? How does the integration of religious activism into an expanding commercial culture transform the nature of religious debate?

To address these questions we need to understand how Islam recently acquired the symbolic and normative force to serve as an alternative basis for community constructions. To account for its place in official discourse on political legitimacy and belonging, I retrace the recent history of the shifting and tenuous relationship between official constructions of a national community and Islam as a source of moral order. This provides the backdrop for the subsequent assessment of the implications of mass-mediated, competing constructions of community and moral authority.

The Nation as Political Community or as Moral Void?

In the area of present-day Mali, families of religious specialists (labeled marabouts by the colonial authorities) never gained an influence in the colonial political arena comparable to the standing that religious authorities had in other West African countries, such as Senegal and Nigeria. Large segments of the population converted to Islam only during the colonial period, that is, after the 1920s. The political influence of lineages associated with Sufi orders, which played an important role in organizing Muslim practice and knowledge in West Africa, was confined to some urban areas in the French Sudan, among them Timbuktu, Gao, Mopti, Djenne, Segu, and Nioro. Some of these religious lineages were able to expand their political influence in the colonial era (Soares

1997; Stewart 1997; Triaud 1997), largely because the French colonial authorities built them up as a stronghold against a new generation of "Wahhabi" merchants and intellectuals with ties to the Arab-speaking world.[10] The new generation of Muslim intellectuals was considered a threat to political stability both by the colonial authorities and by established families of religious specialists whose "non-Islamic" practices and distortions of the true teachings of Islam the young critics attacked as instances of "unlawful innovation" (bidᶜa) (Amselle 1985; Brenner 1993a, 1993b, 1993c).

The social basis and political influence of established families of religious specialists were weakened when the PSP[11] party was defeated in the legislative elections in 1959. It lost further political terrain after independence in 1960, when Modibo Keita and his party, US-RDA,[12] reached power. Very soon many of their former Muslim opponents, the merchants with business ties to the Arab-speaking world, who had originally supported US-RDA militants in their struggle for independence, changed sides, too. The growing opposition of these merchants, which substantially weakened Modibo Keita's regime and ultimately contributed to its fall in 1968, was a response to the socialist regime's economic policy and treatment of religious matters. While Modibo Keita's regime never went as far as to denounce the influence of Islamic clerics on local politics, his secularist policy sought to neutralize them.[13] By appealing to "African culture" as the unifying principle of the new political community, the new leaders of independent Mali reproduced the tensions inherent in the conception of a shared, public interest formulated by liberal Western political theory (Warner 1992).[14] "Culture" became the register through which claims to equal participation in the new political community were expressed, and internal difference and hierarchy denied. Modibo Keita's explicit recognition of religion as individual faith distinguished his "African path towards socialism" from the Marxist-Leninist model (Snyder 1967, 85–86). Yet the US-RDA never framed its anticolonial, nationalist struggle as a matter of Islamic resistance to the onslaught of Westernization. Instead, religion was considered an individual conviction and relegated to the realm of the private.[15]

Modibo Keita's socialist endeavor never found widespread popular support. It was aborted with the coup d'état in 1968 that brought Colonel Moussa Traoré and his military regime to power.[16] Public celebrations of the new regime replaced previous official appeals to a common nation-building project.[17] The "laissez faire, laissez passer" attitude of the new leadership undermined any existing sense of national unity and belonging. Starting in the late 1970s Islam gained a new momentum. Members of rich and influential Muslim merchant families, often with business connections to the Middle East, expanded their influence in the public arena and yet only rarely were implicated in official party politics. Their capacity to mobilize followers through Islamic welfare networks and institutions was a major reason why President Traoré made substantial concessions to the demands of Muslim authorities, in spite of Mali's secular constitution. Granting them privileges (such as reserving a greater share of broadcasting time for them than for Christians) became part of Moussa Traoré's attempt to extend his control over powerful segments of the religious establishment and over the new group of *arabisants*. The latter, because of their degrees from teaching institutions in the Arab-speaking world, soon occupied leading posts in the state bureaucracy and occasionally entered into competition with more established religious leaders. Moussa Traoré's pro-Muslim policy was instrumental in channeling the substantial financial contributions these Muslim groups received from the Arab-speaking world from the late 1970s on. Sponsored by international public and private money, Islam acquired a strong public visibility in the form of infrastructure (mosques and reformed Quranic schools, the *medersas*) and a stronger discursive representation in the national political arena (Triaud 1988a; Brenner 2000, chapter 5). The official creation of a national association of Muslims, AMUPI, in the early 1980s consolidated state control over the activities of various groups of Muslims by simultaneously suppressing and institutionalizing competition among them.[18] It also enabled Muslim spokespeople to make themselves heard in their role *as* Muslims. In this process, Islam came to be seen by many Malians as an element of an at once "tradition-conscious" and enlightened Malian identity.

In 1989, when a call for democracy and civil liberties swept the African continent and reached Mali, representatives of the Muslim establishment were among Moussa Traoré's closest allies in his confrontation with an oppositional "movement for democracy" organized by teachers, lawyers, and civil servants. After Moussa Traoré's fall from power in 1991, the leader of the putsch, Colonel Toumani Touré, organized the country's first democratic elections. The establishment of new institutions and ideologies of rule went hand in hand with selectively rearranged and partially rejuvenated images of political allegiance and community. "Democracy," "transparency," and the "rule of law" became cornerstones of the common good to which President Alpha Konaré and his party, ADEMA, appealed. This orientation has continued under the new president, Toumani Touré, elected in 2002. Paradoxically current governmental attempts to prove the democratic nature of the new political system, such as the organization of a public debate of individual political reform projects, often undermine the regime's credibility, because the majority of the population perceives public controversy and opposition as an indicator of the state's incapacity to establish "law and order."[19]

One important change generated by the political opening since 1991 is the rise to prominence of a type of Muslim actor that can be labeled "activist" because these players combine their political aspirations with a publicly declared Muslim identity. Among them are the above-mentioned *intégristes* who contest the institutional and ideological foundations of the secular state. But they are relatively few in number and have not acquired significant momentum in the national arena. The ties between *intégristes* and other *arabisants* and Muslims with close ties to the Arab-speaking world are tenuous. Many Muslim activists who defend "Arab-inspired" readings of Islam do not agree with the *intégristes'* political agenda and define, instead, their own role as that of a moral watchdog removed from the interested stratagems of politicians. Haidara exemplifies this position. His claim not to "meddle with (party) politics" counts among the most important reasons for his astounding popularity, a popularity that *intégristes* and his other Muslim critics observe with dismay and allegations of mindless populism. Thus Haidara's movement, *Ansar Dine*, not only reflects the diversification of Muslim positions and the transformation of Islamic faith into a publicly proclaimed standpoint. It also illustrates that Muslim leaders may win popular support precisely because they frame their political and social aspirations as a disengagement from immoral politics.

Muslims who support the current trend toward an Islamic moral renewal (*tajdid*) organize themselves in associations, located primarily in urban areas, that have been mushrooming since 1991. Many leaders of these associations enter strategic and sometimes shifting alliances with the current political and economic elites from whom they often receive major financial contributions. While these devout Muslims become more and more visible and audible in the public arena, Islam's place in public life turns into an issue of ever growing contention. This is partly the outcome of the highly ambivalent attitude of current government officials toward Islam, an attitude that undercuts their otherwise explicit secularist orientation. In a situation of widespread discontent with the regime in power, party politicians and state officials cannot afford to antagonize prominent representatives of the Muslim establishment whose informal political influence in towns and in the countryside is based on kin-related and clientelistic allegiances. President Touré, as well as other members of the current government, regularly perform rituals expressing their loyalty to Islamic values, in the presence of renowned representatives of the Muslim establishment, and thus gloss over the difference between a national and a Muslim identity.

The social basis of current Muslim activism is characterized by coexisting types of mobilization. Urban-based Muslim neighborhood associations (sometimes styled after NGOs funded by Western donor organizations) are run according to a rationality in which clientelistic and redistributional considerations intermingle with the logic of the market. Many group leaders once occupied leading positions in the administration and government under the former president. They generally benefit from their former influential positions to enter into clientelistic relations with state officials and politicians. Their strategies illustrate the absence of any clear dividing line between the state and civil society, and stand in tension to the rhetoric of a "civil society against the state" that they employ. Some groups have an impressive number of followers. But people of various socioeconomic and educational backgrounds look upon them and their civil society rhetoric with suspicion. They argue that, similar to NGOs sponsored by Western donor organizations, the only raison d'être for the Muslim associations is "economic interest." Other critics, mostly intellectuals, surmise that Muslim neighborhood associations are used by their leaders and sponsors to mobilize gullible voters.

Other networks stretch from rural groups to urban Muslim patrons. Although they are based on conventional notions of trust and mutual obligation, the conditions under which they come into existence show that they are not instances of primordial social organization but result from recent reconfigurations and reappropriations of social and political alliances. These networks tend to mobilize the disenfranchised, that is, people who remain by and large excluded from clientelistic connections that link the administrative-political centers in town to the rural hinterlands. Haidara's movement, *Ansar Dine,* shares many features with this type of network. *Ansar Dine* originated among the urban lower classes, but it is currently expanding into the surrounding areas of rural towns. It is based on trust and mutual obligation, and yet its social backbone is structured along connections that transcend conventional ties of kinship and patronage. *Ansar Dine* provides services and therefore creates securities, which the state is incapable of delivering. It does not offer its members substantial donations from wealthy patrons but constitutes a network for commercial activities and mutual support that reaches out to neighboring countries, to the Ivory Coast in particular, and increasingly to immigrant communities in France and the United States.

Broadcast Media and Competing Claims to Authoritative Knowledge

Similar to developments in other areas of the Muslim world, current changes in the social basis of religious authority and knowledge are played out in conflicts among competing Muslim factions (see Eickelman 1992, 2000). These changes presently concur with the spread of broadcasting technologies, especially those of small media, that, among other factors, broaden the access to religious knowledge and facilitate individual interpretation. In Mali the origins of these changes date back at least to the 1940s, when individual Muslim reformists sought to adapt traditional religious training to the new demands of the colonial social and political environment. Already at this time access to religious learning became less restricted and pedagogy inspired by the French-language schools transformed conventional forms of learning, thereby weakening the existing foundations of religious authority (Brenner 2000, chapters 3, 4).

Mass higher education in French plays a comparatively minor role in effecting these changes.[20] But the trend toward a secularization of the Arabic language, the expansion of its use to mundane matters and domains, crucially contributes to the undermining of the basis of traditional religious authority. This trend was initiated in the reformed Quranic schools since the 1940s and continued through the post-independent integration of these schools as *écoles franco-arabes* into the national educational system. The growing number of *arabisants* who received a degree from institutions of the Arab-speaking world since the 1980s furthered a diversification of the national field of contestants over authoritative interpretation. Individual access to religious knowledge is also facilitated by the current thriving of vernacular languages promoted by governmental educational policy. Most religious debates are broadcast in *Bamanakan,* a language understood by the majority of the southern population.

Muslim women's learning circles, which have been mushrooming in urban areas over the past twenty years, illustrate some effects of the widening access to religious knowledge. "Muslim women"[21] organize themselves into groups to learn to read, write, and memorize certain *surats* and to learn proper ritual conduct. Until the 1970s few elite women (generally older women from families of religious specialists and merchants) engaged in this form of learning. Now the majority of women in the literacy and prayer groups are from the urban middle and lower-middle classes. This points to a widening access to religious knowledge and to shifts in its mode of transmission. Even though the Muslim women refer to their activities as traditional forms of learning, their new forms and uses of literacy reveal an overlapping of conventional and new paradigms of knowledge transmission. Broadcasting plays an additional role in undermining previous foundations of religious authoritative knowledge. Some leaders of women's learning circles, the *présidentes,* make recordings of their sermons which are then broadcast on local radio or circulate on tape among their followers. In these tape recordings (*caseti wajuli*), *présidentes* sermonize on questions of proper ritual and everyday conduct. While they seem to reproduce a conservative gender ideology, closer scrutiny of their sermons reveals that they respond to concerns triggered by recent changes in gender relations and the undermining of patriarchal family authority (Schulz 2004, chapters 2, 6).

The unsettling of the social basis of religious knowledge, and the new power constellations to which it gives rise, are reflected in current confrontations between Muslim activists and traditional religious leaders who replaced the former elite of experts in Islamic jurisprudence in the early colonial period (Stewart 1997). The confrontations are still presented as disagreements over ritual matters (see Launay and Soares 1999), but the lines of conflict and alliance are changing. Earlier confrontations between influential religious lineages and their Muslim dissidents, whose reformist tendencies were inspired by intellectual trends in Egypt and the *hijaz* (see above), have given way to their joint competition with the *arabisants* whose higher education at institutions in the Arab-speaking world allowed them to occupy influential positions in the state bureaucracy in the later years of Moussa Traoré's rule (Brenner 1993c).

Haidara's movement, *Ansar Dine,* with its uneasy location amid rural- and urban-based networks and its explicit distancing from the realm of politics, adds another dimension of complexity to the shifting alliances that characterize the field of Muslim activism. Haidara, who comes from an unimportant rural branch of a prestigious religious lineage,[22] combines traditional credentials of leadership (such as genealogical prestige) with qualities of charismatic authority (Schulz 2003). For years, representatives of the national Muslim association AMUPI successfully blocked Haidara's attempts to preach on national media, by denouncing him as a rabble-rousing upstart. However, in 2000 they finally had to give in and admit him into a newly created administrative structure, *Haut Conseil Islamique.* Throughout the years of his exclusion Haidara responded to his adversaries' attempts to marginalize him by circulating his opinions on video- and on audio-taped sermons, many of which continue to be broadcast on local radio. He thereby reached a constituency of listeners that stretched further into rural areas than competing Muslim activists do. In other words, he made up for his exclusion from a state-controlled arena of public debate by creating a parallel sphere of discursive exchange. Small media were instrumental but not decisive in this strategic move.

Haidara's stronghold in the countryside manifests itself in numerous letters in which rural listeners address him as their "spiritual guide" and request advice on questions of proper conduct. Haidara's numerous enemies from the Muslim establishment never cease to stress that his training in religious sciences is very thin. Still, they cannot deny that his rhetorical skills and charisma, his extensive use of broadcast technology, and, finally, his ferocious attacks on the Muslim establishment's "hypocritical" position vis-à-vis politicians have earned him a wide following among the urban population. Many men, especially among the urban youth discontented with the unfulfilled promises of "demokrasi," endorse Haidara's denouncing of political and moral corruption as "truthful" and "courageous."

Haidara's embattled positioning in public debate is indicative of a convergence of several processes. His attacks on, and rejection by, prominent clerics illustrate the ongoing struggle over the authoritative use of Islam as a source of moral order. Furthermore, that his participation in public debate is most contested by other Muslims reveals that the strategies of exclusion that structure public debate in Mali do not separate an official secular public from an Islamic "counterpublic." Rather, the practices of silencing and mutual accusation create and reflect the segmentation of the Muslim discursive field. Exclusion is at work within the field of Muslim debate, a field structured by people's unequal access to technologies of media production and to opportunities for consumption. In contrast to the public claimed by Habermas for eighteenth-century Western Europe, Muslim activists in Mali do not simply bring their religious identity to the public arena but, instead, claim, challenge, and incessantly create that identity in public interaction. Muslim actors differ in status and scholarly pedigree, and in their unequal access to the resources and privileges provided by the state.

Given that Haidara mobilizes his followers through networks that operate largely beyond state control, one could surmise that the moral order to which he appeals constitutes a substantive alternative to that constructed in official discourse. The following discussion scrutinizes Haidara's teachings and the kind of moral community he proposes.

Sermons, Argument, and Advertising: Competing Constructions of Community

Haidara's preaching style seems to be inspired by a "rational episteme,"[23] His marked emphasis on the rational character of the Quran, the meanings of which can be debated in a systematic fashion, is reminiscent of Habermas's notion of critical argument as the procedural norm of the bourgeois public.

Haidara's rational approach seems to reflect a similar trend toward the objectification and systematization of religious knowledge as it has been described for other areas of the Muslim world (see Eickelman 2000). Yet a closer look at his sermons reveals that the diffusion of religious debate by the media has more contradictory implications.

Haidara's sermons (*wajuli*) are set up in a dialogue with an interlocutor that bears close resemblance to talk radio programs that are highly popular among urban listeners (Schulz 1999). In response to questions posed by his listeners,[24] Haidara makes extensive use of a rhetorical style generally associated with professional orators (Schulz 2001). His repeated references to the mediated context create a strong sense of immediacy and an audience of an almost palpable presence. In emotionally highly charged dialogues, he appeals to feelings of belonging and sharing, and responds to people's striving for a clearly demarcated frame of ethical reference. The appeal of Haidara's sermons thus resides to an important extent in the illocutionary force of his speech.

Muslims of different orientation and pedigree, who publicly comment on governmental policy, propose versions of moral community that, they claim, counter current official constructions of the nation as a community. The ways in which they frame their political aspirations and the public prominence of their alternative community constructions constitute a comparatively new development in Mali. The increasing permeation of everyday life with mass media supports the shift toward a debate of political and social issues that are generally presented as matters of personal faith and collective well-being. Local radio stations and cassettes enable a broader constituency of consumers to formulate their viewpoints on a range of everyday concerns. The growing importance of media for these opinion-making processes puts an increasing pressure on rival Muslims (and other interest groups) to compete for a public acknowledgment of the validity of their position.

Common to the images of community formulated by various branches of the Muslim establishment and by the *intégristes* is that they merge national and Muslim identities, thereby implicitly denying Christians and people of other religious orientation the right of full participation in the political universe.[25] Haidara's community of "rightful believers," in contrast, is more vaguely defined. It is precisely the diffuse nature of his precepts for a "virtuous life" that makes it so appealing to his followers because it allows them to find various points of identification.

Haidara's indeterminate community construction becomes evident in his reactions to the controversy over the broadcasting of beauty pageants. When Mali hosted the West African beauty pageant "Miss CEDEAO" in Bamako in 1997, a public controversy arose over the question of whether the event should be broadcast on national television. Representatives of the AMUPI and some *intégristes* temporarily allied to denounce what they saw as a governmental endorsement of this instance of moral corruption by Western cultural imperialism. In newspapers and broadcasts on *Radio Islamique,* the AMUPI's private radio station in Bamako, they admonished "decent Muslims, decent Malian citizens" not to watch the pageant on television and to prevent children and women from exposure to "this dishonorable event" which was a "disgrace to the Malian nation and to the dignity of our traditional values." Only a few days after the pageant had been broadcast,[26] Haidara released a tape in which he expressed his concern over the degradation of ethical standards of public conduct. However, the target of his attack was not the government but those Muslim figures who had decried the broadcasting of the event. Without giving out their identity, he characterized them as "Muslims who preach one thing, yet do another" and who "let their daughters go loose," that is, engage in activities that come close to prostitution.[27] If someone was concerned with fending off moral corruption, he argued, it was not the public lip service that mattered. Crucial was "any rightly guided individual's" conduct and that of his (!) daughters. Haidara concluded that the Muslims' interventions constituted a proof of their own hypocrisy.

Haidara's reasoning illustrates that he seeks to present himself as a rightly guided Muslim who espouses the values of education, personal strength, and accomplishment. His attack on "hypocritical Muslims" involved a rhetoric that was simultaneously inclusive and exclusive: exclusive insofar as he appealed to a moral community in which only "true" Muslims could partake (as defined by their virtuous conduct and regular prayer); inclusive because he addressed all "rightly guided" and "sensible" people, a characterization that potentially also included Christians. Haidara's emphasis on the importance of moral integrity deeply resonates with people's sensibilities in a situation in which many urbanites, especially adolescents, feel disillusioned about the unrealized promises of political reform. His oscillation between inclusive and exclusive definitions of community allows him to captivate the moral imagination of listeners, that is, not only of his followers but of a broad range of people who support his cause.

Of similar vagueness were Haidara's comments on the criticisms launched by representatives of the AMUPI in 1991 against the transitory military regime under Colonel Toumani Touré, when the latter publicly announced a decision to keep bars and dancing places open during the month of Ramadan. Haidara publicly denounced "deceitful Muslims" who publicly displayed their righteousness during Ramadan but surreptitiously drank alcohol and engaged in prostitution. Similar to his denouncing of his Muslim brethrens' hypocrisy, he never specified whose behavior was under scrutiny. In his combination of unspecified criticism with a fierce rhetoric of moral righteousness, Haidara made it easy for listeners to view themselves as proper members of an imaginary moral community.[28]

At first sight Haidara's claims appear to perpetuate an older "discourse of truth and ignorance" that reflected and created difference among Muslims in Mali throughout the colonial era (Brenner 2000, chapter 6). But his argumentation also marks a departure from previous assertions of difference. At the heart of Haidara's appeal to an alternative moral community is a void, as he refrains from defining Muslim identity in any substantial terms. In this fashion he leaves the line of demarcation between "true Muslims" and other Muslims porous at best. What seems to matter most is convincingly to enact one's religious faith in a public arena and thereby to assert the truthful nature of one's own conviction. Haidara's way of framing issues suggests a stronger emphasis on individual faith and responsibility, and intimates a move toward a specific, modernist conception of religiosity (see Bowen 1997). Whereas previously being a Muslim was generally perceived as a marker of ethnic affiliation or occupational specialization (Launay 1992), the new identity requires Muslims to publicly enact their individual conviction, that is, to become believers who profess their faith to a broader constituency. Islam needs to be defended against competing normative orders.

The emphasis of Haidara and other Muslims on proper conduct and on the public demonstration of individual virtue shows that they are working within, not outside, the parameters of political modernity. But it is mostly Haidara whose teachings reveal the influence of more than thirty years of secularist state politics that distinguished, at least rhetorically, between private conviction and public interest. In contrast to Muslim activists, such as the *intégristes*, who emphasize the one-ness of public interest and individual ethics, Haidara views religion as a private conviction that only occasionally should bear upon decisions about how to conduct public affairs. Western liberal political thought similarly relegates religion and morality to the realm of the private, that is, to the realm in which faith is first espoused as a component of one's identity and only subsequently brought to bear on matters of public interest (Gobetti 1997; Calhoun 1997).

Concluding Reflections: The Public as Marketplace

The public arena created by broadcast media in Mali constitutes a polycentric field of debate, the dynamics of which are fueled, among other factors, by people's unequal access to state institutions and technologies of mediation. Local radio stations and cassette culture diversify a media landscape that was once almost entirely under the control of the state. Compared to print media and state-directed television, decentralized aural and visual media such as audiotapes, radio broadcasts, and videotapes offer new opportunities to capitalize on the aesthetic force of speech and on the performative qualities of visualization, and they facilitate a mode of persuasion not based on logical reasoning. They create new and favorable conditions for populist leaders who may have only some of the credentials conventionally associated with spiritual leadership in West African Islam (Schulz 2003; see Triaud 1988b).

However, rather than simply favoring a greater transparency of and broader inclusion into critical public debate, small media contribute to its transformation into a marketplace of ideas in which political actors have more opportunities to advertise competing views of community. All actors, state officials, and activists, who claim to offer an alternative reading of the common good, draw on a common pool of symbols and norms. They make use of similar combinations of aurally (and sometimes visually) compelling means and critical-rational argument. They are informed by a neoliberal economist ideology of consumer choice and its progressive, liberating potential. In this process, religious ethics and knowledge materialize in the form of media products to be purchased by enlightened and critical consumers.

This finding sheds light on two points that are critical to current discussions of the interplay between new, religiously inspired movements and the growing mediatization of everyday experience in the postcolonial world. First, it would be misleading to focus the analysis on technological innovation while neglecting the effects of commercialization and the specifics of the current mode of political liberalization. Religious teachings form part of a range of media products that, once they are disseminated on small media, turn into commodities that compete with other forms of entertainment culture. Habermas drew attention to this development when he identified commercial mass media culture as playing a crucial role in the emptying of the bourgeois public of its critical potential. Warner (1992) has rightly pointed out that the potential for this transformation was already inherent in the paradoxical normative foundations of the bourgeois critical public: the claim to disembodied equality was always neutralized by the implicit privileging of the unmarked category of the normal, male, middle-class citizen. The dynamics of Malian public debate suggest that the commodification of media culture and particular power relations provide the context for this critical potential to be realized. In spite of the introduction of multiparty democracy and freedom of opinion, participation in public debate (via national media) and civil society still depends on individuals' access to representatives and resources of the state. That influential Muslim figures successfully capitalized on their position in the national Muslim organization AMUPI to prevent Haidara from accessing national media illustrates the persistent logic of political clientelism in public debate.

This brings me to the second critical point. Small media, rather than unequivocally broadening access to public debate, exacerbate conflicts over participation and often feed into already existing strategies of exclusion engrained (and silenced) in definitions of community membership. In Mali state officials and NGO activists combine their declarations on civil society and democracy with practices that deny broad strata of the population political participation. Strategies of exclusion, presented as matters of doctrinal deviation, are also operative within the public constituted by competing Muslim factions. Haidara's sermons illustrate that Muslim activists currently engage in public debate to assert and contest identities based on claims to moral superiority. They invoke a moral imaginary that simultaneously creates and encompasses difference. Similar to official, ambiguous constructions of Malian citizenship, Haidara's move between different criteria for exclusion and inclusion leaves room for the public negotiation of Muslim identity. In this sense, current public controversies over the definition of the common good (of which Haidara's attacks on the Malian Muslim establishment is only one example) illustrate how religious identities are as much the result of public controversy and not simply the precondition for it. This finding helps to qualify Habermas's contention that the public should serve as a space only for the settling of arguments, not for the articulation of identities. The recent diversification of the media landscape facilitated the public assertion of a plurality of identities, a plurality that Arendt (1958) identified as at once a necessary and inevitable component of the public sphere under conditions of political modernity. In the case of Mali, it is not the formation of political interest groups, or the expression of their aspirations in terms of "identity," that undermines the critical potential of public debate. Instead, this potential is limited by the absence of the institutional preconditions for political participation and of a normative order that would offer an alternative to the one promoted by the current government.

Notes

The article is based on research conducted in San, Segu, and Bamako between 1996 and 2003 (sixteen months altogether). Previous versions of the article were presented at the Free University of Berlin (Department of Anthropology); to the Annual Meeting of the Canadian Anthropological Association in Montreal, 2001; to the Alexander von Humboldt Foundation Summer Institute "Muslim Identities and the Public Sphere," Berlin, July 2001; and to the conference "Religion, Media, and the Public Sphere" in Amsterdam, organized by Birgit Meyer and Annelies Moors in December 2001. I thank my colleagues at the Free University, the participants of the Summer Institute (in particular Dale Eickelman and Armando Salvatore) and the participants of the Amsterdam conference, especially Annelies Moors and Birgit Meyer, for their critical comments. The research on which this paper is based would not have been possible without the assistance and patience of numerous *Ansar Dine* devotees. I owe a special gratitude to Madame Diaby Adam Dembele and her husband for their hospitality and readiness to engage in a dialogue.

1. Alpha Konaré and his party, ADEMA (Alliance pour la Démocratie au Mali), won the first democratic elections and were reelected in 1997. In June 2002 Colonel Toumani Touré, the leader of the military putsch of 1991, was elected president.

2. My analytical perspective contrasts with Soares's (2004) use of the notion of "public" in his account of forms of Islamic piety in postcolonial Mali. Soares dismisses the relevance of Habermas's concept for his own material by observing that Habermas underestimated the role of religious associations and values in the emergence of the eighteenth-century public sphere in Western Europe (see Zaret 1992). I posit that especially Habermas's insistence on the interlocking of changes in the economy and in the nature of "publicness" warrants important insights into recent changes in public debate in Mali, and into the place of religion in these debates.

3. At the same time there is an increasing need for the state to create or to reinvent itself discursively and performatively, as the central locus of political power and as the guarantor of a "commonwealth" that transcends class and sectarian interests (also see Harvey 1989, 108; Comaroff and Comaroff 2001, 37–40).

4. While the term *arabisants* refers to a common educational background, *intégristes*

specifies the political agenda of a group of Muslim activists. Still, it is impossible to clearly set the *intégristes* apart from other *arabisants*, and they are often conflated in popular discourse (Brenner 1993b).

5. One incident of public confrontation occurred in 1994, when the government of Alpha Konaré signaled its dedication to the implementation of the platform of Bejing. A more recent incident was the debate of the reform of family law (Schulz 2003b).

6. Only about 2 percent of the Malian population are Christians. Authors disagree over the exact percentage of Muslim believers. Some statistics speak of 95 percent (e.g., *Encyclopedia of Subsaharan Africa* 1997, 100), while Brenner (1993b, 71) estimates that only 70 percent of the population espouse the Islamic faith. This discrepancy exists because, given the various combinations of animistic and Islamic practices, it is difficult to draw a clear distinction between "real" Muslims and nonbelievers. In rural areas of the south (where most people converted to Islam only during the colonial era), many interlocutors described their religious practice as "walking on two feet," that is, as strategically "supplementing" their Islamic faith with non-Islamic rituals.

7. Unless indicated otherwise, all foreign terms are rendered in Bamanakan, the lingua franca of southern Mali.

8. Haidara's movement thrives most in towns in which historically the political influence of traditional religious leaders has been limited.

9. People's distinction between traditional forms of power (*fanga*) and modern politics (*politiki*) dates back to the late colonial period. The notion of "politicking" (that is, the excesses of *politiki*) acquired a new salience after 1992, when particularly older people interpreted multiparty competition as an indicator of the weakness of the central state (Schulz 2001, chapter 3).

10. Brenner (1993b, 60–62; 2000, chapter 5) notes that the popular practice of labeling this internally diverse group of merchants and students "Wahhabi" is misleading (they refer to themselves as "Sunnis" or "ahl-Sunna," that is, those who follow the example of the Prophet [Sunna]). In spite of their heterogeneous composition, they share an inspiration from the Saoudi Wahhabi movement toward ritual and doctrinal purity, and an opposition to established scholars, clerics, and merchants whose influence often dates back to the colonial period.

11. Parti Socialiste du Progrès.

12. Union Soudanaise Rassemblement Démocratique Africain.

13. This containment of Islamic influence was most prominently played out in the field of education. Traditional and reformed institutions of Islamic learning were not granted the same status as French-language schools. Some of the reformed schools were integrated into the national educational system (cf. Brenner 2000, 169–173).

14. This representation glossed over considerable differences in political traditions and historical experiences of different peoples contained in the new nation-state. Also, it did not account for the fact that Islam had historically been more firmly entrenched in the northern societies of Mali.

15. One reason for the limited role of Islam in the nationalist ideology was that Muslim interest groups were given only a marginal place in the party structures when the Marxist-oriented branch took control (cf. Brenner 2000, 171–172).

16. An alliance between established families of religious specialists and some representatives of a new generation of "Wahhabi" businessmen formed the social basis of the growing resistance to Modibo Keita's socialist policies which significantly contributed to the destabilization of Modibo Keita's regime and led to the coup d'état (Amselle 1985).

17. This celebration revolved primarily around the display of emblems of conspicuous consumption and of the regime's capacity to exert physical violence.

18. The officially declared motivation for the creation of the *Association Malienne pour l'Unité et le Progrès de l'Islam* (AMUPI) was to reconcile the two major wings of the Muslim camp (established families of religious specialists and their opponents, the "Wahhabi" merchants and scholars) whose competition had resulted in open hostilities and confrontation (Brenner 1993b).

19. Popular disillusion with the governmental rhetoric of popular participation and discontent with its seeming lack of authority comes out most clearly in the widespread representation of "demokrasi" as anarchy (see Schulz 2001, chapter 3).

20. Also see Eickelman 1992, 2000. For a different situation in northern Nigeria, see Reichmuth 1996.

21. Group members call themselves simply "Muslim women" (*silame musow*), thereby setting themselves apart from "other women" (*muso tow*) who have not (yet) engaged in a quest for religious virtue.

22. For the social standing of the Haidara lineage in the area around Segu, see Manley 1997.

23. According to Brenner (2000), the "rational episteme" gradually but never fully replaced the esoteric episteme of religious knowledge in the colonial period, under the influence of the pedagogy and ideological value of French-language schooling and literacy.

24. Many letters come from neighboring countries and from France and the U.S. Other listeners send audio-recordings of their questions to Haidara.

25. This is not to say that they are static, internally fully consistent, or always comply with "Islamic principles." For example, during the reform of the family law, representatives of AMUPI sometimes defended a regulation as "Islamic" that was, in fact, a local, non-Islamic rule, such as the prohibition for a woman to exercise a trade without her husband's authorization (Schultz 2003b).

26. The Ministry of Communication finally authorized the broadcasting of the entire event, except for the round in which the mannequins presented themselves in bathing suits.

27. As he declared, not only had he enjoyed watching the pageant but he also made the broadcasting accessible to neighbors and followers by placing his three television sets in the street. Rather than holding the government responsible for offering a "free ticket" for moral corruption, Haidara appealed to his listeners' individual consciousness and their obligation to make their daughters aware of their responsibilities as mothers and wives. This position contrasts with the conservative and patriarchal gender ideology Haidara endorses otherwise and in which he depicts women as less reasonable beings who need the guidance of men.

28. Haidara's explication of the differences between his "path" and that of the Qadiriyya and Tijaniya orders illustrates the diffuse nature of the common good to which Haidara appeals, and his ambivalent positioning vis-à-vis established Sufi orders. Asked whether doctrinal or ritual disagreement were at the origin of his departure from his original initiation into (Tijaniyya) practice, Haidara asserted that doctrinal differences mattered less than the propriety of individual conduct. He thereby subtly called into question some traditional credentials on which the authority of established religious lineages is based. At the same time Haidara repeatedly capitalizes on his own genealogical prestige by stressing his descent from a highly renowned religious lineage (see Schulz 2003a).

References

Amselle, J.-L. 1985. Le Wahabisme à Bamako (1945–1985). *Canadian Journal of African Studies* 19 (2): 345–357.

Appadurai, Arjun. 1990. Disjuncture and Difference in the Global Cultural Economy. *Public Culture* 2 (2): 1–24.

Arendt, Hannah. 1958. *The Human Condition.* Chicago: University of Chicago Press.

Bowen, John. 1997. Modern Intentions: Reshaping Subjectivities in an Indonesian Muslim Society. In *Politics and Religious Renewal in Muslim Southeast Asia,* ed. Robert Hefner and Patricia Horvatich, 157–182. Honolulu: University of Hawaii Press.

Brenner, Louis. 1993a. Introduction: Muslim Representations of Unity and Difference in the African Discourse. In *Muslim Identity and Social Change in Subsaharan Africa,* ed. L. Brenner, 1–20. Bloomington and Indianapolis: Indiana University Press.

———. 1993b. Constructing Muslim Identities in Mali. In *Muslim Identity and Social Change in Subsaharan Africa,* ed. L. Brenner, 59–78. Bloomington and Indianapolis: Indiana University Press.

———. 1993c. La culture arabo-islamique au Mali. In *Le radicalisme islamique au sud du Sahara,* ed. R. Otayek, 161–196. Paris: Karthala.

———. 2000. *Controlling Knowledge: Religion, Power and Schooling in a West African Muslim Society.* Bloomington and Indianapolis: Indiana University Press.

Calhoun, Craig. 1992. Introduction to *Habermas and the Public Sphere,* ed. C. Calhoun, 1–48. Cambridge, Mass.: MIT Press.

———. 1997. Nationalism and the Public Sphere. In *Public and Private in Thought and Practice,* ed. Jeff Weintraub and Krishan Kumar, 75–102. Chicago: University of Chicago Press.

Comaroff, Jean, and John L. Comaroff. 2001. Millennial Capitalism: First Thoughts on a Second Coming. In *Millennial Capitalism and the Culture of Neo-Liberalism,* ed. Jean Comaroff and John L. Comaroff, 1–56. Durham, N.C.: Duke University Press.

Encyclopedia of Subsaharan Africa. 1997. Edited by John Middleton. Vol. 3. New York: Scribner's.

Eickelman, Dale. 1992. Mass Higher Education and the Religious Imagination in Contemporary Arab Societies. *American Ethnologist* 19 (4): 643–655.

———. 2000. Islam and the Languages of Modernity. *Daedalus* 129 (1): 119–136.

Eickelman, Dale, and Jon Anderson, eds. 1999. *New Media in the Muslim World.* Bloomington and Indianapolis: Indiana University Press.

Esposito, John. 1984. *Islam and Politics.* Syracuse, N.Y.: Syracuse University Press.

Fraser, Nancy. 1992. Rethinking the Public Sphere: A Contribution to the Critique of Actually Existing Democracy. In *Habermas and the Public Sphere,* ed. C. Calhoun, 109–142. Cambridge, Mass.: MIT Press.

Geschiere, Peter, and Francis Nyamnjoh. 2001. Capitalism and Autochthony: The Seesaw of Mobility and Belonging. In *Millennial Capitalism and the Culture of Neo-Liberalism,* ed. Jean Comaroff and John L. Comaroff, 159–190. Durham, N.C.: Duke University Press.

Gobetti, Daniela. 1997. Humankind as a System: Private and Public Agency at the Origins of Modern Liberalism. In *Public and Private in Thought and Practice: Perspectives on a Grand Dichotomy,* ed. Jeff Weintraub and Krishna Kumar, 103–133. Chicago: University of Chicago Press.

Habermas, Jürgen. 1962. *Strukturwandel der Öffentlichkeit.* Frankfurt am Main: Suhrkamp.

Harvey, David. 1989. *The Condition of Postmodernity: An Enquiry into the Origins of Cultural Change.* Oxford: Blackwell.

Hock, Carsten. 1998. Muslimische Reform und staatliche Autorität in der Republik Mali seit 1960. Die Ausbreitung der Wahhabiya in einer Situation der politischen Blockade gesellschaftlichen Fortschritts. Ph.D. dissertation, Department of Anthropology, University of Bayreuth.

Kepel, Gilles. 1991. *La revanche de Dieu: Chrétiens, juifs, et musulmans à la reconquête du monde.* Paris: Éditions du Seuil.

Launay, Robert. 1992. *Beyond the Stream: Islam and Society in a West African Town.* Berkeley: University of California Press.

Launay, Robert, and Benjamin Soares. 1999. The Formation of an 'Islamic Sphere' in French Colonial West Africa. *Economy and Society* 28 (3): 476–478.

Manley, Andrew. 1997. The Sosso and the Haidara: Two Muslim Lineages in Soudan Francais, 1890–1960. In *Le temps des marabouts: Itinéraires et stratégies islamiques en Afrique occidentale française v. 1880–1960,* ed. David Robinson and Jean-Louis Triaud, 319–336. Paris: Karthala.

Manuel, Peter. 1993. *Cassette Culture: Popular Music and Technological Change in North India.* Chicago: University of Chicago Press.

Meyer, Birgit, and Peter Geschiere, eds. 1998. *Globalization and Identity: Dialectics of Flow and Closure.* Oxford: Blackwell.

Otayek, Réné. 1993. Introduction to *Le radicalisme islamique au sud du Sahara,* ed. Réné Otayek, 7–20. Paris: Karthala.

Rajagopal, Arvind. 2001. *Politics after Television: Religious Nationalism and the Reshaping of the Public in India.* Cambridge: Cambridge University Press.

Reichmuth, Stefan. 1996. Education and the Growth of Religious Associations among Yoruba Muslims: The Ansar-ud-Deen Society in Nigeria. *Journal of Religion in Africa* 26 (4): 364–405.

Roy, Olivier. 1994. *The Failure of Political Islam.* Cambridge, Mass.: Harvard University Press.

Sanankoua, Bintou. 1991. Les Associations Féminines musulmanes à Bamako. In *L'enseignement islamique au Mali,* ed. Bintou Sanankoua and Louis Brenner, 105–125. Bamako: Editions Jamana.

Schulz, Dorothea. 1999. In Pursuit of Publicity: Talk Radio and the Imagination of a Moral Public in Mali. *Africa Spectrum* 99 (2): 161–185.

———. 2001. *Perpetuating the Politics of Praise: Jeli Singers, Radios and Political Mediation Tradition in Mali.* Cologne: Rüdiger Köppe.

———. 2003a. "Charisma and Brotherhood" Revisited: Mass-Mediated Forms of Spirituality in Urban Mali. *Journal of Religion in Africa* 33, 2: 146–171.

———. 2003b. Political Factions, Ideological Fictions: The Controversy over the Reform of Family Law in Democratic Mali. *Islamic Law and Society* 10 (1): 132–164.

———. 2004. "God Is Our Resort." Islamic Revival, Mass-Mediated Religiosity, and the Moral Negotiation of Gender Relations in Urban Mali. *Habilitation* thesis, Free University of Berlin.

Snyder, Francis. 1967. The Political Thought of Modibo Keita. *Journal of Modern African Studies* 5 (1): 79–106.

Soares, Benjamin. 1997. The Spiritual Economy of Nioro du Sahel: Islamic Discourses and Practices in a Malian Religious Center. Ph.D. dissertation, Northwestern University.

———. 2004. Islam and Public Piety in Mali. In *Public Islam and the Common Good,* ed. Dale Eickelman and Armando Salvatore, 205–226. Leiden: Brill.

Sreberny-Mohammadi, Annabelle, and Ali Mohammadi. 1994. *Small Media, Big Revolution: Communication, Culture, and the Iranian Revolution.* Minneapolis: University of Minnesota Press.

Stewart, Charles. 1997. Colonial Justice and the Spread of Islam in the Early Twentieth Century. In *Le temps des marabouts: Itinéraires et stratégies islamiques en Afrique occidentale française v. 1880–1960,* ed. David Robinson and Jean-Louis Triaud, 53–66. Paris: Karthala.

Triaud, Jean-Louis. 1988a. After Fodé Doumbia. Bamako, la ville aux deux cents mosquées, ou la victoire du 'secteur informel' islamique. *Islam et Sociétés au Sud du Sahara* 2 (1): 166–177.

———. 1988b. Khalwa and the Career of Sainthood: An Interpretative Essay. In *Charisma and Brotherhood in African Islam,* ed. Cruise O'Brien and Christian Coulon, 53 66. Oxford: Clarendon.

———. 1997. Introduction to *Le temps des marabouts: Itinéraires et stratégies islamiques en Afrique occidentale française v. 1880–1960,* ed. David Robinson and Jean-Louis Triaud, 11–29. Paris: Karthala.

Warner, Michael 1992. The Mass Public and the Mass Subject. In *Habermas and the Public Sphere,* ed. C. Calhoun, 377–401. Cambridge, Mass.: MIT Press.

Zaret, David. 1992. Religion, Sciences and Printing in the Public Spheres of 17th Century England. In *Habermas and the Public Sphere,* ed. Craig Calhoun, 212–235. Cambridge, Mass.: MIT Press.

Zubaida, Sami. 1989. *Islam, the People, and the State: Essays on Political Ideas and Movements in the Middle East.* London: Routledge.

7 Media and Violence in an Age of Transparency: Journalistic Writing on War-Torn Maluku

Patricia Spyer

> The war takes place in black and white. For those on the sidelines that is. For those who are actually in it there are many colors, excessive colors, too bright, too red and orange, too liquid and incandescent, but for the others the war is like a newsreel—grainy, smeared, with bursts of staccato noise and large numbers of grey-skinned people rushing or plodding or falling down, everything elsewhere.
>
> She goes to the newsreels, in the movie theatres. She reads the papers. She knows herself to be at the mercy of events, and she knows by now that events have no mercy.
>
> —Margaret Atwood, *The Blind Assassin*

Prominent among the various emergent publicities in post-Suharto Indonesia is one that crystallizes around the term "transparency" as the imagined future for a new more democratic nation. Hijacked from International Monetary Fund (IMF) discourse in the heady days of student rebellion and calls for *reformasi*[1] in the spring of 1998, the discourse on "transparency" as it relates to journalistic practice has gone hand in hand with the mushrooming of watchdog media groups and journalist organizations as well as the proliferation of forums, seminars, and training sessions devoted to the professionalization of media practitioners or to specific topics like "peace journalism" (*jurnalisme damai* or *jurnalisme kasih sayang*) or reporting on AIDS, women's issues, and the like (Ispandriarno 2001, 6).[2]

This paper considers some contradictions in the deployment of the concept of "transparency"—specifically the narrative strategies developed by a number of Indonesian journalists within the wider space of transactions, dilemmas, desires, and revisions that more generally describe the place of the media in post-Suharto Indonesia. Advocates of democratic ideals of transparency and journalistic practice and active in a range of *reformasi*-inspired media initiatives, these men invented a minimalist form of reporting on violence with the aim, in their view, of foreclosing a negative form of media agency within the Moluccan conflict at the far eastern end of Indonesia—one, in other words, that would foster rather than alleviate hatred and violence.

In addition to their own arguments and strategies, I reflect on the possible effects of such a proactive, stripped-bare form of reporting both as a politics and a form of mass mediation. Much like war watched from the sidelines, I suggest how the black and white language of such writing—bereft of the liquid, incandescent colors, shadows, messy contingencies and contexts describing the experience of those "actually in" the war—facilitates a reading of the conflict in the starkest of terms. In the case of Maluku, it provides the language and thereby also the means for glossing over—under the readily available rubric of "religion"—a very complicated, fraught, mobile terrain made up of histories, grievances, friendships, alliances, long-standing rivalries, customs of trust and accountability, power structures, political economy, and, last but not least, the legacies of New Order cultural politics. I also speculate on how the spectralization of violence, which I see as paradoxically enabled by the particular form of proactive journalism discussed here, may, in turn, produce more violence.

Transparencies

In May 2000, during a brief visit to Manado, the predominantly Christian capital of the province of North Sulawesi, I spoke with two of the three journalists who had been directly involved in the project of the new daily *Radar Ternate,* which was subsequently given the more geopolitically comprehensive name of *Radar Kieraha* in honor of the four mountains cum early sultanates of Ternate, Tidore, Bacan, and Makian in North Maluku. As a member of the editorial team of *Manado Pos* which produced the paper, Pak A. had supervised the new daily from the distance of Manado. Pak S., in charge of reporting on the goings-on in the city of Ternate, the DPRD (*Dewan Perwakilan Rakyat Daerah*) or regional government, the police, or, as he summed it up, "issues of government," had been based in Ternate from September 1999 until December 28 of the same year when violence in this city forced *Radar Kieraha* to stop its circulation. A third journalist who dealt with matters of economics and development, and as of May 2000 had relocated to Gorontalo, another city in North Sulawesi, had, along with Pak S., been based in Ternate.

Besides, as I was told, reasons of "bisnis," the idea behind the launching of *Radar Kieraha* was essentially twofold: to give a *kado* or gift to the new province of North Maluku and to provide people (*masyarakat*) in an area where they "do not understand the role of the press" with their own daily newspaper.[3] The ideological underpinning of this move, as it was explained to me, is that in the era of *reformasi* (reform) the role of the people would also be articulated through a media controlled by the people who, specifically, would "exercise supervision on the (actions of the) government" and "criticize things that are wrong." Already from September 1999 on, however, when Pak S. arrived in Ternate, a succession of political problems and conflicts undermined this ideal vision of the relationship between press and people. First and foremost among these were the competition surrounding the governorship of the new North Maluku province, the outbreak of violence between the communities of Kao and Malifut on the neighboring island of Halmahera, the circulation of an illicit and forged letter allegedly issued by leaders of the GPM (*Gereja Protestan Maluku*) or Protestant Church of the Moluccas and calling for the Christianization of Maluku,[4] and the movement into the area of refugees and other persons with recent histories of displacement and violence or complex agendas of retaliation and retribution, or both.

Pak S. explained how under increasingly tense circumstances the newspaper appealed to "the people" to guard against being influenced by the events and how together—newspaper and people—they should take care to subdue and diminish the situation. Notwithstanding such gestures, however, or the practice of "weighing against each other the side of the whites and the side of the yellows whenever an article went to press," Pak S. claimed that both the forces of the Sultan of Ternate or "yellow" (*kuning*) and those of "white" (*putih*), a combination of Makianese and Tidorese—accused the paper of partisanship. The result, as he put it, was that "even we were swept up by the event [*kasus*]." *Radar Kieraha* went to press for the last time on December 27, 1999. Circulation on the 27th was already difficult, and that night, during the height of the confrontation between "yellow" and "white," Pak S. fled to the police station. Either that same night or subsequently the office of the newspaper was vandalized (in early May 2000 when we first spoke it had been occupied by refugees from the North Moluccan island of Halmahera), phone lines in the city were dead, and much of the city had been burned to the ground.

Both Pak S. and Pak A. recognized the limitations of the kind of proactive journalism they preached and put in practice. Pak A. insisted, for instance, on the much larger and immediate reach of television and especially radio broadcasting[5] in an area where newspaper circulation was limited, and the economic and intellectual level of the local population—as they put it—"lower than the prevailing one" so that even if "we publish a news item to cool down the atmosphere it is not sure that they will read it, also even if they know how to read maybe their region cannot be reached." At the same time they did their utmost in their reporting to intervene in the conflict with the aim of diminishing the chances of additional outbreaks of violence.

Reporting now from Manado, Pak S. explained,

> We make comparative news like here, its like this, life in Manado is like this, the newspaper is sent there, like this, so that whatever thing happens there we just obliterate it, what I mean is just let it be since they are already so violently implicated, we shouldn't articulate anything . . . just hush it up, to prevent the Muslim community from killing Christians or the Christian community from killing Muslims but that should not be in [the newspaper] . . . but once a violent outbreak happens which causes so many dead, so many dead, so many dead, it should not be said who did it only that there was a violent outbreak here, don't say Christians died, don't, just say how many died, directly, the number of dead.[6]

Pak A. elaborated, saying,

> [The idea is] to give information about current events but not in a transparent manner, if for instance there is a conflict between inhabitants of a place, between people, between members of a different ethnic group or religion it is not necessary to mention the ethnic group or religion so that this does not cause injury or provoke revenge from another side, so yes there were people killed, yes there was an incident, OK, but who was behind this, who caused this incident does not have to be written so that the information does not spread to the other side.

Pak S. broke in with additional clarification:

> For instance, where, let's see, between Malifut and Kao, we report that there was a clash between the people of Malifut and those of Kao in which five people were killed, that's it, enough said, there was a house of worship burnt down, don't say it was a mosque, don't say it was a church. In this way, we take a kind of action which is objective yet constructive, the end all of it is constructive. If we want to be objective in a transparent manner then this will in fact be destructive because it will trigger conflicts. If that is the case then it would be better not to report at all. So we have two alternatives, either not to report at all or to report in a way that is objective and constructive.

Besides the amount of self-reflection among journalists and other media practitioners in the post-Suharto era that the foregoing indicates, there are a number of other remarkable aspects of the discourse on proactive journalism or constructive objectivity that I would like to highlight. Quite striking is the rapid evolution of the notion of transparency in relation to the political as evidenced in my conversation with the two *Manado Pos* journalists. As James Siegel (1998a, 75, N1) points out, the term "transparency" was co-opted by Indonesian students in their earliest calls for *reformasi* from IMF discourse where it indicated full access to the state and the activities of financial institutions. Rapidly, however, "transparency" came to describe "the desirability of political events also being open to view" (ibid). By extension, those aspects of political, social, and economic life that remained hidden were regarded as corrupt and glossed under the rubric of *KKN* or "*korupsi, kolusi, nepotisme*" (ibid.). By the summer of 2001, when I returned again to Indonesia, "transparency" had entered everyday parlance and enjoyed multiple application—as, for instance, when Moluccan refugees from different camps in the Manado area complained at a meeting that the flow of their Supermie Noodle supply was insufficiently *transparan*. In other words, they suspected that some sort of *KKN* was intervening in the rations they received from the provincial government.

In the conversation with Pak A. and Pak S., this relationship between what should be brought to public view or, in their case, reported on, and what should remain hidden, be obliterated, or hushed up seems entirely reversed; that is, much of what makes the political the political or the violent perhaps somewhat locatable is left out of the picture with the aim of a constructive and responsible journalism. Only the starkest outlines of a violent occurrence make it into the newspaper and hence, also, into public view—the fact of a clash or conflict, the number of dead or wounded resulting, and the destruction of property. Left out are the grievances, historical relations, as well as ascribed/assumed identities of those persons and groups directly involved in a conflict—their ethnicity, religion, race, and class or the kind of potentially politicized difference gathered by the Suharto regime under the acronym SARA[7]—as well as the triggers, causes, background, and unfolding of a given violent happening. The latter, it is important to note, is the kind of information that might help one to fill out the picture, identify the stakes in the conflict and the range of issues that have brought the parties involved into conflict, or, more complexly, begin to understand what makes people re-cognize their identities in moments of crisis in terms of religion, ethnicity, or other collective subjectivities, along with the forms and manners in which they do so (Spyer n.d.). In short, the kind of specificity and unfolding dynamics that necessarily form the starting point of any attempt to come to grips with the complex ways in which otherwise ordinary people perpetuate the most extraordinary atrocities on one another is erased. Lest I be misunderstood, I do not mean in the first instance the "context" or "history" that all too often is unproblematically marshaled as the explanatory backdrop to the outbreak and chronic perpetuation of violence but rather the very form that violence assumes in specific situations.[8] What is called for and figures centrally in the larger project of which this paper is a small part is a radical rethinking of the very notion of context—here, specifically, with respect to how a range of mainstream mass as well as smaller, more tactical media, together with other factors, intervene, jolt, reshuffle, and co-produce the volatile runaway topographies in which violence erratically unfolds.[9]

Regarding the two men from the *Manado Pos,* my point is not to criticize their journalistic practice. Admirably they were highly concerned and engaged with the ongoing crisis in Maluku and in their country more generally. Both were trying to find a way to translate their concerns into a proactive form of journalism. And both were right on target in foregrounding the role of the media in the production of current events and in their acute awareness of how the news, say, that a mosque or church had been burned down (whether true or false), could easily set off another spiral of violence. Indeed, in Maluku, rumors that something has happened have frequently preceded, made possible, and thus prophesized particular violent happenings (Spyer 2002).

Significantly, however, while the journalists emphasized the possible damage or danger to others that a more "transparent" reporting might precipitate, they were silent when it came to the risks that they themselves potentially ran in assigning to particular actors the responsibility for violent occurrences, that is, in naming their source. Beyond the elusive categories of *provokator, pihak tertentu* (certain parties), and *elit politik* populating the pages of *Radar Kieraha* as those of other Indonesian newspapers and media sources, any identification of those persons or groups who would either be invested in the sheer fact of violence and political chaos or in ensuring particular outcomes is by and large also obliterated.[10] I do not believe that the elision of this dimension in their conversation with me or, more generally, in their journalistic practice was either explicit or calculated. Yet neither do I believe it arbitrary that the "transparency" of the political demanded by students during the heyday of *reformasi* was, by May 2000, no longer regarded as a serious possibility within a political climate where the space for democratic reform and the political will to put it in place were increasingly compromised. In such circumstances along with political conviction, prudence as well as perhaps customary practice for those who had worked under the constraints of the New Order fostered self-censorship.[11]

Specters and Spectacles of Violence

Here I would like to reflect further on what the possible consequences are of this journalistic practice of erasure for the relationship between representations of violence and its actual collective and individual occurrences; or what, in other words, a violence that is subject to such erasure does to the understanding or practice of violence on the ground, that is, what kinds of possibly violent social and political effects such representations might have—and, by extension, what form of public such practices might help to put in place. Perhaps because of the continuity of some of the same constraints on "transparency" as those operative under the New Order, the abstraction of violence out of the circumstances in which it is produced and made meaningful and its effect—the representation of a violence without a clearly identifiable origin—dovetails in certain important respects with the production and representation of violence under the former New Order regime.

Take, for instance, Petrus, an acronym for the so-called "Mysterious Killings" (*Pembunuhan Misterius*), a paramilitary operation of the early 1980s aimed at eliminating underworld figures, gang members, and petty criminals (*gali-gali*), and resulting in the point-blank killings of at least four thousand persons. Initially "mysterious," when they first began the killings took place under the cover of anonymity, were carried out at night by masked men, and followed a pattern, as Barker (1998, 18) puts it,

> very similar to less violent operations which were such a prominent feature of New Order life: operations against *becak*, drugs, prostitution, vagrants, women's fertility (i.e. Family Planning), and the like. Just as the *operasi* aimed at drugs, for example, the agents descended on their targets and removed them from the scene in order to maintain an image of order. The removal was then followed by the staging of a spectacle in which the targeted objects or people were shown to have been truly eliminated (the dead bodies displayed for all to see and the drugs crushed or burned).[12]

On the one hand, then, the spectacle prepared for public consumption of the corpses of those persons killed were left exposed, often for many hours, in public places, and, on the other, what Siegel calls "the structure of blindness that leaves criminals out of sight" meant that the corpse, and the excessive violence that produced it, was supposed to be read as a sign of something beyond it (Siegel 1998b, 119). Following Siegel, the violence of the criminals killed and the fear they generated while alive, an "uncontrollable origin," was symbolically recuperated by the Suharto state following a complex trajectory that began with the spectacle of the corpse, led through the excessive violence of the killing in which the state as perpetrator mimicked and, crucially, exceeded the criminal violence of those killed, and became therewith, ideally, not only "a new criminal type in Jakarta" but the mother of all criminal types and, somewhat reassuringly, the source of a generalized fear (ibid.). If the corpse was thus turned into a sign, it was—as any other sign—always unstable and in excess of its possibilities of signification. But if the Petrus corpse did not at all times and for everyone open up the communicative chain leading back to the state, this state under New Order conditions was more generally available to reassure anyone who needed it that fear, having an origin, also had an ultimate source of control.

By the time of the next wave of mysterious killings, less than half a year after Suharto's May 1998 stepdown, the so-called ninja killings in east Java that targeted *dukun santet* (sorcerers) and, much like Petrus, were carried out by unidentified masked men, often in the dead of night, show, in Barker's opinion, "no clear signs of having established a symbolic recuperation" (Barker 1998, 42). Put somewhat differently, it was no longer clear who or what one should fear. Under new circumstances and with a state in crisis, the relationship between violence and its recuperated origin had been severed. The result of the rupture of this relationship is a violence set loose, free-floating, and no longer traceable back to an easily identifiable or ready-made origin. This is also the failure of terms like *elit politik, pihak tertentu,* and *provokator.* Too amorphous and elusive to serve as an origin *elit politik* oscillates between an old *elit politik* that is/is not in the picture and a new (emergent) one that is not clearly consolidated, *pihak tertentu*/certain parties remain "certain" but unnamed, while a *provokator* as an extension of violence rather than something beyond it is only known in retrospect after the fact of a violence "provoked."[13] Nowhere locatable and thus potentially everywhere, violence roams like a specter in the post-New Order landscape of Indonesia.

One can surmise that the logic of the politics outlined here and that of mass media more generally collaborate in the spectralization of violence. Add to this the practices of the *Manado Pos* journalists which take the generalizing, universalizing, indeed spectralizing impulse of mass media—both print and perhaps even more televisual—to a last extreme. If the mass media need and feed on events, they also transform the events they seize upon—which, like crime and like violence, are necessarily eventful.[14] Concerning this tendency, Ernst Jünger observes,

> Today wherever an event takes place it is surrounded by a circle of lenses and
> microphones and lit up by the flaming explosions of flashbulbs. In many cases,
> the event itself is completely subordinated to its "transmission": to a great degree,
> it has been turned into an object. Thus we have already experienced political trials,
> parliamentary meetings, and contests whose whole purpose is to be the object of a
> planetary broadcast. The event is bound neither to its particular space nor to its

particular time, since it can be mirrored anywhere and repeated any number of times. These are signs that point to a great distance. (Quoted in Cadava 1997, xxii)

Jünger described this deracinating effect of mass media—the abstraction of the event from particularities of time and space, its transformation into a dislocatable, exchangeable, circulatable, repeatable, serialized entity or, in Marxist terms, its commodification or definition in terms of exchange value, and, relatedly, the subordination of the event to the fact of its mass-mediability—already in 1934, the year of the Nuremburg rallies. If at this relatively early moment Jünger could write of the production of an event for a planetary broadcast, then it goes without saying that the movement of global capital and the explosion of televisual possibilities owing to the communications revolution have, if anything, only aggravated and magnified the processes of which he spoke (Allen 1999, 37).[15]

While media language post-Suharto has been changing, approximating more closely in certain respects everyday, popular, and regional forms of speech, new kinds of standardization have also set in and, notably, in the expanding vocabulary of violence. Words like *provokator, pihak tertentu, kasus* (event/case), *isu* (issue), or the acronym SARA serve not only to standardize the language of violence but also to universalize the events and social actors they describe—across newspapers but also websites, chat groups, and so on, as well as on the radio and television. And they do so even with respect to media sources that cater to the identitarian-bounded interests of specific audiences and social groups which in other important respects are involuted—physically within a divided Ambon boasting its own "Gaza Strip" (*Jalur Gaza*), ideologically, and also to some extent—given the split and doubling into a "Christian" and a "Muslim" media—in terms of what people on either side see, hear, and read.

I have focused here on print media. In the context of Mbembe's new "geography-in-the-making" (Mbembe 1999, 15), across the ever more porous boundaries of the nation-state and beyond the limitations of national language, the televisual media especially play a dominant role in the process of standardizing and codifying what counts as violence and, importantly, what it looks like. Increasingly today, violence must not only be seen to be believed but only exists when it can be seen—and then, over and over again. "Forms of violence that are not 'telegenic,' that are not selected by the media for transmission tend to be ignored and, in the process, forgotten or devalued" (Weber 1997, 82). Along with other dimensions to the spectralization of violence that I have touched upon here, this figuring of the violent as increasingly televisual is part and parcel of a globalized situation in which politics and history need increasingly to be comprehended in terms of their derivative and secondary relationship to telecommunications (Ronell, cited in Cadava, xxiii).

The epigraph at the opening of this paper, from Atwood's *Blind Assassin*, evokes the unreal blur of war watched from a distance, a war waged two dimensionally in black and gray, a war of the time past of World War II. One can only wonder about the distance of those on the much more immediate sidelines of the violence, say in Manado, and if for them the violence at times threatens to dissolve before their eyes into a black on white, abstract series of *provocator, isu,* and *kasus,* number after number of casualties, or of yet more generic houses of worship going up in flames. This is certainly a possibility. This reading also supports the logic according to which serialized categories like "religious conflict" (in Maluku), "ethnic strife" (elsewhere in Indonesia), or simply the New Order acronym SARA circulate widely, are continually reproduced, and become inserted into highly mediatized if diverse scenes of chronic violence and war. There, taking on a life of their own, they become "good to think" with, providing a ready-made, on-hand appropriable clarity for those on the sidelines and often, too, for those immersed in war's destructive messiness. The easy availability of "religion" to explain violence builds upon the cultural politics and policies regarding religious practice introduced by the New Order regime— specifically "religion's" codification as *agama* for particular ends, too complicated to go into here. Nor should one underestimate the value of such facile, primordialist explanations which leave the state, the army, the police, and other common instigators of violence in Indonesia comfortably out of the picture.

There may be another important effect of the streamlining and spectralization of violence that I have tried to characterize here. One can imagine that when violence comes to be seen as lacking an identifiable origin, when it lurks both nowhere and potentially everywhere, when its source is largely unseen, that this can engender a terrible fear. Without a clear object to fix on or turn to for reassurance, the response to such an engulfing fear may, in the right circumstances, be a recourse to violence. In an age of transparency, when violence proliferates and events have no mercy, terror sets in to precipitate more violence. As if above and beyond it all, the media then step down from the immediate sidelines to enter the spiral of more merciless events.

In the preceding pages I have lifted one strand out of the highly complex, vigorously contested, and expanding post-Suharto mediascape of Indonesia. Drawing on my conversations with several journalists involved in the aborted project of the newspaper *Radar Kieraha,* on my perusal of examples of this paper, and of the page bearing the same name that was subsequently inserted in North Sulawesi's *Manado Pos,* I have suggested what the phantom implications of the advocated pruned-back media prose might be. One may object, however, that the consequences of such stark reports, codified language, and bare-boned enumeration depend considerably on how they are received—that is, actually read, talked about, and used. While this is something I have not pursued, it is clear that such reading and talk from Manado to Maluku would necessarily be somewhat different. Moreover, as a practice, a politics, and a form of public imagination emergent in the post-Suharto era, I find this kind of proactive journalism itself intriguing for what it reveals of the processes of reflection and the dilemmas faced by media practitioners in our own general times of avid publicity and proclaimed transparency.

Surrounded on all sides by areas of conflict, Manado prides itself on being a haven of relative tranquility or, as Pak S. pointed out in a follow-up conversation in July 2001, we are hemmed in by Posso to the south in Central Sulawesi, the provinces of Maluku and North Maluku to our east, and Kalimantan, another site of vicious "ethnic" warfare, to our west.[16] Maluku, by contrast, and especially the city of Ambon, has, since the outbreak of violence there in January 1999 up through the Malino II Peace Agreement of early 2002, itself been the scene of chronic warfare. In both Manado and Maluku, stripped-down media reports such as those produced by my journalist friends operate alongside other media—both print and electronic, regional, national, and international, as well as mass media forms versus smaller, more covert, tactical genres produced and circulated beyond the grid of the country's conventional media institutions.

In terms of media, Ambon is an especially dense and murky terrain, a swirl of highly ideologized images, vocabularies, sound bites, slogans, and vectors introducing during the war a host of mediated and mediatized "elsewheres" into the mobile, charged scene of urban confrontation (Spyer 2002). If and when they entered this space, the "objective but not transparent" reports of *Manado Pos*'s journalists become part of a much larger arena of conflicting messages, fragmentary information, representational immediacy, and stark clear-cut abstraction. They shared the same space with phantom letters that proved incendiary enough to trigger large-scale violence. One especially infamous incident, mentioned earlier, involved a letter allegedly issued by Ambon's Protestant Church and calling for Maluku's Christianization which, once multiplied, read aloud over megaphones, and spread about, led directly to the dislocation and deaths of numerous North Moluccas—and indirectly to the demise of the new province's newspaper, *Radar Kieraha*. Such "dark" circuits, also traced by inflammatory video CDs produced on both sides, competed for attention with partisan descriptions of the local press, with village gossip presented as truth on Christian and Muslim websites, with Christian-inclined state radio vying with illegal Muslim radio, the latter dominating at one point all the airwaves in Ambon, crowding out other channels, and even infiltrating the handy-talkies of priests. Add to this the state of civil emergency declared in Maluku and North Maluku provinces in June 2000, with its severe curtailment of civil liberties, not the least those of the press, and the lag of two to three days before national newspapers reach Ambon and their exorbitant prices once they do, and one may well wonder what, and if, people in this city were actually reading. Once again, in the summer of 2001, Pak S. insisted that in Manado, with strife on all sides, "we must direct our discussions as journalists to how we should act, and how to check the influence of *provokator* from outside," thereby invoking the proactive practice of minimal description. Another journalist, a Moluccan who worked for a year in Ambon following the outbreak of war and subsequently in the tense, post-conflict environment of Kei, Southeast Maluku, observed that a more neutral source, like the pro-peace writing of Pak S. was quickly marginalized once it appeared in Ambon. In the volatile, polarized setting of the war-torn city, alongside phrases like "Muslim cleansing" and other vivid, slanted versions of war, such neutrality appeared ludicrous by contrast.

Epilogue: One Slip of the Pen . . .

All the above begs the question of how to write and what to write about violence—perhaps especially violence elsewhere—and whether to write about violence at all. This includes, of course, my own writing of this modest piece. An Indonesian colleague and fellow Maluku watcher insists that in writing about such situations, whether we are partisan or neutral, the language itself limits our descriptions and forms of argumentation. If one writes, say, about the ill-fated and now infamous pro-peace Public Service Announcement "Speaking from the Heart: Acang and Obet" aired some months after the war in Ambon began and refigured subsequently as a source of important emblems of enmity on both sides—the names of its sentimentalized child protagonists, Acang and Obet, becoming those for both the Christian and Muslim enemy—this writing itself, or so the argument goes, reproduces the war's bitter, bloody divide. "Ambon is itself bloody," my colleague commented, "you mention Ambon and you mention blood—one slip of the pen and . . . " Since people's desires, fears, and imagination are even more sharply tuned in extraordinary situations than otherwise, a slip of the pen is often not needed to turn a writer or filmmaker's intentions considerably awry. Yet even the kind of not-writing advocated by the *Manado Pos* journalists can, I argue, conceal its own phantom dangers which, in certain circumstances, may contribute to producing more violence. In the end I believe it is often best to write. In this age of publicity, airing and exposing conflict has undoubtedly its own obvious as well as unforeseen dangers, but media exposure, as in the case of former East Timor, can also, eventually, contribute to peace. If writing is a kind of violence, not writing and varieties of not-writing occasionally risk being so, too.

Notes

This essay is based on three months of fieldwork in Manado, Yogyakarta, and Jakarta, Indonesia, in 2000 and 2001. It was carried out in the context of a four-year interdisciplinary research project on "Indonesian Mediations," which in turn is one of four subprojects within a larger "Indonesia in Transition" Program funded by the Royal Netherlands Academy of Sciences. My own research concerns the dynamics of mass and small media in the imagination and production of violence and peace in the Moluccas. I would like to thank the Royal Netherlands Academy of Sciences for its support of this research and the Research Centre Religion and Society at the University of Amsterdam for its support of a preliminary field trip to Indonesia in May 2000. Versions of this essay have been presented as papers at conferences at Leiden University, University College London, University of Amsterdam, Harvard University, and at the Association for Asian Studies meetings in April 2002. I would like to thank the audiences of these different venues for their comments. Special thanks go to Webb Keane, P. M. Laksono, Birgit Meyer, Annelies Moors, Rafael Sánchez, and Henk Schulte Nordholt for their helpful suggestions. I also acknowledge gratefully the assistance of Ibu Bian Loho-Unsulangi, Broeder Corne, Sister Josefa, and Sister Angela of the DSJ (Dina Santo Josef) in Manado, and, last but not least, that of the journalists without whose time and patience this essay would not exist.

1. All foreign terms are derived from Bahasa Indonesia, the national language of the Republic of Indonesia.

2. Lukas Suryanto Ispandriarno (2001) mentions that, for print media alone, for instance, more than one thousand new newspapers and magazines have arisen in the two years following Suharto's downfall. For an assessment of the role of print media in the "Moluccan disaster," see the special issue of *Pantau* 9 (2000) on "Petaka Maluku." Numerous seminars and publications supported by local institutions and nongovernmental organizations (NGOs) as well as international organizations such as UNESCO, USAID, and the British Council are currently devoted to journalistic practice and professionalism as well as to specific foci like peace journalism.

3. The *Manado Pos* is a subsidiary of the Surabaya daily, *Jawa Pos*, and, as such, is part of the country's largest press empire. Following Sen and Hill (2000, 58–59), the *Jawa Pos* is, importantly, the only paper outside the capital Jakarta that has focused on the development of provincial markets.

4. See Nanere 2000, 63–80, for a facsimile of the letter and discussion of the incident; see also Komkat KWI 2000, 75.

5. Alongside Christian-inclined state radio in Ambon, several illegal radio stations operating in this capital of the province of Maluku have been seen as a source of provocation in the conflict. See "Maluku Leader Dies of Gunshot Wounds," *Jakarta Post*, March 22, 2001. In July 2001 I was told by several people that the Muslim extremist *Laskar Jihad* Radio Station, the SMPP or *Suara Perjuangan Muslimin Maluku*, had managed to control all the airwaves in Ambon for approximately the previous three months. As it was explained to me, all radios in Ambon exclusively received the SPMM station while even handy-talkies (HT) were infiltrated by the channel's broadcasting. Elsewhere the activities of radio stations in conditions of war have been inflammatory, for instance, during the genocide in Rwanda. See Saine 1998.

6. The issue of numbers, not surprisingly, is an extremely contentious and debated subject in the context of the conflict. Some activists I spoke to insisted that it is preferable not to mention any figures publicly. On the other hand, as Robert Cribb points out in a sensitive piece on the problem of reporting the numbers of dead in massacres, numbers are necessary to get a grasp on mass killing but, given the enormous problems involved in putting numbers on political casualties, the utmost caution is advised in using them. There are also, he writes, serious moral consequences in getting it wrong—"if we overstate the number killed we commit blood libel on those we accuse, if we understate it we deprive victims even of the recognition that they died." See Cribb 2001, 94–95.

7. An acronym for Suku, Agama, Ras, Antar-golongan or ethnic group, religion, race, and class.

8. For an excellent and now classic discussion of representing violence, see Pandey 1992.

9. On the notion of "runaway topographies," see Spyer 2000, esp. 36–40.

10. The literature on violence in Indonesia is growing. A selection includes the insightful piece on Indonesian modalities and figurings of violence by Sidel (2001), Henk Schulte Nordholt's helpful historical genealogy of especially New Order violence (2001), the collections of essays by Colombijn and Lindblad (2002), and Wessel and Wimhofer (2001).

11. On control of and actions taken against the press under the New Order, see Human Rights Watch 1994. On the press more generally during this period, see Sen and Hill 2000, esp. chapter 2, "The Press: Industry and Ideology."

12. More generally Barker (1998) offers a perceptive analysis of some of the New Order's policies and strategies of surveillance. For further information on various waves of "mysterious killings," including those of *dukun santet*, see also Kees van Dijk 2000, 359–377.

13. On the "newspeak" of Indonesia's *reformasi* era post-Suharto and, specifically, on the renewed social currency of the term *provokator*, see Dirk Vlasblom "Megafoons en gefluister: Vademecum van de 'reformasi' in Indonesia," *NRC Handelsblad,* 4 March 2000 (in Vlasblom 2002); also see Kees van Dijk 2000, 282–283.

14. For an illuminating analysis of the "more than incidental" relationship between mass media and crime, see Ivy 1996, 12.

15. Allen foregrounds the impact of dramatic changes in news media technology available since the 1980s on the practices of journalists, politicians, and aid agencies. Equipment that allows film to be rapidly transmitted from one part of the world to another, together with the increasing demand for real-time news coverage, the intense competition for dramatic images, and the decrease in opportunities for more investigative forms of journalism, collaborate to make a certain kind of international reporting the norm and to reduce the scope for subtlety and insight.

16. The sizable population of especially Christian refugees from Maluku (the Muslims from this area having largely fled to Muslim-dominated South Sulawesi) housed in camps in and around Manado contributed to the tangible presence of this region—including its troubles—in North Sulawesi.

References

Allen, Tim. 1999. Perceiving Contemporary War. In *The Media of Conflict: War Reporting and Representations of Violence,* ed. Tim Allen and Jean Seaton. London: Zed.

Barker, Joshua. 1998. State of Fear: Controlling the Criminal Contagion in Suharto's New Order. *Indonesia* 66:7–42.

Cadava, Eduardo. 1997. *Words of Light: Theses on the Photography of History.* Princeton, N.J.: Princeton University Press.

Colombijn, Freek, and J. Thomas Lindblad. 2002. *Roots of Violence in Indonesia.* Leiden: KITLV Press.

Cribb, Robert. 2001. How Many Deaths? Problems in the Statistics of Massacres in Indonesia (1965–1966) and East Timor (1975–1980). In *Violence in Indonesia,* ed. Ingrid Wessel and Georgia Wimhofer. Hamburg: Abera-Verlag.

Dijk, Kees van. 2000. *A Country in Despair: Indonesia between 1997 and 2000.* Leiden: KITLV Press.

Human Rights Watch. 1994. Three Strikes against the Press. In *The Limits of Openness: Human Rights in Indonesia and East Timor.* New York: Human Rights Watch.

Ispandriarno, Lukas Suryanto. 2001. Problems, Pressures and Threats in Constructing Realities for Media and Journalists. *Jurnal ISIP* 3 (1): 1–9.

Ivy, Marilyn. 1996. Tracking the Mystery Man with the 21 Faces. *Critical Inquiry* 23:11–36.

Komkat KWI. 2000. *Mediator Dalam Kerusuhan Maluku.* Jakarta: Komkat KWI.

Mbembe, Achille. 1999. Africa's Frontiers in Flux. *Le Monde Diplomatique,* November.

Nanere, Jan, ed. 2000. *Halmahera Berdarah: Suatu Upaya Mengungkap Kebenaran.* Ambon: Bimaspela.

Pandey, Gyanendra. 1992. In Defense of the Fragment: Writing about Hindu-Muslim Riots in India Today. *Representations* 37 (winter): 27–55.

Saine, Pap. 1998. African Media and Conflict. In *Conciliation Resources,* ed. Onadipe and David Lord. Available online at http://www.c-r.org/pubs/occ_papers/af_media/saine.shtml.

Schulte Nordholt, Henk. 2002. *A Genealogy of Violence in Indonesia.* Lisboa: CEPESA.

Sen, Krishna, and David T. Hill. 2000. *Media, Culture and Politics in Indonesia.* Oxford: Oxford University Press.

Sidel, John T. 2001. Riots, Church Burnings, Conspiracies: The Moral Economy of the Indonesian Crowd in the Late Twentieth Century. In *Violence in Indonesia,* ed. Ingrid Wessel and Georgia Wimhofer. Hamburg: Abera-Verlag.

Siegel, James T. 1998a. Early Thoughts on the Violence of May 13 and 14, 1998, in Jakarta. *Indonesia* 66:75–108.

———. 1998b. *A New Criminal Type in Jakarta: Counter-Revolution Today.* Durham, N.C.: Duke University Press.

Spyer, Patricia. 2002. Fire Without Smoke and Other Phantoms of Ambon's Violence: Media Effects, Agency, and the Work of Imagination. *Indonesia* 74:21–36.

———. 2000. *The Memory of Trade: Modernity's Entanglements on an Eastern Indonesian Island.* Durham, N.C.: Duke University Press.

———. n.d. Seriality Unbound: Some Thoughts on Religion, Media, and Violence in Indonesia. Invited lecture at the International Institute for Asian Studies (IIAS), Leiden University, May 2000.

Vlasblom, Dirk. 2002. Megafoons en gefluister: Vademecum van de "reformasi" in Indonesia. *NRC Handelsblad,* March 4, 2000.

Weber, Samuel. 1997. Wartime. In *Violence, Identity, and Self-Determination,* ed. Hent de Vries and Samuel Weber. Stanford, Calif.: Stanford University Press.

Wessel, Ingrid, and Georgia Wimhofer. 2001. *Violence in Indonesia.* Hamburg: Abera-Verlag.

8   Mediated Religion in South Africa: Balancing Airtime and Rights Claims

Rosalind I. J. Hackett

At one level this essay on religious broadcasting in South Africa addresses the heightened relevance of the media sphere in today's global network society for the identity and survival of religious collectivities (see Castells 1996). But it is perhaps more concerned with the growing significance of the local and global media in shaping attitudes of religious tolerance or intolerance, and in managing religious diversity.[1] Recent scholarship on religious discrimination and persecution more generally demonstrates the particular vulnerability of new religious movements and minority religious groups in this respect (Adams 2000; Richardson 1995, 2000).[2] In fact, British legal scholar Malcolm Evans (2000, 182) goes so far as to claim that "the origins of contemporary forms of human rights protection flow from attempts to protect the religious freedoms of certain identified and vulnerable religious communities."

Hent de Vries (2001, 21) frames these interconnections well when he argues that "the relationship between religion and media sheds light on the question of how cultural identity and difference are constituted, as well as on how they relate to the aims of sociopolitical integration" (cf. Spitulnik 1993, 300). Because of its paradoxical universalizing and particularizing tendencies, "religion . . . forms the condition of possibility *and* impossibility for the political." Rightly chiding Casanova for his neglect of the media sphere, he suggests that "the mediatized return of the religious" illustrates "an increasingly complicated *negotiation* between the private and public spheres" (de Vries 2001, 17). This accounts for some of the new forms of regulation of expression of religious communities being developed by both state and nonstate actors.[3]

Studies of Africa's rapidly expanding and diversifying media sector, notably of the cultural and religious dimensions of media production, distribution, reception, and consumption, are growing apace (see chapters 6 and 14, this volume). However, insufficient attention has been paid to the ways in which media institutions and representations may constitute an important site of conflict between religions and the state, and between religious groups. So recognizing with Debra Spitulnik (1993, 303) that "the mass media are extremely potent areas of political struggle," this chapter examines the case of South Africa and the various negotiations—at times acrimonious—over public religious broadcasting at the South African Broadcasting Corporation (SABC). These debates came to a head as South Africa moved into its post-apartheid phase in the 1990s. The literature on the role of religious organizations, predominantly the Christian churches, in this political process is extensive (Cochrane, Gruchy, and Martin 1999; Gruchy 1995; Gruchy 1995; Kilian 1993; Villa-Vicencio 1992; Moosa 2001; Sundkler 1991; Johnston 1994; Oosthuizen 1999; Tayob 1998; Chidester 1996; Gifford 1988; Graybill 1995; Walshe 1995).[4] The education sector as a politically strategic location for religious representation is also well documented (Chidester 1994, 2001; Dlamini 1994; Mitchell 1993; Steyn 1999; Stonier 1998; Sachs 1993). So, too, is the significance of the media sector in facilitating the new political dispensation (Tomaselli, Tomaselli, and Muller 2001; Netshitenzhe 1999).[5] Less well analyzed is the religious dimension of public broadcasting, for example, the emerging policy questions surrounding religious programming, and issues of control and representation (Baker 2000; Nkosi 1994).

The chapter thus seeks to document and explore this neglected interrelationship of religion and media in the South African context not just because of the light it throws on the role of public religion in a nation-state in political transition but also because it provides an important insight into the mechanics of religious representation in the mediated public sphere. This "production and management of meaning" occurs not just at the formal, institutional level but also as the result of internal (and, in the case of South Africa, external) debates and conflicts (cf. McLagan 2000). Discussions are primarily limited to public broadcasting, and the medium of television, in particular, for reasons of space. As Graham Mytton (2000, 28) observes, most broadcasting in Africa is still "centralized, national and state-dominated."[6] This is especially the case for television (see Teer-Tomaselli and Tomaselli 2001, 140). Thus despite current scholarly trends to link the electronic mass media with global scapes and flows (Urry 2000, 161), and to favor "conceptualizing the world as a whole," I have chosen to focus on a nationally constituted society as a unit of analysis (King 1997, viii). Transnational and translocal forces are clearly active in South Africa through the agency of religious and media institutions, which can serve to deterritorialize the process of the imagining of communities. Michael Herzfeld (2001, 312) comes to the rescue by arguing that "the various kinds of media, ethnographically studied in context, can provide a very close look at the interaction of the local, the national and the international" and that anthropology's "subversive localism" can unmask globalization for the "realist fiction" it has become (see, esp., Gunsburg, Abu-Lughod, and Larkin 2002).

Broader Contextual Issues

My ongoing research on religious conflict and violence in Africa more generally (Hackett 2004), and in Nigeria specifically (Hackett forthcoming), notably in connection with the imposition of Shari'a by northern states, clearly indicates the instrumentality of the media sphere in relations between religions and the state, between religions, and between religious organizations and their followers (Hackett 2003). Conflict between religious groups is commonly linked to rights of access to the national media. Because of the asymmetry of resources, capacity, and influence, some religious organizations find themselves at the head of the media table while others may not even enjoy the crumbs from underneath it. These patterns of exclusion and inclusion, coupled with issues of fair representation, have been exacerbated by the processes of democratization and liberalization. While I am not addressing here media representations of religion(s), nor the content of mediated messages, it is worth noting that government and legal authorities can be influenced by negative portrayals of non-mainstream groups (Richardson 2000, 125 n. 30) (Dillon and Richardson 1994). Bias and misinformation affect whether airtime is accorded to minority groups. It is popular to oppose the "cult menace" (Richardson 2000, 115). We should not underestimate the influence of globalizing discourses of Satanism and anti-cultism which emanate principally from U.S. courts and the media, as well as religious and para-religious organizations (Richardson 1996). Currently several European countries, notably France, have jumped on the anti-cult bandwagon (Hervieu-Léger 2001) (for Africa generally, see Hackett 2002; on South Africa, see Faure 2000).

In most postcolonial African states the stakes of religious coexistence have changed (cf. Haynes 1996, 1995; Gifford 1998). Mainstream religious organizations that enjoyed the patrimony of colonial and independence governments now find themselves threatened by newer religious formations, notably of the revivalist type. These minority groups are often acutely aware of their rights to freedom of religion and freedom of expression.[7] They claim these rights in the new spirit of communal self-determination, constitutionalism, and the global lingua franca of international human rights that is sweeping the African continent.[8] In post-apartheid South Africa, this is commonly referred to as the new "rights culture" or the new "human rights dispensation." Furthermore, the liberalization of the media sector has opened up all sorts of new outlets for expression, many of which escape government control in relation to balancing and nondiscrimination. With the growing dominance of the market paradigm, airtime is frequently bought rather than meted out. In other words, ownership and commercial interests of media institutions increasingly trump respect for national diversity (Tomaselli, Tomaselli, and Muller 2001). This causes frustration to many religious organizations that maintain a state-centric mentality; but savvy religious leaders, usually of the younger and more entrepreneurial variety, know that a good media presence is proselytizing writ large in a competitive religious environment and are prepared to foot the bill (Hackett 1998).

The right to disseminate one's religion easily surpasses the freedom to believe and to practice one's religion as the most controversial aspect of religious freedom.[9] African constitutions may not accord the same primacy to free speech as is the case in the United States, where the judicial protection of free speech has increasingly guided the protection of related constitutional principles (Richards 1999, 14). However, the structural connections between free speech and religious freedom or liberty can be noted (ibid., 9). Almost all African states have included in their constitutions a bill of rights (van der Vyver 1999, 110). Religious freedom features prominently in one form or another in those constitutions, although it is often subject to various conditions. The media sphere constitutes a critical "test site" where the interpretation and implementation of these "new" rights can be publicly evaluated by all concerned.

Contestation and Consultation: The Story of Religious Broadcasting in South Africa

South Africa offers an illuminating case for considering the relation between religion, media, and the public sphere. Since the first universal franchise election in 1994, there has been a widespread effort at every level of society "to introduce new and better, more democratic, more demographically equitable, more politically and gender sensitive ways of doing things" (Teer-Tomaselli and Tomaselli 2001, 123). There has been an accompanying debate about how to manage cultural diversity in a way that reflects constitutional ideals ("united in . . . diversity") and does not evoke negative historical memory (Tayob 1998). The reform of the media has been central to these sociopolitical changes in the "new South Africa," for, in the words of leading media analysts Ruth Teer-Tomaselli and Keyan Tomaselli, "newspapers, magazines, television and radio are both the *sites* and the *instruments* of transformation" (Teer-Tomaselli and Tomaselli 2001, 123). As "sites" of transformation, the structures, management, ownership, and workforce of the media industries have been subject to debate and reform. As "instruments" of transformation, the media provide the platforms for debate, the stories, the images and visions of personal and national identity, both real and ideal.

Within the contested power relations of the mass-mediated public sphere, religious broadcasting policy and practice constitute a significant micro-sphere. Given the former close ties between the apartheid regime and the Dutch Reformed Church, the reapportioning of airtime for the country's diverse religious groups has been a key element in the refashioning of the South African state. David Chidester highlights the transformation in state broadcasting as offering not just "new possibilities for broadening the representation of South African religious communities in public media" but also as a "growth area for the future of the study of religion in South Africa" with its critical potential for "analyzing symbols, myths, and rituals that generate powerful moods and motivations" and engaging structures of power (Chidester 1998, 17–18).

Under apartheid, the SABC, as a tool of the state, offered only Christian programming. Despite the political constraints of the time, several religious broadcasters objected to the juxtaposition of news and religious programs as a strategy for displacing "the actual context of conditions" (Teer-Tomaselli and Tomaselli 2001, 105).[10] The very conservative orientation of the programming and restrictions on preaching with political content drove a number of English-language churches in 1979 to challenge the racism and narrowness of the SABC. Under the auspices of the South African Council of Churches (SACC), they even appealed to the wider Christian community to boycott the SABC and to consider alternative broadcasting facilities. While they failed to counter the intolerance and extreme right-wing views of the organizer of religious television programs, they took advantage of the greater flexibility of radio with its live broadcasts. Some preachers were able to address socially relevant and politically sensitive issues through such rhetorical devices as allegory and analogy (ibid., 107).

In one of the few published analyses of religious broadcasting policy in South Africa, Russell Baker, a research associate at the main hub of media studies in South Africa, the Centre for Cultural and Media Studies at the University of KwaZulu-Natal, Durban, directed by Keyan Tomaselli, aptly describes it as characterized by "contestation and consultation" as well as "progressive developments" (Baker 2000, 237). He traces these developments through various policy documents specifically oriented to the coverage of religion, devoting particular attention to the more recent phase of religious broadcasting policy. He notes the role played by the SACC in establishing a discussion forum—the Independent Forum for Religious Broadcasting (IFRB)—aimed at addressing the problems associated with religious broadcasting and SABC's consultative process (ibid., 242). This resulted in the production of the IFRB's Charter for Religious Broadcasting in 1984. The forum consisted of members representing the various Christian churches (Afrikaans, English, and African Independent), as well as the Hindu, Muslim, and Jewish communities. They advocated "fundamental changes in the relationships between religions and churches and the SABC" and "both equitable distribution of broadcasting time and greater theological control over the content of religious programmes" (ibid., 242–243).[11]

In response to these public concerns and the new democratic dispensation, SABC circulated a Working Draft Policy on Religious Broadcasting to religious organizations in October 1994 (for the text, see Baker 2000, 238–241) and established the Religious Broadcasting Panel (RBP) in the same year.[12] The RBP met several times between 1995 and 1998, serving as interface between the SABC and religious communities.[13] It set up committees to address concerns of individual communities, such as traditional African religious groups, who complained about being included in the category of African independent churches, or as nothing else but culture (see Mndende 1998). Steps were taken to cultivate interfaith programming, and to improve training and development for staff from previously disadvantaged communities.[14] The head of Religion from the British Broadcasting Corporation conducted workshops at the major centers. Suleiman Dangor notes that one of the most heated debates in the RBP was over time allocation (see below).

Public Storm and Independent Criticism

A particularly revealing source regarding the contentious exchanges between SABC and the religious communities is the retiring chairman's report to the annual forum of the IFRB delivered on November 16, 1998.[15] In this report Bishop Peter Lee refers to the mandate of the IFRB, namely, "to make religious representation on behalf of the religious community into the broad process of broadcast policy revision in South Africa." He alludes to the "considerable public controversy" related to religious broadcasting between 1996 and 1998, a controversy he attributes, first, to SABC's unilateral decision "to breach the agreement solemnly made with the religious community regarding religious broadcasting" and, second, to the "drastic" reduction in the amounts of time available for religious programs. He blames this decision for raising a "public storm" about the place of religion generally on the airwaves not just of the public broadcaster but also those of commercial and community license holders. The chairman also talks of the "bad faith" created by SABC's reneging on its earlier commitment to the religious community, its public lies, and its poor treatment of the RBP. This panel, according to Bishop Lee, "suffered huge frustration and eventually found itself sidelined within the SABC"—a situation he claims was ongoing. He also criticizes the lack of transparency regarding some of the later elections to the panel. Furthermore, he strongly bemoans the lack of reference to religious broadcasting in a government White Paper, despite representations by the IFRB at various broadcasting policy colloquia and the earlier "furore" over religious programming.

Bishop Lee vehemently criticizes the "secularizing tendency of the present management" for ignoring the grassroots influence of religious organizations and for "overriding the spirit of the Constitution." He goes on to cite section 31 of the Bill of Rights in the Constitution which guarantees the rights of cultural, linguistic, and religious groups. Despite this provision, the broadcasting White Paper still ominously omits the category of "religious" groups while referring to cultural and linguistic ones. Lee also regrets the lack of serious treatment of religious issues in a published discussion paper on a code of conduct for broadcasters, limiting consideration to "blasphemy and possible offence to religious sensitivities." He ends the report by pledging to lobby the government on these issues and by urging the respective religious groupings to challenge this continuing "process of being sidelined by public policy."

When SABC announced cutbacks to cultural and religious programming in 1997 (75 percent reduction to 106 minutes per week, or 0.5 percent of its total output), and informed the public that in the future all magazine programs would be sourced from outside the Corporation, an "enraged public and religious community" joined the fray of confused and upset staffers and independents.[16] Rev. Martin Frische, chairperson of the Association of Christian Broadcasters, graphically accused the SABC of cutting the tree on which it sat by ignoring the (moral) importance of religion in society. Dr. Ed McCain, acting president of United Christian Action, spoke of the "high-handed, dictatorial attitude" of the SABC in failing to consult with religious bodies over the cutbacks. The outraged response was not just limited to the Christian constituency. Abie Dawjee, a spokesman for Jamiatul Ulama (KwaZulu-Natal) (a council of Muslim theologians) and a member of IFRB, stated: "We are appalled at this cut. The religious majority, a vast share of the population, will be deprived of broadcasting." He went on to bemoan the loss of the small gains that the Muslim community had made in the face of Christian-dominated broadcasting.

Mediating State and Religious Interests: SABC as the "Pulse of Africa's Creative Spirit"

From 1998 on, following the revision and approval of the Religious Broadcasting Panel, SABC, in its annual report (for 1997–98), described its (new) role with regard to religious programs as follows:

> The SABC, in its role as a public service broadcaster, has an obligation to reflect all faiths in an unbiased and appropriately representative manner. This, therefore, sees the presence of dedicated religious broadcasts on both radio and television. These cover the various formats of devotional, worship service, magazine, panel discussion, phone-in and music programmes catering to a wide spectrum of ages and preferences, and in all 11 of the official languages.[17]

Referring to the RBP, "which tries to ensure respect for all religions and equitable representation for the expression of each faith within the total amount of religious broadcasting air time" (ibid.), the SABC report further states that "the total amount of time allocated to religious broadcasting should be such that those religions with the smallest ratio of air time enjoy meaningful and sufficient programming on a faith-specific basis" (ibid.). The report also indicates the adjustment in guidelines for the allocation of airtime for the various religions:

Christianity	70% (as previously)
Hinduism	7.5% (increased from 5%)
Islam	7.5% (increased from 5%)
ATR	10% (increased from 5%)
Judaism	5% (increased from 3%)[18]

By the following year, the 1998–99 annual report had dropped the reference to the goal of reflecting "all faiths in an unbiased and appropriately representative manner" and, significantly, it did not feature in any of the subsequent reports. In the report of 2000–2001, the mention of "respect for all religions and equitable representation" has disappeared, yet the report describes the "positive impact on television audiences" of religious programs as they "continued to educate and inform viewers about the various religions and the life of their

Religious programmes for all faiths

The SABC's religious programmes reflect a mix of South Africa's major religions — Christianity, African Religion, Islam, Hinduism and Judaism

Fig. 8.1. Religious programs for all faiths. SABC programming reflects a mix of South Africa's major religions—Christianity, African Religion, Islam, Hinduism, and Judaism. *SABC Annual Report, 2002–2003.*

communities."[19] It vaunts the fact that the program *Crux,* on the life of the Church, was one of the first magazine programs in South Africa to avail itself of virtual reality technology, and that the program *Crossing the Divide* brought together a pagan and an occultist on air. The highlighting of this particular encounter seems to trivialize an otherwise important and innovative program.

The noticeably slicker website in the 2000–2001 report was clearly seeking to reflect the diversity of the South African religious scene, and one could see images of black Zionist Christians, with a woman drumming in the foreground, and the Torah. On the page outlining plans for the future, there was a composite graphic with images of a multitude of religious leaders and practitioners. Apart from the Pope, the majority of faces were non-white, with Hindus and Zulu traditional worshipers in the foreground. The 2003 report has less complex images, but there is a stunning full-page illustration of a female Zionist worshiper.

A number of tradition-specific programs were developed for television in the post-1994 period, but these were consolidated under the rubric of the popular and award-winning multifaith documentary *Issues of Faith* or featured as documentaries.[20] Some Christian programs retained their separate status—an option preferable to the more conservative end of the Christian spectrum. A new development is the Sunday morning breakfast show (*Spirit Sundae*) which aims to be "inclusive of the full spectrum of religion in South Africa."[21] With its more creative and flexible approach, it covers topics "ranging from current affairs to the arts, religious festivals, cooking and holistic healing." In addition, there are worship programs and evening devotions for each of the main religious traditions (e.g., *Jewish Voice, Aum, Izwi Labantu, Reflections on Faith*), as well as morning devotions in various languages (Afrikaans, Sotho, Nguni) which reflect the variety of expressions of Christianity around the country. These devotional programs continue to claim the highest audience ratings.

In terms of "multifaith" programs (and "faith" is clearly the SABC term of preference nowadays), there are the *Issues of Faith* documentaries on SABC2, which discuss topics such as liberation, caste, *ubuntu,* or African humanism, and human rights in relation to different religious communities. On SABC1, which aims to reach more youthful audiences, there is *Tapestries of Faith.* Along these lines, SABC1 broadcasts *You Gotta Have Faith* every Friday morning. This is billed as a "life orientation program" which discusses the way religion affects the choices people make in life. A 2001 program series, *Paul and the Menu: Cooking with Spirit,* explored and celebrated religious multiculturalism through food under the aegis of a zany Anglican priest.[22] The popular *Free Spirit,* a program trendily described as "less about religion and more about spirituality," and destined "to enhance the lives of spiritually open South Africans," is the brainchild of Religion Commissioning Editor Yashika Singh.[23] It is not only repeated midweek but also has a related website.[24] Music programs tend to have a Christian emphasis, such as the award-winning *Gospel Gold* and the ever popular BBC classic *Songs of Praise.* A gospel talent show, *Gospel Star* has also been added to the *Crux* (the Christian magazine program) slot on SABC1.

Wanting to be seen as promoting national harmony and integration, rather than division and conflict, producers may opt for a pastiche of viewpoints, rather than allowing direct confrontation. The current (global) trend toward framing news and issues more in the guise of entertainment and human interest may also mitigate conflictual differences between religious positions, and neutralize any "prophetic" critique of the state by religious leaders. Although, to SABC's credit, they air some hard-hitting documentaries, such as the one (in 2001) on the controversial Nigerian Pentecostal miracle worker T. B. Joshua, who has been attracting supplicants from southern Africa.

Current Challenges

In addition to trying to balance the (devotional and informational) needs of South Africa's diverse religious constituencies and promote (inter)religious understanding and tolerance in the interests of nation building, two of the most contentious issues SABC has had to face on the religious broadcasting

Fig. 8.2. *Gospel Gold*: Among the top performing religious programs on television, it provides a platform for South Africa's gospel music industry. *SABC Annual Report, 2002–2003.*

front have been outside funding and "the neglect of African culture in the public media."[25] The question of funding became critical in the late 1990s when drastic cutbacks occurred, forcing creative measures on the part of the religious broadcasting staff.[26] For a time American Christian programming took up the slack (as it has in many other African countries), but this was eventually seen as compromising the democratization process in the country. Moreover, there was reluctance to allow religious groups to use independent funding as a means of securing additional broadcast time. However, owing to financial considerations, a decision was taken to allow selective sales of airtime, sponsorships, and classical advertising as long as "profits from such endeavors enable SABC to fund more of its own local religious productions" and "such contracts do not in one way or another compromise either the editorial independence or integrity of the SABC or its Policy on Religious Broadcasts" (cf. Nkosi 1994).[27]

The second challenge for religious broadcasting in South Africa has been to contextualize and reflect African reality.[28] The SABC Policy on Religious Broadcasting (revised and approved by the SABC Board in 1998) alludes to some of the battles fought over the place of traditional African religion: "In order to correct further neglect of African culture in the public media, special attention should be given to African Traditional Religion (ATR) and traditional cultures." This needs to be seen against the background of the African Renaissance movement launched by President Thabo Mbeki in the late 1990s (see Makgoba 1999).[29] For several analysts, the capacity of the media to serve as facilitators of democracy and African cultural self-determination is closely linked both to structures of ownership and to diversification of production (Baker 2000; Netshitenzhe 1999).

One of the strongest voices on behalf of traditional African religions and fiercest critics of discriminatory practices by political and religious authorities has been Nokuzola Mndende. A former parliamentarian and freelance presenter turned educational consultant, and armed with higher degrees in religious studies to boot, she has campaigned forcefully to expose the racism "now clothed in religious attire" (Mndende 1999). Because of the failure to include ATR in educational policies, civic events, and the Truth Commission, Mndende refers to the present government as "nothing else but Christianity at prayer." She vehemently criticizes the SABC for referring to *indigenous* African religions as "minority religions" and for not censoring the negative portrayals of these religions in their programming.[30]

Mndende (1999, 48) strategically resorts to rights talk when criticizing the then chair of the Human Rights Commission (Anglican cleric Dr. Barney Pityana) for disbelieving that there are Africans who can practice African religion without Christianity: "How can we speak of human rights when my right to believe and my freedom to practice my religion is still controlled and despised?" In the same vein, she opines that "to define African Religion from a Christian perspective violates the rights of its followers to have complete freedom of religion: when a particular way of seeing the truth is imposed on others it violates their freedom to seek the truth" (49).

The RBP has also had to deal with complaints from several religious groups about the scheduling of many religious programs on Sunday—to which SABC replied that weekday evenings were reserved for prime-time programming which religious programs did not fit into. In addition, the panel has received requests from various groups to be treated as separate entities, as in the case of the Mormon Church.[31] While the RBP feels that it achieved some success in transforming religious programming in the SABC, the panel made less headway with radio broadcasting which is traditionally more decentralized and predominantly Christian.[32]

While Muslim groups in South Africa have made advances in the political and media spheres, in March 2000 concern was still being voiced about negative representations and reporting. A Muslim media group, Media Review Network, reported to the South African Human Rights Commission in Johannesburg that the South African media were generating "Islamophobia" through their demonizing and stereotyping, notably in connection with the bombings in Cape Town.[33] This is an ongoing problem, as evidenced by the group's comments to the SABC on the latter's Draft Editorial Policies in 2003, notably regarding the "special vocabulary list" ("fundamentalist," "extremist," "fanatic," "terrorist,") used by the media almost exclusively in reference to Muslims.[34] The Muslim community has also complained to the RPB about documentaries portraying Islam in a bad light (cf. Baderoon 1999).

Religious programmes on SABC
radio and television also cater for
people who adhere to African
Traditional Religion (ATR).

Fig. 8.3. Seeking to cater to those who adhere to African Traditional
Religion (ATR). *SABC Annual Report, 2001–2002.*

Rainbow Nation: Actuality or Mirage?

From the above discussion one can see that the negotiations over the public, mediated presence of religion in a culturally and religiously pluralistic democracy such as South Africa are increasingly informed by appeal to the globalizing discourse of rights. Yet some critics, such as South African scholar of religion Ebrahim Moosa, are skeptical of the constitutional arrangements for freedom of religion in the South African context (and one could extend the argument to other African states also) (Moosa 2001, 132–134). Moosa claims that expectations of freedom are never realized because religion is reduced to the status of "junior partner" with the state. He attributes the "fiction of the sovereignty of religion" to the framing of religious rights in binary terms (public/private, secular/profane, belief/practice, etc.) which reflect imported liberal and modernist constitutional values rather than the consensus values of the majority community (ibid.).

Other analysts point to the precarious nature of both the rights to freedom of religion and freedom of expression in the face of new strategies by state and nonstate actors in many parts of the world, not least some European countries, to curtail these freedoms.[35] Moves to re-regulate the media in terms of access, licensing, and censorship may be interpreted as a consequence of the loss of control by states over religious pluralization and diversification, or as an effort by politicians to diminish the influence of the religious sector. Some governments see media censorship as a more feasible option for co-opting or excluding unpopular or subversive religious ideologies. In some cases this can be effected by encouraging the market forces which are reconfiguring religious power relations across Africa. Keyan Tomaselli, who has written extensively on the political economy of the South African media, has warned of the vulnerability of the electronic and print media in South Africa's public sphere in the face of globalization of capital, media, and markets.[36] He has underscored the need to pursue critical media education, and the adoption of civil charters such as The People's Communication Charter. The Windhoek Charter on Broadcasting 2001, among other things, calls on states to transfer regulatory powers on the airwaves and telecommunication structures to publicly constituted bodies under a three-tier system composed of public service, commercial, and community operators.[37] An important landmark in this connection for South Africa is the Media Development and Diversity Agency Act of July 8, 2002, which provides for a statutorily recognized body, to be funded by government and the media industry, for the development of community and independent media.[38]

For religious broadcasting policy in particular, Baker argues that, in the age of (post)modern technologies and ideas, "simple objectivity," based on "dubious membership figures," is seriously challenged by the "emerging multi-channel, multi-media environment" (Baker 2000, 228–229, 232).[39] He rightly considers that the "goal of impartiality will have to be addressed more in terms of the satisfaction of the needs of the full spectrum of the South African audience" (232). In this regard he underscores the need to incorporate those on the "fringe of formal religions" and advises against excessive normative limitations being placed on religious programs.[40] While such constraints (such as on proselytizing and discrimination) obtain in other locations, he considers the South African religious scene to be too diverse to enforce such restraints and the resultant "bland uniform programming" to be undesirable (245).[41] Instead, he favors the democratic "right to reply" system, while acknowledging that such responsibility may conflict with the racist and sexist teachings still propounded by some religious groups (246). This concurs with efforts by the Africa Region of the World Association for Christian Communication (WACC) to encourage churches to work toward more "democratic communication" and to treat their constituencies as "active participants in articulating social/spiritual problems" (Esaya 1992, 82–83).

Because of the intimate relationship between the country's political and economic history and the ongoing divisions and differences of the South African religious landscape, Baker argues that SABC's religion department should proactively target economically disadvantaged groups, such as the African independent churches, previously marginalized by the mainstream media (Baker 2000, 241). This problematic heritage of religious conservatism and exclusion came up at a series of seminars on "Religion, Liberation and Transformation through the South African Experience" held at the Parliament of the World's Religions, Cape Town, in December 1999.[42] Under discussion was research conducted at the University of Stellenbosch in 1990 and 1996–97 which has shown that people with religious affiliations (except for Jews) were more likely to be politically intolerant (in terms of according civil rights to groups they did not support or agree with) than those who did not profess to be religious. So seminar participants called for religious leaders and communities to develop new attitudes of tolerance, given their power to socialize communities. They were enjoined to promote the African concept of community or *ubuntu* (one can only be human through relationships) and rediscover the emancipatory ecumenism that brought down the apartheid regime.[43]

The South African case demonstrates that the fields of identity and action for religious groups are increasingly located in, and defined by, the interface of modern media, both local and global. It also further confirms Bourdieu's observation that the "journalistic field," most notably television, profoundly modifies power relations in other fields of cultural production (Bourdieu 1996, 68). There have been, and continue to be, great hopes for the modern media to help realize the African Renaissance, in whatever modality that is imagined—cultural pride, academic recognition, spiritual rediscovery, moral renewal, informational accuracy, political freedom, economic growth, or social harmony (Boateng 1999; Chinweizu 1999; Teffo 1999; Tomaselli and Shepperson 1999).[44] In that regard, the particular focus in this essay on religious broadcasting demonstrates the strategic role that the state can, and should, play in transitional democracies such as South Africa, in promoting religious tolerance. It has further provided a revealing, yet salutary, window onto the entanglements of religion, democracy, and capitalism in one of the world's most strategic nation-states. Yet the story of this "rainbow nation," to use Archbishop Tutu's enduring symbol, and its quest to balance democratic nationalism with cultural and religious pluralism, and what Achille Mbembe calls "struggles over autochthony," is clearly far from over.[45]

Notes

I am grateful to Keyan Tomaselli and Ruth Teer-Tomaselli for their critical reading of this essay, and to Paul du Plessis for obtaining the SABC illustrations.

1. Both the U.S. State Department Annual Report on International Religious Freedom (http://www.state.gov/g/drl/rls/irf/) and an earlier survey of how religious freedom is understood, protected, or denied around the world (Boyle and Sheen1997) highlight the importance of the media in this connection.

2. See the special issue of *Nova Religio* 4, no. 2 (2001) on this topic; see also Lucas and Robbins 2004.

3. Two excellent sources are Human Rights Without Frontiers, particularly their news service on "Religious Intolerance and Discrimination" (http://www.hrwf.net), and Index on Censorship (http://www.indexonline.org).

4. Also of note are the annotated bibliographies on the different religious traditions of South Africa compiled by David Chidester and his team at the Institute for Comparative Religion in South Africa, University of Cape Town (Chidester, Tobler, and Wratten 1997a, 1997b; Chidester et al. 1997).

5. On "Media and Human Rights," see the special issue of *Critical Arts: A Journal for South-North Cultural and Media Studies* 16 (2001). Available online at http://www. und.ac.za/und/ccms/publications_default.htm.

6. But see Fardon and Furniss 2000 for the diversification of radio broadcasting across the African continent. It is regrettable that such a useful work could not include any serious treatment of religious radio stations, long active in many parts of Africa.

7. This is affirmed by Knut Lundby (1997, 38) for rural Zimbabwe at least in his comparative study of media, religion, and democratic participation in two small-scale communities, located at a distance from metropolitan centers in Zimbabwe and Norway.

8. See, for example, Ilesanmi 2001; Mutua 1999, 2001; An-Na'im 1990, 1999. On southern Africa there is an abundance of sources: Ackermann 1992; Boschman 1996; Chidester 1994; Dlamini 1994; Gruchy 1995; Kilian 1993; Mamdani 2000; Mitchell 1993; Moosa 2001; van der Westhuizen 1993; Villa-Vicencio 1996, 1999–2000; Walsh and Kaufmann 1999; Villa-Vicencio 1992.

9. See the series on Proselytism published by the Law and Religion Program at Emory Law School, and especially the volume on Africa (An-Na'im 1999).

10. Although it should be noted that for many years the religious broadcasting department formed part of Television News Productions (Baker 2000, 232).

11. Cf. similar efforts by the powerful coalition, the Campaign for Independent Broadcasting, to ensure that the SABC was wrested from the control of the old National Party apartheid regime and instead serve as a tool for diversity and democracy (Minnie 2000). For excellent analytical overviews of the contours and ideological battles of the

South African media scene, pre- and post-1994, see Teer-Tomaselli and Tomaselli 2001; Tomaselli and Tomaselli 2001.

12. On the importance of such independent review bodies, see Boafo 1992, 49.

13. I am indebted to Dr. Suleiman Dangor, of the University of Durban-Westville, South Africa, for valuable information on the Religious Broadcasting Panel on which he served. He made minutes of the meetings available to me. He also presented his experiences at a panel on "Religious Broadcasting in South Africa" at the Eighteenth World Congress of the International Association for the History of Religions, Durban, August 11, 2000, in a paper entitled, "Transformation of the SABC from a Christian Broadcaster to a Multifaith Broadcaster."

14. The category of "free allocation" (12 percent), originally intended for the coverage of festivals and interfaith issues (Baker 2000, 240), disappeared with the renegotiated allocations of airtime.

15. Forwarded to the ANDERE-L list from the World Conference on Religion and Peace, Durban Chapter, February 25, 1999.

16. Andrew Worsdale, "SABC's Dire Straits," Mail and Guardian, June 20, 1997. This appears to have been increased, for the 1999–2000 annual report states that 2 percent of broadcasting schedule time is devoted to religious programs on television across the three channels (SABC1, SABC2, and SABC3), and 7.5 percent for radio broadcasts. There are no such statistics in the 2000–2001 annual report.

17. Available online at http://www.sabc.co.za/annual/religious.htm (accessed July 28, 2002).

18. According to the 1996 census, 74.1 percent of the population of more than 42 million claim to be Christian. "Other faiths" total 7.7 percent. Hindus and Muslims each account for approximately 1 percent, and about 0.4 percent are Jewish. A sizable minority of the population, more than 18.3 percent, does not belong to any of the major religious traditions, and may be practitioners of traditional religion or have no specific religious affiliation (see Hendriks 1999).

19. Available online at http://www.sabc.co.za/annual/annual2000/religion.pdf (accessed July 28, 2002).

20. See http://www.sabc.co.za/rel/index.htm for the range of programs.

21. Available online at http://www.sabc.co.za/annual_03/index.html (accessed August 24, 2004).

22. Available online at http://www.suntimes.co.za/2001/10/14/arts/durban/aned01.asp (accessed August 25, 2004).

23. See http://www.suntimes.co.za/2002/03/31/arts/durban/aned04.asp (accessed August 25, 2004).

24. The website is at http://www.freespiritsa.co.za/ (accessed August 25, 2004).

25. See SABC Religious Policy at http://www.sabc.co.za/rel/index.htm.

26. Information from Ed Worster, Commissioning Editor, and Yashika Singh, Producer, SABC Johannesburg, at the "Religion and the Media" panel at the Parliament of the World's Religions, Cape Town, December 1999. An anonymous independent producer contracted to the SABC put a more positive spin on the cutbacks, saying it was a useful exercise to rid SABC of mediocre and unimaginative producers. See, "SABC's Dire Straits," Mail and Guardian, June 20, 1997.

27. On the growing difficulties facing African television stations with regard to local production, see Bourgault 1995, 103–152.

28. More generally Ebrahim Moosa points to the recurring tensions between local, indigenous values and worldviews and the globalizing (predominantly Western) le-

gal and political order as it is domesticated in non-Western cultures, not least in post-apartheid South Africa (Moosa 2001, 122–123, 130–131). He shows how traditional African values, such as *ubuntu*, were included in the 1993 Interim Constitution but omitted in the 1996 Constitution.

29. Teer-Tomaselli and Tomaselli (2001, 147 n. 29) note that the SABC, as expressed in its new publicity as the "pulse of Africa's Creative Spirit," exceeded its national mandate and "in the spirit of global (or at least supra-regional) enterprises took on the challenge of spiritually revitalizing the entire continent."

30. Based on her remarks at the panel on "Religious Broadcasting in South Africa" at the IAHR Eighteenth World Congress, Durban, South Africa, August 11, 2000. She was also a member of the Religious Broadcasting Panel but claims that it was a mistake and that she was only included because the RBP thought she belonged to an African independent church (!).

31. Information from Dangor, personal communication, 1999.

32. See "Religious and Cultural Programmes on PBS Radio"; available online at http://www.sabc.co.za/annual/annua12000/religion.pdf (accessed August 23, 2004).

33. This group is by no means representative of the entire South African Muslim community. Information from Keyan Tomaselli, personal communication, June 23, 2000.

34. Available online at http://www.mediareviewnet.com/comments%20on%20sabc%20policies.htm (accessed August 25, 2004).

35. Kevin Boyle, "Religious Intolerance and the Incitement of Hatred"; available online at http://www.article19.org/docimages/975.html (accessed August 23, 2004).

36. See his reported comments in "Report from the Working Group on 'Freedom of Expression'" (1998); available online at http://www.und.ac.za/und/ccms/media/naphrc.htm (accessed February 4, 2001). See also Tomaselli and Nkosi 1995.

37. "Widen Scope of Press Freedom in Africa, Conference Urges." Panafrican News Agency, May 6, 2001. See also Kizito 1992.

38. Media Development and Diversity Agency (Pretoria). Press release, July 23, 2002.

39. His and Bishop Lee's fears have been borne out, as the political scene has hardened. Mainstream religions still dominate the SABC airwaves and Rhema and TBN broadcast on Dstv. Information from Keyan Tomaselli, e-mail, August 26, 2002.

40. The SABC 1999–2000 annual report refers to the need to include programs that reflect the "Shembe and Bahai faith [*sic*]." Note: *Shembe* refers to the renowned Zulu independent church, founded by Isaiah Shembe, the Nazaretha Baptist Church. Incidentally the African independent churches form the largest grouping within the Christian category, according to the 1996 census, although the greatest market share growth goes to the Pentecostal/Charismatic group (Hendriks 1999, 79).

41. But consider John Urry's argument, in the context of a wider discussion on (global) citizenship, that "paradoxically it may be that aspects of global homogenisation, consumerism and cosmopolitanism, are necessary conditions for preventing social divisions in the contemporary world" (Urry 2000, 187).

42. *Journal of Theology for Southern Africa* 106 (April 2000): 61–83.

43. See Bernstein 2002, 204–210, for a discussion of the vagueness of the concept and the ambivalence of black South African elites toward their cultures of origin.

44. For a critical review of this "brilliant marketing concept," see Bernstein 2002, 230–243.

45. A very valuable set of studies and reflections on these questions by a number of South Africa's leading scholars of religion and some German researchers can be found in a special issue of *Journal for the Study of Religion* 11, no. 2 (September 1998), on "Re-

ligion and Politics in South Africa." On the cultural politics of territories, borders, and identities in Africa, see Mbembe 1999.

References

Ackermann, Denise. 1992. Women, Human Rights and Religion: A Dissonant Triad. *Journal for the Study of Religion* 5 (2): 65–82.

Adams, Nathan A., IV. 2000. A Human Rights Imperative: Extending Religious Liberty beyond the Border. *Cornell International Law Journal* 33 (1): 1–66.

An-Na'im, Abdullahi A., ed. 1999. *Proselytization and Communal Self-Determination in Africa*. Maryknoll, N.Y.: Orbis Books.

An-Na'im, Abdullahi A., and Francis M. Deng, eds. 1990. *Human Rights in Africa: Cross-Cultural Perspectives*. Washington D.C.: The Brookings Institution.

Baderoon, Gabeba. 1999. Muslims and the Media in 1998: Covering and Uncovering Masks—Race and South African Media. *Annual Review of Islam in South Africa* 2:16–19.

Baker, Russell. 2000. Policy Considerations for Religious Broadcasting. In *Public Service Broadcasting: Policy Directions towards 2000*, ed. A. Mpofu, S. Manhando, and K. Tomaselli, 225–249. Johannesburg: Anthropos.

Bernstein, Ann. 2002. Globalization, Culture, and Development: Can South Africa Be More Than an Offshoot of the West? In *Many Globalizations: Cultural Diversity in the Contemporary World*, ed. P. L. Berger and S. P. Huntington, 185–249. New York: Oxford University Press.

Boafo, S. T. Kwame. 1992. Mass Media: Constraints and Possible Solutions. In *Communication and Human Rights in Africa: Implications for Development*, ed. R. N. Kizito, 41–52. Nairobi: World Association for Christian Communication—Africa Region.

Boateng, Edward. 1999. The Role of Information in Promoting Economic Development in Sub-Saharan Africa. In *African Renaissance: The New Struggle*, ed. M. W. Makgoba, 386–403. Cape Town: Mafube.

Boschman, D. R. 1996. Religious Freedom in Botswana: The Cases of the Zion Christian Church and the Nazareth Church of Botswana. In *African Independent Churches Today: Kaleidoscope of Afro-Christianity*, ed. M. C. Kitshoff. Lewiston, N.Y. Edwin Mellen.

Bourdieu, Pierre. 1996. *On Television*. New York: New Press.

Bourgault, Louise M. 1995. *Mass Media in Sub-Saharan Africa*. Philadelphia: University of Pennsylvania Press.

Boyle, Kevin, and Juliet Sheen, eds. 1997. *Freedom of Religion and Belief: A World Report*. London: Routledge.

Castells, Manuell. 1996. *The Information Age: Economy, Society and Culture*. Vol. 1, *The Rise of the Network Society;* Vol. 2, *The Power of Identity;* Vol. 3, *End of Millennium*. Oxford: Blackwell.

Chidester, David. 1996. *Savage Systems: Colonialism and Comparative Religion in Southern Africa*. Charlottesville: University of Virginia Press

———. 1998. Embracing South Africa: Internationalizing the Study of Religion. *Journal for the Study of Religion* 11 (1): 5–33.

———. 2001. Multiple Voices: Challenges Posed for Religious Freedom in South Africa.

In *Religious Education in Schools: Ideas and Experiences from around the World,* ed. International Association for Religious Freedom, 26–31. Oxford: International Association for Religious Freedom.

Chidester, David, Gordon Mitchell, A. Rashied Omar, and Isabel Apawo Phiri, eds. 1994. *Religion in Public Education: Options for a New South Africa.* 2nd ed. Cape Town: University of Cape Town.

Chidester, David, Chirevo Kwenda, Robert Petty, Judy Tobler, and Darrel Wratten, eds. 1997. *African Traditional Religion in South Africa: An Annotated Bibliography.* Westport, Conn.: Greenwood.

Chidester, David, Judy Tobler, and Darrel Wratten, eds. 1997a. *Christianity in South Africa: An Annotated Bibliography.* Westport, Conn.: Greenwood.

———. 1997b. *Islam, Hinduism, and Judaism in South Africa: An Annotated Bibliography.* Westport, Conn.: Greenwood.

Chinweizu. 1999. Towards the African Renaissance Media. In *African Renaissance,* ed. M. W. Makgoba. Cape Town: Mafube and Tafelberg.

Cochrane, James, John de Gruchy, and Stephen Martin, eds. 1999. *Facing the Truth: South African Faith Communities and the Truth and Reconciliation Commission.* Athens: Ohio University Press.

Dillon, Jane, and James Richardson. 1994. The "Cult" Concept: A Politics of Representation Analysis. *Syzygy: Journal of Alternative Religion and Culture* 3 (3–4): 185–195.

Dlamini, Charles. 1994. Culture, Education and Religion. In *Rights and Constitutionalism: The New South African Legal Order,* ed. D. van Wyk, J. Dugard, B. de Villiers, and D. Davis, 573–598. Kenwyn, South Africa: Juta.

Esaya, Menkir. 1992. Content and Context of Christian Communication: Implications for Development. In *Communication and Human Rights in Africa,* ed. R. N. Kizito. Nairobi: World Association for Christian Communication-Africa Region.

Evans, Malcolm D. 2000. Religion, Law and Human Rights: Locating the Debate. In *Law and Religion in Contemporary Society: Communalism, Individualism and the State,* ed. P. W. Edge and G. Harvey, 177–197. Aldershot, U.K.: Ashgate.

Fardon, Richard, and Graham Furniss, eds. 2000. *African Broadcast Cultures: Radio in Transition.* Oxford: James Currey.

Faure, Veronique. 2000. L'occulte et le politique en Afrique du Sud. In *Dynamiques religieuses en Afrique australe,* ed. V. Faure. Paris: Karthala.

Gifford, Paul. 1988. *The Religious Right in Southern Africa.* Harare: University of Zimbabwe.

———. 1998. *African Christianity: Its Public Role.* Bloomington and Indianapolis: Indiana University Press.

Gunsburg, Faye, Lila Abu-Lughod, and Brian Larkin, eds. 2002. *Media Worlds: Anthropology on New Terrain.* Berkeley: University of California Press.

Graybill, Lynn S. 1995. *Religion and Resistance Politics in South Africa.* Westport, Conn.: Praeger.

Gruchy, John de. 1995. *Christianity and Democracy.* Cambridge: Cambridge University Press.

Gruchy, J. W. de, and S. Martin, eds. 1995. *Religion and the Reconstruction of Civil Society.* Pretoria: University of South Africa.

Hackett, Rosalind I. J. 1998. Charismatic/Pentecostal Appropriation of Media Technologies in Nigeria and Ghana. *Journal of Religion in Africa* 26 (4): 1–19.

———. 2002. Discourses of Demonization in Africa and Beyond. *Diogenes* 199.

———. 2003. Managing or Manipulating Religious Conflict in the Nigerian Media. In

Studies in Media, Religion and Culture, ed. J. Mitchell and S. Marriage, 47–63. Edinburgh: T & T Clark.

———. 2004. Prophets, "False Prophets" and the African State: Emergent Issues of Religious Freedom and Conflict. In *New Religious Movements in the 21st Century,* ed. Philip C. Lucas and Thomas Robbins, 151–178. New York: Routledge.

———. Forthcoming. *Nigeria: Religion in the Balance.* Washington, D.C.: United States Institute of Peace.

Haynes, Jeff. 1995. Popular Religion and Politics in Sub-Saharan Africa. *Third World Quarterly* 16 (1): 89–108.

———. 1996. *Religion and Politics in Africa.* London: Zed.

Hendriks, H. J. 1999. Religion in South Africa: Census '96. In *South African Christian Handbook,* ed. M. Froise, 47–91. Welkom, South Africa: Christian Info.

Hervieu-Léger, Daniele. 2001. France's Obsession with the "Sectarian Threat." *Nova Religio* 4 (2).

Herzfeld, Michael. 2001. *Anthropology: Theoretical Practice in Culture and Society.* Oxford: Blackwell.

Ilesanmi, Simeon O. 2001. Constitutional Treatment of Religion and the Politics of Human Rights in Nigeria. *African Affairs* 100:529–554.

Johnston, Douglas. 1994. The Churches and Apartheid in South Africa. In *Religion, the Missing Dimension of Statecraft,* ed. D. Johnston and C. Sampson, 177–207. New York: Oxford University Press.

Kilian, J., ed. 1993. *Religious Freedom in South Africa.* Vol. 44. Pretoria: University of South Africa.

King, Anthony D., ed. 1997. *Culture, Globalization and the World-System.* Minneapolis: University of Minnesota Press.

Kizito, Robert N., ed. 1992. *Communication and Human Rights in Africa: Implications for Development.* Nairobi: World Association for Christian Communication—Africa Region.

Lucas, Phillip Charles, and Thomas Robbins, eds. *New Religious Movements in the 21st Century: Legal, Political and Social Challenges in Global Perspective.* Expanded and updated edition. New York: Routledge, 2004.

Lundby, Knut. 1997. Media, Religion and Democratic Participation: Community Communication in Zimbabwe and Norway. *Media, Culture, and Society* 19:29–45.

Makgoba, Malegapuru William, ed. 1999. *African Renaissance.* Cape Town: Mafube and Tafelberg.

Mamdani, Mahmood, ed. 2000. *Beyond Rights Talk and Culture Talk: Comparative Essays on the Politics of Rights and Culture.* Cape Town: David Philip.

Mbembe, Achille. 1999. At the Edge of the World: Boundaries, Territoriality, and Sovereignty in Africa. *CODESRIA Bulletin* 3/4:4–16.

McLagan, Margaret. 2000. Spectacles of Difference: Buddhism, Media Management, and Contemporary Tibet Activism. *Polygraph: An International Journal of Culture and Politics* 12:101–120.

Minnie, Jeanette. 2000. The Growth of Independent Broadcasting in South Africa. In *African Broadcast Cultures: Radio in Transition,* ed. R. Fardon and G. Furniss. 174–179. Oxford: James Currey.

Mitchell, G. 1993. Education and Religious Freedom. In *Religious Freedom in South Africa,* ed. J. Kilian, 113–124. Pretoria: University of South Africa.

Mndende, Nokuzola. 1998. From Underground Praxis to Recognized Religion: Challenges Facing African Religions. *Journal for the Study of Religion* 11 (2): 115–124.

———. 1999. From Racial Oppression to Religious Oppression: African Religion in the New South Africa. In *Religion and Social Transformation in Southern Africa*, ed. T. G. Walsh and F. Kaufmann, 143–156. St. Paul, Minn.: Paragon House.

Moosa, Ebrahim. 2000. Tension in Legal and Religious Values in the 1996 South African Constitution. In *Beyond Rights Talk and Culture Talk: Comparative Essays on the Politics of Rights and Culture*, ed. M. Mamdani, 121–135. Cape Town: David Philip.

Mutua, Makau. 2001. Savages, Victims, and Saviors: The Metaphor of Human Rights. *Harvard International Law Journal* 42 (1): 201–245.

———. 1999. Returning to My Roots: African "Religions" and the State. In *Proselytization and Communal Self-Determination in Africa*, ed. A. A. An-Na'im, 169–190. Maryknoll, N.Y.: Orbis.

Mytton, Graham. 2000. From Saucepan to Dish: Radio and TV in Africa. In *African Broadcast Cultures: Radio in Transition*, ed. R. Fardon and G. Furniss, 21–41. Oxford: James Currey.

Netshitenzhe, Joel. 1999. The Media in the African Renaissance. In *African Renaissance: The New Struggle*, ed. M. W. Makgoba, 376–385. Cape Town: Mafube.

Nkosi, Daniel J. J. Nhlanhla. 1994. The Future of Public Religious Broadcasting in South Africa. MA thesis, Media and Cultural Studies, University of Natal, Durban.

Oosthuizen, Gerhardus C. 1999. Indigenous Christianity and the Future of the Church in South Africa. In *Religion and Social Transformation in Southern Africa*, ed. T. G. Walsh and F. Kaufmann, 157–173. St Paul, Minn.: Paragon House.

Richards, David A. J. 1999. *Free Speech and the Politics of Identity*. New York: Oxford University Press.

Richardson, James T. 1995. Minority Religions, Religious Freedom, and the New Pan-European Political and Judicial Institutions. *Journal of Church and State* 37 (1): 1–59.

———. 1996. Brainwashing Claims and Minority Religions outside the United States: Cultural Diffusion of a Questionable Legal Concept in the Legal Arena. *Brigham Young University Law Review* 4:873–904.

———. 2000. Discretion and Discrimination in Legal Cases Involving Controversial Religious Groups and Allegations of Ritual Abuse. In *Law and Religion*, ed. R. J. Ahdar, 111–132. Aldershot, U.K.: Ashgate.

Sachs, Albie. 1993. *Religion, Education and Constitutional Law*. Cape Town: Institute for Comparative Religion in Southern Africa.

Spitulnik, Debra. 1993. Anthropology and Mass Media. *Annual Review of Anthropology* 22:293–315.

Steyn, H. Christina. 1999. The Role of Multi-Religious Education in the Transformation of South African Society. In *Religion and Social Transformation in Southern Africa*, ed. T. G. Walsh and F. Kaufmann. St Paul, Minn.: Paragon House.

Stonier, Janet. 1998. A New Direction for Religious Education in South Africa? The Proposed New RE Policy. *Journal for the Study of Religion* 11 (1): 93–115.

Sundkler, Bengt. 1991. African Independent Churches and Their Political Roles. In *Religion and Politics in Southern Africa*, ed. C. F. Hallencreutz and M. Palmberg, 85–88. Uppsala: Scandinavian Institute of African Studies.

Tayob, Abdulkader. 1998. Managing Cultural Diversity in Democratic South Africa: Is There a Surplus Value to the National Project? *Journal for the Study of African Religion* 11 (2): 99–114.

Teer-Tomaselli, Ruth, and Keyan Tomaselli. 2001. Transformation, Nation-Building and the South African Media, 1993–1999. In *Media, Democracy and Renewal in Southern*

Africa, ed. K. Tomaselli and H. S. Dunn, 84–152. Colorado Springs: International Academic Publishers.

Teffo, Lesiba. 1999. Moral Renewal and African Experience(s). In *African Renaissance*, ed. M. W. Makgoba, 149–169. Cape Town: Mafube and Tafelberg.

Tomaselli, Keyan G., and Fr. Nhlanhla Nkosi. 1995. Political Economy of Televangelism: Ecumenical Broadcasting vs. Teleministries. *Communicare* 14 (1): 65–79.

Tomaselli, Keyan, and Arnold Shepperson. 1999. Media Studies and Practice Reborn: Recovering African Experiences. In *African Renaissance: The New Struggle*, ed. M. W. Makgoba, 404–414. Cape Town: Mafube.

Tomaselli, Keyan, and Ruth Tomaselli. 2001. Between Policy and Practice in the SABC, 1970–1981. In *Currents of Power: State Broadcasting in South Africa*, ed. R. Tomaselli, K. Tomaselli, and J. Muller. Denver, Colo.: Academic Books.

Tomaselli, Ruth, Keyan Tomaselli, and Johan Muller, eds. 2001. *Currents of Power: State Broadcasting in South Africa*. Vol. 1, *Critical Studies in African Media*. Colorado Springs: International Academic Publishers.

Urry, John. 2000. *Sociology beyond Societies: Mobilities for the Twenty-first Century*. New York: Routledge.

Villa-Vicencio, Charles. 1992. *The Theology of Reconstruction: Nation-Building and Human Rights*. Cambridge: Cambridge University Press.

———. 1996. Identity, Difference and Belonging: Religious and Cultural Rights. In *Religious Human Rights in Global Perspective*, ed. J. Witte Jr. and J. D. van der Vyver, 517–538. The Hague: Martinus Nijhoff.

———. 1999–2000. Christianity and Human Rights. *Journal of Law and Religion* 14, 2: 579–600.

Vries, Hent de. 2001. In Media Res: Global Religion, Public Spheres, and the Task of Contemporary Religious Studies. In *Religion and Media*, ed. H. de Vries and S. Weber, 3–42. Stanford, Calif.: Stanford University Press.

Vyver, J. D. van der. 1999. Religious Freedom in African Constitutions. In *Proselytization and Communal Self-Determination in Africa*, ed. A. A. An-Na'im, 109–143. Maryknoll, N.Y.: Orbis.

Walsh, Thomas G., and Frank Kaufmann, eds. 1999. *Religion and Social Transformation in Southern Africa*. St. Paul, Minn.: Paragon House.

Walshe, Peter. Christianity and Democratisation in South Africa: The Prophetic Voice within Phlegmatic Churches. In *The Christian Churches and the Democratisation of Africa*, ed. P. Gifford, 74–94. New York: Brill.

Westhuizen, J. V. van der, and C. H. Heyns. 1993. A Legal Perspective on Religious Freedom. In *Religious Freedom in South Africa*, ed. J. Kilian. Pretoria: University of South Africa.

9 Rethinking the "Voice Of God" in Indigenous Australia: Secrecy, Exposure, and the Efficacy of Media

Faye Ginsburg

Fire in the Projection Booth

Expository and observational films, unlike interactive or reflexive ones, tend to mask the work of production, the effects of the cinematic apparatus itself, and the tangible process of enunciation, the saying of something as distinct from that which is said . . . a disembodied *Voice-of-God* commentary . . . [creates] the evasive lure of a narrative that seems to issue from nowhere, that can simply announce, through an anonymous agency, "Once upon a time . . . "

—Bill Nichols, *Representing Reality*

In 1988, shortly after returning to New York City from my first field trip to Central Australia to study the nascent development of indigenous media in remote Aboriginal communities, I went into the 16-mm film archive in the Department of Anthropology at New York University (NYU) where I had just started working, to remove from the collection those films that had been made of Aboriginal ceremonies. I wanted to carry out the rules that had been put in place in Australian archives over the prior decade, out of respect for community protocols that prohibit the viewing of restricted aspects of Aboriginal religious life by people who had not been initiated, a prohibition that had been extended to film. In Australia, film recordings of indigenous practices had been made by white anthropologists and their fellow travelers, beginning with the work of Alfred Cort Haddon with Torres Straits Islanders in 1898, who saw their work as "salvage anthropology" documenting what were then looked upon as disappearing worlds. While filmmaking practices became more technologically sophisticated, this epistemological approach still prevailed when the Australian Institute of Aboriginal Studies, as it was then called, created an ethnographic Film Unit in the early 1960s when the Institute was established. As the filmmaker and scholar David MacDougall (1987, 55) has pointed out: "The institute was founded in the early 1960s primarily to carry out salvage anthropology, documenting what was then often looked upon as a moribund culture . . . to record Aboriginal ceremonies which it was thought might never be performed again." The works produced by the Film Unit exquisitely embodied in practice the appropriative relationship of the settler society to the cultural/religious practices of Australia's indigenous inhabitants. At that time the Institute's research paradigm (although contested by some) bracketed the contemporary political realities of Aboriginal people in favor of creating film records of indigenous ceremonial life in remote areas but separated out from the broader social conditions they faced. The Film Unit focused in particular on recording men's restricted rituals, producing more than a dozen films based on these activities between 1964 and 1969 (Peterson 2003, 133). Despite doubts raised about the strict rules governing the circulation of certain kinds of sacred knowledge in traditional communities, the Institute felt that as long as these were only seen by academic audiences in Australia's cities, this prohibition was being honored, not taking into account the possible circulatory reach of film and photographic materials until the 1970s when the filming of secret ceremonies was stopped (Peterson n.d., 1).[1]

In part this was because of the ways in which Aboriginal religious practice has been positioned in social science since Durkheim's classic treatise (1912), as an incredibly elaborated cultural system despite the simplicity of their every-day material culture. Following in that tradition of scholarship, the aim of the Institute and its filmmakers was to document key rituals and ceremonies that form the core of Aboriginal religious expression in an effort to obtain a record for continued scientific study. These classic ethnographic films were made out of a concern that traditional cultural practices were disappearing (Langton 1993, 77). For Aboriginal subjects, the production of films for the Institute often became the occasion for elders and others to revisit sacred sites, sometimes located on lands they no longer occupied, an opportunity that, at the time, in-evitably elicited cooperation.

However, the indigenous communities represented in the colonial film ar-chives failed to disappear as predicted, although traditional knowledge of cere-monial life declined. Aboriginal Australians managed to survive the onslaughts of violent settler colonialism of the nineteenth and early twentieth century, and the assimilationist policies that prevailed from the 1930s until the 1970s under a regime that Jeremy Beckett (1988) aptly calls welfare colonialism. By the mid-1970s those films of Aboriginal traditional life that had been made under the sign of their possible cultural erasure became part of a material legacy to which indigenous activists claimed rightful ownership. Realizing that their relatives and ancestors might not have cooperated under conditions resembling what to-day we would call "fully informed consent," Aboriginal activists began to protest the use and circulation of these archival filmic images outside indigenous sys-tems of control.

Their protests were based on a number of concerns. First, many of the people in the films were now dead; Aboriginal protocols prohibit the circulation of names and that protocol has been extended to the showing of film and photo-graphic images of those who have passed on, especially in the vicinity of their relatives.[2] Second, certain cultural practices—totemic designs, songs, and cere-monial dances—should only be seen by those who have been initiated and introduced to an understanding of their significance through appropriate ritual practices. As a result, many of the films documenting restricted aspects of ceremonial life held in the Film Archive of the Australian Institute of Aboriginal and Torres Straits Islander Studies were eventually removed from the available archive except with the permission, or at the request, of members of the appropriate Aboriginal communities. As Ian Bryson (2002) comments in his history of that archive:

> Scientific recording was thus brought face to face with the realities of the practice of Aboriginal religion. . . . Aboriginal people in urban areas sought to protect the rights of those living in remote areas and therefore create a pan-Aboriginal political space in which to operate. Regardless of who was doing the politicking, *the issue of concern in the 1980s was how could religious systems heavily reliant on the controlled transmission of knowledge go on allowing the recording of stories, paintings, dances and songs on a communication medium that had mass distribution of information as a central tenet.* (148, emphasis added)

While I was well aware of the restrictions and complex histories of these films, somehow, far away in New York, those restrictions did not seem to apply to me in quite the same way that they would have in Australia. In 1988, when I was asked to start a program in ethnographic film at NYU (which eventually became the Program in Culture and Media which I currently direct),[3] it was my lot to sort out the past from the future epistemologically and pedagogically, and, as it turned out, materially. One of my first tasks was to get the desultory and neglected ethnographic film collection into proper order since, until my arrival, it had been stored in an old refrigerator (along with wine, beer, and lunch bags), turning a number of color classics a soft shade of red. Among the works in the archive were several films on Aboriginal ceremony that I had never seen, films that NYU had acquired prior to the embargos placed on their circulation—*Emu Ritual at Ruguri* (1966–67), *Pintupi Revisit Yaru Yaru* (1971), *Pintupi Revisit Yumari* (1971), and *A Walbiri Fire Ceremony: Ngatjakula* (1977)—all directed by Roger Sandall, the key filmmaker for the Australian Institute of Aboriginal Studies during the 1960s. Determined to do the right thing, I pulled out the film cans holding the now prohibited films but then hesitated before pulling them from circulation. Since I was starting to work with some of the communities where the films had been made, especially with Warlpiri people from Central Australia, it seemed reasonable that I might view at least one of the films before removing them.

I had heard about the quality of the work, the first ethnographic films shot in remote Australia to use 16-mm color stock with sync sound of Aboriginal participants talking and singing. They were of another era—signified for scholars of documentary film by the aptly (and in this case ironically) named "Voice of God" narration track, in which the authoritative expert explains in a voice external to the visible action the meaning of the activities to which the presumed non-Aboriginal audience is a virtual witness. While there is "wild sound" of general talk, there is no synchronous dialogue with participants used to

Fig. 9.1. Warlpiri men during a Ngatjakula ceremony, August 1972. Photograph by Nicolas Peterson. Used by permission.

structure the film or to address the audience directly, formal conventions that routinely shape contemporary documentary style. Despite these signs of hegemonic control over Aboriginal life audible in the explanatory sound tracks by anthropologists who structured these films, these works were also considered classics of observational cinema, "characterized by a commitment to record whole events, spatially and temporally" (Dunlop 1983. 16). Like Pandora of mythological fame, I could not contain my curiosity and thought I owed it to myself as a researcher and scholar to view at least one of the films in the privacy of the department's projection booth.

I threaded the 16-mm projector with the 1977 ethnographic classic *A Walbiri Fire Ceremony: Ngatjakula,* made by Roger Sandall with anthropologist Nicolas Peterson who offers commentary on the role of this spectacular ceremony in restoring social order, directed to a presumed non-Aboriginal audience.[4] The ceremony is both about settling up grievances (in which fire plays a crucial, cleansing role) and a statement of Aboriginal ownership of land, told through stories of the journeys of ancestral beings and the places they visited, all of which are represented in songs, dances, body designs, and painting (Langton 1993, 75–76; Peterson 1970).

The event culminates at night with one group of ritual participants (*kirda*), elaborately painted and arrayed with dry brush, dancing toward a large fire while being ritually beaten with burning torches by *kurdungurlu,* their ritual "managers" and key moiety counterparts in the cosmological orchestration of Warlpiri ritual life. The climax comes when huge towers of brush are ignited, creating a spectacular and almost out of control conflagration, which, in one Western observer's words, "satisfies the most extreme European appetite for savage theatre, a morality play of the sort Artaud describes" (Michaels 1987, 58).

As I watched the film, absorbed in the scenes of fire, I gradually became aware of the distinctive odor of overheated celluloid. The projector had jammed, and the smell of film on the verge of burning filled the tiny room. In a panic, and with considerable effort, I managed to retrieve the film from the projector and put it back in its box. However, I could not get the projector to work again. Chastened by what I regarded as the destructive results of my hubris, I have never reopened those film cans.[5] This moment still stands in my memory as a visceral recognition of the limits to and particularity of knowledge under certain regimes of value, in contrast to the model of the Habermasian public sphere that presumes the transparency, rationality, and free flow of communication as an ideal (Habermas 1989). And while that position has been critiqued for its bias toward the historical circumstances it attempted to theorize, even the productive discussions of counter public spheres (Fraser 1993) are not able to encompass the epistemological vertigo produced when quotidian Western media technologies are taken up in profoundly different cultural circumstances.

Far from simply being about different content, the fire in the projection booth brought home to me the ways in which the very "looking relations" (Gaines 1988) embedded in media practices around different cosmological worlds are far more epistemologically complex than I had imagined. In an effort to gain some grasp on how these encounters between filmmaking, revelation, and secrecy have been negotiated, in this chapter I examine the legacy of efforts from the 1970s through the 1990s to use moving image technologies to document Warlpiri fire ceremonies, during a period when ethnographic filmmaking was, to some extent, being displaced by indigenous media production. What unintended consequences emerged through this historically changing encounter between indigenous Australian religious practices and the use of media such as film, video, and television to document them?

Re-enchanting the Archive

When some archivist [in the dystopic future] wandering through the ABC film library chances on an old undocumented copy of the Peterson Fire Ceremony film . . . [imagine that] something truly momentous happens. In pursuit of a moment of "primitivism," the tapes go to air, via satellite, to thousands of communities at once, including those of its subjects, their descendants, their relations, their partners, in ritual exchange, their children, their women (or men). One more repository guarded by oral secrecy is breached, one more ceremony is rendered worthless, one more possible claim to authenticity is consumed by the voracious appetite of the simulacra for the appearance of reality. At Yuendumu, this already causes fights, verbal and physical, even threatened payback murders, in the hopeless attempt to ascribe blame in the matter, to find within the kin network the one responsible, so that by punishing him or her the tear in the fabric of social reproduction can be repaired. . . . [T]apes and broadcasts reach forward and backwards through various temporal orders, and attempt somehow to bridge the Dreaming and the historical.

—Eric Michaels, For a Cultural Future:
Francis Jupurrurla Makes TV at Yuendumu[6]

In 1983 the American researcher Eric Michaels arrived at the Warlpiri community of Yuendumu in Australia's Central Desert,[7] the place he chose as his field site for a study he had been hired to carry out on the impact of film and television on this and other remote communities. The set of assumptions that undergirded the production of films on Aboriginal ceremonial life from the 1970s had been overturned, as Aboriginal activists—both remote living and urban—began to demand control over their own media representations (Langton 1993, 9).[8] In part because of a more activist zeitgeist, as well as his training with the prescient media scholar and filmmaker Sol Worth (1997 [1972]), Michaels became far more interested in working with local people to help them create their own forms of media. Rather than simply studying what they thought about the dominant forms of television being imposed on them, the project resulted in the formation of the Warlpiri Media Association, a locally based group that produced video for and about Yuendumu, and narrowcast to the community. Appropriately Michaels called his study of that process the *Aboriginal Invention of Television: Central Australia, 1982–86* (1986). One of his key findings was to see how quickly the practice of making video was socialized into Warlpiri ritual practice. Central to the social organization of ritual (and video) was the division of people into mutually dependent semi-patrimoieties that are each necessary to all ceremonial matters: *kirda* (owners of the land and active performers of ritual) and *kurdungurlu* (managers of the land who observe and serve as guarantors that rituals are being carried out properly). In the initial translation from orality to electronics, video making quickly was assimilated into the tasks assigned to *kurdungurlu* whose primary role is as authorizing witnesses who affirm the truth of religious activities carried out by *kirda* ritual actors (Michaels 1986, 65).

While working at Yuendumu, Michaels familiarized himself with the films made with Warlpiri people under an earlier paradigm, in which native religious life was documented on film primarily as texts for Anglo-European consumption and study. To his surprise, the version of the Warlpiri Fire Ceremony, Ngatjakula, captured with such drama on Sandall's 1977 film, apparently had not been performed since that time, despite the fact that it was considered an important part of Warlpiri spiritual life and "law" (the word used in English to designate *Jukurrpa,* the cultural rules that govern Aboriginal society and cosmologies, also referred to by some as the Dreamtime, because of the ancestral temporality it evokes).[9] At that time Michaels wrote,

the Fire Ceremony seemed little more than a memory. This is despite the fact that it is one of the great traditions of the Warlpiri and was once widespread throughout Central Australia. . . . There seemed to be some recognition among the Warlpiri that the Fire Ceremony was essentially incompatible with the expectations of settlement life, and the impotent fantasies of dependency and development they were required to promote. The Fire Ceremony was an explicit expression of Warlpiri autonomy, and for nearly a generation it was obscured. (1987, 59)[10]

In 1984, while at Yuendumu, Michaels was invited to join a meeting of male elders in the video studio. At Michael's urging, they had written to the anthropologist Nicolas Peterson, asking for a copy of the Sandall Fire Ceremony film, narrated by Peterson (on whose research it was based). They had received a copy and now were there to review it. Michaels describes the scene:

I set up a camera and we videotaped the session. As it was clear that many of the on-film participants would now be dead, how the community negotiated this fact in terms of their review was very important. . . . Following a spirited discussion, the men . . . came to the decision that all the people who died were "in the background":[11] the film could be shown in the camps. Outside, a group of women elders had assembled, and were occasionally peeking through the window. Some were crying. They did not agree that the deceased were sufficiently backgrounded, and it made them "too sorry to look." These women didn't watch the film but didn't dispute the right of the men to view or to show it. (ibid., 61–62)

Soon after the screening of the earlier film, it became clear that the virtual viewing of the ceremony had been catalytic. Remarkably the decision was made to perform another version of the Fire Ceremony, the Jardiwarnpa (or snake dreaming) again for the first time in a generation.[12] As preparations proceeded, the Sandall film played an increasingly important role. Rather than seeing it as a patronizing relic of an earlier era, the film was unexpectedly resignified and actively appropriated as authoritative by certain senior men. When the Warlpiri Media Association finally made their own video recording of the Fire Ceremony in 1986, the male elders insisted that they tape the same scenes in precisely the same order in which they were seen in the film made by Sandall a decade before (ibid., 62): "The question arises," Michaels' commented at the time, "as it does also in accounting for the ceremony's recent revival: what role did introduced media play in this history?" (ibid., 60).[13]

The resulting new tapes that they made circulated quickly around Yuendumu; within twenty-four hours they were presented to members of the nearby Warlpiri-speaking Willowra community. Eventually, because of the death of one of the central ritual leaders, the tapes were removed from the archive because of the prohibition on viewing images of those who have passed away (Michaels 1987, 64). In 1987, shortly before Eric Michaels died, he speculated on the "cultural future" of those tapes and Warlpiri ritual practice:

When the mourning period for that old Japangardi is passed, his relations will take the Fire Ceremony tape from the "not to look" shelf and review it again, in regard to the presence or absence of recent performances of the ceremony. . . . They might declare this a "proper law tape," and then go on to perform the ceremony exactly the same, but different. I expect that in the highly active interpretative sessions that these attendances have become, there will be much negotiation necessary to resolve apparent contradictions evoked by the recorded history. (ibid., 74)

As it turns out, he wrote with great prescience. In this case, clearly, mechanical reproduction, contrary to Benjamin's predictions, in no way diminished the aura of these representations of Warlpiri ritual. If anything, the film seemed to have the effect of "re-enchanting" the ceremony through its objectification of it.

Revelation, Secrecy, and National Television

The concept of the "Indigenous public sphere" is intended to describe the highly mediated public "space" for developing notions of Indigeneity, and putting them to work in organizing and governing the unpredictable imme-diacy of everyday events. Thus far, the Indigenous public sphere has hardly been under the control of Indigenous people. Indeed, it is a peculiar example of a public sphere, since it precedes any "nation" that a public sphere nor-mally "expresses" as it were; it is the "civil society" of a nation without borders, without state institutions, and without citizens.

—John Hartley and Alan McKee, *The Indigenous Public Sphere: The Reporting and Reception of Aboriginal Issues in the Australian Media*

By 1989 the Warlpiri senior men at Yuendumu were concerned that with the death of many older members of the community it was increasingly important that they have a more complete and high-quality record of the Jardiwarnpa ver-sion of the Fire Ceremony, so that what they regarded as proper versions of religious and cultural traditions could be safeguarded for future generations. The earlier two versions—of the Ngatjakula shot by Sandall in 1966 and of the Jardiwarnrpa made by the Warlpiri Media Association in 1986—could not yet be shown at Yuendumu because of the recent deaths of participants in the films. The Warlpiri men also wanted to make two versions: one for initiated men and one that could be shown to the public by editing out some of the more restricted elements of the ceremony. For central desert people, the circulation of ceremonies and ritual media (such as painting) that are not restricted is seen as enhancing their cultural and cosmological power; the revelation of ancestral truths is seen as a performative, accomplishing in its very display a strengthen-ing of the connection to Aboriginal cosmological knowledge and law. Although the efficacy and significance of the latter may vary depending on the audience and form of mediation, the circulation of knowledge augments its value (Dus-sart 2000; Langton 1993, 79). At the same time, the level of knowledge that can be displayed, and for whom, is constantly being negotiated, as a number of scholars have made clear in their works discussing the impact of circulating Aboriginal ritual performance and art into new, non-Aboriginal regimes of value (Dussart 2000; Myers 2003). As one analyst of the use of media in Yuendumu has argued,

> Old people are *not* recording that knowledge which they consider to be the most highly valued *for Warlpiri consumption,* because ultimately, *they do not regard these processes of recording to constitute a Warlpiri medium of exchange.* This is the case regardless of whether the cameraman is Warlpiri or European. Importantly, this observation points . . . to a burgeoning inter-cultural domain in which Warlpiri people interact enthusiastically with recorded images of their cultural practices, past and present, which is viewed as in some respects distinct and separable from the domain of the "really sacred." (Hinkson 1999, 176)

In 1991, with these multiple motivations, members of the Warlpiri Media Association approached filmmaker Ned Lander and his partner, Rachel Perkins, an urban Aboriginal filmmaker, who at the time was in charge of indigenous productions at SBS, Australia's national multicultural station, to see if they would work with them to make the new Jardiwarnpa video. Rachel is the daughter of the late Charlie Perkins, a leader of the Aboriginal civil rights movement, a man whose family had originally come from Arrernte people, living to the east of Warlpiri lands in Central Australia. Because of her kinship connections, Rachel began her work as an indigenous media maker in that region. By the late 1980s she joined with other Aboriginal activists from urban areas who were particularly vocal in demanding a positive and creative indigenous presence on Australia's two state-run television channels, resulting in the establishment of indigenous units at both the ABC and the SBS in 1988. When Rachel moved from Central Australia to Sydney to produce Aboriginal media for national audiences at SBS, she made a strong commitment to include not only urban aboriginal people in her stories but also the lives of more traditional and remote-living Aboriginal people. Based on the interest of Yuendumu elders in filming the Jardiwarnpa version of the Fire Ceremony for a national audience, she and Ned Lander took the opportunity to collaborate with them, as producer and director, respectively, and invited the Aboriginal anthropologist and activist Marcia Langton to prepare the treatment. They hoped to "whet the audience's appetite for further information about the issues rather than to provide a mass of detail which could not be absorbed in a one hour format" (Perkins 1991, 4; cited in Bryson 1995).

The project required constant consultation with the community about which versions of the ceremony would be shown in local, national, and international contexts (Langton 1993, 80), a strategy consistent with the kind of negotiation of knowledge discussed above.

> Elders supervised and guided the crew, participated in the editing, and reviewed all material. Constant viewing and screening of the material took place [at Yuemdumu]. . . . The tracks leading in and out of the grounds were open and the building had doors on each side so people could leave to comply with kinship avoidance relationships. Cassettes were also circulated in the community and aired through

Fig. 9.2. Still of senior Warlpiri men from the documentary *Jardiwarnpa: A Warlpiri Fire Ceremony,* 1993. Used by permission.

the television transmitter so that viewings could take place at people's homes. (Langton 1993, 80)

Other questions addressed finance and copyright for all parties to the negotiations: the ritual authorities for the ceremony, the SBS producers, Warlukurlangu (the Warlpiri Artist's Association), and the Australian Film Finance Corporation. These negotiations were particularly significant in light of prior media made in Aboriginal communities that disregarded their rights to their own images and entitlement to compensation for use of their intellectual property.[14] When *Jardiwarnpa* was due to be rebroadcast on SBS in 1995, negotiations took place over how to manage images of people who had died since its completion in 1993. An arrangement was made so that those people's images could be digitally blocked, allowing the film to be shown in its unedited version without violating protocol (Hinkson 1999, 112). Overall the project made clear the potential value of a co-production between urban and rural Aboriginal media makers.[15]

The making of *Jardiwarnpa* raises once again the question Michaels had posed in 1987 regarding the impact of introduced media on ritual practice. Based on the producer's documentation, they thought that "the process would actually motivate people to organize and perform the ceremony. . . . It can be

Fig. 9.3. Still of senior Warlpiri woman preparing for a ritual performance from the documentary *Jardiwarnpa: A Warlpiri Fire Ceremony.* Used by permission.

said that the presence of the camera and the intent of the filmmakers launched a cultural revival which was centered around an attention to fine ceremonial detail" (Bryson 1995, 3–4). The resulting hour-long documentary, entitled *Jardiwarnpa*, was part of a national series on SBS called *Blood Brothers* (1992), which grouped four one-hour documentaries focusing on the lives of four prominent Aboriginal men.

The broadcast of *Jardiwarnpa* (along with circulation of other forms of Aboriginal art, dance, music, writing, crafts, and so on) has helped to establish and enlarge a counter public sphere in which Aboriginal concerns—cosmological as well as political—are central and emergent, constituting a new form of cultural capital. *Jardiwarnpa* demonstrated how Aboriginal ritual and cosmological worlds could be represented on mass media, more or less on their own terms. As Melinda Hinkson noted in her research on Warlpiri response to media in the late 1990s, "Warlpiri people are extraordinarily experienced when it comes to presenting certain layers of knowledge and withholding others, particularly in situations involving non-Aborigines" (Hinkson 1999, 176). Furthermore, the presence of indigenous claims to culture and land, presented in high-quality broadcast format on national television, enables this contested domain of cultural assertion to address a national audience, and to find a place in Australia's national narrative. Media theorists John Hartley and Alan McKee comment on how the presence of such work in the national mediascape is part of a steadily increasing Aboriginal presence that, they argue, is helping to produce an indigenous public sphere, even under the regime of Prime Minister John Howard which, since he took office in 1996, has been decidedly negative toward the support of indigenous cultural production.[16] Writing in 2000, Hartley and McKee sustained an optimistic tone:

> Historically, European narratives have given agency to Europeans, construing "natives" as passive recipients . . . but only rarely and grudgingly giving agency and a "speaking part" to the "other" of their imaginings. . . . Indeed, it may be that the "Indigenous public sphere" is evidence that "Australia" is indigenizing its narrative sense of self as a whole. Thus, the current period may be characterized as an intense dialogue between Aboriginal and Australian components of the overall Australian "semiosphere," the outcome of which is not yet resolved. (4)

Much has changed in the representation of Australian Aboriginal religious practices since the 1970s, transformations that mirror the shifting place of indigenous people in the Australian national imaginary more generally. Tracking the changes in the mediation of Aboriginal religious life on film, video, and television reveals how these representations of ritual become re-signified in changing social practices as indigenous control over these forms of cultural production grows in significance (though not unproblematically) from local to national arenas of circulation. A central feature of that process is the increase in Aboriginal control over media representations of their own cosmological worlds. Indeed, the repatriation of archival films made under the salvage paradigm, discussed in the first section of the chapter, is an important dimension of that effort to build an indigenous public sphere that resignifies relations in the past as well as in the present. As Hinkson observed in 1999,

> When VHS video tapes of Roger Sandall's 1977 documentary *Ngatjakula: A Warlbiri Fire Ceremony* arrived in the township . . . at a time when a version of this ceremony was in the process of being re-enacted, the copies were quickly snapped up by a number of ritual leaders. At one camp-based viewing . . . more than 100 people gathered around a video player to watch the film, a number of Warlpiri residents saw images of their parents and grandparents for the first time since their deaths. . . . The arrival of such material tends to generate a great deal of interest intergenerationally among Warlpiri people and often feeds into debates about current-day problems and differences between the past and the present. Audio-visual recordings have come to play a critical role as repositories of the Warlpiri past. Their now prominent place in Warlpiri daily life has transformed the process by which collective memory is constituted. (1999, 112–113)

Clearly, by the 1990s, video and television have been incorporated into older formal traditions of religious mnemonics and representation—such as sand and body painting and ritual performance—as regularized features of Warlpiri forms of practice and objectification.

This process, understood as part of broader struggles for self-determination and cultural recognition of indigenous Australians, characterizes efforts on the part of Aboriginal cultural activists to control their own traditions—and their representations—within the changing context of Australia's national narrative. That narrative has been reshaped over the last half century with the (at least partial) eclipse of the salvage paradigm of colonial social science that prevailed during the early-twentieth-century period of European settlement of Australia, and the assimilationist cultural policy that followed. As part of a widespread movement for indigenous rights, local media production developed in response to Aboriginal movements for cultural autonomy but continued to operate under strict protocols through which rights to see and know certain forms of esoteric knowledge revealed in certain rituals are negotiated. These negotiations are particularly clear in tracking the various film and video versions of Warlpiri Fire Ceremonies, beginning with the 16-mm ethnographic film, *Ngatjakula,* in which the anthropologist's voice stood in for "the Voice of God," exemplified in the work of Roger Sandall in the 1960s and 1970s, to the video of the Jardiwarnpa version of the Fire Ceremony made by the Warlpiri Media Association as part of local indigenous production in the 1980s. In the 1990s the creation of a documentary of the Jardiwarnpa Fire Ceremony for Australian national television as a co-production between traditional Warlpiri elders and urban Aboriginal and non-Aboriginal filmmakers, became an occasion for negotiating secrecy as well as revelation of Warlpiri cultural knowledge. Indigenously made film and television productions have served as interventions into the Australian national imaginary, and indeed onto the world stage as indigenous Australian filmmakers and their work are seen at film festivals in Cannes, Berlin, New York, Toronto, and elsewhere, linking them to transnational articulations of indigenous identities.

In Aboriginal cosmologies, the circulatory reach of media can enhance the cultural power mobilized through the "showing" or display of sacred sites, designs, dances, songs, and other ceremonial practices. Their revelation helps establish local hegemony for particular groups by asserting the truth of their dreaming stories and—significantly—demonstrating culturally sanctioned rights to land to which the stories as well as political claims are inextricably linked. Countering these benefits of the media circulation of ritual practices either locally or more broadly are taboos and protocols against showing certain sacred activities, sites, designs, songs, or dances to those who are uninitiated. Additional sanctions forbid the viewing of images of those who have recently died, particularly in the vicinity of relatives, although these are increasingly negotiable. Thus media forms such as film and video that can escape local control are particularly problematic, even as they are highly desirable as a new aspect for the reproduction of Aboriginal religious life. Even critics of Habermas's exclusionary and overly rational framework nonetheless concur in their acceptance of the presumed absolute good of the ever increasing free flow of information. The Aboriginal case usefully complicates these ideas by making evident, instead, that moving image media technologies carry within them contradictory potentialities regarding the significance of revelation and secrecy for societies in which knowledge of certain ceremonies, rituals, and objects is both valorized and restricted. This case, then, raises key questions for us regarding religion, media, and the public sphere, and offers a cautionary tale regarding the profound ethnocentrism that too often blinds the ways in which we understand media and its relationship to collective religious expression.

Notes

Thanks to Birgit Meyer and Annelies Moors who encouraged me to write this essay and inspired its improvement through their 2002 Conference on Religion, Media, and the Public Sphere at the University of Amsterdam. I am deeply grateful to anthropologists Nicolas Peterson and Françoise Dussart for their comprehensive comments on this essay, and to Nicolas Peterson for the use of his 1972 photos and to Cheryl Furjanic for her help in digitizing them. Thanks as well to Barbara Abrash, Rayna Rapp, Angela Zito, and, in particular, Fred Myers, as ever, for reading various drafts of this essay.

1. As anthropologist Nicolas Peterson writes: "Initially the project appeared quite unproblematic, but by 1975 the program of filming ceremonies, particularly men's secret ceremonies, was virtually abandoned. In less than a decade, social and political change among Aboriginal people and a developing interest in film and media among anthropologists made the enterprise impossible" (n.d., 1).

2. Recently those protocols have become less strict regarding the circulation of film and photographic images, especially among younger people (Deger 2004; Hinkson 1999; Dussart and Peterson, personal communication).

3. For further information on this program, a joint project of the Graduate Programs in Anthropology and Cinema Studies, please see our website at http://www.nyu.edu/gsas/dept/anthro/programs/cultmedia.

4. According to Ian Bryson's 2002 history of the Film Unit, Sandall had gone out to the Central Desert to film in August 1967. He had planned to film a Warlpiri Ceremony at the community of Lajamanu (Hooker Creek) later that year. However, on arriving at Yuendumu, their ceremony was already in progress so he filmed that instead. Sandall regarded the footage as technically flawed—he had left the wrong filter on—and so only edited an archival print. In 1977 Kim McKenzie, a recent arrival at the Institute, worked with anthropologist Nic Peterson, an expert on Warlpiri life, and edited a release print in 1977 (Bryson 2002, 38).

5. At the time, and until quite recently, it was my understanding that this film was not appropriate for circulation. When I sent a copy of this essay to Nicolas Peterson to be sure I had gotten the details right, he informed me that everything they filmed was considered a public ceremony; the restricted parts of the ceremony had not been filmed.

6. According to anthropologist Nicolas Peterson (2004, personal communication), "This quotation from Eric is his sensationalizing of the Warlpiri (payback murders). There were aspects of the ceremony that should not be shown in public such as blood letting . . . , and singeing pubic hair, but neither of these was shown."

7. Located in the Tanami Desert in Central Australia, Yuendumu was established as a government settlement in 1946, and has been self-governing since 1978. The popula-

tion, which is still semi-nomadic, may vary from five hundred to one thousand people at any given time, a number that also includes white workers (Peterson 2004, personal communication; Langton 1993, 59).

8. According to Bryson, Roger Sandall resigned from the Film Unit in 1973. Furthermore, at that time the new Whitlam Labor government ushered in a period of rapid change in Aboriginal affairs, supporting increased political activism among Aboriginal people and the foundations of a pan-Aboriginal movement, all of which had considerable impact on the Film Unit and the kind of work it undertook (Bryson 2002, 52). Beth Povinelli (2002) has written a discouraging critique of the limits of Australia's multicultural frameworks that, she argues, rule out the recognition of nontraditional Aboriginal subjects.

9. The Fire Ceremony, in fact, has several versions. According to Nicolas Peterson, there are at least three at Yuendumu, and other versions in the Tanami, to the north. In any case, each celebrates and enacts the exploits of ancestral beings such as the Jardiwanpa (the Snake) or the Yankirri (the Emu), and is controlled by a different semi-moiety, for different "country" (Peterson 2004, personal communication). In Aboriginal law, the revelation of ancestral tracks through the display of this esoteric knowledge establishes rights to land in those areas indexed by the ceremony, and re-created iconically in dances, body designs, and sand paintings (Langton 1993, 76).

10. Concerning this point, Nicolas Peterson writes: "Just why, indeed even whether, the Ngatjakula ceremony had not been held for fifteen years is more problematic. Michaels canvases a range of relevant issues but his query is predicated on the notion that the ceremony should be held more frequently, which there is no reason to suppose is correct. Ceremonies are held to achieve specific purposes: in particular, the fire ceremonies are held to resolve disputes, remove tabus on sexual relations for widows, and to commemorate the dead. Further . . . there are four versions of the ceremony, one for each semi-moiety" (n.d., 7).

11. The prohibition on viewing images of the deceased is regarded as an extension of Warlpiri application of *kumanjayi*, a generalized term that replaces the name of an individual so that the person can be referred to without saying his or her actual name.

12. According to the anthropologist Françoise Dussart, who was there at the time, the moratorium on the performance of the Jardiwanpa was the result of many of the male ritual leaders having passed away. In 1984 senior women urged the men to stage a Jardiwanpa in order to release widows from the taboo that prevented them from remarrying (Dussart 2004, personal communication).

13. Nicolas Peterson disputes this observation, pointing out that "the film of the Ngatjakula lasts 25 minutes whereas the ceremony is held over several weeks or months, with singing and dancing lasting through most of the last night: through the course of the ceremony, as many as a hundred or more different verses will be sung but less than half a dozen are included in the film. . . . This is not to say that a film . . . cannot be part of a cultural reproduction but it cannot be a vehicle for the reconstitution or revival of ceremony as it was at the time of the filming. Most mysteriously of all is the unwitting suggestion that one version of the fire ceremony, the Jardiwanpa version, could be revived by looking at a film of a different version, the Ngatjakula, which is associated with different heroic ancestors" (n.d., 8).

14. Peterson points out that Jardiwarnpa still uses a voice-over commentary, although the voice is that of an Aboriginal man. He also notes that "senior owners of the Jardiwarnpa ceremony complained that they had not been paid properly by the filmmakers, only getting $200–$300 each. . . . Making money has always been a central con-

cern in having the Jardiwarnpa ceremony filmed as the documents attached to the fund-raising prospectus make clear" (n.d., 12).

15. Regarding this film, Peterson writes: "Langton is critical of the Ngatjakula film for having a voice of God narrative by myself and lacking any interviews with the participants. By contrast, the film she was involved in has an Aboriginal voice of god and includes limited direct translation of exegesis and conversation by Warlpiri people involved in the film. . . . There is no evidence that the Warlpiri controlled the whole process of the making of the film or that their comments make what is going on much more transparent: indeed it could be the reverse" (n.d., 10–11).

16. In May 2004 John Howard abolished the Aboriginal and Torres Straits Islander Commission (ATSIC), the main indigenously run bureaucracy through which most funds have been distributed to indigenous communities and projects. Not surprisingly this reversal of political sentiment has emanated largely from right-wing critics of hard-won principles of Aboriginal autonomy articulated by indigenous activists since the 1960s, ideas that offer hope and a foundation for an Aboriginal future beyond the non-choices of total assimilation or a frozen traditionalism.

References

Beckett, Jeremy. 1988. Aborigines and the State in Australia. *Social Analysis,* Special Issue Series 24 (December).

Bryson, Ian. 2002. *Bringing to Light: A History of Ethnographic Filmmaking at the Australian Institute of Aboriginal and Torres Strait Islander Studies.* Canberra: Aboriginal Studies Press.

———. 1995. Jardiwarnpa: Fighting Fire with Fire. Unpublished paper.

Deger, Jennifer. 2004. Shimmering Screens: Media, Mimesis, and a Vision of Yolngu Modernity. Ph.D. dissertation, Department of Anthropology, Macquarie University, Sydney, Australia.

Durkheim, Émile. 1912. *The Elementary Forms of Religious Life.* Translated and edited by Joseph Edward Swain. New York: Collier.

Dussart, Françoise. 2000. *The Politics of Ritual in an Aboriginal Settlement: Kinship, Gender, and the Currency of Knowledge.* Washington, D.C.: Smithsonian Institution Press.

———. 2004. Shown but not Shared, Presented but not Proffered: Redefining Ritual Identity among Warlpiri Ritual Performers, 1990–2000. *Australian Journal of Anthropology* 15 (3): 273–287.

Fraser, Nancy. 1993. Rethinking the Public Sphere: A Contribution to the Critique of Actually Existing Democracy. In *The Phantom Public Sphere,* ed. B. Robbins, 1–32. Minneapolis: University of Minnesota Press.

Gaines, Jane. 1988. White Privilege and Looking Relations: Race and Gender in Feminist Film Theory. *Screen* 29 (4): 12–27.

Habermas, Jürgen. 1989. *The Structural Transformation of the Public Sphere.* Translated by Thomas Burger, with Frederick Lawrence. Cambridge, Mass.: MIT Press.

Hartley, John, and Alan McKee. 2000. *The Indigenous Public Sphere: The Reporting and Reception of Aboriginal Issues in the Australian Media.* Oxford: Oxford University Press.

Hinkson, Melinda. 1999. Warlpiri Connections: New Technology, New Enterprise, and

Emergent Social Forms at Yuendumu. Ph.D. dissertation, Department of Anthropology, La Trobe University, Victoria, Australia.

Langton, Marcia. 1993. *"Well, I Heard it on the Radio and I Saw it on the Television."* Sydney: Australian Film Commission.

Lander, Ned (director, coproducer), and Rachel Perkins (coproducer). 1993. *Jardiwarnpa: A Warlpiri Fire Ceremony.* Blood Brothers Series, SBS (55 minutes). Sydney: Film Australia.

MacDougall, David. 1987. Media Friend or Media Foe? *Visual Anthropology* 1 (1): 54–58.

Michaels, Eric. 1986. *Aboriginal Invention of Television in Central Australia, 1982–86.* Canberra: Australian Institute of Aboriginal Studies.

———. 1987. *For a Cultural Future: Francis Jupurrurla Makes TV at Yuendumu.* Art and Criticism Monograph Series. Melbourne: ArtSpace.

Myers, Fred. 2003. *Painting Culture: The Making of an Aboriginal High Art.* Durham, N.C.: Duke University Press.

Bill Nichols. 1992. *Representing Reality: Issues and Concepts in Documentary.* Bloomington and Indianapolis: Indiana University Press.

Peterson, Nicolas. n.d. Reproduction, Appropriation, and Ethnographic Film. Unpublished manuscript.

———. 1970. Buluwandi: A Central Australian Ceremony for the Resolution of Conflict. In *Australian Aboriginal Anthropology,* ed. R. M Berndt, 200–215. [Nedlands]: University of Western Australia Press, Australian Institute of Aboriginal Studies.

———. 2003. The Changing Photographic Contract: Aborigines and Image Ethics. In *Photography's Other Histories,* ed. Christopher Pinney and Nicolas Peterson, 119–145. Durham, N.C.: Duke University Press.

Sandall, Roger. *A Walbiri Fire Ceremony: Ngatjakula.* (16-mm film, 21 minutes). Canberra: Australian Institute of Aboriginal and Torres Straits Islander Studies.

Worth, Sol, John Adair, and Richard Chalfen. 1997 [1972]. *Through Navajo Eyes.* With a new introduction, afterword, and notes by Richard Chalfen. Albuquerque: University of New Mexico Press.

Part Three | *Religious Representations and/as Entertainment*

10 Synchronizing Watches: The State, the Consumer, and Sacred Time in Ramadan Television

Walter Armbrust

There is another group who fasts like everyone else, but who are as far as can be from understanding the point of fasting, or the virtues of Ramadan. Either they sleep during the day, or they sin with an ugly word, harsh withdrawal from society, a criminal gaze, or uncouth thoughts. At night they gather in places of pleasure and amusement, and indeed, of sin and obscenity. Gluttonously they eat every manner of food, filling their bellies. For them Ramadan is the month of good eating, fine drink, long nights in bars, and partaking in all sorts of entertainment.

—Hasan al-Banna, circa 1940[1]

And now, after you've been keeping yourself all day from everything bad, please allow me to join you from now until dawn so that we can watch together everything that is provocative and contemptible, as we make you forget the merits of the fasting that you've done with God's permission. Now, a silly commercial interlude followed by the popular program, "What the Stars Do from the Time They Wake Up until the Time They Go to Sleep."

—Cartoon television hostess "Sonya," 2002

As the above quotation from Hasan al-Banna's sermon indicates, a perceived failure to correctly observe the Ramadan fast can be an occasion for censure. Al-Banna's understanding of Islam is not necessarily normative, but his disapproval of covering Ramadan excess with a fig leaf of fasting comes close to a broad consensus among Muslims that in contemporary societies the meaning of the Ramadan ritual is structured by self-denial. "Sonya," a red-haired imagined television hostess drawn by cartoonist Muhammad Sami (2002) approximately sixty years after al-Banna's sermon, makes the same point: nominal observance of the Ramadan fast during daytime does not license bad behavior at night. In his heyday al-Banna cast bad behavior as gluttony in the fleshpots of the big city. The more contemporary "Sonya" associates bad behavior intriguingly with mass media—"watching everything that is provocative and con-

temptible" following a "silly commercial interlude"—suggesting powerful institutional backing rather than individual deviance. Paradoxically television,
the state-dominated institutional basis for promoting excessive consumption
during the nonfasting hours of Ramadan, is also a vehicle for promoting piety.
To some extent excessive behavior and proper ritual observance define each
other contrastively. But the two are also used together to construct an apparent confluence between the interests of the state, business, and religion. The
daily change in social status between fasting and nonfasting defines the ritual,
but it is also an opportunity for the state to act as master of the ceremony. Furthermore, the programming of the commercials mentioned by the fictional
"Sonya"—*hadha al-fasil min al-iʿlanat* (this interlude of advertisements)—is a
crucial part of the process.

This essay examines the orchestration of time during Ramadan in the context of an Egyptian television program broadcast at the time called *Fawazir
Ramadan. Fawazir* means riddles (the singular is *fazzura*). The program posed
a riddle each night of the month of Ramadan. The riddle was not just stated but
was performed in lavish song-and-dance routines broadcast roughly an hour
after the *iftar*—the breaking of the fast just after sundown. *Fawazir Ramadan*
is no longer produced every year.[2] It is now a semi-moribund production lost in
an ever larger sea of holiday programming. But for years the *Fawazir Ramadan*
program was an important component in a complex of practices that promote
an association of corporate-sponsored materialism with morality. Although the
program itself has been superseded, the association of morality with materialism, of which it was a powerful example for decades, is stronger than ever. By
associating morality with materialism the program did not legitimate materialism. It did, however, put the state in the position of orchestrating the relationship between the two.[3] My essay examines this association through the lens of
a single episode of *Fawazir Ramadan,* the sequence of programming in which
it is embedded, and its interaction with the ritual character of Ramadan.

Plainly *Fawazir Ramadan* was not an "Islamic" program in terms of its content. It was not, and did not pretend to be, representative of Islam in any formal
sense. The program was, however, geared to the Islamic calendar and certainly
affected the way many people approached Ramadan. In Egypt and elsewhere
much media attention is given to the "lighter" nonreligious accompaniments to
Ramadan. By contrast, most direct commentary on Ramadan, in books, web
sites, and, indeed, state-sponsored television discourse, takes the form of sober
examinations of "the meaning of fasting." Aside from considerations of such
matters as how to fast, the conditions under which one can be excepted from
fasting, and what can potentially invalidate a fast, the emphasis in direct discourse on Ramadan focuses on values: piety, humility, uniformity of the Islamic
community, sincerity, and struggle in the Way of God. In other words, in direct
religious discourse the central element of the ritual, fasting, is constructed by
self-denial. But self-denial itself is not the point.[4] In contemporary literature on
Ramadan fasting is not meant to be an extreme form of asceticism, nor is it
meant to be a simple reversal of normal activities—one is not supposed to sim-

ply sleep during the day and stay awake at night. But *Fawazir Ramadan* was part of an ongoing practice of doing just that—staying awake, celebrating, consuming excessively. In religious discourse a "correct" fast is not necessarily the most austere, but there is no question that excessive consumption during Ramadan, even during the nonfasting hours, can be interpreted as contrary to the "true meaning" of the ritual, as delineated in modern instructional literature. As one Internet site put it (echoing Hasan al-Banna and the cartoon television announcer "Sonya"):

> Excessive intake of food is avoided (this regulates the stomach from being pot-bellied and distinguishes Muslims from kaafir whom Qur³an describes as those who eat like cattle (47:12); etc. All these good things which Ramadan fast teaches Muslims are the means to attain piety. This is why the verse on Ramadan fast says: "O ye who believe, fasting is prescribed for you . . . so that you will (learn how to attain) piety." (2:183)[5]

The *Fawazir Ramadan* episode described below is antithetical to such recommendations of moderation and sobriety, and must be understood in relation to it. Juxtapositions of apparently contradictory Ramadan practices have been observed in other parts of the Muslim world (Bennani-Chraibi 2000; Adelkhah 2000; Salamandra 2004; Christmann 2000). Such juxtapositions construct piety through systematic and institutionalized contrast with various kinds of counter-piety. This process deserves greater attention, as it draws out the wider context of a perceived intensification of religiosity in Muslim societies usually seen through such categories as "political Islam." Media orchestrate this complex and promote its commodification. Hence Ramadan becomes both an occasion for advocating communal leveling through the production of a discourse of pious moderation and an occasion for producing social distinction.

Commercial Sponsorship in Ramadan

The alliance of commercialism and state interest and the ritual aspect of Ramadan come together in households. The television sequence described below occurs typically in a middle-class home just after the *iftar*. After eating, the dishes are cleaned, and everyone is usually sitting in some common room chatting. Anyone present is stuffed from having consumed an abnormally large meal on an empty stomach. Most people have not yet left the home for their customary visits to friends and relatives or, indeed, to resume working lives rearranged by the necessity of observing the fast.[6] Before the main riddle program comes a "pre–*Fawazir Ramadan fazzura*" ("pre-'Ramadan Riddles' riddle"). This is essentially a warm-up before the main event. After that comes a commercial interlude, which at least in Egypt is an important and under-analyzed aspect of television consumption. After the "little *fazzura*" and the commercials comes the introduction to the *Fawazir Ramadan* song-and-dance routine, followed ultimately by the main event: the evening's installment of the main *Fawazir Ramadan* program.

The "little *fazzura*" described below is from Ramadan in 1990. It was sponsored by the Nasr Company for Consumer Chemicals. Judging from the company's product line—insecticides, detergents, and cheap perfumes—the presumed audience was broad, and probably of modest means. The program was hosted by Fayza Hasan, a cheerful woman wearing Western clothes, who was reminiscent of the cartoon announcer "Sonya" quoted at the beginning of the chapter. Her appearance, like almost all female television announcers, contrasts sharply to the substantial majority of middle-class Egyptian women who wear the neo-Islamic *hijab*. Ms. Hasan began the program as follows:

> Ladies and Gentlemen, happy holidays. The Nasr Company for Consumer Chemicals gives you its best wishes for the blessed month of Ramadan. The company presents to you each day of the month after the Arabic *musalsal* [dramatic serial] caricature riddles. The Nasr Company for Consumer Chemicals offers valuable prizes:
> —*Hajj* and *Umra* tickets
> —A color television
> —A full automatic washing machine
> —A four-burner stove
> —Ten bicycles
> —Five tape players
> —100 prizes from the products of the Nasr Company for Consumer Chemicals
> Before we tell you the riddle we'll see it together in a caricature. Pay close attention, because the solution to the riddle is contained in the drawing.

Then comes a series of cartoons which the audience sees being drawn in fast motion, punctuated by shots of the artist smiling at the camera. The cartoons were all designed to evoke a certain kind of food being eaten in humble circumstances. As a riddle it was absurdly easy. The first thing the cartoonist drew, in fact, was some letters being pulled out of a *ful* pot and formed into the words *al-ful sadiqi* ("fava beans are my friend"). It was a "Beans Are My Friend" caricature riddle. Anyone who was minimally literate, of course, already knew that the answer was "*ful*"—fava beans. The *ful* beans cartoons themselves were all very simple and obvious. From the look of them one might have surmised that the goal of the program was entertainment for young children. On the other hand, one wonders just what a toddler would do with the prizes. A four-year-old winning *hajj* tickets? A four-burner stove?

After the cartoonist finished, Fayza Hasan came back on and restated the riddle in a poem:

> Shall we say the riddle?
> ʿ*Amm* ("uncle") Zaghlul al-Zanati
> When the cannon sounds says "Woman, bring me some meat
> I feel like some protein from the kabab restaurant."
> She smiles, and says to Zaghlul al-Zanati:
> "We have some vegetarian protein
> Its scientific name is *vichya faba*
> Food of the poor
> Add a bit of lemon and oil, and dig in

Everyone eat, and whoever gets full should thank the Lord
For a loaf of bread and the *vichya faba*."

After stating the riddle Ms. Hasan told the audience the terms of the contest: "We hope the riddle is easy, and we wait for you to send the answers to Egyptian television, and don't forget to attach to the answers two coupons for products from the Nasr Company for Consumer Chemicals. The company wishes you good luck."

Something that can easily be inferred from this program is that *fawazir* put a premium on localized imagery. *Ful,* or fava beans (the *vichya faba* alluded to in the poem) is the butt of jokes at home, as the cheapest and most humble food on the market. However, as a "typical Egyptian food," *ful* is also potentially an object of nostalgia abroad—a symbol of identity made effective through its in-group associations.[7] The localizing strategy of televised *fawazir* was characteristic also of the far more elaborate *fazzura* that I will describe in a moment, although in that case it is less obvious. The entire Ramadan complex of hedonistic consumption and entertainment is understood by most Egyptians as local custom, as opposed to formal religion. But it should also be noted that in this case, for some, the homely local imagery of this riddle might have seemed a perversion of sentiments voiced a generation earlier. The "Beans Are My Friend" *fazzura* recited by Fayza Hasan echoed a poem composed in the 1970s by the leftist poet Ahmad Fuʾad Nigm and sung by his frequent artistic collaborator, the blind singer Sheikh Imam. In Nigm's "*Mawwal al-Ful wa-al-Lahma*" (Song of beans and meat), "*Duktur Muhsin al-masʾul*" (Dr. Muhsin, the official) takes the place of ʿAmm Zaghlul al-Zanati's wife. Dr. Muhsin tries to convince a skeptical listener that *ful* is "vegetarian protein not found at the kabab restaurant (*lahma nabati wa-la fi al-hati*), and that meat is in fact bad for one's health" (Nigm 1986). The listener replies, "Leave us to die with our meat; And you all live and eat your *ful;* What do you think, Captain Muhsin? Isn't that more reasonable?" (Nigm 1986, 859).[8] Nigm's 1970s poem protests the lot of the poor, who must eat "vegetarian protein," in a direct address to those fortunate enough to be able to afford meat but too callous to care about those who cannot. By the 1990s "vegetarian protein" had become a quaint device for selling bug spray. The combativeness of Nigm and Sheikh Imam in the 1970s makes a striking contrast with the 1990s alliance between the state and commercial interests.[9] The "Beans Are My Friend" caricature program, a minor instance of Ramadan entertainment, expresses no political agenda. But like the whole state-orchestrated complex of Ramadan festivities, it is a hegemonic articulation that effects a suture of disparate interests.

Advertising and Flow

Before we examine the *Fawazir Ramadan* program—the lavish "main event" of Ramadan festivities so to speak—it is important to consider the advertising interlude that precedes it. Advertisements are part of the "flow" of television programming. The concept of "flow" was described by Raymond Williams (1975) and is an often-cited phenomenon in television (e.g. Abu-Lughod 1995, 206; Mankekar 1999, 91). Williams suggests that television differs from other media in that viewers tend to experience it as a flow, or an organized sequence, rather than as the staging of discrete events. According to Williams, the key to creating a sense of flow, rather than of event, is filling the "interval" between programs in such a way that the television-watching experience, including both "content" and advertising, is continuous. The point is to make the distinction between content and advertising as seamless as possible. Announced programs grade into one another and into unannounced advertising. Williams suggests that in the United States viewers no longer even have a sense of the space between programs constituting a break, because the programs are sponsored by intrusive advertisers, whose presence is felt throughout a show, and because later shows are continually foreshadowed in whatever show one is watching. Of course this form of television is hardly inevitable and is not the only way that programming can be organized. As Williams (1975, 90) puts it, "What is being offered is not, in older terms, a programme of discrete units with particular insertions, but a planned flow, in which the true series is not the published sequence of programme items but this sequence transformed by the inclusion of another kind of sequence, so that these sequences together compose the real flow, the real 'broadcasting.'" Although Williams undoubtedly overstates the confusion caused by televisual flow, and too easily discounts the obviously common practice of television watching that *is* event-oriented, his argument that television spectatorship differs qualitatively from other kinds of spectatorship is nonetheless valuable.[10] Advertising certainly is an integral part of television programming in many places, and the programming of advertising surely changes the nature of television events.

In much Egyptian television the advertising does not fall within programs but rather occur in blocs of time between shows. In the early to mid-1990s, and substantially still today, advertising intervals could last up to half an hour.[11] Then, as now, longer advertising segments were grouped before the most desirable television events, such as the main prime-time dramatic serials of the evening. Prices for prime advertising time rise, and the period before prominent Ramadan programs commands some of the highest rates of the television calendar.

Williams (1975, 95) suggests that the "central television experience" is of flow, not of event. He also pointed out that there are various ways to structure flow. He had in mind the differences between British and American television (at a time before British television had begun to incorporate elements of American programming patterns). In Egypt, advertising is an increasingly important part of programming, although the system is far more state-dominated than television is either in the United States or Britain. But in all cases the analysis of television flow hinges crucially on the intentions of planners. In U.S. television, commercial programmers have to structure the flow so that it continually flashes forward from the event being aired at any given time to upcoming events. Ideally shows should have an exciting first segment to keep the viewer watching. The programmer has to balance between keeping the viewers interested in the station's own programming and distributing advertising time to sponsors.

Although Egyptian television sells advertising time, the pattern of structuring flow in Egyptian television differs markedly from American or European television. Some of the difference is attributable to the fact that Egyptian television is a state monopoly. Hegemonic discourse that seeks to make political agendas invisible alternates with direct state messages presented more explicitly than would be the case in the United States or Britain. The insertion of advertising is connected to the state's free-market economic policies, but the television system itself is a hybrid. Much of the programming is privately produced, but all programming is ultimately controlled by the state.

The analysis below of the pattern of advertising leading up to the *Fawazir Ramadan* is based on a recorded segment. Ideally one would examine the process from the perspective of the programmers, but thus far I have been unable to do so.[12] However, I have been told by an Egyptian acquaintance in the advertising industry that certain assumptions one might make about American television advertising might not pertain to advertising in Egypt. My informant is the owner of an audio recording studio, which I happened to be visiting during the making of a television advertisement for chocolate-covered croissants. The creative process began with the studio owner playing various tunes on his synthesizer until the advertising agent heard one that he liked. This was the melody to "The Twist" by Chubby Checker. Then a singer was brought in and words were made up on the spot, having to do with a sad man dragging himself through his morning until eating a delicious chocolate-covered croissant, at which point the "Twist" music kicked in. It took about an hour and a half for the studio owner, in consultation with the advertising agent, to fine-tune the lyrics, and for the singer to perform it to everyone's satisfaction. The tape was made and sent on to the television studio, where someone else would have the responsibility of creating visuals to go with the music.

My studio-owner informant insisted that the process of making advertisements such as this one was as haphazard as it appeared. According to him, one of the main reasons for operating in this way is that the state does not permit marketing research.[13] It is true that advertisements were by no means my informant's true love; he only worked on them because piracy in the music business had made it difficult to make a living purely as a performer. His lack of commitment to advertising as a business may therefore have contributed to his disdain for it. Nonetheless his opinion that the advertising executives had absolutely no idea if the advertisements really worked was striking. He believed that for many of the companies who produced advertisements for television the advertisements were entirely a product of vanity. By the logic of capitalist enterprise this sounds counterintuitive. Television advertising time in the U.S., for example, is an expensive high-stakes business. Why invest in advertising if the effectiveness of such publicity is dubious?[14]

Audience reaction to advertising is similarly open to question.[15] In the mid-1980s, when I first began spending time in Egypt, it was sometimes said that many people considered the advertising segments more interesting than the programs. At that time television advertising was less ubiquitous than it is now. If it was ever true that advertising segments were an "event" in and of themselves, it seems unlikely that anyone would consider them so in the much more advertising-saturated environment of the present. In Ramadan of 2003 (1424 A.H.) the advertising drew little commentary and did not seem an object of great attention for anyone I knew. One advertising producer I met, who was inactive in this business in 2003, remarked sourly in a casual conversation that all the advertising that year would be for food and mobile phones, as opposed to a more diverse and lucrative range of products. From the television I saw and recorded that year he appeared to have been roughly on the mark.[16]

In 1990, between the low-budget "caricature" riddle program described above and the broadcast of the much more elaborate and expensive *Fawazir Ramadan* program, there came approximately twenty minutes of advertising, commencing just after ʿ*isha*ʾ—the evening call to prayer. Although most of the advertisements were not tailored specifically to Ramadan, their placement vis-à-vis the prayer times appears to be deliberate. During the rest of the year the *adhan* (call to prayer) came in the middle of films, dramatic serials, news broadcasts, and advertising intervals. Whatever happened to be on was interrupted at the correct time for the *adhan*. But the post-*iftar* television flow suggests that certain programming principles were employed. The most important elements of the experience were both televisual and ritual. They were, first, the *maghrib* call to prayer that marks the end of the daily fast; second, the ʿ*isha*ʾ call to prayer that occurs at some fixed interval (roughly an hour and a half later, depending on the length of time between twilight and evening at a given latitude); and, third, the *Fawazir Ramadan* program that occurs after the ʿ*isha*ʾ. I consider the *Fawazir Ramadan* program to be the end of the segment by virtue of how audiences watched it. There was a strongly marked convergence of ritual and social action, on the one hand, with television programming, on the other. In a nutshell, Egypt resembles many other Muslim societies in that Ramadan is a time of enhanced sociability. But many people in Egypt begin visiting friends and relatives only after the end of the *Fawazir Ramadan* program. Social practice indicated a strong suture of the secular *Fawazir Ramadan* program with Ramadan religious ritual.

The marking of religious time on a daily basis in the television flow was not comparable to anything in American television programming. The most fixed items in the Egyptian television program were not programs (dramatic serials, news shows, sports events, etc.). On the contrary, the announced schedule of these programs were rarely adhered to strictly, as one soon discovered when trying to videotape programs using a timer. The recording often missed the beginning or end of the program. Calls to prayer, by contrast, were fixed and interrupted whatever was in progress. Programming therefore operated by a kind of fuzzy logic overlaid with more firmly structured ritual time. During Ramadan one of these fixed moments provided a reference point to which the entire television schedule could be resynchronized.

The "reset point" for this synchronization was the *maghrib* call to prayer. In Cairo the end of the daily fast was customarily signaled by a cannon blast (now broadcast on television and radio), announcing the *maghrib* prayer, after which food was served. The period from *maghrib* until the end of the *Fawazir Ramadan* program consisted, in effect, of a distinct bloc of television-watching time for millions of people. This bloc was not exactly an event, or at least not analogous to the experience of a play or a film—in other words, it was the non-televisual experience that Williams contrasts to the televisual "flow." In the *maghrib*-to-*Fawazir Ramadan* programming block people were not just "watching television" (as Williams [1975, 94] described it), nor were they watching precisely a television "event." The events (the *maghrib adhan* and the ensuing *iftar*) were of a ritual nature. Television programming and spectatorship was therefore consciously linked to ritual time. In effect, the overall structure of the post-*iftar* television segment facilitated a transition from fasting time to "normal" time. The main *Fawazir Ramadan* program—the culmination to the programming sequence, featuring imagery that was not just nonreligious, but aggressively secular—occurred after the last call to prayer of the day. From the *ʿishaʾ* until the next day's *fajr* prayer people had the greatest possible license to indulge in activities forbidden during the fast.

The television segment analyzed here began just before the *ʿishaʾ* prayer and continued to the *Fawazir Ramadan*. The ostensibly child-oriented (but highly commercialized) "caricature" *fawazir* described above came first. Between that program and the *adhan* was a brief interval filled not by advertising but by a religious song. The song was perfectly ordinary devotional music sung by a woman who wore a scarf over part of her light-brown hair—not exactly a *hijab* but at least a nod to what most people regard as modest dress. As she sang, the image of her face faded to scenes of a Sufi order circling a tomb (that of Husayn, grandson of the Prophet Muhammad, in Cairo). Given the relatively ancient veneration of Husayn, the choice of song to go with the image was odd. It was arranged with harmony, which gave it a sound resembling a Christmas carol. It ended with the *shahada* (the witnessing of the unity of God) sung in harmonized rounds, suggesting pealing bells far more than either Quranic recitation or any recognizably Arabic style of music.[17]

This overproduced, harmonized, and lavishly orchestrated Sufi song functioned as a transitional buffer to the call to prayer. In normal television time, as previously mentioned, the call to prayer would simply have been inserted into whatever program was in progress. In Ramadan time perhaps more care was taken to juxtapose the sacred with officially sanctioned imagery. In many ways this devotional song was an expression of the state's modernist vision of a domesticated nonoppositional Sufism that nonetheless evoked only shallow appeal at best (Gilsenan 1982, 238–243).[18]

The buffering function of the song was emphasized by blending it into the *adhan*. While in normal television programming the *adhan* can occur anywhere, during Ramadan, at that time, there appeared to be greater sensitivity to juxtaposing religious discourse with the highly commoditized post-*iftar* discourse. Such sensitivities have been observed in other contexts. In an article on the political economy of religious commodities Gregory Starrett (Starrett 1995, 53) notes:

> As religious commodities are to be understood as material things, they have two networks of signification in which they can act as markers of difference: first, with regard to other objects defined as religious, and second with regard to the field of commodities as a whole.

Consequently, according to Starrett, religious objects are often placed in spaces of high visibility, but protected from disturbance (ibid., 53). Something similar occurred with this call to prayer. The *adhan* was not a religious commodity, bought and sold like an amulet, calendar, or clock inscribed with religious formulas. Nonetheless on television, and particularly in a programming structure that juxtaposed one of the most commoditized television events of the year— the *Fawazir Ramadan*—with religious discourse, surely programmers ran a risk of making too close an association between objects that should remain apart.[19] The "field of commodities as a whole," as Starrett calls it, must be taken into account, particularly if the televisual "flow" has the effect Williams suggests it has, namely, of causing the viewer to implicitly mix images, thereby insinuating overt commercial content with narrative programming. Hence the need to provide a "protected space" for religious discourse during Ramadan programming.

The call to prayer in this case was long (during normal time it was as brief as a window inserted in one corner of the screen showing first a clock and then the subtitle *adhan al-maghrib, adhan al-ᶜishaʾ*, etc.). Visuals broadcast with the *adhan* included scenes of pilgrims circumambulating the Kaᶜba (amplifying the previous image of a Sufi order circling the tomb of Husayn) and the recitation of an appropriate *hadith*.[20] After the call to prayer a family planning advertisement featuring an authoritative white-jacketed female doctor-figure provided a further step from religious to commercial content. This transition continued with an advertisement for Bank Faysal al-Islami, which was one of the few ads specifically tailored to Ramadan. It extolled the bank's charity work and gave holiday greetings to the audience. After Bank Faysal al-Islami came an advertisement for wedding dresses by ᶜAbudi. There was still a connection between the product (wedding dresses) and the season (Ramadan). Weddings do not occur during Ramadan, as it would be impossible for newlyweds to engage in intercourse during fasting hours. Typically, just after the completion of the month of fasting, there is a spate of weddings, and hence the sale of wedding dresses can be seen as still connected to Ramadan. ᶜAbudi is followed by a quick spot for *Tafsir al-Qurtubi*—a Quran commentary by a thirteenth-century Islamic scholar.

From al-Qurtubi to the end of the advertising segment, all the ads were completely secular and materialistic. Chicken bouillon, al-Ahram locks, Toshiba VCRs, Riri baby formula, the Filfila restaurant (long a favorite of tourists but now aggressively marketed to Egyptian consumers as a haven for sanitized "folk-lore"); then a delightful Meatland advertisement in which chickens and cows cluck and moo to the tune of the "1812 Overture" as their carcasses are efficiently hacked up in a clean industrial packing plant; juice concentrate, corn oil, smokers toothpaste, more wedding dresses, crystal chandeliers. In an intriguing Juhayna Yogurt advertisement a cow metamorphosed into a beautiful spinning woman. A perfume ad showed a woman who appeared to be going out on a date (she is shown waiting to be being picked up by a handsome man in a red sports car).[21] And, finally, the advertising segment ends.[22]

In terms of flow, the overall effect was that the handful of state-sponsored and religious messages blended into a veritable sea of commercialism. If, as Raymond Williams (1975, 92) argues, television programming creates an "irresponsible flow of images and feelings," then as a whole this segment sutured religious discourse with commoditization, even as, in more formal terms, it sought to set off the formally religious from the commercial.

Fawazir Ramadan

When I first watched Fawazir Ramadan in 1986 the program attracted a large audience. In that year I often attended iftar with a lower-middle-class family. This particular family had two daughters, and although the Fawazir were an aggressively secular counterpoint to a religious holiday, it would not be far wrong to say that they watched them religiously, missing few, if any, episodes. They were also trying to guess the answers to the riddles, for reasons we will come to shortly.

In 1986 Fawazir Ramadan (not, I should note, the program broadcast in the year described below) was a mass ritual. I generally joined the iftar, then stayed through the Fawazir, which began about an hour and a half after iftar (just after the ʿishaʾ call to prayer) and lasted for roughly an hour. After the Fawazir I returned home or went on to other social engagements. The family I was visiting found it odd if I tried to leave early, and it appeared that their pattern was typical. When the sign-off music of the Fawazir program played I said my good-byes and headed for the street. When leaving their apartment the streets were usually empty but filling rapidly. Everyone seemed to be leaving at the same time. On the occasions when I did leave early the streets were abandoned, and the program could be heard wafting from many a window.

The popularity of the Fawazir Ramadan is not constant. In 1994, for example, the Fawazir program was either losing its hold over audiences or was perhaps getting lost in an increasingly large shuffle of programming.[23] My own perception of the popularity of the program might also have been affected by segmentation of the audience. By 1994 most of my friends and acquaintances were male college students. In all likelihood homebound people (disproportionately women) are more avid watchers than those who enjoy higher mobility (i.e., men). It is also probable that the Fawazir Ramadan more effectively hailed a lower-class audience than an affluent one.

Fawazir Ramadan was clearly an "invented tradition" and, as proved in later years, an impermanent one. Among my informants there was a consensus that the practice of telling riddles in a mass-mediated format on each night of the holiday dates to the 1950s. Some suggested that its origins were further in the past—in the 1930s. Others believe that the custom of telling riddles during Ramadan is ancient, although the capacity of modern holiday practices to create nostalgia through very recent practices ought to make one cautious about claims to the antiquity of Ramadan riddle-telling practices.

The mass-mediated version of the program has been attributed to be the brainchild of the vernacular poet Salah Jahin and a radio hostess named Amal Fahmi, who became known by the phrase "*wi niʾul kamaan*" ("and we'll say it again," after which the riddle was repeated).[24] The phrase was also used by Fayza Hasan in the caricature *fazzura* "Beans Are My Friend" mentioned above, and the repetitive riddle-telling formula was replicated in the structure of the lavish *fazzura* described below. Ten years after the 1950s radio incarnation of *Fawazir Ramadan* the program migrated to television.[25] In 1975 it metamorphosed into *Sura wa Fazzura* (A picture and a riddle). This was the first time that the riddle was enacted by a vivacious dancer known on the stage as Nelli.

Also in 1975 the manager of the electronics company Casio began to offer digital wrist watches as a prize for guessing the riddles. He was later trumped by the owner of the local BMW dealership, who offered a luxury car. In the mid-1980s the Islamic investment companies (al-Rayan and al-Saʿd, among others, later accused of massive fraud and dissolved) used their sponsorship of the *Fawazir* to promote their businesses.[26] Since then the sponsors have again been corporations.

Nelli, the main performer in the 1990 episode described here, was introduced by the announcer as *al-fannana al-istiʿradiyya* (the revue-show artiste). She was essentially a dancer but not of the "oriental" type. Some of my informants opined that Nelli, though vivacious and often presented in form-fitting outfits, was considered more "cute" than "sexy." She had a flair for comedy and seemed to have a special appeal to children.

One final observation: each year the *Fawazir* had a theme. It was always secular. One year it was "folk proverbs." In another it was tales from *A Thousand and One Nights*. In the *Fawazir* program discussed here, the theme was "paper"—birth certificates, graduation diplomas, marriage licenses, and the like.

Fawazir 1990: World of Paper, Paper, Paper

Fawazir Ramadan of 1990 was introduced by an attractive un-*hijab*ed woman, as is typical of all Egyptian visual media (and in sharp contrast to most of the female viewers it addresses): "Ladies and gentlemen: *Ramadan Riddles*, by the title 'World of Paper, Paper, Paper.'" The program consists of thirty pieces of paper that have special significance in our lives. The star of the show is the "revue artiste" (*al-fannana al-istiʿradiyya*) Nelli (and various other important contributors to the project are named). Then came a grandiose (and perhaps deliberately retro) animated sign-on for the Egyptian Radio and Television Union, Economic Section, which produced the program. This consisted of an image of the well-known Radio and Television Building, which occupies a prominent space along the Nile Corniche.[27] But before the program could actually begin, another advertisement was inserted into the flow. At the time this was an innovation—in the early 1990s when I recorded the segment the practice was criticized by my informants. Now it is quite common. In this case the inserted advertisement was for that year's sponsors of *Fawazir Ramadan,* Noritake China, and the Fitihi shopping center in Jidda, Saudi Arabia:

> [a ponderous, authoritative voice, with visuals of the product]: Name of the manufacturer—Noritake; type of product—fine quality china; name of the manufacturer—Noritake; place of sale—Fitihi Center, Jidda; . . . [repetition of the same lines] . . . The Fitihi Center in Jidda presents LE 30,000 in cash prize money for *Fawazir Ramadan.* Good Luck.

This was followed by a surreal introductory dance segment—the longest part of the show—which had Nelli dressed in a luxuriant variety of outfits (always the subject of pre-Ramadan speculation in fan magazines). She danced with a sparkly-blue overall-clad male ensemble, a Turkish Pasha, a fleet of baby carriages pushed by chic women, and various other assemblages of glitzy male and female dancers. All the while she sang about ʿalam waraʾ waraʾ waraʾ (world of paper, paper, paper). Dressed at the end of the introductory segment as a gypsy, and speaking in a heavy "gypsy" accent, she told the riddle to a different character each night. In this episode the riddle was directed to the captain of "The Love Boat"—a direct reference to the American comedy series. The riddle itself, like that of the caricature riddle "Beans Are My Friend," was easy (the answer was a boat ticket). Nelli asks the riddle and then enacts it as a stowaway on the Love Boat, ending the spectacle dancing in a ballroom with the captain. Then she returns to her gypsy persona and restates the riddle:

> *At the beginning of the dance, Gypsy to the captain:*
> There's a piece of paper in your life captain—not a passport or a map or a card. Your trip doesn't start until you've gotten one from everyone who has one. Get it, captain?
> *At the end of the dance (and in a slightly more poetic style):*
> The train travels and pulls into the station,
> The Love Boat arrives at a foreign port
> Even a plane landing on the ground, sweetie.
> There's no difference between first class and some trashy passenger.
> What's more important? The chairs, or getting there?
> Hintish bintish [i.e., "presto" . . .], try and guess. Do you get it, or not?

On the surface the playful anarchy of "World of Paper, Paper, Paper" was a gentle joke about bureaucracy. But the corporate sponsorship and frank materialist attraction of the prizes puts the program in the same category as the "Beans Are My Friend" *fazzura.* Only the scale differs—a local chemical company sponsors the caricature riddle that broadcasts the "Beans Are My Friend" images, while Noritake China, together with a Saudi shopping center, sponsor Nelli's elaborately choreographed and expensive paper riddles. Both tie consumers to local identity, although it is not as immediately obvious in "World of Paper" as it is in "Beans Are My Friend." Nelli's tie to local custom lay, however, in her status as a media tradition. She herself did this program many times, and always her performance was associated with breaking the fast during Ramadan. The repetitiveness of the ritual makes it part of Egyptian Ramadan. Even now that the *Fawazir Ramadan* program is no longer produced, the older generation (really two older generations) mention it frequently as part of their fond memories of Ramadan. The much more fragmented satellite-driven television of the present still broadcasts *Fawazir* "Greatest Hits" during Ramadan. For the older generation, *Fawazir Ramadan* is now conflated with local customs: *fawanis* (Ramadan lanterns that children play with); *kunafa* (a sweet pastry) and various other foods associated with the way Egyptians observe Ramadan; certain songs and poems; the *misahharati* going around the neighborhood waking everyone for their final predawn meal; the cannon going off to signal the end of the fast; and now *Fawazir Ramadan*. The program functions (or, as time goes by, functioned) much like *Frosty the Snowman, How the Grinch Stole Christmas,* or *Miracle on 34th Street* function at Christmastime on U.S. television.

Of course, as with Christmas, it is entirely possible that the commercial side of the package goes entirely unnoticed by the audience, particularly a young audience more fascinated by the dances than by the prizes or riddles. This invisibility of economic and ideological interest by no means negates the importance of bundling commercial and state ideologies with entertainment. Indeed, such invisible suturing of disparate interests is the mark of effective hegemony. One challenge that the *Fawazir Ramadan* presents for us is to resist dismissing the program as "inauthentic." Stephen Nissenbaum notes that the idea of "invented tradition" is inescapable in the context of highly commercialized holidays. But he warns against the tendency to let obvious inauthenticity be the end point of an analysis:

> The easiest and most tempting way to abuse the idea of invented traditions may be to believe that if a tradition is "invented," it is somehow tainted, not really authentic. There are several reasons why such a belief is false. But the most important of them is that it is based on a profoundly questionable assumption—that before there were "invented" traditions, there were "real" ones that were *not* invented. (Nissenbaum 1996, 315)

A crucial part of this phenomenon is that the materialism of the newly invented rituals helps focus a discourse of disapproval. There are a variety of manifestations of such disapproval. In 1986 one man I knew adamantly refused to watch the *Fawazir,* calling them *al-fawazir al-burgwaziyya* (the bourgeois riddles). Basically the suture of materialism, corporate, and state interests to religious ritual was plainly visible to him. His indignation at the bourgeoisification of ritual resembles demands in U.S. society for a counter-traditionalism to the accretions of pagan and Victorian celebrations that became Anglo-American Christmas.[28]

Of course, the parallel between Christmas and Ramadan lies primarily with the linking of morality to commercialism, and in the centrality of media to this process of linkage. In the case of Ramadan, a ritual of communal solidarity and religious merit is clearly expressed in scripture. Of course, whether contemporary calls for a stricter adherence to scripture is a return to tradition or an expression of modernity is a familiar question. To some extent the existence of a profane Other makes the articulation of a purified Ramadan easier. It may be simpler to promote a vision of what Ramadan is when there are such blatant and omnipresent examples of what it is not. All the same, it seems likely that the coupling of materialism with moral value is intensifying. In effect, a religious holiday blurs into a ritual of mass consumption. In mass-mediated public culture the religious obligation of fasting during the month of Ramadan has become the twin of the holiday Ramadan. Ramadan the holiday is associated with Ramadan the period of ritual fasting. The two are not exactly the same, but it is becoming increasingly difficult to pull them apart.

Notes

1. The passage in the first epigraph to the chapter is available from a 1970s publication of al-Banna's sermons (al-Banna n.d.). Al-Banna died in 1949; hence the statement must be from the 1930s or 1940s. The second epigraph, a quote from "Sonya," the cartoon hostess drawn by cartoonist Muhammad Sami, is from the "For Islam" website, http://www.forislam.com/ar/main/modules.php?op=modload&name=My_ eGallery&file=index&do=showpic&pid=27&orderby=hitsD (accessed August 10, 2002).

2. The *Fawazir Ramadan* program ceased production around 2001. In 2003 (1424 A.H.) an attempt to revive it under the direction of veteran filmmaker Muhammad Khan met with little success.

3. This is consistent with a widespread tendency in many Muslim societies for Ramadan to be a focal point for cultural politics (Adelkhah and Georgeon 2000). The program is classically hegemonic in the sense that it expresses "dispersed and fragmented historical forces" ideologically as "an organic and relational whole, embodied in institutions and apparatuses, which welds together a historical bloc around a number of basic articulatory principles" (Laclau and Mouffe 1985, 67).

4. Contextualizations of Ramadan fasting can be found in Antoun 1968; Bakhtiar 1995; Buitelaar 1993; Fallers 1974; Wagtendonk 1968; and Yamani 1987.

5. Available online at http://sunnah.org/ibadaat/fasting/fast.html. As-Sunna Foundation of America (accessed December 8, 1999).

6. Not all shifting of work to the nonfasting nighttime hours is caused by unacknowledged attempts to avoid the fast. Daytime work schedules must be truncated simply to give employees time to get home through traffic jams of increasingly epic proportions. This means that work that cannot be delayed until after Ramadan must often be done at night. For example, when I was asked in 2003 to contribute an article on my impressions of Ramadan to the weekly magazine *Sabah al-Khayr* I was asked to come to the office at 10:00 P.M., well after the day's fast had been broken. The magazine was a beehive of activity—virtually everyone was working at night. Nonetheless the following

day on Nile TV, a state-run station created to address foreigners, I watched a program in which a young journalist was queried about Ramadan practices for the benefit of his presumed non-Muslim audience. He said, completely straight-faced, that practicing Muslims were not allowed to shift work schedules into the night hours. The reality is very different, although the reasons for working at night are not entirely reducible to fast avoidance.

7. The use of *ful* as a national symbol in the "Beans Are My Friend" caricature riddle recalls the notion of cultural intimacy described by Herzfeld (1997). Herzfeld's example of an in-group practice that binds people together in private, but is embarrassing when adopted by outsiders as a "typically" Greek custom, is breaking plates after a meal. *Ful* functions similarly here.

8. "The Song of Beans and Meat" was originally published in 1974, when many of Ahmad Fuʾad Nigm's poems were being performed by the blind dissident singer Sheikh al-Imam. My thanks to Clive Holes for pointing out the similarity between "The Song of Beans and Meat" and the poem recited in the caricature riddle.

9. The suppression of class conflict in the television reworking of Nigm's "beans and meat" theme echoes the Syrian state's strategy of removing class, ethnic, and religious conflict from Ramadan television discourse (Christmann 1996, 2000). Salamandra (1998; 2001, 163–203), however, argues convincingly that the state's efforts to erase ethnic and regional differences sometimes produce the opposite effect, and that expressions of social distinction are still central to the production and consumption of Syrian television.

10. Williams's point, however, is unnecessarily limited. He himself conceived "flow" as specific to television. But his concept of flow was a variant of montage theory—juxtaposing two unrelated images to create a third meaning, albeit in this case an imperceptible merging of meanings rather than a narrative line. More important, the same effect of a hegemonic suturing of content (of various sorts) with commercial and (in the Egyptian television case discussed here) state interests can be seen in other media such as illustrated magazines (Stein 1989). It is an important technique for insinuating hegemonic articulation into all sorts of communication processes.

11. It is noteworthy that the programming techniques employed in Egyptian and Arab television are far more diverse in the satellite-driven mediascape of today than they were in the early 1990s, when the programs discussed here were produced. But it is nonetheless true that most programs available to Egyptian audiences even now conform to the distribution of content and advertising described in this chapter.

12. An interview with Nadir al-Tayyib, head of the advertising department of the economic section of the Egyptian Radio and Television Union (ERTU) (October 3, 2003) revealed little of the practice of distributing programming. Mr. Al-Tayyib did help crystallize for me the basic framework of advertising rates and was also informative on the importance of Ramadan programming to the overall operation of Egyptian television. But he was understandably circumspect about the actual relationships of the ERTU and its advertising clients.

13. His statement must be qualified. In the mid-1990s marketing research in Egypt may have been poorly developed, but a number of marketing-research companies do operate in Egypt today. However, there are many questions about the quality of research on television-watching habits (and hence on advertising potential) in the Arab world (Sakr 2001, 113, 114).

14. I do not discount the notion expressed by my informant that vanity was a strong

motivation in advertising. Possibly the same motivation plays a role in European and American advertising. But vanity does seem to be very close to the surface in Egyptian advertising. During the Ramadan of 2003 (1424 A.H.) one of the most lavishly produced advertisements run during prime Ramadan time was for a company that produced structural steel for buildings. There are few consumers for such a product. I asked those I was watching television with about the ad. It struck everyone as an act of vanity rather than as an attempt to sell a product.

15. Television advertising—or, indeed, any form of advertising—is not a popular subject for academics. There is, however, a good analysis of the effect on domestic relations between a husband and wife of the marketing of cooking oil as opposed to the more traditional *sanma* (ghee) (see Seymour 1999). Diase (1996) does not address advertising directly but does provide an excellent analysis of the politics behind the production of a US AID–funded dramatic serial designed to disseminate social policy to rural audiences (see also Abu-Lughod 2004, for an analysis of Egyptian television— for the most part not including advertising—from the perspective of both producers and audiences).

16. His comments, and his withdrawal from the advertising business, points to the likelihood that further research on advertising in the Arab world might well have to account for an interesting disjuncture between forcefully expressed assumptions about the undesirable *ubiquity* of advertising (often described in the idiom of complaints about the overbearing influence of "money") in contemporary Arab societies and the possibility that advertising in Arab, or at least Egyptian, media may well be *less* prevalent than in many other societies. For example, music video stations, the most apparently commercialized satellite television programs, run advertising mainly for their own products, that is, singers, as well as mobile phones, which the programs' youthful audiences use to send each other SMS ("short message service") text messages which flow across the screen as the music videos play. The stations do not appear to be "sponsored" in the same way as, for instance, dramatic serials on American television.

17. By contrast, in the sensational Ramadan hit *musalsal* "Umm Kulthum" of 1999, the greatest Arab singer of the twentieth century is depicted singing religious songs in *maqam* style, without harmony, and with no instrumental accompaniment.

18. In Ramadan of 2003/1424 A.H. the song was still broadcast on television, but the visuals had changed. The Sufi imagery was gone, as were the images of the singer herself (Fayza Ahmad). Only men, nature scenes, and much more austere and less Sufi-oriented images were included. Fayza Ahmad died in 1983, so even my first (1990) recording of her must have already been old. But the visuals clearly can be adapted to new (and in this case more austere and Islamist) tastes.

19. Starrett (1995) contends that utilitarian objects are mostly incompatible with religious discourse. Note that the call to prayer comes between a program sponsored by a chemical company selling everything from bug spray to dish detergent, and a segment of advertising which, as we will see shortly, focuses strongly on utilitarian objects, but only after another set of buffering messages of a less utilitarian nature.

20. *Sahih al-Bukhari* 24, vol. 3, book 31, no. 127: [Narrated by Abu Huraira] "The Prophet said: 'Whoever does not give up forged speech and evil actions, Allah is not in need of his leaving his food and drink'" (i.e., God will not accept his fast).

21. All the advertisements featured women not wearing the neo-Islamic headscarf (*hijah*). However, it should also be noted that with the exception of the perfume ad, every woman in the sequence was depicted in domestic space where women (in real life, if not in advertising) would not have to wear *hijab*.

22. Sakr (2001, 116–117) notes that, in satellite television advertising, a substantial proportion of the ads are for American- or European-owned companies. This also seems to be the case, in most instances, for advertisements in this terrestrial broadcast.

The full sequence of the tape, from *Fazzura* to *Fazzura,* is this:

1. *Karikatir* ("Beans Are My Friend" riddle)
2. Sufi song, 9:00
3. *Adhan,* 11:30
4. Family planning ads, 16.56
5. Bank Faysal al-Islami, 18:26
6. Wedding dresses (Abudi), 19:26
7. Tafsir al-Qurtubi, 19:57
8. Crystal. 2:25
9. Chicken bouillon 20:56
10. al-Ahram locks, 21:25
11. Toshiba, 21:55
12. Riri baby formula, 22:25
13. Samna, 22:55
14. Pasta, 23:26
15. Abnuri window blinds, 23:54
16. Tatou tomato paste, 24:22
17. Kubi tomato paste/sauce, 24:43
18. Filfila, 25:14
19. Meatland, 25:43
20. Juice concentrate (sharbat), 26:42
21. Dura corn oil, 27:01
22. Smokers toothpaste, 27:31
23. Adel Abu Hemila wedding dresses, 28:01
24. Crystal Asfour (gives Ramadan greetings), 28:49
25. Juhayna Yogurt, 29:19
26. Perfume (woman going out on a "date"), 29:49
27. Saʿd cars, 30:20
28. Announcer for *Fawazir Ramadan,* 30:50
29. Radio and TV logo, 31:30
30. Noritake ad, 31:40
31. Back to ERTU introduction, 32:09
32. *Fawazir,* 32:38; end of *Fawazir* introduction, 38:27; end of *Fawazir* story, 51:05; end of *Fawazir* program, 54:37.

23. Although the types of programs available on television have increased dramatically, still the most prominent form of Egyptian Ramadan television, in local terms and in terms of academic writing, is the *musalsal*—a dramatic narrative broadcast in fifteen to thirty episodes. For more on narrative television, and also for an examination of a non-narrative Ramadan program, see Abu-Lughod 1993, 1995, 1999, 2004; Armbrust 1996, 11–36; Diase 1996; Seymour 1999; and Gordon 1998.

24. Bayram al-Tunsi, another prominent vernacular poet, may also have been involved in these broadcast *fawazir.* He published a collection of riddles under the title *Fawazir Ramadan* (al-Tunsi 1962).

25. In its initial migration to television, *Fawazir Ramadan* was performed by the

comedy trio Samir Ghanim, George Sidhum, and Dayf Ahmad. The program was suspended in 1967 because of the June war and was revived after a five-year hiatus.

26. For this history of *Fawazir Ramadan* I am indebted to Khaled el-Shami, Thomas Gorguissian and El-Sayyid el-Aswad.

27. The Radio and Television Building is on the edge of the lower-class neighborhood of Bulaq. In recent years the state has sought to remove longtime residents of this highly visible (to foreigners) neighborhood to make way for high-profile modern developments geared to the global economy (see Ghannam 1998).

28. Calls to "put the Christ back in Christmas" are historical nonsense. A more accurate demand, as Nissenbaum (1996) implies, might be to "put the carnival back in Christmas."

References

Abu-Lughod, Lila. 1993. Finding a Place for Islam: Egyptian Television Serials and the National Interest. *Public Culture* 5:493–513.

———. 1995. The Objects of Soap Opera: Egyptian Television and the Cultural Politics of Modernity. In *Worlds Apart: Modernity through the Prism of the Local,* ed. Daniel Miller, 190–210. New York: Routledge.

———. 1999. The Interpretation of Culture(s) after Television. In *The Fate of "Culture": Geertz and Beyond,* ed. Sherry Ortner, 110–135. Berkeley: University of California Press.

———. 2004. *Dramas of Nationhood: The Politics of Television in Egypt.* Chicago: University of Chicago Press.

Adelkhah, Fariba. 2000. Le Ramadan comme négociation entre le public et le privé: Le cas de la République islamique d'Iran. In *Ramadan et politique,* ed. Fariba Adelkhah and François Georgeon, 97–112. Paris: CNRS Éditions.

Adelkhah, Fariba, and François Georgeon, eds. 2000. *Ramadan et politique.* Paris: CNRS Éditions.

Antoun, Richard. 1968. The Social Significance of Ramadan in an Arab Village. *Muslim World* 58 (1–2): 36–42, 95–104.

Armbrust, Walter. 1996. *Mass Culture and Modernism in Egypt.* Cambridge: Cambridge University Press.

Bakhtiar, Laleh, ed. 1995. *Ramadan: Motivating Believers to Action: An Interfaith Perspective.* Chicago: Institute for Traditional Psychoethics and Guidance.

al-Banna, Hasan. n.d. *Nafahat Ramadan; Din wa-siyasah; al-Banna yutalibu bi-hukum al-Islam.* Bayrut (?): n.p.

Bennani-Chraïbi, Mounia. 2000. Le Ramadan au Maroc: Sacralisation et inversion. In *Ramadan et politique,* ed. Fariba Adelkhah and François Georgeon, 41–54. Paris: CNRS Éditions.

Buitelaar, Marjo. 1993. *Fasting and Feasting in Morocco: Women's Participation in Ramadan.* Oxford: Berg.

Christmann, Andreas. 1996. An Invented Piety: Ramadan on Syrian TV. *Diskus* 4 (2). Available online at http://www.uni-marburg.de/religionswissenschaft/journal/diskus/christmann.html (accessed August 12, 2002).

———. 2000. Une piété inventée: Le Ramadan dans les mass media syriens. In *Ramadan et politique,* ed. Fariba Adelkhah and François Georgeon, 55–80. Paris: CNRS Éditions.

Diase, Martha. 1996. Egyptian Television Serials, Audiences, and the Family House: A Public Health Enter-Educate Serial. Ph.D. dissertation, University of Texas, Austin.

Fallers, L. A. 1974. Notes on an Advent Ramadan. *Journal of the American Academy of Religion* 42 (1): 35–52.

Ghannam, Farha. 1998. The Visual Remaking of Urban Space: Relocation and the Use of Public Housing in "Modern" Cairo. *Visual Anthropology* 10 (2–4): 265–280.

Gilsenan, Michael. 1982. *Recognizing Islam: Religion and Society in the Modern Arab World.* New York: Pantheon Books.

Gordon, Joel. 1998. Becoming the Image: Words of Gold, Talk Television, and Ramadan Nights on the Little Screen. *Visual Anthropology* 10 (2–4): 247–264.

Herzfeld, Michael. 1997. *Cultural Intimacy: Social Poetics in the Nation-State.* New York: Routledge.

Laclau, Ernesto, and Chantal Mouffe. 1985. *Hegemony and Socialist Strategy: Towards a Radical Democratic Politics.* London: Verso.

Mankekar, Purnima. 1999. *Screening Culture, Viewing Politics: An Ethnography of Television, Womanhood, and Nation in Postcolonial India.* Durham, N.C.: Duke University Press.

Nigm, Ahmad Fuʾad. 1986. Mawwal al-Ful wal-Lahma. In *Diwan Ahmad Fuʾad Nigm,* 857–859. Dimashq: Talas.

Nissenbaum, Stephen. 1996. *The Battle For Christmas: A Cultural History of America's Most Cherished Holiday.* New York: Vintage Books.

Sakr, Naomi. 2001. *Satellite Realms: Transnational Television, Globalization and the Middle East.* London: Tauris.

Salamandra, Christa. 1998. Moustache Hairs Lost: Ramadan Television Serials and the Construction of Identity in Damascus, Syria. *Visual Anthropology* 10 (2–4): 227–246.

———. 2004. *A New Old Damascus: Authenticity and Distinction in Urban Syria.* Bloomington and Indianapolis: Indiana University Press.

Sami, Muhammad. 2002. Al-Tilifizyun. From "For Islam" website, http://www.forislam.com/ar/main/modules.php?op=modload&name=My_eGallery&file=index&do=showpic&pid=27&orderby=hitsD (accessed August 10, 2002).

Seymour, Elizabeth. 1999. Imagining Modernity: Consuming Identities and Constructing the Ideal Nation on Egyptian Television. Ph.D. dissertation, State University of New York at Binghamton.

Starrett, Gregory. 1995. The Political Economy of Religious Commodities in Cairo. *American Anthropologist* 97 (1): 51–68.

Stein, Sally. 1989. The Geographic Ordering of Desire: Modernization of a Middle-Class Women's Magazine, 1914–39. In *The Contest of Meaning: Critical Histories of Photography,* ed. Richard Bolton, 145–162. Cambridge, Mass.: MIT Press.

al-Tunsi, Bayram. 1962. *Fawazir Ramadan.* Cairo: Sharikat Dar al-Nashr al-Muttahida.

Wagtendonk, K. 1968. *Fasting in the Koran.* Leiden: Brill.

Williams, Raymond. 1975. *Television: Technology and Cultural Form.* New York: Schocken Books.

Yamani, Mai Ahmed Zaki. 1987. Fasting and Feasting: Some Social Aspects of the Observance of Ramadan in Saudi Arabia. In *The Diversity of the Muslim Community: Anthropological Essays in Memory of Petere Lienhardt,* ed. Ahmad al-Shahi. London: Ithaca.

11 Becoming "Secular Muslims": Yaşar Nuri Öztürk as a Super-subject on Turkish Television

Ayşe Öncü

The phenomenal expansion of transnational media markets throughout the 1990s has unleashed two contradictory tendencies in different parts of the world. On the one hand, the visual technologies and commodity logic of popular media have ruptured the seamless totality and imagined homogeneity of national cultures by lending voice and visibility to a plurality of alternative political visions. Television, in particular, with its ontology of "liveness" and lexicon of plentitude and choice—"free" entertainment, "free" opinions, "free" rights— has made it increasingly difficult to harness the dispersal of cultural identities in the public realm. The production of national subjects has become fraught with ambiguities. It is now commonplace to argue that developments in global media culture have eroded state hegemony in the cultural realm, making the fragmentation and dispersal of cultural identities inevitable.

Simultaneously, however, the explosive growth of commercial media have brought into the foreground new modes of identification with the abstract nation. The nation assumes a form of paramount reality, as its icons and narrative tropes circulate in an endless variety of commodity forms, across consumer and media markets. Belief in "the people" is reborn in two minutes of television time, through the remarkable achievements of individuals, be they football players, international award winners, or ordinary people who succeed in the face of insurmountable odds. The idea that the nation exists as a totality, and that "we" are in it, is confirmed daily as news reports identify the adversaries/ enemies who threaten its integrity, who endanger its well-being, health, and morals. This mode of linking to the abstract nation reaffirms "the people," without, however, the imagination of a collective agency. It has come under criticism as "consumer citizenship" among social analysts, and embraced as "positive nationalism" by the transnational advertising industry.

The unfolding of the 1990s, then, has accentuated two opposing tendencies inherent in the current expansion of transnational media markets. How the ensuing tensions of fragmentation and affirmation have been played out in different national/cultural sites, is historically contingent and politically mediated.

For the *political site* of struggles unleashed by these opposing trends continues to be the *national*, not the post-national or transnational.

What follows is an attempt to pursue this line of thinking in the context of Turkey's "televisual moment"—roughly ten years in chronological time. Specifically I am interested in how one of the most trenchant motifs of Turkish nationalism, *we are all secular Muslims*, has been simultaneously destabilized and reconfigured in the political conjuncture of the late 1990s. My main concern is not the insurgent politics of Islam per se or how it has challenged the mythologies of Turkish nationalism but rather the contradictory tendencies which have come into play. What I hope to trace is how the normative fiction of a *secular Muslim* has been reanimated and reaffirmed through commercial media, at a moment in time when its inherent ambiguities were highlighted and politicized by the growing visibility of Islam in the political arena.

My entry point of investigation into the dense political landscape of the late 1990s in Turkey will be to focus on the metamorphosis of a divinity professor into a super-subject on commercial television—"the phenomenon of Yaşar Nuri Öztürk." The centerpiece of my analysis will be how the chimera of a "secular Muslim" was constituted on a particular talk-show program which was on the air for more than five years, featuring Yaşar Nuri Öztürk as a regular guest every Friday morning. But, first, a parenthetical caveat on the generality and specificity of the "televisual moment" in Turkey.

The Unfolding of the "Televisual Moment" in Turkey

What defined the televisual moment in Turkey, as in many parts of the postcolonial world, was the historical coupling between the explosive growth of neoliberal discourses and the phenomenal expansion of commercial media markets.[1] The dramatic failure of state-led development efforts to deliver its promise of national progress was already apparent by the 1980s, in a range of countries as diverse as India, Indonesia, and Turkey.[2] The blowing winds of neoliberalism from the transnational arena, with its rhetoric of "freedom from state controls," "opening to the outside," and "integration to the global economy," promised the dawn of a new era. But what lent hope and optimism to such a utopian possibility was the ease with which satellite technologies penetrated across space, suggesting that integration to a world of plentitude and choice waiting "outside" would be effortless, once "state barriers" were removed. It is all too easy to forget, with the hindsight of the present, that "the dismantling of state controls" was executed, at least initially, in the spirit of a heroic new beginning. The immediate burst of energy in media and consumer markets seemed to lend this hope tangibility, however brief, before it was displaced by the disillusionments of neoliberalism.[3]

In its broader outlines, the eventful history of Turkey's televisual moment is one variant of this narrative. It began sometime in the mid-1980s, with deregulation in financial and capital markets that spearheaded the "opening of the economy to the outside." The breakup of the Soviet Union in 1989, which spawned a set of new "Turkic" states in Central Asia, fostered dreams of Turkey's impending leap into the global arena. Coupled with a cycle of exuberant growth in the domestic economy, Turkey's neoliberal turn became a showcase for success in international circles.[4]

Thus the year 1990—when a satellite venture, beaming from Germany, broke through state broadcasting monopoly—was a moment of heady optimism. The banking and advertising industries were already integrated into global markets through partnerships and joint ventures. Consumer markets were flooded with goods and brand names from distant parts of the world. The boom in domestic consumption, coupled with an unprecedented expansion in advertising markets, made investments in commercial television highly attractive. A series of commercial networks were launched in rapid succession, followed by a spate of buying and selling to gain common control of newspapers, television, and magazines. The broadcasting industry expanded at a frenzied pace, becoming a hotbed of mergers and acquisitions, with growing concentration of corporate control within and across various commercial media markets. By 1994—the precise date when the provisions of a new law re-regulating commercial media markets went into effect—media markets had already undergone a dramatic transformation, and mainstream Turkish audiences had become familiar with the seductions of infotainment and tabloid television.[5]

The downturn to Turkey's neoliberal episode was equally swift and dramatic. From around the mid-1990s on, the country began to suffer "economic uncertainty"—to use the favorite catchphrase of Turkish journalism—which became an endless topic for public debate. A succession of coalition governments began to follow one another in a game of musical chairs, lending credence to the diagnosis that "political instability in Ankara" was the main culprit for "economic uncertainty."[6] And, most important, insurgent politics of Islam and of Kurdish nationalism seemed to escalate concomitantly, bringing the Turkish nation on the brink of being drawn and quartered.

The fifteen-year conflict between armed Kurdish dissidents and the Turkish military, which claimed more than thirty thousand lives, was never officially recognized. The official rhetoric of "anarchy" and "the fight against terrorism," which was deployed from the mid-1980s until the end of the 1990s, cast a cloak of silence over the political trauma of mass deportations, empty villages, and large cities flooded by refugees from the war zone. The military—its budget, operations, and expenditures—remained (and remains) outside the boundaries of public debate. Direct censorship of news about the war—in which more than 2.5 million young men were immediately involved in the fighting—meant that reporting was confined to the ups and downs of seemingly scattered "terrorist incidents."

By contrast, the growing significance of Islam in electoral politics (especially after a succession of landslide victories in large metropolitan centers beginning with Istanbul in 1994) became an incessant topic of public discussion and television "chat," next to none other than "economic uncertainty." In the ensuing debates, the centralized Directorate of Religious Affairs became a focal point of controversy. As the representative of official Islam in Turkey, the Directorate of Religious Affairs is one of the largest and best financed state institutions in Turkey, with control over mosques, religious education, and a vast network of religious endowments and charities.[7] Ignoring the details of a complicated history, it might be said that its emergent scope and powers are bound with the project of Turkish modernity and nationalism, aimed at creating "secular Muslims." Two sets of state practices were involved in this process of social engineering. On the one hand, the Turkish state attempted to purge (with various degrees of vigilance or success or both at different times) all autonomous loci of Islamic thought and activity embedded in communal networks. On the other, it has sought to define and produce, under state auspices, the universal principles of Islamic doctrine and ritual for all Turkish citizens. The onus of interpreting the doctrinal and ritual injunctions of Islam was delegated to the State Directorate of Religious Affairs, along with the responsibility of training, certifying, and monitoring *imams* who preach in mosques, and, most important, the task of educating all Turkish citizens in the religious and moral precepts of Islam as part of the national educational curriculum. So the Directorate has evolved into one of the most powerful institutions in Turkey, with an organizational reach (as well as budget) next to none other than the Ministries of Education, Interior, and Defense. Needless to say, its doctrinal and ritual injunctions as well as its educational policies have been subject to the viscidities of party politics since the 1950s. But its institutional centrality and primacy in defining and supplying what constitutes public knowledge of Islam in the "secular" republic of Turkey was never seriously challenged until the 1990s.

In the political conjuncture of the 1990s the Directorate became a major target of attack for nearly all strategic groups in the political arena. Most immediately it was targeted by radical discourses emanating from Islamic circles, denounced as an anomalous product of Kemalist authoritarianism and state repression of Islam, in the guise of "secularism." The Directorate was identified as the site of state coercion, as opposed to "civil" formations of political Islam. Simultaneously the Directorate also came under vociferous attack by the gathering momentum of "secularist" forces, this time for allowing "Islamists" to infiltrate state bureaucracy and to benefit from its dispensations. Public outcry centered on the growing numbers and the expanding student population in schools for training religious functionaries (*imam-hatip* schools), where female students attended segregated classes in "covered" uniforms. The Directorate was accused of promoting a parallel educational system based upon *sheria* principles, through state funding and tutelage. Concurrently critical voices emanating from Turkey's hitherto invisible *Alevi* minorities (an estimated 20 percent of Turkey's population) began to be heard in the political arena. Threatened by the growing momentum of political Islam, *Alevi* minorities began to publicly criticize state policies for promoting Sunni-Islam as the official state religion, under the guise of "secularism." The Directorate was accused of using public tax money to subsidize an expanding network of Sunni-Orthodox mosques and schools, not to mention a vast centralized bureaucracy from which *Alevi* minorities have been excluded by definition. Thus, in the neoliberal conjuncture of the 1990s, at a moment of dramatic reductions in state expenditures for welfare and education, not only the ideological role but also the budget and expenditures of the Directorate became a matter of heated controversy—furnishing rich material for columnists, talk show hosts, as well as academics in the media-saturated environment of the moment.

The Metamorphosis of Yaşar Nuri Öztürk into a "Super-subject" on Turkish Television

In discussing the relationship between television and knowledge in general, John Ellis (1999) emphasizes the dialectic between two extremes of disorder and control. Television, he suggests, does not provide an overall explanation; it comes to no conclusions. Instead, it produces an unstoppable flood of events, spectacles of conflicts, intimations of crises of all sorts, people in desperate circumstances—unfolding before our very eyes in "real time" with cameras deliberately focusing on action. It also offers an enormous amount of "chat"— musings about what may have happened, what may be about to happen, or what may be the result if events were to take a certain turn. We, as audiences, are desperate for some sort of conclusion, but the more bits of information we acquire, the more the complexity and contradictions. Television's perpetually shifting agendas leave us adrift in a sea of doubt and contingency.

This was certainly the case toward the end of the 1990s in Turkey, when the body politic of the nation appeared to be dissolving symbolically and literally, as a series of calamitous events—"shock news" in the language of tabloid journalism—began to tumble upon one another on television screens. The ongoing civil war between Kurdish independence fighters and the armed forces of the state remained invisible on television screens, apart from officially authorized references to terrorist activities. But as the death toll continued to increase, visual images of mothers crying over the funeral caskets of their sons, who died defending their nation, began to intrude with increasing frequency. Then there was a series of shock events involving "reactionary Islam"—young girls falling into the clutches of heterodox sects (Fadime Sahin event of 1996); provincial towns falling prey to Iranian extremists (Sincan event of 1997); the infiltration of the "bloody" Hizballah network into the heartlands of the nation (Hizballah event of 2000)—which brought the nation to the brink of disaster. Last but not least was a series of political scandals (uncovered by investigative journalists) which revealed the hitherto unsuspected existence of a "deep state," involving linkages between high-level state officials, drug cartels, and Kurdish tribal networks. For mainstream audiences, watching these "disastrous events" unfolding before their very eyes, interspersed with tabloid news on the "ordinary lives of the super rich" (the subject matter of innumerable tele-magazine programs) and the "extraordinary sufferings of ordinary people" (featured "live" on "reality shows"), there seemed little doubt that the Turkish nation was on the verge of disaster.[8]

In this climate of doubt, contingency, and speculation, what mainstream infotainment broadcasting in Turkey (as elsewhere perhaps) offered audiences was a limited set of "super-subjects" who speak the truth as they say it.[9] Such super-subjects address viewers in the category of the person, balancing out the moral and immoral, the acceptable and the unacceptable, the right and the wrong, even as events tumble upon us and there are no second guesses. Among them are a selected number of news anchors, some notables from the business community, some politicians (very few), and Yaşar Nuri Öztürk. These are not television stars or celebrities—"show biz" in the conventional American sense of the term. Nor are they merely representatives of particular channels, the media world in general, or "the public interest"; rather, they seem to represent a complex nexus of them all. They speak as the "I" (analogous to the "I" in a sentence), and their messages perform the "magic" of binding different elements and cultural institutions together to form a coherent "reality." The super-subject (at least on Turkish television) is not a "narrator" in the classical sense of the term, organizing "live" events and orchestrating them toward a particular resolution. He (*not* she) does not provide narrative resolution but, by his very presence, seems to stabilize the chaos, discord, and disorder of the world beyond our immediate experience.

Yaşar Nuri Öztürk, then, is one among the limited number of such super-subjects on Turkish television and, akin to them all, stands in a category all its own. He has an impressive cachet of credentials as a scholar as well as positional authority—a theology professor at Istanbul University who specializes in Islamic philosophy—which empower him as an "expert." His prodigious writings include more than forty books, both scholarly works and popular "best-sellers." He is fluent in Arabic, Persian, and English; has committed the entire Quran to memory; holds a (secular) Law degree; and is equally at home with quotations from Nietzsche, Afghani, or Mevlana.[10]

In addition to his scholarly/intellectual credentials, Yaşar Nuri Öztürk has a lengthy history of engagement with the popular media. He started writing "Friday columns" for daily newspapers in the 1970s, starting with *Son Havadis,* later *Tercuman,* then moving up to *Hurriyet* (the largest circulating mass daily) in the 1980s. From 1987 on, he began to appear regularly on the *World of Belief* program, broadcast on state television on Friday evenings. But it was the advent of multichannel commercial broadcasting that catapulted Yaşar Nuri Öztürk into the national limelight, transforming his name into a household word, sweeping his books to the top of best-seller charts, and turning him into a highly visible public persona.

Since the mid-1990s Yaşar Nuri Öztürk has become the most sought after "guest" in innumerable studio debates, talk shows, and arena programs. He has prepared and presented such regular programs as *Isiga Cagri* (Call to Light) or *Kuran ve Insan* (Quran and the Human Being) for various commercial channels, which have since been recycled endlessly, particularly during Ramadan. He gives close to one hundred scheduled talks annually in settings ranging from five-star hotels in Istanbul to provincial towns and cities in various parts of the country. He is available on the Web to answer questions (paid) from the public seeking advice on a variety of issues. His most recent book, based on the most frequently asked questions on the Internet, entitled *I Am Answering*, is currently on sale in supermarkets and R&D chains, along with other popular bestsellers of the moment. And his personal life, ranging from his "hip" dress style (polo-shirts, suits with ties or foulards) and his daily workouts, to his "modern" home-style and "uncovered" wife, has become an endless source of fascination in the magazine press.

The Superstar of White Islam?

Perhaps the simplest way of thinking about the phenomenon of Yaşar Nuri Öztürk is how he embodies (literally and metaphorically) the blended culture of global consumerism. His public image is very much in tune with the spirit of the times—Muslim but with a difference: Muslim Lite. Ever since mass tourism took off in the mid-1980s Turkey has been marketing itself with a montage of images intended to convey its spirit—whirling dervishes, sizzling kebabs, sandy beaches, belly dancers, graceful minarets, and diners drinking red wine. This cultural pastiche, constituted through the optics of the global tourist industry, has been embraced as "multiculturalism" by the affluent and well-to-do classes of the neoliberal era, now associated with a mythical "Ottoman" past. Thus among the more striking features of Turkey's entry into the global culture of consumerism has been the circulation of "Ottoman cultural heritage" in a variety of commodified forms. So it is possible to interpret the phenomenon of Yaşar Nuri Öztürk as part of the same process—the rediscovery of Turkey's Muslim identity through the optics of global consumerism. When viewed from the bird's-eye vantage point of global consumerism, Yaşar Nuri Öztürk encapsulates the summation of incompatibles—hybridities—which is the essence of what might be thought of as a "global culture."

Still, Yaşar Nuri Öztürk is, first and foremost, a political figure—an active combatant in the battleground of cultural politics in Turkey. His fame and popularity on television cannot be divorced from the deepening cleavages of the neoliberal era, which became increasingly apparent from the mid-1990s on. The year 1994 was an important watershed, because a series of landslide victories in local elections (including in Istanbul) revealed the growing success of political Islam in developing a popular moral discourse of opposition—based on justice, honesty, and abstemiousness—while simultaneously incorporating the language of "human rights" and "civil society" from neoliberal discourses of the moment. Thus, in the political conjuncture of the late 1990s, the "classical" divisions of Turkish politics between the "progressive" left (secularist) and the "conservative" right (religious) were reconfigured. Political Islam succeeded in defining itself as the voice of "civil" society, the major force of (progressive) opposition

Fig. 11.1. A portrait of Yaşar Nuri Öztürk.

Fig. 11.2. Yaşar Nuri Öztürk: Superstar of white Islam?

against the secularist (conservative) establishment, with vested interest in maintaining the status quo.[11]

Within this increasingly polarized cultural-cum-political scene of the late 1990s in Turkey, Yaşar Nuri Öztürk has emerged as a crusader for a Kemalist-modernist version of Islam in Turkey. He is, in this sense, "the superstar of White Islam" (to directly quote the weekly *Aktuel,* January 1998). But as I try to demonstrate below, matters are somewhat more complicated than this. For on commercial television, which has become the primary arena of endless debate about who "we" are and what "our" culture is, Yaşar Nuri Öztürk, even when he draws upon and articulates the cultural themes and symbolic linkages of Kemalist-modernist Islam, recasts them in a different mold. Before proceeding further, therefore, I will attempt to provide a "close-up" of Yaşar Nuri Öztürk by focusing on a particular "talk show" program where he has been a regular participant for more than five years. This will allow me to discuss, in the last section of this chapter, how his polemical style and assertions have (re)politicized, in the public realm, a series of explosive issues that have (re)divided Turkey's Muslims.

A Close-up of Yaşar Nuri Öztürk on the Ayşe Özgün Talk Show

Every Friday morning for more than five years (between 1996 and 2001) Yaşar Nuri Öztürk has been an "expert guest" on a talk-show program hosted by Ayşe Özgün. The program itself is modeled after a very successful television genre (usually recognized as having been invented by the American Phil Donahue) which brings audiences into the studio as "real people"—an "audible public"—to create a sense of participation in a communal event. In its formulaic form, the talk-show format simulates a sort of town-hall meeting where topical social, moral, and political issues are debated among "ordinary people," with the host or hostess dashing about with a microphone in hand to catch different speakers, who give voice to different opinions among the members of the (studio) audience. Visually the studio audience is constructed as the focus of the show, and the ultimate success of the program is contingent on the audience's involvement in controversy and argumentation—each person representing him- or herself to express reactions based on personal experience—on a variety of topics ranging from problems of working women to drug abuse among youth and criminality. The role of the host or hostess is that of "mediator," allowing everyone to speak his or her mind, while simultaneously orchestrating the discussion so that officially invited "guests" (luminaries often sitting in panel formation) are invited to contribute their expert opinion.

Needless to say, there can be an enormous range of variation within this formula. The size and composition of studio audiences can vary from a "living room" with predominantly middle-class women, for instance, all the way to "town meetings" with a conscious mix of gender and age groups from different class backgrounds. Studio audiences may engage in a shouting match among themselves, or they may act as polite commentators, or their function may be limited to a select few who wait their turn at the microphone to recite a prepared statement on a particular position. The implied dynamic between "expert guests" (representing scientific knowledge) vis-à-vis studio audiences (representing ordinary common sense) can be that of one-sided deference. Or the entire program may be orchestrated (by the host or hostess) so that the status of expertise is challenged by real-life testimonials and exposed as trivial or pompous. And since the host or hostess is the trademark of the talk-show genre, his or her choice and handling of topics, as well as performative style, is crucial to the success of the formula. (Carpignano et al. 1990; Livingstone and Lunt 1994).

Home-grown versions of nearly all these variants have proliferated across television screens in Turkey. But Ayşe Özgun remains the first successful talk-show hostess, both as the "trademark" and also the producer of her own programs. Her talk show has been remarkable for its longevity, aired every morning on one of the major infotainment channels for more than five years. Although her show is scheduled at a time when networks target female viewers, Ayşe

Özgün's own proud claim is that her home audiences include many men—which is possible, given the numbers of retired and jobless in Turkey. Regardless, however, her choice of "social issues" for discussion (such as public health, municipal services, and crime rates) as well as performance style imply a mixed home audience. Her studio audiences are consciously gender and age mixed. The "expert guests" she invites differ according to the choice of topic and the exigencies of programming—except every Friday morning, when Yaşar Nuri Öztürk is the unchanging and indisputable authority.

Below I focus on the Friday morning program exclusively, to illustrate the dynamic between Yaşar Nuri Öztürk (as the expert), Ayşe Özgün (as the hostess), and the studio audience (as a protagonist), such that particular kinds of knowledge are constructed. For analytical purposes, I take up "the performance" and Yaşar Nuri Öztürk's own discourse and rhetoric as different "layers" that operate separately.[17]

The Performance and the Players

On Friday mornings the show begins as usual, with generics and music followed by camera shots of Ayşe Özgün's face addressing home audiences directly as "our dear" or "very dear viewers" as well as "our respected viewers." Ayşe Özgün, as the producer and hostess of the program, is, of course, a "celebrity" herself; after all, the show bears her name. She is a hefty woman in her fifties, with a cherubic face, elaborately coiffed and costumed in brightly colored matching ensembles—who appears on camera as if she had just walked out of a Brazilian telenovella (to my mind at least). Her appearance, as well as the dynamism she projects as she rushes around with a microphone in her hand, seemingly caught up in the heat of the discussion and eager to give everyone in the studio audience a voice, makes her performance one of the main objects of watching during the show.

But the program proceeds with a solemnity that befits Yaşar Nuri Öztürk's status and knowledge. Ayşe Özgün's own performance is a skilled combination of "sincerity" and "congeniality"—enacted somewhat differently when addressing studio/home audiences and Yaşar Nuri Öztürk himself. She is "sincerely" ignorant on matters pertaining to "Islam"—which allows her to be awkward when posing questions to Yaşar Nuri Öztürk (on behalf of audiences). But because she is "honestly" concerned about what she is asking, "lack of knowledge" is transformed into an emotional appeal.

She addresses Yaşar Nuri Öztürk as *hocam*, a word that has been assimilated into everyday Turkish as a general term of respect for someone of learning, but much less distant than the alternative *sayin* which acknowledges official stature, as in the English "sir." She seeks "illumination" in the third-person plural "we," but lapses into "I" when emotionally moved.

But in addition to the "we," for those of "us" in the studio and at home who seek illumination, Ayşe Özgün periodically brings into the picture "poor

Fig. 11.3. Talk-show host Ayşe Özgün.

people" or "people who are in very difficult economic circumstances" or "people who live in villages" by raising questions that begin with the words, "What about those people . . . ?" So there are always disadvantaged "others" whom "we" need to think about ("others" who are also watching the program). These are "our other people" (*bu insanlarımız*), who might find the ongoing discussion either too abstract or irrelevant. So Ayşe Özgün is concerned about sending "the right message" to "these people."[13]

The "studio audience," chosen to simulate "a bus full of people in Istanbul" (according to Ayşe Özgün), sit in rows facing the front. On Friday mornings only a selected few stand up to ask questions individually (obviously coached), rather than engaging in discussion among themselves. Most of the time they are "quiet moral sitters," facing Yaşar Nuri Öztürk.

Yaşar Nuri Öztürk sits behind a small desk throughout the program, rarely moving until he begins to talk. In the opening long shots, he appears dwarfed by the large bouquet of fresh flowers placed on the desk, totally incongruous against the background of wallpaper decorated with leaves, butterflies, and the program logo—Ayşe Özgün's own signature blown up in pink—with a generic music reminiscent of soap operas. But as the camera moves in to show him close-up and he begins to answer, explain, and elaborate his arguments, he is transformed into a figure of immense power. Thus when the studio audience bursts into spontaneous applause after one of his impressive soliloquies, the sense of watching a contrived performance is transformed into a shared moment of "togetherness."

Apart from these "electric" moments (which I discuss later), Yaşar Nuri Öztürk's discursive style is much closer to classroom lecturing than to sermonizing intended to inspire emotional leaps of faith. His claim to authority and self-framing is that of a "man of scientific learning" (*bilim adamı*) as distinct from a "man of religion" (*din adamı*). He continuously promotes "reason" and "logic" (*akıl ve mantık*) against "muddled thinking" (*kafa karışıklığı*).

In the overall progression of the program itself, Ayşe Özgün's own "muddled thinking" serves to highlight Yaşar Nuri Öztürk's "reasoned" explanations, giving him the opportunity to sort out the significant from the irrelevant, and to expound the real issues (*esas meseleler*). To illustrate:

[following upon a series of comments-cum-questions from the audience]

Ayşe Özgün: We are doing something that Allah does not want. To bring us together, he has sent the book, he has sent the prophet, we are sharpening the divisions and so if I say something I am afraid of reaction from this group, if I say another from that, is this something good? We are doing something Allah does not want. This is what I see. But how we get out of this situation, that I do not know. Is it with tolerance, I mean getting away from the mentality of imposing our own ideas that I do not know either. But once again after our last week's program many viewers, twelve to thirteen viewers who did not agree with your views, telephoned us. Would you believe it? But one viewer called in such anger, thanking Allah for those who give us correct or wrong religious information. Now this is where I am flabbergasted. I mean, what does it mean to be thankful for wrong information, this I do not understand, this kind of thinking. . . . You say the truth but I do not want to accept it, it is true according to one side of course and this viewer of ours was raising hell last week. So thirteen telephone calls came like this. Now this is my question to you: Is it wrong or right to say thank God for wrong religious information as well as right religious information?

Yaşar Nuri Öztürk: If someone makes a mistake out of ignorance, I would not blame him. Even when he telephones in anger, if he is not deliberately misleading but believes in what he says, what could we say? Wake up.

AÖ: No. Let us wake up but life is continuously changing.

YNÖ: Ayşe hanim, let us not trivialize matters. There are those who deliberately lie and mislead the people. A person may lack knowledge, may not have enough education, but believes in something. If he says "salt" instead of "sugar," this should not be exaggerated. Now this is not the issue. This is not the problem Turkey is facing. This is never the real issue. The real problem is that people who know the Quran do not reveal all of it. Or people who say the Quran says this, but such and such important man says something else. This is the issue. This is the destruction. Is our religion to be revealed by the Quran, or by others? This has to be decided. We have been saying for years that there two religions in the Islamic world as well as in Turkey. Of course, there are many distinctions, but two main religions that go under the name of Islam. There is the Islam that has been brought down by the Quran, and then there is the Islam that has been invented. Do you know how long this division has existed in the Islamic world? . . . [continues uninterrupted for ten to fifteen minutes]

The excerpt above is typical of how Yaşar Nuri Öztürk responds to "muddled questions" from Ayşe Özgün, which she invariably poses in binary form. He does this in a highly polemical style, rephrasing Ayşe Özgün to formulate and answer his own questions, bringing in scholarly references, points of fact, examples from everyday life. What is lost in (my own) translation is the ease with which Yaşar Nuri Öztürk alternates between religious language and everyday colloquialisms while speaking. Each soliloquy is a tour de force, an exercise in reduction and simplification, delivered with "inner conviction" by someone authorized to speak the truth as "a man of scientific learning." The program ends with Yaşar Nuri Öztürk's speech amid enthusiastic applause.

Yaşar Nuri Öztürk's Discourse and Rhetoric

During his lengthy soliloquy's on television Yaşar Nuri Öztürk adopts various overlapping frames of self-representation—always speaking in the first-person plural (rarely "my" or "I"), for instance, which simultaneously asserts his indisputable authority as a theologian, and also underscores his self-certainty when speaking as a social diagnostician who provides explanations of and remedies for social as well as personal ills. And, of course, he acts as a dedicated "educator," who never tires of clarifying abstract ideas by using everyday metaphors "to reach the masses." The skill with which he alternates between these different frames of self-reference, taking time to articulate a set of "reasoned" arguments and explanations, simultaneously informing and convincing his viewers, is undoubtedly the key criterion that makes his performance worth watching for "educated" viewers.

But the "interpretive contract" between Yaşar Nuri Öztürk and his wider, more heterogeneous audiences is based, I would suggest, on the anticipation that there will come a crucial moment in his performance when he will adopt a "combative" or "fighter frame." Nearly every Friday morning there comes a dramatic moment when he loses patience and bares his knuckles—boldly standing up (metaphorically) to state the truths that audiences know from elsewhere. This is when Yaşar Nuri Öztürk lapses into "I" (or when "we" becomes an all-inclusive term rather than self-referential) and he is transformed into a passionate fighter in a battleground of political adversaries, fighting on "our" behalf—not only those in the studio or at home but seemingly for the whole nation. During such "exceptional" moments the hiatus between Yaşar Nuri Öztürk's "expert" knowledge and the "lay" epistemology of audiences seems to disappear, and the studio participants burst into spontaneous applause (rather than respectful clapping). But, of course, it is precisely the anticipation of such "exceptional" moments that lends interest to his television performance and constitutes the highpoint (for lack of a better term) of the *Ayşe Özgün Show* for most viewers.

Yaşar Nuri Öztürk's statements during such moments of high drama are framed within a master binary opposition, which he repeats almost every week, as in the quotation above: "There are two kinds of Islam, one which has been sent by Allah and the other invented." And the only way of learning the Islam sent by Allah is for everyone to *read* the Quran.

Thus, for instance:

> YNÖ: I have been telling this *millet* to examine the Quran's original for the past twenty years. I tell them to take it out of the chests, to bring it down from the attics, and to read it. But the man who is supposed to read it does not know Arabic. They have told him, the perpetrators of this racket, don't touch it if you do not know Arabic. This racket, to protect itself, has sanctified Arabic. Now, according to these people, what is holy is not Allah's word. It is Arabic letters that are holy. We are saying that what is sacred is the message Cenab-i Hak has sent us. And we can learn this message when we read the Quran in the language we understand. The citizen listens to me and telephones the *müftü* offices. Can I read the Quran in Turkish? No permission, no such possibility.

Yaşar Nuri Öztürk's emphasis on *reading* the Quran rather than memorizing and reciting it in Arabic is obviously a very modernist stance. Ayşe Özgün interprets this as follows: "Hocam, you want everyone to acquire a *Kuran'i Kerim* and read it from beginning to end." But as the paragraph above reveals, Yaşar Nuri Öztürk continues to say much more than this. Not only does he bring up the politically charged issue of "vernacularization" and attack its opponents—as "perpetrators of a racket"—but refers directly to the office of the *müftü* (which is part of the centralized Directorate of Religious Affairs in Turkey).

When Yaşar Nuri Öztürk begins to attack "those" or "they" who benefit from "invented Islam," not only do they seem to increase in numbers but we discover that they are in "our midst." There are, for instance, the "*seytan evliyasi*" (the devil's saints or emissaries) who are the "profiteers" from Islam.

> YNO: Now they have brought this contemptible Islam into our midst. Now a Muslim cannot be close to Allah without paying a commission, without mortgaging his mind and belief. Now I am asking this mass, wasn't this mass Muslim before these profiteers came onto the scene? Now no one should expect to get anywhere by bowing [*secde*] to the devil's saints [*seytan evliyasi*]. If the Islamic world were to get anywhere by bowing, it would have become the leader [*efendi*] of the world. Turkey would have become the leader of the world. A mosque is being built

every six hours. In the six centuries of the Ottoman Empire, the number of mosques built was around fifteen thousand, in the sixty-five years of the Republic, the number of mosques has exceeded one hundred thousand. Why are they being built? There is something wrong here. Muslims must free themselves from those who first put artificial distances between themselves and God, and then ask for a commission to remove them.

The illustrative excerpts above are chosen from particular moments in Yaşar Nuri Öztürk's performance, when his facial expression and gestures imply that he has cast aside what he had come prepared to talk about (as an expert guest), and his voice and intonation suggest that he is now speaking "spontaneously." Within the anticipatory framework of the *Ayşe Özgün Show,* "we" (studio audiences, viewers at home, as well as Ayşe Özgün herself) expect and wait (respectfully) for the moment when Yaşar Nuri Öztürk will assume a "fighter" frame, lashing out against the enemies of "real Islam" rather than elaborating on what "real Islam" is.

Ayşe Özgün, as a shrewd and experienced producer, knows that such "electric moments" (her term) are crucial for her program ratings. During the interviews she narrated a "mistake" during the second year of the program: "We decided that instead of telling people to read the Quran, we would read it together on the program, chapter and verse. Our ratings fell immediately, so we gave up after two weeks." She lamented that "people were not interested in learning the Quran," immediately qualifying that she would never admit this in public.

Overall, during the five-year period when this particular program was on the air every Friday, Yaşar Nuri Öztürk's language and attacks have become progressively sharper, along with his growing visibility on commercial channels, in a range of other programs. When asked, program directors have one answer: "ratings."

A Heroic Fighter against "Fake" Islam?

Moving outward from the microcosm of the *Ayşe Özgün Show* to draw conclusions about Yaşar Nuri Öztürk's "ratings" on commercial television in general is obviously a hazardous task. The foregoing analysis suggests that a crucial component of "watching" him on television is his readiness to assume "a fighter" frame—cutting across different groups of viewers to engage them in a melodramatic conflict between "real" Islam and "corrupt" Islam. What lends him credibility as a "lone fighter" against forces of corruption is the recognition, on the part of diverse audiences, that he is a man of "scientific learning"—that is, that his scholarly knowledge of "real Islam" is formidable. So regardless of how ambivalent or even confused perhaps "we" (as his viewers or as Turkish people) might be about "real Islam," there can be no doubt about Yaşar Nuri Öztürk's own qualifications as a man of prodigious scholarship (since he continuously refers back to his own writings) and his perfect recall of the entire Quran (since he quotes exact words and phrases in Arabic along with their interpretations in Turkish). But, most important, of course, is the *urgency* of the ongoing battle in the present, which demands united opposition on the part of different groups of viewers.

When Yaşar Nuri Öztürk situates himself within a melodramatic conflict between "real" versus "invented/fake" Islam, he does not target "political Islam" directly but only "those people" who distort "real Islam" for their own gain. His true enemies are the "racketeers" or "profiteers" (*tezgahlar*), which might be translated into the everyday experience of his viewers in a variety of ways. In Turkey of the 1990s "they" might include Islamic Financial Houses that attract clients by offering "interest-free" banking. Or "those people" may be offshoots of religious orders that channel "great wealth" through foundations (*vakıf*). And, as in one of the direct quotations I have given above, "they" might also include people who solicit contributions from "innocent" believers to build a new mosque every other day. So each time Yaşar Nuri Öztürk begins to attack "profiteers" and "racketeers" (combined with the viewing experience itself), the timeless opposition between "real" versus "fake" Islam, one good, the other bad, both acquires fresh urgency and becomes an immediate problem calling for united opposition.

But why are (some) "Turkish people" deceived by these profiteers? Why don't they "wake up"? The answer appears to reside in "muddled thinking" based either on hearsay (*kulakdan dolma bilgiler*) or "superstition" (*hürafe*)—terms Yaşar Nuri Öztürk often uses interchangeably in his television performances. He frequently dismisses questions about the morality of everyday practices (such as the appropriateness of handshaking between men and women or the permissibility of men and women swimming together at the beach) as trivial because they amount to no more than "hearsay" rather than being based on true knowledge of the Quran. He continuously berates his audiences for believing what they hear from others, instead of reading the Quran to decide for themselves by "reasoning." Similarly he dismisses such "popular" rituals as visiting shrines of holy men or seeking help from healers as *hürafe*—superstitions that corrupt "real Islam." But the distinction between "muddled thinking" and *hürafe* (an assimilated word from Arabic) also connotes a symbolic hierarchy, between (modern) literate people who are simply confused and the (traditional) illiterate masses who *remain* steeped in superstition. Hence the word *hürafe* captures the time immemorial opposition between the literate culture of Sunni Orthodox Islam and the popular Islam of the periphery,[14] as well as its numerous reincarnations throughout Republican history enlightened elite versus uneducated masses, urban versus rural, modernity versus tradition. So, once again, Yaşar Nuri Öztürk's battle against *hürafe* in the immediate urgency of the present becomes part of a ceaseless struggle between Orthodoxy and heresy, between enlightenment and backwardness.

Yaşar Nuri Öztürk's struggle to rescue "real Islam" from *hürafe* and *tezgahlar*, then, invokes the familiar tropes of Turkish nationalism while simultaneously recasting them in the immediacy of the present. In the act of watching him on television, the contradictions, ambivalences, and ambiguities of the couplet "secular Muslim" recede into the background, as "we" *become* united in the fight against those perpetuating "fake Islam."

The "Young Turk" of the Divinity Establishment?

Public arguments acquire their meaning from what is known and anticipated on the part of those who listen, read, or watch. But their public nature means that they enter into circulation in cross-reference to other arguments, as part of a broader field of citations, controversies, and emissions. To assert an argument "publicly" means entering a field of interplay with other discourses, or what Warner (2002) describes as "a cross-citation field of many other people speaking." Circulation of arguments in public is therefore a "reflexive process" he suggests, rather than one of passive relay and mechanical diffusion. Arguments acquire "talk value" as they move in different spaces of circulation, mobilized, reframed, or challenged by interested strategic actors, both dominant and subordinate.

What has lent "talk value" to Yaşar Nuri Öztürk's polemical arguments—beyond his immediate appeal to television audiences—has been his readiness to publicly challenge the official stance of Turkey's Directorate of Religious Affairs on a variety of issues. Since he himself is a product and prominent member of the same establishment, he has come under heavy criticism within its closed circles as a "sensationalist" and "publicity seeker," accused of trivializing serious theological debates for the sake of ratings. But his arguments have found wider public resonance, because they came into public circulation at a time when the centralized Directorate of Religious Affairs was under growing political criticism, from multiple vantage points.

Yaşar Nuri Özturk's polemical arguments entered the public field amid a multiplicity of critical discourses that targeted the official stance and practices of the Directorate of Religious Affairs. The silence of Turkey's Divinity Establishment amid raging political controversy—or, more accurately perhaps, its efforts to maintain its official status above and outside public debate by refusing to respond to any and all public criticism—created a chasm, a silence if you will. Within this vacuum Yaşar Nuri Öztürk's solo voice was amplified, resonating beyond his immediate audiences, to be picked up and reframed by various strategic actors in the public arena. His ideas began to make headlines as "sensational news"—*because* they contradicted the official injunctions of the Directorate. And Yaşar Nuri Öztürk himself, ever the publicity seeker, seemed to bask in media attention as his arguments were interpreted and framed as "breaking taboos." Public speculation began to center on whether he was—as the popular weekly *Aktuel* put it boldly on its cover story in 1988—"the Young Turk of the Divinity Establishment?" or "the Ventriloquist of the Military?"

So the drama of "Yaşar Nuri Ozturk *versus* the Directorate of Religious Affairs" acquired an autonomy of its own as a public text, open to alternative political readings. Many of the "radical" ideas he propounded had a lengthy history of ideological struggle behind them. His arguments for vernacularization, for instance—such as translating the Arabic call to prayers (*ezan*) into Turkish, conducting mosque worship in Turkish, or reciting daily ritual prayers (*namaz*) in Turkish—have been subject to intense debate, negotiation, and compromise since the formative decades of Turkish nationalism. But when retold in the media-saturated environment of the 1990s, they *became* something new—the litmus test of political standing in the immediacy of the present. And, as such, they were transposed onto a different plane, reconfigured in the public arena in terms of "people's choice *versus* state controls." Whether Yaşar Nuri Öztürk was a "hero" or a "false hero" in this struggle remains open to question. But the drama itself, by repudiating the functionaries of the centralized state, and calling them to account for interfering with people's choice, offered the potential possibility of "freely choosing" to become united as "secular Muslims." Perhaps the "magic" of Yaşar Nuri Oztürk in the political conjuncture of the 1990s resided in making this impossible dream sound plausible.

In terms of substance, what produced the "phenomenon of Yaşar Nuri Öztürk" was a double-dynamic. His television audiences embraced him as a way of affirming who "we" are and "what we stand for" as secular Muslims. His statements were mobilized by different constituencies to concretize ongoing struggles over the issue of "whose interests" the Directorate of Religious Affairs promoted and "what it stood for" in the secular Republic of Turkey. Neither of these is reducible to the other, in the sense of what came before and what came after, or which was primary and which was secondary. What linked them together, in mutual feedback, was the historically specific ways in which "the affair of state" and "the affairs of religion" continue to be entangled in Turkey. The "phenomenon of Yaşar Nuri Öztürk" was both a product of this entanglement and part of its renegotiation in the political conjuncture of the 1990s in Turkey.

I began this essay by proposing the notion of a "televisual moment" as a way of capturing both the generality and also the specificity of the 1990s in Turkey. In the broadest sense, this was a historical moment when the blowing winds of neoliberalism in the transnational arena coincided with declining optimism and faith in the utopian promise of state-led development and progress in much of the postcolonial world. The entry of television into history at this particular moment, I suggested, brought into the foreground two opposing tendencies associated with the global expansion of media and communication networks. On the one hand, it revealed the fragility of a phalanx of "modern" institutions associated with the nation state, undermining official scripts of who "we" are and "what we stand for." On the other hand, it brought into play new modes of identification with the abstract nation, by annexing familiar motifs and themes from narratives of nationalism, and reproducing them through visual formats and popular genres of global media culture.

Focusing on the "phenomenon of Yaşar Nuri Oztürk" was a way of "cutting" into the dense political landscape of the late 1990s in Turkey, to explore how one of the key motifs of Turkish nationalism—"we are all secular Muslims"— was being reanimated through the visual formats and commodity logic of television. Rather than reinventing the unanswerable question of who is a secular Muslim, I assumed that, like all cultural identities, its boundaries are inherently blurred. By situating myself in the terrain of the present—wherein insurgent cultural politics of Islam, and of Kurdish nationalism, were intermingled with political discourses of neoliberalism and its anti-state rhetoric—I hoped to avoid the conceptual pitfalls of a genealogical account. Instead, I started out with the metamorphosis of Yaşar Nuri Öztürk into a "super-subject" on television, and tried to plot the overlapping constituencies for whom he "made sense" and the intersecting social spaces wherein his voice was amplified.

Yet even as I tried to map out the multiple meanings of what he was saying and the competing interpretations being constructed around them, additional aspects of the phenomenon I was investigating came into focus. The object of my analysis seemed to recompose itself as my search for situated knowledge continued. I had begun by thinking of him as a "super-subject" on television—addressing viewers in the first person to stabilize the perpetually shifting agendas of the moment, performing the "magic" of balancing out the moral from the immoral, right from wrong. Was this because audiences embraced him as a sermonizer in tune with the spirit of the times—a happy blending of Islamic theology, aerobics, the Internet, English, and a "modern" (uncovered) wife? His own self-positioning, however, was that of an eminent scholar. The primary content of his lengthy soliloquies on television, reminiscent of classroom lecturing, seemed to be pitched to literate, urban, middle-class audiences. So what was the secret of his magical "ratings"? How did he cut across multiple audience segments to bring them in front of the television set? This line of questioning led me to focus on moments of passionate intensity in Yaşar Nuri Öztürk's performance, when he assumed a "fighter frame" to lash out against the enemies of "real Islam." What brought diverse audience segments in front of the television set, and knit them together, I concluded, was the desire to watch him fight the perpetrators of "fake Islam"—the identities of whom invoked a shared fund of knowledge based on narratives of Turkish nationalism. The question of who "we" are and "what we stand for" *as secular Muslims* acquired facticity in the ongoing moral struggle between "real" and "fake Islam," even as the term, as an abstract concept and political practice, became more meaningless, implacable, and illusive. What seemed an impossible illusion to sustain—"we are all secular Muslims"—was fabricated in the heroic fight against "those" who benefited from "fake Islam."

If the line of questioning I pursued led me to a more layered understanding of his "magical" relationship with audiences, it also revealed the terra incognito of my research. What about the way that his arguments underwent public circulation? During the course of my research I had become increasingly aware of the difference between the primary content of Yaşar Nuri Öztürk's "political" sermons (addressed to viewers) and the way that his statements were selectively picked up and amplified as they entered public circulation. His "magical" television ratings and the "talk value" of his statements in public circulation were obviously linked. This link, however, was not a matter of temporal ordering in time (first one, then the other) but was politically defined and interactive. There existed (already) a range of controversies surrounding the centralized Director-ate of Religious Affairs in the political conjuncture of the late nineties. I risked the crudities of an abbreviated account in order to emphasize the preexistence of strategic interests (both dominant and subordinate) whose political agendas were at odds with the official policies of the Directorate. Within this politically charged context, the television persona Yaşar Nuri Öztürk proved to be a readily accessible signpost, lending concrete form to ongoing debates. His public ad-dresses provided a repertoire of statements likely to prove "controversial," which were immediately picked up, abridged in the journalistic catchphrases of the moment, and reproduced as the latest installment in an ongoing drama—Yaşar Nuri Öztürk versus the Directorate of Religious Affairs. I termed this a "public text," because it provided a popular idiom of "circulation," one that allowed for multiple, divergent interpretations of what the Directorate stood for and whose interests it served.

Returning to the notion of a "televisual moment," there is a *tension* between two opposing tendencies of fragmentation and affirmation that are embedded within the "televisual moment." How this tension *unfolds*, however, is "open-ended" in the sense that it is bound with prevailing power configurations, con-tingent events, and emergent resistances. Television is obviously not some sort of trans-historical agency, capable of lending direction to events. But it is far more than décor or wallpaper against which players enact their rehearsed parts. The claim of television to "reach everybody" opens up new discursive spaces and maps out new constituencies, augmenting some political voices and choices while muffling others. Thus any attempt to move beyond the generalities of a "televisual moment," to trace and unpack its unfolding in specific contexts, necessitates particularizing, or what William Sewell has named an "eventful" history.

Epilogue

As I was trying to knit together various strands of my research into a narrative conclusion, the incumbent coalition government fell apart, and new elections came on the political agenda. Yaşar Nuri Öztürk succumbed to the lure of publicity (very predictably) and announced his political candidacy on the ranks of the CHP (Republican People's Party) amid a media blitz. He was elected to parliament, on November 3, 2002, to be precise. He is currently seated (presumably) on the back benches of the national assembly, suffering the com-mon fate of all deputies from opposition parties, namely, oblivion. He is unlikely to be heard of again unless he becomes involved in corruption or a sex scandal. So outworking of political events have relegated Yaşar Nuri Öztürk, the person, into obscurity. He is now part of the very recent history of the present.

The landslide victory in the November 3 polls belonged to the AK (Justice and Development Party), which was defined by its critics as "Islamist." Having won a comfortable two-thirds majority in parliament, the newly inaugurated

AK government immediately rejected the label "Islamist." Both AK's new prime minister (Abdullah Gül) and its charismatic chairman (Recep Tayyip Erdogan) affirmed their belief in the separation of religion and state, and declared their vision of a new future—a modern, democratic, economically prosperous, secular, Muslim Turkey. This summation of incompatibilities suggests that the divisive issues that produced the "phenomenon of Yaşar Nuri Öztürk" will continue to haunt Turkish politics in the coming decade, in ways that remain to be investigated.

Notes

1. I use the notion of "a televisual moment" so as to avoid the universalistic connotations of the concept of a "millennial moment" developed by Comaroff and Comaroff (2000). So I have come up with a phrase that reiterates their emphasis on the significance of neoliberal discourses, and also highlights the concomitant boom in domestic media and consumer markets.

2. I refer to India and Indonesia specifically, because accounts of the changing media scene during the 1990s seem so remarkably similar to the Turkish case (Pendakur and Kapur 1997; Sen and Hill 2000; Rajagopal 2001).

3. Tsing (2000, 115) describes the 1990s decade in Indonesia as follows: "From the top of what was called a 'miracle,' Indonesia fell to the bottom of a 'crisis.' . . . So recently an exemplar of the promise of globalization, overnight became the case study of globalization's failures."

4. There is a vast literature on Turkey's neoliberal turn. For an overview and extensive bibliography, see Cizre-Sakallıoglu and Yeldan 2000. On the rise of an "Islamic economy" during this period, see Buğra 1999, 1998; Öniş 1997.

5. For a discussion on the interaction of markets and politics in the transformation of the media scene during the 1990s decade in Turkey, see Öncü 2000; forthcoming.

6. The expressions within quotation marks are all direct translations from Turkish. That they sound so familiar reveals how rapidly catchphrases from the global language of neoliberalism were appropriated by Turkish journalists and entered into public discourse as well as everyday language.

7. The paucity of research on the history of the Directory of Religious Affairs is remarkable. For a notable exception, see Tarhanli 1993.

8. What Langer (1998) describes as "the other news" or "tabloid news" has been main fare of prime time news programming since the mid-1990s in Turkey.

9. The concept of a "super-subject" was developed by Morse (1986). with specific reference to television news personalities. Although television producers use the word "magic" to describe Yaşar Nuri Öztürk's appeal to audiences, I prefer to avoid Weber's notion of charisma, used by Marshall (1999) to discuss the celebrity phenomenon in general. Morse's concept of a "super-subject" emphasizes the significance of direct address on television, in the subjective, conversational mode, which brings into play the powerful codes of equality and reciprocity in everyday talk. She suggests that when a super-subject speaks to *me,* the truth conditions or rules of verification of "secondary" or mediated experience are suspended, and what he says assumes the paramount reality

of direct experience. On how this is accomplished through visual signs, see Johansen 1999.

10. For a discussion of how Yaşar Nuri Öztürk's scholarly credentials set him apart, both from the notables of the state divinity establishment in Turkey (a closed community of scriptural scholarship) and also the publicly visible "Islamist intellectuals" whose antiestablishment "radical" rhetoric identifies them with political Islam, see Özcan 2000.

11. For three excellent books that offer grounded analyses of how Islam has penetrated the public culture and everyday experience of the 1990s decade in Turkey, see Saktanber 2002; Navaro-Yashin 2002; and White 2002. For a broader comparative perspective on politics of Islam in Turkey, see Zubaida (1996, 2000).

12. The "analysis" I offer is essentially based on video recordings of ten programs broadcast on different Fridays between 1998 and 2000, "randomly" selected by the archivists of ATV channel. I have transcribed these into writing, as well as watching them repeatedly—alone, with students, as well as with colleagues willing to spare the time. I have also interviewed Ayşe Özgün at length, and had to "reciprocate" by becoming an "expert guest" on one of her programs. I have deliberately avoided interviewing Yaşar Nuri Öztürk himself.

13. Ayşe Özgün describes her involvement with television in terms of "reaching the people." She "wants to do something for this country." But she also admits that "we have not been able to reach the mass [kitleye inmeyi başaramdık]." Here is one of her illustrations: "I was in the south, stopped and got out of the car. People were picking cotton in the heat with Omo [detergent] cartons on their heads. They all came rushing to embrace me. They watch my program. But when I ask, 'do you do what we say?' they mumble 'things are different here.'" So Ayşe Özgün is the prototype—almost a caricature—of modern/modernizing woman of her generation. Her life story and the ingredients of her success as a talk show hostess are interesting in their own right but are beyond the immediate concerns of this essay.

14. According to Mardin (1969) the word hürafe has been in circulation since the end of the nineteenth century, with more or less the same connotations; that is, it is used to dismiss all popular beliefs and practices associated with oral traditions of "folk" Islam as "superstition."

References

Bayat, Asef. 2002. Piety, Privilege and Egyptian Youth. *ISIM Newsletter* 10 (2): 23.

Buğra, Ayse. 1999. *Islam in Economic Organizations,* Istanbul: TESEV Publications.

———. 1998. Class, Culture and State: An Analysis of Interest Representation by Two Turkish Business Associations. *The International Journal of Middle East Association* 30 (4): 521–539.

Carpignano, Paolo, and R. Andersen, S. Aranowitz, W. Dizazio. 1990. "Chatter in the Age of Electronic Reproduction: Talk Television and the 'Public Mind.'" *Social Text*, no. 25/26: 33–55.

Cizre-Sakallıoglu, Ümit, and Erinç Yeldan. 2000. Politics, Society and Financial Liberalization: Turkey in the 1990s. *Development and Change* 31: 481–508.

Comaroff, Jean, and John Comaroff. 2000. Millennial Capitalism: First Thoughts on a Second Coming. *Public Culture* 12 (2): 291–343.

Ellis, John. 1999. Television as Working-Through. In *Television and Common Knowledge,* ed. Jostein Gripsrud, 55–70. London: Routledge.

Johansen, Anders. 1999. Credibility and Media Development. In *Television and Common Knowledge,* ed. Jostein Gripsrud, 159–172. London: Routledge.

Langer, J. 1998. *Tabloid Television: Popular Journalism and the "Other News."* London: Routledge.

Livingstone, Sonia, and P. K. Lunt. 1994. *Talk on Television: The Critical Reception of Audience Discussion Programs.* London: Routledge.

Mardin, Şerif. 1997 [1969]. *Din ve İdeoloji.* Istanbul: Iletişim.

Marshall, P. D. 1999. *Celebrity and Power: Fame in Contemporary Culture.* Minneapolis: University of Minnesota Press.

Morse, Margaret. 1986. The Television News Personality and Credibility: Reflections on the News in Transition. In *Studies in Entertainment: Critical Approaches to Mass Culture,* ed. T. Modleski, 55–79. Bloomington and Indianapolis: Indiana University Press.

Navaro-Yashin, Yael. 2002. *Faces of State: Secularism and Public Life in Turkey.* Princeton, N.J.: Princeton University Press.

Öncü, Ayşe. 2000. The Banal and the Subversive: Politics of Language on Turkish Television. *European Journal of Cultural Studies* 3 (2): 296–318.

———. Forthcoming. Interaction of Markets and Politics: The Remaking of Turkey's Media Industries in the 1990s. *Boğaziçi University Journal,* Istanbul.

Öniş, Ziya. 1997. The Political Economy of Islamic Resurgence in Turkey: The Rise of the Welfare Party in Perspective. *Third World Quarterly* 18 (4): 743–766.

Özcan, Esra. 2000. New Configurations of Islam in Contemporary Turkey: The Case of Yaşar Nuri Öztürk, Unpublished master's thesis, Boğaziçi University, Istanbul.

Pendakur, Manjunath, and Jyotsna Kapur. 1997. Think Globally, Program Locally: Privatization of Indian National Television. In *Democratizing Communication? Comparative Perspectives on Information and Power,* ed. Mashoed Bailie and Dwayne Winseck, 197–217. London: Creskill Champton.

Rajagopal, Arvind. 2001. *Politics after Television: Religious Nationalism and the Reshaping of the Indian Public.* Cambridge: Cambridge University Press.

Saktanber, Ayse. 2002. *Living Islam: Women, Religion and the Politicization of Culture in Turkey.* London: Tauris.

Sen, Krishna, and David T. Hill. 2000. *Media, Culture and Politics in Indonesia.* New York: Oxford University Press.

Tarhanli, İştar B. 1993. *Müslüman Toplum, Laik Devlet: Türkiye 'de Diyanet İşteri Başkanlığı.* Istanbul: Afa Yayincilik.

Tsing, Anna. 2000. Inside the Economy of Appearances. *Public Culture* 12 (1): 115–144.

Warner, Michael. 2002. Publics and Counterpublics. *Public Culture* 14 (1): 49–90.

White, Jenny B. 2002. *Islamist Mobilization in Turkey: A Study in Vernacular Politics.* Seattle: University of Washington Press.

Zubaida, Sami. 1996. Turkish Islam and National Identity. *Middle East Report,* April–June.

———. 2000. Trajectories of Political Islam: Egypt, Iran and Turkey. In *Religion and Democracy,* ed. David Marquant and Ronald Nettler. Oxford: Oxford University Press.

12 Gods in the Sacred Marketplace: Hindu Nationalism and the Return of the Aura in the Public Sphere

Sudeep Dasgupta

Mankind loses religion as it moves through history, but the loss leaves its mark behind.

—Max Horkheimer, *Critical Theory*

Mass media imagery has become a seductive site where one glimpses the complexity of the "Nostalgia for the Present" (Jameson 1994, 279) in contemporary society. And what better place to begin than with that postmodern phenomenon par excellence—television. Let us begin, then, with a fragment from Indian television. The glitzy, hybrid globalized programming that preaches the resurgence of local, pan-Indian identity and India as an equal (if not superior) partner in global culture can be glimpsed in a popular MTV music video entitled "Jai Jai Shiv Shankar." From the opening close-up shot of a pair of feet that casts off its wooden *chappals* to don Adidas sneakers, the video speeds through a high-tempo song that combines the rhythms of the *ghatam*, techno, and Bollywood musical styles as it narrates the happy marriage of tradition and modernity and, in the process, calls both into question. The little novice monk in his Adidas shoes is speeding through the landscape toward the door of a matronly, white-haired Indian woman, where he delivers the message that she has just won the "Video Ga Ga" contest. As she collapses to the ground in pleasurable disbelief, a muscular bare-chested man clad in a *dhoti* launches into the first chords of "Jai Jai Shiv Shankar" aided by his buxom muse. As the man and woman swap clothes ranging from golden swimsuits and mini-skirts to rural clothing reminiscent of Ram's exile in the forest, a bemused ascetic under a banyan tree rocks to the infectious beat. Mobile phones, Karl Lagerfeld sunglasses, gym-toned male and female bodies all vie for space among the faces of religious figures in the acoustic space of folk drumbeats and the popular verses of old Hindi-film classics redone as a techno-mix. The enduring popularity of such representations of modern India where traditional markers of a recrudescent past are

Fig. 12.1. Moments of Transition. From wooden slippers to Adidas trainers (screen capture, *Jai Jai Shiv Shankar MTV*).

coeval with the high-tech lifestyles of urban India exemplify the mass-mediated imagination of a syncretic worldview.

Rather than focus on the seductive appeal of cross-cultural mish-mash evidenced in such a video clip, and move from an analysis of visual culture at the surface to grand pronouncements of the "postmodern social condition," this chapter probes below the surface of such visual proliferation and relationally considers how processes of identity-formation, the constitution of the public sphere, and the question of the aura are symptomized in visual culture. An empirically concrete historical analysis of the present, then, would situate and conceptualize how resurgent discourses of religious identity within the public sphere can be analyzed through and with changes in visual culture. To do a "history of the present" thus implies a critical distance from the fascinating imagery of consumer culture in order to consider how "tradition" is currently being re-invoked. Fredric Jameson reminds us that "historicity is . . . neither a representation of the past nor a representation of the future . . . it can first and foremost be defined as a perception of the present as history; that is, as a relationship to the present which somehow defamiliarizes it and allows us that distance from immediacy" (1994, 2984). The key words in this quotation ("representation," "perception," "relationship") underline the conceptual frames of the analysis of Hindu nationalism and consumerism that follow. "Critical distance" is crucial in order to defamiliarize the seductive appeal of such imagery so as to situate what our relationship is to the representations of the present which the mass media now provide. Such a defamiliarization would enable revisiting the contemporary discourses on marginality, postcolonial identity, and especially the "return of religion" within public discourse.

Intellectually savvy commentators for some time now have rightly rejected the triumphalist and teleological *grands récits* of historical inevitability and progress that subtended the discourse of Western Enlightenment. Their political investments in rescuing the margins (and the "marginal") from obscurity and dragging them into the light of day might nevertheless have opened a Pandora's box. For if a univocal and transcendental logic that found expression in the "voice from nowhere" must now be abandoned, there is no guarantee that "alternative discourses" might not slot in as easily, if not more complexly, within the rejected paradigm. Religious nationalism, to take one potent example circulating in popular and intellectual circles, is now (problematically) cast as a "return of the repressed," the dark underbelly of postmodernity, that threatens the stability of a vocal discourse of triumphalist capitalist globalization. In this chapter I want to look at one visual discourse that vocalizes its alterity to the reigning hegemony of contemporary globalization. However, as my own narrative is cobbled-together, it should become apparent that discourses of hybridity, "the margin," and "the politics of minoritization" do not possess any a priori, ontological claim to resistance against discourses of modernization and linear progress. The theoretically informed empirical study below, then, is ranged at two targets: the political discourses of contemporary religious nationalism, as well as the hegemonic discourses of hybridity, migrancy, and liminality within the academy.

Visual culture analyses have yielded an impressive set of diagnoses of the contemporary postmodern condition. In a sense, the phenomenological intensities of reading images as they circulate through the complex spatial and temporal dimensions of contemporary "global culture" have provided eloquent arguments for the destabilization of notions of identity, the making of meaning, and wholeness. But what if this fluidity of contemporary visual culture were perceived through the seemingly organic, identitarian, and narrow logic of religious discourses? By focusing on the complex interplay between the ecology of global media in India, and the stridently identitarian discourse of Hindu nationalism, I will explore how the political and cultural explanations thus generated construct notions of cultural identity that ground themselves on the complex dialectical processes of the local and the global. Methodologically it is by analyzing the concept of the "aura" in Walter Benjamin's texts that my analysis will track the nexus between economic and cultural value in the creation of a fluid and complex notion of Hindu Indian identity. The argument I present briefly connects our considerations around Benjamin's notion of the "aura" to Habermas's articulation of the "public sphere." Such an articulation provides the entry point for an analysis of the political and economic purchase of the discourse of cultural identity within contemporary Hindu nationalism.

The Aura of Modernity, the Poverty of Experience

Benjamin's reflections on the concept-metaphor of the aura were located at those changing media that were seen as prime signifiers of modernity. Most commentators have been tempted, therefore, to see his reflections on the aura as a final farewell to that politically conservative dimension of cultural production whose death knell had been sounded by technical reproduction. Hence it is necessary to immediately point out that Benjamin's concern with the aura predated the "Work of Art" essay by at least four years. In his "Little History of Photography" from 1931, Benjamin's fascination with the epistemological and ontological character of the photographic image's political dimensions were already sufficiently dialectical so as to preclude the populist readings of his work in cultural studies (Benjamin 1927–34, 507–530). Benjamin argued that "the photographer was confronted in the person of every client, with a member of a rising class equipped with an aura that had seeped into the very fold's of the man's frock coat" (ibid., 517). What could provisionally be called the "content" of the photograph prior to its being caught in the play of light is thus endowed with an aura. Here Benjamin underlines that the particular symbolic meanings attached to the *object* of the photographer's lens provide the photograph with an auratic appeal. In the case above, the authority conferred on the photograph is the result of the particular object being represented—a member of "a rising class" and the accoutrements ("the frock coat") which signify a certain social standing of respectability and power at a particular historical moment. Hence it is worth emphasizing that, if the object of a work of art (including photography, film, or television) has particular symbolic meanings which signify power and authority, the fact of it having been mechanically reproduced does not *necessarily* mean that the result is a "loss of the aura."

Further, the aura, rather than being erased in the act of mechanical reproduction, is also reconstructed through the techniques of re-presentation; thus,

> the most precise technology can give its products a magical value, such as a painted picture can never again have for us. After 1880, though, photographers made it their business to simulate the aura which had been banished from the picture with the suppression of darkness through faster lenses, exactly as it was banished from reality by the deepening degeneration of the imperialist bourgeoisie. They saw it as their task to simulate this aura using all the arts of retouching, and especially the so-called gum print. (ibid., 517)

Benjamin emphasizes that a "magical value" can be layered onto an artwork through certain techniques—for our moment, one can see this in the sphere of advertising, for example, where technical possibilities enable certain "ideals" of beauty to be represented, or in media like MTV where special effects and digital technology are not just technical facts, but their increasing visual sophistication are used to attract larger audiences and have a symbolic value that implies being on the "cutting edge."

It is crucial at this point to point out that, for Benjamin, the aura is "a strange weave of space and time: the unique appearance or semblance of distance, no matter how close it may be" (ibid., 518). The aura, then, is understood primarily in the fact that the object perceived is placed at a certain spatial and temporal remove from its intended audience. This "distance effect" (for example, a particular painting exists in only one place so that one goes to the Louvre to see da Vinci's *La Gioconda*) confers a particular authority on the artwork. The "aura" that accrues to a work of art is understood primarily in terms of the legitimation of authority, given that only certain people have access to the artwork, and that access signifies, for instance, a particular class—enabled privilege. The aura also signifies authority in that its distanciation from its audience confers a socially recognized privilege on those sanctioned to maintain this distance—for example, the priest (and hence the church) to whom proximity to the holiest parts of the altar is sanctioned gives these spaces within the church an auratic appeal, whereas parishioners are denied that proximity and thus implicitly recognize the authority of clerical power.

The aura of a work of art derives from it singularity in terms of its specific location in a particular time and place, and the fact that this time/space dimension is unique—"Even the most perfect reproduction of a work of art is lacking in one element: its presence in time and space, its unique existence at the place where it happens to be" (Benjamin 1968, 220). It is in ritual and religion that Benjamin locates the particular retention of the aura of the unique work of art. The conditions of possibility for the aura is thus linked to the specificity of its time-space dimension. With technical reproduction this uniqueness of the work of art is eroded given that it becomes available for experience in more proximate and varied situations. The question that immediately arises regards the function of the aura in relation to temporality and spatiality, and its place in history as a source of legitimation for linear narratives of progress (hence the relevance of a discussion of the aura for a critique of modernity as "development"). As will become evident below, the particular time-space nexus that accrues around images under globalization results precisely in the recoding of the auratic rather than its disappearance.

Benjamin insists that technical reproducibility degrades the aura of traditional art, in the sense that the specific time and place of the appreciation of an art piece, concretized first through ritual and then religion, is lost at present, given that, "that which withers in the age of mechanical reproduction is the aura of the work of art . . . the technique of production detaches the reproduced object from the domain of tradition. . . . And in permitting the reproduction to meet the beholder or listener in his own particular situation, it reactivates the object produced" (ibid., 211).[1] This short quote is dense in its suggestions. First, tradition, located for Benjamin in ritual and religion, loses its hold in time and place on the work of art. Here it must be stated that, for Benjamin, tradition is not some fixed static object. As he puts it, "The uniqueness of a work of art is inseparable from its being embedded in the fabric of tradition. This tradition is thoroughly alive and extremely changeable" (ibid., 223). The work of art, however, when released from its place in a changeable tradition (the relevance for religious media is evident) is not left to free-float outside the grasp of the aura. It is re-embedded in "the particular situation" of its reception, and, in the process, is "reactivated." This last point is crucial. The reactivation of the aura of the work of art in mass-mediated society is not the same aura as in antiquity or the classical age. However, this dimension is reinvigorated not by its proximity to a fixed time and place but rather by its relationship to the particular power relations within which it is re-embedded. It is in the reception of an artwork that the aura can be reactivated, as a result of the particular symbolic meanings that accrue to it and that are related to its subject matter and its mode of presentation at a specific historical moment. It would be a mistake to assume that the aura vanishes with technological mediation; rather, its character changes given its displacement from the time and space of tradition in ritual and religion to the mobile and fragmented temporality and spatiality of modern experience (*Erlebnis*).[2]

From the above discussion of Benjamin's understanding of the "aura" one could summarize as follows: the possibility (rather than necessity) of the reappearance of the aura; that such a reactivation of the aura is necessarily a politically interested act at a particular historical moment; that such an act serves to legitimize social authority through the medium of visual culture; that this act is made possible through the selection of a certain subject matter and decisions about its mode of representation. It should be emphasized that, for Benjamin, this persistence of the aura is not an ontological given but instead is the result of *the aestheticization of politics* in the interests of dominant social classes. A great deal more can be said about the aura, but I focus on these aspects above not only because they hardly see the light of day within contemporary intellectual culture but also because they complicate the more celebratory aspects of Benjamin's own argument in the "Work of Art" essay. It is important to note that even in that essay he has a properly dialectical understanding of the technologically mediated work of art, whose reception cannot be guaranteed in politically progressive terms and as an escape from social authority—after all, he did not fail to point out that it was fascism that had most effectively harnessed these media through the inculcation of an aesthetics of contemplation rather than action.

Sophisticated technological developments, then, have the capability of underwriting the positions of power of dominant social groups within the contemporary moment through particular modes of representation and of certain subjects. For the purpose of my argument, the question of history is critical—but history not as some easily accessible and representable "object" but as the unrepresentable horizon within which we understand the politics of representation and legitimation of social authority. For obviously neither the modes of representation nor the objects to be represented remain the same, and decisions on the above two dimensions are necessarily imbricated in questions of power.

Benjamin's attack on historicism (the teleological and linear nature of which was the target of our contemporary intellectual critique) must therefore be conjoined to our investigation of visual culture's auratic appeal, for it would be nonsensical and ahistorical to make any historically blind claims for the ontological status of the politics of the image. Often it is precisely this sort of ahistorical and historicizing move that has been exemplified in cultural criticism that takes the death of the aura as a sign for populist cultural studies. For any claim for the death of the aura must be situated at a particular historically specific moment within a social formation whose conflictual character requires the legitimation of dominant social classes.

It is this question of domination and social power that inspired Jürgen Habermas's investigation into the *bürgerliche Öffentlichkeit* that emerged in the eighteenth century with the rise of generalized commodity exchange, an educated reading public, and mass media.

> The bourgeois public sphere may be conceived above all as the sphere of private people come together as a public; they soon claimed the public sphere regulated from above against the public authorities themselves, to engage them in a debate over the general rules governing relations in the basically privatized but publicly relevant sphere of commodity exchange and social labor. The medium of this political confrontation was peculiar and without historical precedent: people's public use of their reason [*öffentliches Räsonnement*]. In our [German] usage this term i.e., *räsonnement* unmistakably preserves the polemical nuances of both sides: simultaneously the invocation of reason and its disdainful disparagement as merely malcontent griping. (Habermas 1989, 27)

In the light of the preceding discussion, the link between the politics of representation and the representation of political authority within the public sphere becomes readily apparent. For our discussion, the "medium" in question is not just Reason but its own remediation through technologically reproduced mass media such as satellite TV. Further, Habermas's own formulation is nuanced enough to signal that Reason is not exercised at the expense of what we now call "affect" but that the passions play an important role in this process. If this is a generous reading of Habermas, it is worth recalling that, in his own attempts to justify the moral bases for intersubjective communication, he is left with no alternative but to defer to the ongoing process of the community in question's own consensual mechanisms that cannot be purely "rational" in dispassionate fashion. While Habermas's position cannot be cast as some kind of postmodern, libidinal, and nonrational theory for intersubjective communication (and his argument is all the stronger for that), neither can it be circumscribed as a purely dispassionate attachment to the exercise of the cognitive capabilities of participants in a conversation. Having framed the analysis that follows in terms of the aura in Benjamin and the role of media in Habermas's formulation of the political character of the public sphere, here I briefly lay out the historical conjuncture within which Hindu nationalism articulates its claims to identity and alterity within the complex narratives of globalization.

Screening the Past

It is because we want to be modern that our desire to be independent and creative is transposed on to our past.

—Partha Chatterjee, *"Our Modernity," The Present History of West Bengal: Essays in Political Criticism*

The complicated social and economic history of the Indian nation-state is all but erased within the contemporary public discourse in the mass media and among mainstream political leaders. Presenting the current moment as a narrative is necessarily, then, a political coding of the value of cultural and economic identity, often in religious terms. After Independence in 1947, the Indian nation-state was largely defined in economic and political terms as part of the Non-Aligned movement. Refusing, at least in political discourse, the paths of capitalist and communist development, it sought to chart an independent passage through the stormy waters of first- and second-bloc political and economic hegemony. In terms of the discursive constitution of the nation, then, independence from integration into either the free-market or the state-led economic systems was avowed with a simultaneous assertion of sovereignty in political matters and international détente. In the sphere of culture, the state propagated a discourse of secularism and recognition of difference under the slogan "unity in diversity." The state-controlled mass media, particularly All-India Radio and Doordarshan (DD) television, were the organs for the constitution of a notion of public belonging to the nation in terms of a secular nationalism that emphasized unity as well as group specificity in terms of language, religion, geographical region, and so on. Most important, for our purposes this relationship between the state, the media, and an affective belonging to the nation was strongly anti-consumerist. It is worth recalling that the first prime minister of India, Jawaharlal Nehru, initially had serious reservations about the introduction of television which he saw as a luxury the country could ill afford given the many serious problems it confronted in delivering basic needs to the majority of the population. Thus when DD began its function as a state organ it was strongly pedagogical, anti-consumerist, and directed primarily to those target audiences seen as needing help through education.

The introduction of commercial advertising within the DD structure already marked the beginning of a sea change in the role of TV as a medium. The first educational soap opera, *Hum Log* (*We People*), formulated to spread family planning behavior, quickly became the vehicle for the phenomenal marketing success of Nestle's Maggi Instant Noodles.[3] Commercially sponsored programming led to a Leavisite condemnation of popular culture in certain intellectual and bureaucratic circles. The increasing reliance on the market, particularly during the years of Rajiv Gandhi's leadership, opened the floodgates and the mass media, especially TV, exploded into a plethora of satellite TV networks from within the country but most noticeably from major international players such as Rupert Murdoch's STAR Network and Time-Warner's CNN, BBC, and others. The crucial shifts in this period beginning in 1990, during the U.S.-led Iraq Gulf War, could be seen in terms of ownership, kinds of programming, and audiences. From a primarily state-controlled media environment, the new ecology of globalization led to an influx of programming previously unseen and primarily U.S.-produced such as *Dynasty, Baywatch,* and *Phil Donahue.* Later this content was to shift dramatically to indigenously produced programming and a localization of the broadcasting from the global players. Further, given that such programming was satellite-based, the primary clientele were urban, middle-class households, often part of housing colonies that shared one satellite dish. What currently marks the TV scene in India is that the most popular programming content is that which is considered "hybrid," featuring "Hinglish" as its language and owned by Indians and nonresident Indian corporations such as Zee TV, SET (Sony Entertainment Television), and STAR (with Murdoch now holding a minority share). These highly popular programs include TV serials, televised religious epics, and film-based musical programming. Most strikingly, the earlier discourse against consumerism and in favor of "building the nation" through education and information has all but disappeared. Rather, the logic of the commodity form has penetrated not just advertising-led programming but the content as well, through strategies such as prizes for viewers, lifestyle programming like interior decoration and fashion shows, and the most popular program of all, *Kaun Banega Krorepati? (Who Wants to Be a Millionaire?),* hosted by aging film icon Amitabh Bachchan.

The hybrid mix of religious imagery and consumer sacrality visualized in the MTV clip that opened this chapter cannot be understood without placing it within a historical horizon which shifted dramatically in economic terms from the earlier, relatively sequestered period of partial state control to the present wholesale wooing of foreign capital and consumer goods. Crucial for the purpose of this argument is an insistence that this switch in economic conditions was not the result of a rationally thought-out strategy for increasing prosperity but instead was precipitated by a series of global crises such as the rise in oil prices after the Gulf War and the consequent burgeoning internal debt of the state. Thus it was the crisis situation within the economy and the inevitable turn to foreign lending institutions such as the World Bank that led to a massive influx of consumer goods and foreign capital investment into the country, often on terms most beneficial to the emergent Indian petite bourgeoisie and multinational corporations. Some important points need to be made with regard to this observation.

The historicist narrative that underwrites present triumphalist discourses of the reinvigorated nation dissimulate this crisis and recode it as the "natural" consequence of the development of the "Indian nation." It is precisely here that Jameson's call for critical distance and Benjamin's attack on teleological historicism become particularly relevant. Further, this discourse of newfound consumption-fueled prosperity is often transcribed in the form of religious belonging. However, as opposed to discourses of the "return of the repressed" of religion under capitalist modernity, this discourse of religion in India is grounded on vague notions of "culture" understood as *sanskriti*, rather than through some foundational texts. This polyvalence that structures religious discourse allows religious nationalism a fluid modality that can happily engage in the most pronounced consumerist practices of Western-led globalization without feeling in the least dissipated by "materialism" which was anathema to Nehruvian socialism. This development is, of course, partly to be understood as a consequence of the very impossibility of granting "Hinduism" some kind of objecthood as a firm, unitary, and historical thing. It has also to do with the specific political strategies and electoral bases through which it came to dominate the Indian political scene since the late 1980s.

The Sacred Market and the Profane Temple: Descartes as Guru

After the debacle of Indira Gandhi's corruption-ridden reign, and her son's inept attempts at "modernizing" the nation-state, the precipitous economic crises in the country in the late 1980s coincided with the emergence of the Hindu rightists' Bharatiya Janata Party (BJP) as a powerful player on the national scene (Hansen 1998, 291–314). It is crucial to remember that the BJP has traditionally been a party against state involvement in the economy, spoken consistently in the name of "the people" as opposed to the Congress—an undertaking of constructing the people in a pedagogic project—and has shifted its strategies of political mobilization depending on particular conjunctures. The dominant social groups within the Hindu Right (itself a deeply fragmented but nevertheless powerful social bloc) have thus been in favor of greater involvement in the global economy, have come from positions of relative power in terms of disposable incomes, and have often couched their political rhetoric in terms of their "Hinduness" (*Hindutva*).

The chief ideologue of the Hindu Right, Deendayal Upadhyaya, always maintained that the core of Hindutva and the nation lay in its "*Chiti*" or soul, which must remain unchanged whatever the shifts in culture (*sanskriti*), since the latter must not deviate from the former (Upadhyaya 1992 [1962]). This wonderfully elastic philosophical duality has consistently grounded the Hindu Right's "constructive engagement" with metropolitan capital and global TV while still claiming an increasingly masculinist and aggressive religious nationalism. In the context of its integration into the BJP's *economic* platform in their document "Humanistic Approach to Economic Development," the relationship between discourses of cultural purity and global capitalism have important implications for notions of cultural homogenization. In this case, discourses of the "nature" of a nation's "ethos" can be characterized as expressions of cultural autonomy, particularly since they are framed in opposition to the "Western" discourses of secularism and "socialism" that the supposed elites of the country have propounded. Thus Hindutva claims an embattled position in relation to the "establishment" and speaks the language of populism, while positing an "authentic" culture. Further, the focus on the "all-round welfare of the human personality" and the insistent critique of the concentration of economic and political power in favor of decentralization coincides neatly with the insistence of organizations like the International Monetary Fund (IMF) on the retreat of the state from the functioning of the market and the free play of market forces (Jaffrelot 1996, 18). The ideology of individualism and humanism (retooled in the guise of an "Indian ethos") coincides neatly with the ideology of the "free market" and consumerism. What is crucial is that this constitution of "Indian Culture" is integral to the dynamic of global capitalism, rather than in opposition to the dynamic of "cultural imperialism."[4]

The Hindu Right has successfully used the mass media to mobilize public support: in terms of press exposure, it has at least one publication in each language, a nationwide network of correspondents, sophisticated use of video technology, particularly by the VHP, incorporating themes and genres from popular culture as well as well-known film celebrities, live performances, and the use of popular music modeled on film songs. Much of the success of communal organizations in mobilizing popular support has been through their successful insertion into the *secular* activities of rural and urban communities, by providing much needed recreational, cultural, and welfare services. The widening of the appeal of the Hindu Right is thus closely related to the failure of the state in guaranteeing public welfare, a failure that has been accelerated by its further retreat as a consequence of the imperatives of the "free market" and deregulation.

Religious discourse and ideology has always lent itself to a trans-local modality, whatever its pretensions. In the present context, the contact zone opened up by globalization in all its forms not surprisingly sees a "return to the source." However, this return cannot be framed as the revenge of the repressed but rather as the production of an already existing *modality* of the religious as a spatially and temporally expansive and mobile discursive formation. Hindu nationalism, in fact, simultaneously invokes scriptural authority to finance its traffic with the economic and technological imperatives of globalization, and justifies globalization in its contemporary capitalist expansion as the culmination of what "Hindu philosophy" has been saying all along—the *Dasein* of Capital concretized in the lived reality of Indian society. As Walter Benjamin noted, however, the lived reality (*Erlebnis*) of modernity derives its "richness" precisely in the shock of the ever new, the paradoxical enervation of affect that extinguishes the fullness of experience (*Erfahrung*) amid the phantasmagoria of continual consumption.[5] The necessity of constellating a materialist critique of the sacral signifier of Hinduism and the virtual promises of endless consumption under globalization increases the more that religious doctrines and political practice assert their absolute separation from the concreteness of socioeconomic processes and circumscribe themselves in the idealized realm of statecraft and culture. The Hindu Right in India, through a variety of strategies, always shifting and contingent to the field of political practice, alternately invokes scripture here, "culture" there, bemoans the materialism of the West while sanctifying the free market in the idiom of "native tradition."

At present, Hindu "missionaries" are being trained and sent abroad to work among diasporic populations, projects that yield lucrative financial benefits. The Internet is being used to construct a "nation of Hindutva" that spans the globe and on which services ranging from access to political speeches and government documents of the ruling party to "cyber-rituals" find a place. The "nation of Hindutva" group argues that

> the primary weapon in the defense of the Hindu Rashtra has been identified as information and publicity. This is achieved by targeting all forms of media and promoting the cause of the Hindu Rashtra through the various media channels. With the incredible surge in popularity of the Internet as one of the major forms of publication, it is essential that the Hindu community are [sic] able to keep up with things. The vast array of anti-Hindu and anti-Indian propaganda being spread around via the medium of the Internet means that it is becoming increasingly necessary for this disinformation to be countered. It is here that the Nation of Hindutva website aims to strike, and by publishing information, as well as acting as a resource center to various other related sites on the WWW, the website aims to promote the cause of the Hindu Rashtra internationally.[6]

The Rashtriya Swayamsevak Sangh (RSS; a leading Hindutva organization) now offers *cybershakas* (physical drills) on the Internet where one can sit in one's room anywhere in the globe and participate in the regular exercises and drills of the organization using one's computer. E-Prarthana, an Internet site, provides the faithful with the daily opportunity to offer prayers ("click on a deity"!) to more than 450 temples in India "for all your personal and business needs and get the blessings shipped to you."[7] For every archana performed, devotees are guaranteed two free gifts such as a designer Ganesha clock, while the site's "shopping mall" provides the instantaneous purchase of statues, books, cassettes, and CDs. The dissemination of Hinduism throughout the globe, through the activities of the Vishwa Hindu Parishad, the Overseas Friends of the BJP, the RSS calling itself the Hindu Swayamsevak Sangh (HSS) outside India, and several affiliate organizations and networks of support such as the American Hindu Students' Council and other "cultural heritage" organizations, as well as numerous religious groups and foundations set up by diasporic Indian Hindu communities, particularly in the West, are clear evidence of the bankruptcy of a view that sees narrow, sectarian, national or subnational, and premodern responses as the necessary outcome of globalization.

If Hindutva has gained and is exploiting the hi-tech dimensions of globalization, particularly among diasporic groups, the discourse in India itself around accelerated consumerism and questions of identity are increasingly couched in terms of Hinduism. For example:

> The BJP believes in a new social and economic order which is non-exploitative, cooperative and harmonious, and which provides full play to individual initiative and dignity. The multifarious urges and aspirations—spiritual, intellectual, eco-

nomic and social—of the citizens have to be reconciled and harmonized. This approach follows from our national heritage and from the concepts of Gandhiji's Ram Rajya and Pandit Deen Dayal Upadhyaya's Integral Humanism. The holistic, total and comprehensive philosophy must suffuse all of us in national effort toward all-round economic development. (*BJP Economic Resolutions* 1995, 1–2)

The focus on individualism is seen as a response to the stultifying consequences of the traditional socialist state while at the same time linking this individualism to an organic notion of "Hindu" culture.

The discursive consolidation of a transnational Hindu identity is embedded with the economic and political dimensions of globalization, and this can be seen in numerous discourses around the place of Hindu wisdom in a transnational context. On the eve of the millennium, Francois Gautier, writing in the *Indian Express* proclaimed:

> But there is something infinitely more important, which India can bring to the West. And that is her spirituality. India is a vast and ancient land which alone has managed to keep within herself thanks to the stubborn will of her people and by the silent *tapasaya* of her yogis hidden in their Himalayan caves the immaculate truth, the ultimate knowledge, the secret of our destiny. At a time when the world has never been as disoriented as it is now; at a time when mankind is erring on the road to evolution; at a time when man has forgotten the "why" and "how" of his existence and all religions have failed, India holds the key to man's future. And what is this knowledge? It is not some mystical, faraway and smoky Utopia, but a pragmatic, down-to-earth, Cartesian knowledge which can be put immediately into practice. Take *pranayama*, for instance, the most exacting, precise, mathematical, powerful breathing discipline one can dream of. Its effects and results have been observed and categorized by Indian yogis for millennia and it brings in, very quickly, wonderful results in both the well-being of the body and the quietude of the mind. (Gautier 2000)

Further, Gautier reminds us, in his enthusiasm for Hindutva as the panacea of the ills of contemporary life, that "India is also a bastion of the pro-western, open-minded, English-speaking, highly cultured upper and middle classes. . . . No western nation could wish a friendlier country than India, whose elite dreams of sending their sons and daughters to study in Harvard!" (ibid., 37).

Visual Culture and the Modernity of the Aura

Given the above discussion it should be apparent that, by insisting on its alterity precisely through its engagement with global capital, technology, and cultural hybridity, the proponents of Hindu nationalism cannot be understood as occupying a "minor" position within the teleological *grand récit* of the end of history with the collapse of the Soviet Union. As a powerful player in both the national and regional geopolitical sphere and now as a prime economic ally and political game player (especially after the events of 9/11), Hindu nationalism is imbricated within the very triumphalist discourses of progress. How does this relate to visual culture? The relationship can be seen by looking at both the upsurge in the sort of hybrid programming that marries the sacred marketplace to the profane religiosity of the moment, as well as certain engagements with technology.

It is in the current heated debate around Direct-to-Home (DTH) transfer that the lineaments of the flexible logic of Hindu nationalism, or what I term "digital Hinduism," comes to the fore in the clearest fashion. DTH technology enables the reception of satellite transmission directly from the satellite broadcasting TV network, thus effectively cutting out the cable operator, whose dish at present is the hub through which satellite feed is cabled into subscribers' homes. DTH is also the technological platform for the provision of other services such as e-mail, the Internet, visophony, and telephone and cyber commerce. According to the vociferous attacks on foreign broadcasting from the Hindu Right, such a development would further distance government control of programming (itself limited to the Cable Network Regulation Act which merely requires cable operators to register with the post office and makes no programming demands, although some are currently being made such as a minimum number of DD channels). However, it is in fact the BJP Information and Broadcasting Minister Pramod Mahajan who shows the most support for DTH. "The air is open to all, the sky is the limit" is his opening salvo in the heated debate around DTH. But this expansiveness toward technological change is argued forcefully as follows: "DTH actually means viewing the channels with a 12 inches [*sic*] antenna instead of a 12 feet [*sic*] antenna. We cannot oppose technology. We must learn to use them [*sic*] to our best advantage. And whoever comes first is bound to have the early bird advantages" (Mahajan 1999, 11).

By couching the discussion around DTH in purely technological terms (six feet to six inch receivers), Mahajan neatly sidesteps the discourse of his own party in its vociferous attacks on foreign networks, the "air attacks" on the nation's *Chiti*. The realpolitik sentiment of "first come, first serve" hides the fact that in terms of either financial resources or programming material, the state broadcaster DD would be unable to compete effectively with global networks such as NewsCorp which have already taken up the cudgels against the Indian government for its restrictive law on a maximum foreign participation of 20 percent in broadcasting. NewsCorp, CNN, and other networks have been lobbying the U.S. State Department on this issue for some time. At stake are millions of dollars in advertising revenue, and the pond is big enough for major Indian satellite networks to dip into. Mahajan's "open skies" policy, besides its convenient framing in terms of keeping up with technology, is paralleled by the RSS public organ, *The Organiser*, framing a feature article discussion of the DTH issue in the sanskritized tones of Hindutva: "An no bhadrah kritavo yantu vishwatah (Let noble thoughts come to us from all sides)—Rg Veda" (Mishra 1999, 9). Here the native subject of nationalism is constructed and strengthened in its moral, cultural superiority through the deployment of precisely those signifiers of modernity which have been traditionally understood to belong elsewhere. More important, in the context of Hindutva and its philosophical underpinnings, the belief in development, holistic thinking and its execution through

Fig. 12.2. The seduction begins. When Hinduism meets *MTV* sponsored by Coca-Cola (logos top right/left).

high technology, the free-market and institutions such as the World Bank, the World Trade Organization, and related organizations is seen as a recognition on the part of the West of what was already embodied in "Hindu philosophy."

In terms of programming, the market-temple nexus is evident in many different forms. First, given that most epics are telescoped into each other, televising one religious epic often provides the alibi for representing another. This stretches the length of the serial and proves highly profitable since advertisers are lining up for such programming. Second, while general programming has been openly wooing audiences through prizes including cash, automobiles, jewelry, and the like, religious programming has been following the same format, although in less conspicuous and more sacred ways. When Dheeraj Kumar, producer of the top mythological *Om Namah Shivay*, got in on the act, irate devotees reacted angrily to the commercialization of the program. Kumar hastily withdrew the contest and replaced it with a request to viewers to write a ten-line "moral" for each episode telecast, and the rewards were Prasadam, Shiv Jyotirlingas, Angavastaram, Rudraksha, and a "mega prize" of a Jyotirlinga yatra with "gold moments of Lord Shiva."[8]

In a thought-provoking piece on the sea change in the media landscape in India, and particularly on modes of advertising, Swapan Seth, executive director Equus, compares the current situation to the bygone era of planned socialism where India was a "a nation devoid of self-confidence, a nation about to build and create its own fortunes." Such a discourse of the fall of the nation and its resurgence in the era of liberalization bears a striking resemblance to the contours of the familiar rhetoric of the Hindu nation brought to its knees under colonialism and "Western socialism" after Independence. In the field of media and advertising, however, it is the increasing possibilities of consumption, and the wider range of choices, that strike Seth most. "So the consumer had little independence in terms of choosing brands," he argues, yet around the 1970s something changes. "We were aghast when Coca-Cola was banned, Ram-like, from our land" (Seth 1997, 81). The metaphorical transference of consumer availability to Ram's banishment into exile is both provocative and an instantiation of the power of metaphor as a passage, a transfer, and consequently a generative matrix for linking seemingly disparate themes and meanings. Clearly, within such an understanding, neither the product Coca-Cola nor the mythic character Ram retain their originary nature. Functioning rather like fetishes, Coca-Cola becomes a symbol of choice that is counterfactually linked to Indian Independence while the actual circumstances of its banning in the 1970s were precisely those of preserving our Independence! As for Ram, the skyrocketing TRPs (television rating points) for mythologicals provide the ideal platform for a massive commercialization of religion, both as a medium for delivering consumers to advertisers but also in the marketing of objects as rewards for religious devotion and faithful viewing, as was made clear in the example above about *Om Nama Shivay*. A visual representation of this collapsing of the discourses of "local flavor," Independence through choice, and consumption is instantiated in a popular TV ad for Candico on Channel [V]. The camera shakily follows at close range the swiveling head of an enormous Indian water buffalo as it masticates in the confines of a dark shed, to the strumming of a Ry Cooder-esque blues guitar. Suddenly, as the animal's face stares straight into your eyes, a huge pink balloon blows out of its mouth and pops explosively. The punch line on the screen, also heard in voiceover, reads "Your Right to Chew!"

If one were tempted to read Seth's comments as an apology for a whole-hearted turning to Western consumerism, besides his metaphor of Ram's banishment, his reading of the failures of advertising reproduce the familiar theme we have encountered above: the resilience of the nation's *Chiti*, or Soul, in "choosing" the path most consistent culturally with its ethos.

> By the 90s, the winds of change had swept across the consumer continuum. . . .
> But the Indian did not get hypnotized by these events. Having finally got independence as far as choice was concerned, the consumer made pragmatic decisions and evaluated both Indian and global brands with an objectivity that no one expected. So, the customer did not stand weak-kneed in front of Pepsi. She evaluated and uncorked a Thums Up. (Ibid., 82)

Rather than stand at the altar of the all-conquering Western God, our, now interestingly gendered consumer asserts her independence *through choosing an Indian product*. This point is crucial. The terms of the discourse of both Independence and Openness are not couched in terms of Western materialism and

Eastern spiritualism. Rather, like Ram, our Independence through consumption occupies a space *within* the discourse of consumerism. Further, it reproduces a similar logic where technology like DTH is wholeheartedly embraced along Seth's argument for "pragmatic decisions" (ibid., 81). If such a reading would be considered farfetched or too generalized in its claims, witness the following. In "Market Freedom: Tryst with Destiny Again," a special *A&M* feature in its August 15, 1997, annual review, the lead writers open the article thus:

> Ironic. That's just the word. India awoke to "light and freedom" having struck the world dumb with what was perhaps the planet's biggest ever victory of persuasion over might. Then she chose to let people choose their leaders, even religions. And then somehow ended up with an economic system so warped that the allocation of the nation's resources are determined by the mighty, not people's persuasions on what they want to consume. (ibid., 86)

The interpenetration of discourses of a chauvinist Hindu nationalism and economic globalization fueled through the promises of consumerism are central to the evolving cultural nationalism in India. The numerous examples above illustrate this structural homology between religiously oriented culturalist discourse and a future-oriented discourse of globalization. What we see is a harnessing of the new possibilities of technology within a global imaginary in the construction of a particular discourse of the "local." Further, this discourse materialized through the Hindu nationalist-led governments in India, is structured hierarchically, and is fed by a strong demarcation of those who belong to the nation and those who do not. It is undergirded by practices and discourses of militarism, where the conflict in Kargill in Kashmir, for example, is repeatedly used as a sign of the strength not so much of the military but of the militaristic discourse of Hindu nationalism.

Etienne Balibar (1998, 220) has observed that "borders have stopped marking the limits where politics ends because the community ends." As we have seen, the "community of the faithful" for Hindu nationalism obeys no logic of state-defined territoriality, and mapping the borders of nationalism remains a futile task if it sticks to such an emphasis. Balibar rightly argues that the complexity of thinking about borders does not entail the conclusion that we live in a "borderless world." Rather, it is precisely through the global "borderlessness" of Hindu nationalism that borders are being drawn (the ideology of "true Hindus," "true secularists," etc.). The point here is that one must grasp contemporary religious nationalisms on a changing map where "borders are both multiplied and reduced in their localization and their function, they are being thinned out and doubled" (ibid., 220). It is this dialectic of dis-attachment and reattachment across an imaginary landscape where borders remain unfixable in time and space through which Hindu nationalism operates. The mass media, satellite television in particular, lends itself to such an understanding in terms of the "territory" of operation (at a planetary scale beyond state control), the problematic relation to the nation-state, and the affective power of cultural belonging.

In this context the fragmentation of the singularity of the time/space nexus, so central to Benjamin's argument, requires some rethinking in relation to the aura. By positing a "tradition" that is one with the contemporary global imaginary, the value of "cultural heritage" is now reworked, and Hindu nationalism can be seen as a globe-girdling movement that fragments the chronotopic focus of Benjamin's argument around the aura. In other words, precisely because of the spatial separation of numerous audiences that constitute "India," the use of high technology and mediated communication, themselves signifiers of modernity, and the past history of "suppressed consumption" and insularity of the Indian nation-state can Hindu nationalism refashion a discourse of authenticity and difference, of alterity and commonality. Within these de-territorialized dimensions of cultural nationalism as discourse and practice, national identity is re-territorialized in hegemonic, hierarchical, and exclusionary terms. Further, the homologous temporal structures of the "promises of globalization through consumption" and the "promise of redemption through belief" enable a sacralization of the profane and its obverse.

For our present discussion, it is readily apparent that the fragmentation of audiences, programming, spatial dimensions of broadcasting, and the global reach of technological innovations such as the Internet are precisely what have made Hindu nationalism such a powerful force within and outside the country. Part of the success of Hindu nationalism has been precisely to structure the promises of religious chauvinism with those of globalization, marrying an empowered "Hindu" identity to that of consumerism. In this blurring of the sacred and the profane, one encounters a paradoxical reactivation of the aura. Precisely through its embeddedness in discourses of globalization and consumerism, Hindu identity stakes a place in the contemporary world as a supremely modern phenomenon. At the same time the earlier discourses of consumerism as Western decadence are replaced by that of a nation freed from its past mistakes (an insular, secular, and socialist burden) and fully engaged in the fruits of globalization without sacrificing its cultural identity, its "spirituality."

Aura here also has a positive function, because the "appearance or semblance" of the aura is linked to a compensatory mechanism whereby the contingency of history is solidified into an apologia for the status quo. A "true" aura is one that does not succumb to the ideologies of a triumphalist narrative of history as progress, of modernity as modernization: "The peeling away of the object's shell, the destruction of the aura, is the signature of a perception whose sense for the sameness of things has grown to the point where even the singular, the unique is divested of its uniqueness—by means of its reproduction" (Benjamin 1927–34, 519). Here, very clearly, technology is implicated in the predominance of exchange value, in "the sameness of things" that marks capitalist society, so that exhibition value linked to consumption becomes the functional dimension of the image. It is precisely here that the earlier quote around a "warped economy" slots into such a discourse of progress, thereby conferring an auratic appeal on the images of consumption and the consumption of images and products.

The "public" here is constituted just like those aspirational masses of the

Fig. 12.3. Fortuitous (re-)union? Flute-player, mobile phone-wielding grandmum, and traditional village damsel.

1931 World Exhibition in New York City's Democricity (only now the "cultural sensitivity" is glimpsed in General Electric advertising its lightbulbs on television with little Indian girls trying on traditional saris). The authority of these images, we are told, derives from "what people want" while, as Habermas (1989) rightly points out, the public sphere under capitalism is increasingly subsumed under the instrumental logic of exchange value. It is no accident that the neo-Freudian deployment of psychoanalysis marketed by his daughter, Anna, and nephew, Edward L. Bernays, in the 1940s is redeployed in the focus group experiments and market research of TV organizations like Sony Entertainment Television (SET) and ZEE. The transformation of the responsible citizen of the public sphere into the "faithful" consumer of the free market mirrors the coding of economic and cultural value under transnational capitalism. For those of us caught in the "postcolonial moment" in the academy, Gayatri Chakravarty Spivak warns that "unwittingly commemorating a lost object can become an alibi unless it is placed within a general frame" (1999, 1). For this very reason religious nationalism cannot be a "lost object" scripted as a "return of the repressed" in a simplistic form. Rather, by placing it in the "general frame" that includes economic globalization and political change, I argue that the "aura" which legitimates contemporary power relations accrues in even the most profane practices and discourses. Further, my argument evades a continuist argument that traces origins through a linear narrative back into the past, for to do so would be to reproduce the progressivist narratives of both contemporary globalization and religious nationalism.

Finally, this auratic dimension, as Benjamin insisted and Habermas explored, constructs a certain delimited space of public engagement, with the public understood as empowered consumers (or Gods in the sacred marketplace) while those who are merely supplying them with what they want police the boundaries of what is admissible within visual culture. For if globalization and religious nationalism are indeed so all-embracing, why do those on the receiving end not see themselves reflected in the small screen? Clearly they count very little within a definition of the "public sphere" coded in terms of economic value. It is precisely here in the coding of alterity within a narrative of globalization and progress that the aura can be understood as reactivated within a visual culture that fractures the unique space-time nexus that Benjamin understood as its defining mode of being. The epigraph from Max Horkheimer which opened this chapter assumes its importance precisely at this point. For if religion is "lost" to mankind with time it does not disappear in the *grand récit* of modernization, but instead its mark, still retained in the present, survives. Its coded reemergence within the flickering light of the screens of global visuality casts a shadow on our desire for hybridity. The value of culture might reside less in the auratic appeal of profane images and more in the destruction of their tenuous solidity. If "history hurts," then rescuing forgotten histories locked in the images of the past might be one way of resuscitating life into the future that is past.

Notes

I use the term "religious" rather than "religion" in the title to underline that although the focus of this essay is on Hindu Nationalism, the analysis below is less interested in examining "religion" as an object-like thing than in exploring the transnational and historically specific dimensions of the discourse and practice of the "religious." The centrality of faith, futurity, and the quasi-transcendental is thus analyzed here in its concrete specificity. (For a nuanced philosophical discussion of the "religious," see de Vries 2001, 3–42.)

1. Translated by Harry Zohn as *The Work of Art in the Age of Mechanical Reproduction,* the subtlety of Benjamin's formulation, and the substance of his argument, has been seriously degraded, particularly within contemporary cultural studies. While exigencies of space preclude me from engaging with the details lost in the English translation, it is worth signaling here that *Reproduzierbarkeit* should be understood in English as "Reproducibility," not "Reproduction." The sloppy translation has resulted in celebratory accounts in contemporary cultural criticism of the popular and populist possibilities of mass media, without recognizing that the protensive potentiality with which the word "Reproducibility" is marked implies, for Benjamin, the two-edged sword of either fascism *or* revolution. When this potential of the mass media to be turned either way is ignored, and democratic and political liberation announced as the necessary effect of technological innovation, Benjamin's subtle dialectical argument is lost. For both versions of the original essay in German, written in 1935 and revised in 1939, see *Gesammelte Schriften* 1 (2): 431–469, 219–253. See Walter Benjamin 1968, 211, 217–252.

2. Experience as *Erfahrung* is to be distinguished from *Erlebnis*. The latter is related to a punctuated encounter in time and space, such as the sight of a car crash, whereas the former is understood as the unfolding through time of a continuous narrative that has a past, present, and future. The structure of the classical *Bildungsroman* is an example of *Erfahrung*, while the shock of viewing a fleeting image projected on a screen occupies the temporality of *Erlebnis*.

3. For a brief overview of shifts in Indian television, see Rajagopal 1993, 91–111.

4. Arif Dirlik (1994, 341) makes a similar argument in the case of the philosophy of Confucianism and capitalist restructuring in China, in "The Postcolonial Aura: Third World Criticism in the Age of Global Capitalism."

5. See, especially, Walter Benjamin's "The Storyteller" and "On Some Motifs in Baudelaire," in *Illuminations* (1968).

6. Online at http://www.geocities.com/CapitolHill/Lobby/9089/aims.html.

7. Available at http://www.eprarthana.com.

8. "Hook Them at Any Cost," *Screen*, November 21, 1997, 34.

References

Balibar, Etienne. 1998. The Borders of Europe. In *Cosmopolitics: Thinking and Feeling Beyond the* Nation, ed. Bruce Robbins and Pheng Cheah, 216–232. Minneapolis: University of Minnesota Press.

Benjamin, Walter. 1927–34. Little History of Photography. In *Walter Benjamin: Selected Writings*, vol. 2: *1927–1934*, ed. Michael W. Jennings, Howard Eiland, and Gary Smith, trans. Rodney Livingstone et al., 507–530. Cambridge, Mass., and London: Harvard University Press.

———. 1968. *Illuminations. Essays and Reflections*. Translated by Harry Zohn. New York: Schocken Books.

BJP Economic Resolutions. 1995. New Delhi: BJP Publications.

Chatterjee, Partha. 1998. *"Our Modernity": The Present History of West Bengal—Essays in Political Criticism*. New Delhi: Oxford University Press.

Dirlik, Arif. 1994. The Postcolonial Aura: Third World Criticism in the Age of Global Capitalism. *Critical Inquiry* 20:328–356.

Gautier, Francois. 2000. India as a Teacher in a New Era. *Indian Express*, January 3. Courtesy of http://www.VHP.org.

Habermas, Jürgen. 1989. *The Structural Transformation of the Public Sphere*. Cambridge, Mass.: MIT Press.

Hansen, Thomas Blom. 1998. The Ethics of Hindutva and the Spirit of Capitalism. In *The BJP and the Compulsions of Politics in India*, ed. Thomas Blom Hansen and Christophe Jaffrelot, 121–162. Oxford: Oxford University Press.

Horkheimer, Max. 1972. *Critical Theory*. New York: Herder and Herder.

Jaffrelot, Christophe. *The Hindu Nationalist Movement in India*. New York: Columbia University Press.

Jameson, Fredric. 1994. *Postmodernism; or, The Cultural Logic of Late Capitalism*. Durham, N.C.: Duke University Press.

Mahajan, Pramod. 1999. I Am Not in a Hurry but I Cannot Wait for Eternity: Interview with Pramod Mahajan. *The Organiser*, February 21.

Mishra, Anup Kumar. 1999. How Far Is Too Far. *The Organiser,* February 21.

Rajagopal, Arvind. 1993. The Rise of Television of National Programming: The Case of Indian Television. *Media, Culture and Society* 1:91–111.

Screen. 1997. November 21.

Seth, Swapan. 1997. An Eventful Transition. *Advertising & Marketing,* August 1–15.

Spivak, Gayatri Chakravorty. 1999. *A Critique of Postcolonial Reason: Toward a History of the Vanishing Present.* Cambridge, Mass.: Harvard University Press.

Upadhyaya, Deendayal. 1992 [1962]. *Integral Hinduism.* New Delhi: Jagriti Prakashan.

Vries, Hent de. 2001. In Media Res: Global Religion, Public Spheres, and the Task of Contemporary Comparative Religious Studies. In *Religion and Media,* ed. Hent de Vries and Samuel Weber, 3–42. Stanford, Calif.: Stanford University Press.

13 The Saffron Screen? Hindu Nationalism and the Hindi Film

Rachel Dwyer

In his groundbreaking work on Indian anticolonial nationalism, Partha Chatterjee argues that the nationalist struggle in India focused on the state and political power, while cultural nationalism was located in the inner domain of tradition (Chatterjee 1993, 116–134). The current (post-1980s) and dominant form of Indian nationalism is *Hindutva,* or Hindu nationalism. In its latest guise, based on a reworking of earlier forms of Hindu national thought dating back to Veer Savarkar and his followers, it comprises a new politics of militant Hinduism based on ethno-religious mobilization.[1] Hindutva is not about the presence of Hinduism in Indian secular politics but rather is a politics of communal identity.[2] Thomas Blom Hansen argues that it has grown not just through its political organization (Jaffrelot 1996) or through existing religious elements of nationalism (van der Veer 1994) but rather within the domain of public culture. He shows how, since the 1980s, symbolic language and rituals have been used to promote Hindutva ideology, concentrating on *yatras* ("pilgrimages, journeys") and the building of a temple at the birthplace of Rama (*Ramjanmabhumi*), supposedly on the site of a previous temple where a Mughal mosque then stood. Using a Lacanian framework, Hansen locates various Hindutva discourses in already existing forms of subjectivity (1999, 203) around communal identities built on constructions of self, community, and nation with the Muslim posed as Other. He does not, however, discuss India's dominant form of public culture, the Hindi film.[3]

The rise of Hindu nationalism was simultaneous with a media invasion (satellite and cable television since 1991 [Merchant 1996]), a communications revolution (the mobile phone and the Internet), and a flood of Western brands into India. To get its message across, the BJP (Bharatiya Janata Party, the political party of Hindutva) and its allies harnessed the media via televised religious soap operas (Lutgendorf 1995; Mitra 1993; Rajagopal 2001), popular visuals (Kapur 1993), and cheap technology such as the music cassette.[4] Religious soaps that may not have set out with a political agenda or been overtly chauvinistic have been used by Hindutva supporters to foment nationalism.[5]

The simultaneous rise of Hindutva and of the new media has also seen the emergence of new social groups in India. Since the 1970s the middle classes have expanded rapidly, while the "new middle classes" (Dwyer 2000a, chapter 3) have benefited greatly from the economic liberalization of 1991. Many supporters of Hindutva have emerged from this group, which also generates much of India's public culture, both as producers and consumers of television and film. They can be contrasted with India's "old middle classes" or the professional, national bourgeoisie, who deplore this new group's cultural products, which it attacks in the cultural spheres it controls (most educational institutions, the press, and censor boards), and who, on the whole, espouse secular democracy and reject Hindutva.

Film is a major arena of contestation between the two groups, highlighting the difference in their cultural tastes and values. Cinema in India has highly segmented audiences (Dwyer and Patel 2002, 21–22), with the old middle classes being associated with realist cinema, including the "art" cinema of Satyajit Ray et al. and new cinemas that emerged during the 1970s, with the state-sponsored "parallel cinema." The new middle classes largely ignore these forms, preferring popular Hindi cinema, a taste shared by other social groups with less economic and educational capital, which the old middle classes regard as commercial, crass, and vulgar. The new middle classes respond in kind, such as in the Hindi film's caricatures of Congress politicians.[6]

It would be surprising if the Hindi films from the 1990s on, produced and consumed by the new middle classes, did not manifest Hindutva ideology, just as nationalist and Nehruvian ideologies dominated earlier films. Indeed, the old middle classes argue strongly that cinema is in thrall to Hindutva, while the new middle classes often regard them as espousing only "Indian values" (Dwyer 2000b). Distinguishing between these two positions is complex, as both include religiosity (mostly Hindu) and patriotism. Certain images would identify Hindutva clearly (see below), but otherwise the two sets of values can be hard to separate because they are strikingly similar in "real life" as well as in film. This is partly because, although India remains constitutionally secular, practices and symbols of Hinduism remain central to the nation's culture as India's population is overwhelmingly Hindu, comprising around 800 million Hindus, and Hindu representations continue to dominate by default supposedly secular institutions.[7]

This chapter examines the Hindi cinema of the 1990s and, in particular, how religion, culture, and politics are imagined in production, film texts, stars, and the audience. Saffron, long regarded as an auspicious color in Hinduism, is one of the colors of the national flag of the secular Indian state, where it is popularly believed to represent the Hindus of India, whereas the green element is that of Islam. The "saffron flag" has now come to represent Hindutva, although it is also a sign of wider Hindu practices. This chapter examines the question of whether these films are showing signs of Hindutva or whether, as with the saffron flag, general signs of Hindu practices and beliefs are misattributed to militant forms of Hindu nationalism, including Hindutva.

Hindutva in the Film Industry and Film Production

The Hindi film industry in Bombay has long-established connections with politics. Several film stars have become Members of Parliament (MPs)[8] or have joined the Rajya Sabha (Upper House), but there has never been the close connection between political parties and cinema that there is in South India, where cinema is preoccupied with local political concerns.

Yet, even with the rise of Hindutva, most Hindi film industry personnel do not espouse this ideology, although some stars are active in BJP politics. This may be because the industry has always employed many Muslims, the result, in part, of Bombay's sizable Muslim population and also the long tradition of Muslims working alongside Hindus in the arts, notably music. At Partition, a few Muslims from the Bombay industry migrated to Pakistan, such as Noor Jehan, but most remained. Simultaneously the Lahore film industry found itself in the new state of Pakistan, but many of its key personnel migrated to Bombay. The Hindi film industry continues to have many prominent and powerful Muslims as stars, financiers, writers, musicians, and so on, and Muslims work at all levels of the business, while the industry has loose associations with secular, leftist, or Marxist organizations. Although many rituals in the film industry have a clearly "Hindu" base, such as astrological moments of auspiciousness, propitious ceremonies, and so on, these are part of a general South Asian culture and would offend only the most orthodox Muslims.

Until recently Urdu, which is popularly associated with Muslim culture, has been valued over Hindi in the "Hindi" film industry.[9] Hindi cinema is rooted in Urdu traditions, and so Urdu-educated writers are required for dialogues and lyrics as are actors who can deliver Urdu dialogues. This language factor was also important for the dominance of Punjabis in the industry especially after Partition, as Urdu was the main language of culture for all Punjabis before Independence.[10]

This situation changed in the 1990s, as Urdu, while still highly valued in the industry and by the audience, became more isolated from the mainstream. Few of the younger people in the industry know Urdu well, with some notable exceptions, but the great lyricists are still educated in the language, such as Javed Akhtar and the late Anand Bakshi (died 2002). However, the popularity of the light classical *ghazal*[11] and the Sufi *qawwali* has perpetuated the attractions of Urdu. It is seen as a "sweet language," and is still highly regarded as being associated with culture and learning (see Dwyer 2002b).

One of the striking features of the 1990s is the dominance of male Muslim stars, notably the Khans (Shahrukh, Aamir, and Salman, no relation), although female Muslim stars are now rare. In early cinema, stars often changed their names to hide strong caste or regional associations, and several Muslims used Hindu screen names, notably Dilip Kumar (Yusuf Khan). The Muslim background of today's stars—two of whom have Hindu wives—is accepted without comment. When Hrithik Roshan emerged as a new superstar with his first film in 2000, Hindu nationalists were said to have been delighted that a Hindu male star was toppling "those Muslims," even though he is married to one. Shadowy Hindutva forces in Bombay are said to have told Salman Khan not to consider marrying a "Hindu icon" such as Aishwarya Rai, with whom he has been rumored to have a romantic connection.

Yet recent years have seen closer, though vague, connections between the film industry and Hindu nationalist groups. Bombay is located in the heartland of Hindu nationalism, as many Hindutva groups have their origins in Maharashtra, while Bombay itself is home to the Shiv Sena, a localized, plebeian, militant Hindu group (Hansen 2001). Its leader, Bal Thackeray, is rarely directly involved in the industry, but his daughter-in-law, Smita, rapidly became head of the film producers' association. Thus networks and associations may well exist between the Shiv Sena and the industry, but, as suggested above, these are unclear.

The recent (to 2004) BJP government had an active relationship with the film industry, granting it industry status and promoting it vigorously abroad. This does not mean, however, that the industry is a hotbed of Hindutva but rather that it is seeking its own advantage and seems to have found support, for the first time, from the national government.

Censorship

Although industry personnel may not be inclined to make a "Hindutva" film, it seems unlikely that Hindi film could exist in a cultural vacuum, and hence recent films may show traces or condensations and displacements of Hindutva, although it is not clear what a Hindutva film would be.

Supporters of Hindutva are not necessarily anti-Western or antimodern, as many welcome technology and yet are more ambivalent about consumerism, although hoping for an Indianized version. They are clear about the groups they oppose: the Anglicized Indians or old middle classes who support secularism, or, in Hindutva's phrase, "pseudo-secularism." This group is also hostile to the low and scheduled castes supported by Congress and the Mandal Commission and to Christians. However, Hindutva's major target remains Muslims, despite the much-publicized presence of several Muslims in the party and the official line that Muslims should accept benevolent marginalization by the majority community. Among the various positions taken by supporters of Hindutva, the most frequently heard complaints are opposition to India's separate Muslim personal law; anxieties about the higher Muslim population growth; supposed Muslim allegiance to Pakistan and hence to other Islamic states; and the supposed cultural wounds inflicted by the "Muslim period" of Indian history.

Clearly it would be difficult to make a Hindutva film exacerbating such communal tensions given the problems such a film would face with the censors. Appointments to the censor boards are made under the guidance of a chair chosen by the government. *The Report of the Enquiry Committee on Film Cen-*

sorship (1969) suggests criteria that implies membership of the old middle classes (quoted in *Report of the Working Group on National Film Policy* 1980. 75). Although censorship rules are fairly loose, section 5(B) (1) of the Indian Cinematographic Act (1952) provides that "a film shall not be certified for public exhibition if, in the opinion of the authority competent to grant certificate, the film, or any part of it, is against the interest of the security of state, friendly relations with foreign states, public order, decency or morality, or involves defamation or contempt of court or is likely to incite the commission of any offence" (ibid.). This means that any images, narratives, or other manifestations of communalism are likely to be banned. The major concerns of the censor board are with sex and violence, the latter being more important for this study as the parties of Hindutva are seen as communal, that is, as aggressively hostile to non-Hindus.

Since many Hindi films promote "Indian values" and nationalism, there would have to be a distinct presentation to show these as signs and symbols of Hindutva, perhaps by mobilizing other features such as language. Distinctive symbols of Hindutva have appeared in televised mythologicals, such as its images of a muscularized Rama or the saffron flag, which fed into the political images manipulated by LK Advani in his Rath Yatras (traveling campaigns). Such direct symbols are rarely seen in Hindi films, although some are discussed below in the context of *Hey! Ram.* Any filmic representation of communities in conflict is a sensitive topic, and the films mentioned in detail below have all had mixed receptions among minority communities, where they have caused offence as well as pleasure.

The role of censor is also assumed by some of the forces of Hindutva. These may be direct interventions by leaders, such as Bal Thackeray, who "permitted" the screening of *Bombay* (although he suggested that it be renamed *Mumbai*, in accordance with Shiv Sena policy). Sometimes censorship has taken more violent forms such as the Shiv Sena's attacks on theaters screening Deepa Mehta's *Fire* (1996) on the grounds that it depicts lesbianism, which is not an "Indian practice." In 1999 theaters in Delhi screening *Fire*, which depicts sexual intimacy between sisters-in-law, who have Hindu names, were vandalized by female Shiv Sena activists. Protests led to the film being returned to the censor board amid great protest although it was later shown again, uncut.[12]

Religion in Hindi Cinema

Religion and nationalism have been central concerns of the Indian film industry from the very first film in 1913. Three genres that were established during the early days may be loosely labeled "religious" from their titles alone: the mythological, the devotional, and the Muslim social (Dwyer 2005). Through these genres, filmic ways of viewing religious symbols and practices became part of the visual culture of Indian cinema.[13] Although they may have stirred religious sentiment among viewers, they were not regarded as promoting religious nationalism or separatism but were part of a wider Indian culture. While religious and other genres remained popular after Independence, they were largely eclipsed by the epic melodrama (Rajadhyaksha 1993), the omnibus genre of the social film, where a central protagonist seeks to incorporate his romantic love into his family and to fulfill his kinship duties. The social is made in the melodramatic mode, where traditional hierarchies and concepts of the sacred are transposed onto the domain of nationhood and its key icons.[14] It upholds Nehruvian ideology, where secularism is not an absence of religion but a separation of religion and culture from politics as suggested by Chatterjee (1993). The social does not show a plurality of religions but rather the Hindu norm.

The normative role in the Hindi film was usually that of the upper-class, upper-caste, male Hindu. As in the wider sphere, Hindu is loosely equated with Indian. Within the group of religious practices that are labeled "Hindu," it can be hard to distinguish the religious from the cultural. In other words, the presentation of the upper-caste Hindu as the norm dominates the Indian public sphere so it is not surprising to see it also in Indian public culture.

Indian cinema underwent radical changes in the 1970s, associated with the breakdown of a political consensus that led to the Emergency and the weakening of the Congress Party (Prasad 1998). It is striking that the 1970s is the first time ordinary or subaltern Muslims are depicted in cinema, a trend that continued into the 1980s.

Hindutva and Hindi Films in the 1990s

Hindi cinema in the 1990s was dominated by the plushy romance, exemplified by the banners of Yash Raj Films (see Dwyer 2002a), Rajshri and Mukta Arts, whose films promoted the romantic couple under the aegis of the traditional Indian joint family, where consumerist lifestyles are celebrated and religiosity is valued. These values share some features with Hindutva, but this does not automatically make the films locations for Hindutva propaganda.

The social film's focus has always been the family, often as metaphor for the nation or as a location for traditional values, love and happiness, for example. However, in the 1990s the ideal of the joint family came back with a vengeance, none more so than in Sooraj Barjatya's *Hum aapke hain kaun . . . !* (*What am I to you . . . !*) which was entirely plotted around engagement, marriage, childbirth, and death (Uberoi 2000).[15] The younger generation is prepared to sacrifice love for the welfare of their loving and supportive families, who are the entire focus of the film. The hero does not womanize but follows the guidance of his older brother, and drives a jeep emblazoned with the *graffitto* "I love my family." This big-budget, family-oriented film amazed the experts by becoming one of the greatest box office hits of all time.

Religion is present in these films, often as a consumerist lifestyle, with houses containing ever larger and more elaborate *puja* (worship) rooms, where the family gathers, often around the central figure of the mother, suggesting another source of family authority beyond patriarchal economic power. The ethos of consumerism in the film reaches into religious practices which become more and more ostentatious. The heroine may prefer miniskirts to traditional Indian clothes but, when challenged to sing at college, chooses a *bhajan* (devotional song), and wears a sari once married (*Kuch kuch hota hai,* 1998). The gods may intervene in the film, whether indirectly as the crystal images of Ganesh in *Dil to pagal hai* or more directly as in *Hum aapke hain kaun . . . !* when Krishna directs the shades-wearing, Coke-drinking dog to carry a message between the lovers.

Muslims appear rarely in these films: *Hum aapke hain kaun . . . !* has a Muslim couple, a doctor and his wife, who visit the family, whose main function seems to be reciting poetry, a performative version of Muslimness. There are no characters who are only distinguished from the Hindu norm by their names.[16] Only gangster movies show the communities working side by side in their aim to depict the underworld/mafia realistically (*Satya,* 1998). Christians are usually drinkers and small-time racketeers, although several films have shown Christian heroines romancing Hindus with no comment on this as an issue (*Mohabbatein,* 2000; this was most famously seen in Raj Kapoor's seminal *Bobby,* 1973). Sikhs are the closest a minority community comes to being nonperformative, but they may also be figures of fun (as in *Kuch kuch hota hai*), although they are also shown as representing the Indian military, as in *Border* (1997), which depicts their martial prowess.

Yet it would be stretching a point to argue that these manifestations of religiosity and Hindu signs and symbols are symptomatic of the growing presence of Hindutva in Hindi cinema. Another category of films has, however, been more closely identified with such ideology, namely, those that can be described loosely as nationalist, patriotic, or historical, and those that are overtly hostile to Pakistan. Terrorism and security have featured more frequently in films of late, representing the insecurity of the Indian state after the assassinations of two prime ministers (Indira Gandhi in 1984 and Rajiv Gandhi in 1991), and the long-running separatist campaign in Kashmir and conflict with Pakistan. Despite the problems the Punjab faced in the 1980s over issues of separatism, this seems to have largely bypassed the Hindi cinema, despite its predominantly Punjabi personnel.[17]

Hostilities between India and Pakistan have been central to their histories but only very recently have Hindi films mentioned Pakistan by name or shown agents of that state, such as in *Sarfarosh* (*The Willing Martyr;* John Matthews Matthan, 1998). One of the few war films made since Independence, *Border* (J. P. Dutta, 1997) is set during the 1965 war with Pakistan but shows the Indian army's respect for Islam in the daring rescue of a Quran from a burning house.[18] Such films may show Muslims in a negative light not because of their culture but because they are Pakistani. Indian Muslims are shown positively, as in *Ghulam* (1998), where a Muslim police officer complains that he is tired of proving his Indianness to the star, Aamir Khan, a Muslim, who plays a Hindu police officer. *Gadar* (*Turmoil,* 2001), which is a Panjabi film in all but language, has a dramatic scene where the Sikh hero goes to Pakistan after Partition to try to persuade his in-laws to allow his Muslim wife to return to India. Surrounded by the Pakistani army, the hero is willing to convert to Islam but risks his life by refusing to praise Pakistan and curse India.[19]

Mani Ratnam's "Trilogy"

The Tamil separatist issue is not referred to directly in Hindi film,[20] but there are many indirect references in "human bomb" films, which included the "art" film, Santosh Shivan's *Terrorist*, (1999) and Mani Ratnam's *Dil se* (*From the Heart*, 1998). But it is striking that this film is part of Mani Ratnam's "trilogy," the earlier two films being *Roja* (*Rose*, 1992) and *Bombay* (1995),[21] which deal with Kashmir terrorism and the riots in Bombay in 1992–93 after the destruction of the Babri Masjid in Ayodhya by Hindutva supporters. Unlike *Dil se*, Mani Ratnam's only Hindi film, these two earlier movies were both made in Tamil, although they became national successes in their Hindi-dubbed versions. These are among the few films which have engaged with contemporary issues about the Indian nation-state,[22] and it is striking that they are made in the Tamil cinema, which had earlier concerned itself more with local political issues of Dravidianism and anti-Brahminism. These films were made after the assassination of Prime Minister Rajiv Gandhi in 1991, and so may represent a venting of collective guilt by subsuming Tamil nationality into an Indian one (Niranjana 1994, 82). They all feature high-caste, if not Brahminical, figures, who travel throughout India, rehearsing a high-caste Hindu identity of nationalism. The first two films have quite unjustifiably led to Mani Ratnam being attacked as a supporter of Hindutva.[23]

Much of *Roja* is set in Kashmir, which was formerly used as the major location for romance in Hindi movies, drawing on its associations of an earthly paradise, but which features rarely now because of political unrest.[24] One of the most memorable scenes from the film is when the hero, Rishi, is taunted by his captors, Kashmiri separatists, who burn the Indian flag (described at length in Dirks 2000). Rishi throws himself on it and catches fire, to the words of a song by the nationalist Tamil poet Subramania Bharati: "India is dearer to me than life."[25] The film cuts to his impassive Muslim captor at prayer, enforcing the image feared by followers of Hindutva of the disciplined and self-controlled Muslim linked to millions of other Muslims praying in a regimented manner.[26]

Rustom Bharucha (1994) denounced the film as "fascist," and Tejaswini Niranjana (1994), in more moderate language, also noted how it portrays the modern, secular (Hindu), Westernized, middle-class male as representative of Indian nationalism while marginalizing the role of women to the nation and depicting the Hindus as tolerant and the Muslims as fanatical. Ravi Vasudevan (1994) complicates their argument by looking at the text as film, arguing that they have privileged representation over narration, thus reducing its story to one of ideology, while Nicholas Dirks (2000) reminds us of the complexity and even ambivalence of the pleasures of popular film. While the film is retrogressive in its association of Islam with "militants" or "terrorists" and in its gender politics, it certainly cannot be read as a Hindutva text. *Roja* won the National Award for the film best promoting national integration, tax exempt status (which makes the tickets much cheaper), and is regularly screened on Doordarshan (Indian state television) on Independence Day. This happened under the Congress (non-Hindutva) government.

Mani Ratnam's second film in this trilogy, *Bombay* (1995), has a central narrative of an intercommunal marriage between a south Indian Hindu male and a Muslim girl, both hoping to escape communal tensions in Bombay. However, this is 1992 and, following the mobilization of support for Hindutva via Rath Yatras around India, which demanded the building of a temple at Rama's birthplace in Ayodhya, on a site then occupied by a mosque, the mosque was demolished and there were subsequent riots in Bombay in December 1992 and January 1993, which left many dead, mostly Muslims. A film about such recent events, which seemed to threaten the future of India, was a bold move and one unlikely to pass the censors, who made many cuts, including references to the high numbers of Muslim deaths and images of the police shooting Muslims as well as actual footage of the mosque being demolished (Vasudevan 2000a, 195–196). The censors may have thought *Bombay* would not inflame communal sentiments as it shows that Hindus and Muslims were equally culpable (whereas the violence was disproportionately against Muslims) and the violence directed more at property than at people (Vasudevan 2000a). Mani Ratnam met the head of the Shiv Sena, Bal Thackeray, who acted as unofficial censor, authorizing screening in Bombay without protest. However, the film was the object of Muslim protests, and Mani Ratnam's home in Madras was attacked by a gunman. Muslims and secular objectors to the film argued that *Bombay* shows the secular male as the modern citizen, while his wife is a religious, domestic figure. The film enforces many stereotypical images of the Muslim, as aggressor (the girl's father) contrasted with the educated, peaceful Hindu (the boy's father), or images from the Muslim social (Vasudevan 2000a, 200). Again, while many objections to the film may be upheld, apart from the seal of approval from the Shiv Sena, which Mani Ratnam was obliged to obtain, there is no convincing argument that *Bombay* espoused Hindutva. In fact, in the film's final scenes, when the mob threatens to burn the hero alive, he claims he is an "Indian," not a Hindu.

A Hindutva Film?

Hey! Ram (Kamalahasan, 1999), again from the south although made in simultaneous Tamil and Hindi versions, undeniably flirts with Hindutva in a more dangerous manner. This film is nationalistic and historical, a flawed epic. While ultimately carrying a Gandhian message and showing scenes of Hindu barbarity, albeit often retaliatory, the film emphasizes graphically violent scenes depicting Muslim atrocities, inspired directly by Jinnah, while sympathetically portraying the Rashtriya Swayamsevak Sangh (RSS; a leading Hindutva organization). The conversion at the end feels like an afterthought, added after a very serious and deep fascination with forms of fascism. Some of the film's images are the most Hindutva yet seen in Hindi films, especially when the hero, dressed in a *dhoti* and a caste-thread (*janoi*), fires arrows in an image that consciously echoes the chromolithographs of Rama used in the Ramjanmabhumi campaign, showing him as the muscled, angry warrior, very different from his earlier gentle images (A. Kapoor, 1993). Vasudevan (n.d.) notes that it is only the cinematic form that keeps the audience at a distance from identification at this part of the film, and although *Hey! Ram* does not promote Hindutva, it is deeply ambivalent about it.[27]

The Return of the Historical Film

Some of the biggest hits of 2001, which became some of the most profitable films of all time, are historicals, a genre that was considered defunct. These included *Gadar* (*Turmoil*), which is hostile to Pakistan but not to Islam, and the "Oscar"-nominated *Lagaan* (*Once upon a Time in India*), the story of a cricket match between the British and local villagers, including a Dalit and a Muslim, set in the late nineteenth century (Dwyer 2002c). Among a crop of films about nationalist leaders that found little success was one about the founder of Hindutva, *Veer Savarkar, Ambedkar* (dir. Jabar Patel, 2000), which drew a small audience, as did several films on Shaheed Bhagat Singh in 2002. The biggest hit film of 2001 followed the values of the 1990s consumerist films, Karan Johar's *Kabhi khushi kabhie gham*, more popularly known as *K3G*. It directly promotes Indian nationalism or chauvinism, with one of the heroines taking on a humorous role as a promoter of Indian culture in the United Kingdom and a fanatical supporter of the Indian cricket team, within the religiously inclined Hindu joint family. Yet it does not espouse Hindutva overtly, and indeed has a Muslim character and an overtly "Muslim" song, "Yeh ladka hai Allah" ("O Allah, This Boy"). The historical film may once again provide grounds for depicting nationalism, but the Hindi cinema has yet to produce a truly Hindutva film.

The Audiences for Hindi Films

The Hindi film constitutes its audience through its combination of vision and narration which organize forms of knowledge, through its mechanisms of pleasure[28] and involvement. Melodrama plays an essential role in involving the spectator in the film, where music, dance, the star, and structures of the spectacle play their own unique roles. The Hindi film audience is little studied, but some idea of the new middle-class community of Hindi film viewers can be seen in the construction of a community of such readers by the film magazines (Dwyer 2000a, chapter 6). There are many audiences for these films, and it cannot be said that there is any one reading of the films. The problem of interpretation and the location of meaning remains, and so not all mentions of Hinduism and religiosity during the rise of Hindutva necessarily reflect this ideology.

Industry personnel have a clear notion of their audience, seeing it made up of a loose assemblage divided along the lines of class and region (both within India and overseas). The audiences in which they are most interested are the elite metropolitan Indians and the diasporic South Asians, their hope being that within the next decade Hindi films will find a mainstream audience in the West (Dwyer 2002c). The impetus is largely economic as such audiences may pay more than twenty times the price of a ticket than the provincial Indian audience.

Many of those in the Indian metropolitan elite audience belong to the new middle class so closely associated with the Hindutva parties. One might therefore expect a slant toward Hindutva imagery and ideology in these films. However, the filmmakers still wish to maximize their audience, rather than excluding sections, and the proportion of Muslim viewers and others averse to Hindutva policies is significant enough that it is not going to alienate this sector. Nor is the filmmaker going to risk cuts by the censors, as mentioned above. Perhaps the films are also context-driven in that the up-market, aspirational film is more concerned with the Indian's place in the world rather than with domestic communal tensions, and with romance and the family rather than with social problems. This can be dealt with by promoting Indian chauvinism or nationalism rather than attacking minority communities or looking at serious social issues beyond the family. Moreover, many films that show Indians overseas have little reason to take a Hindutva stance, as their romantic and familial concerns rarely allow for relationships with various communities.

The patriotic surge in Hindi films in the 1990s is also part of a wider manifestation of national devotion, which undoubtedly had Hindutva overtones, such as the celebration of India's detonation of a nuclear device in 1998, for which greetings cards were issued with the slogan *"Hum kisise kam nahi"* ("We're not inferior to anyone"). Hindutva has no monopoly on patriotism, and such feelings are more likely a manifestation of insecurity less over Pakistan than with the fear of pan-Islamic resurgence within India and beyond.

While Hindi films are undoubtedly anti-Pakistani, they are not anti-Muslim. This would prejudice sales in the international market, in particular, in the Gulf States where these films have a huge market, as well as the large Muslim South Asian diaspora in the United Kingdom.[29] The film is, as Adorno reminds us, a commodity.

More complicated is the orientation of the Hindi film to the diasporic market. Films featuring diasporic Indians returning "home" have almost become a sub-genre of the social (Dwyer 2000b), which has lately become more concerned with endorsing "Indian values," centered around the family, food, religion, and nationalism, as in *Hum aapke hain kaun . . . !* (Dwyer 2000b). A striking if sometimes heavy-handed approach to the nonresident Indian (NRI) film can be seen in *Pardes* (*Overseas;* dir. Subhash Ghai, 1997), which featured an Indian girl, Ganga (her name is that of the goddess of the River Ganges, implying her purity), whose family want her to marry the son of a wealthy family friend, who lives in America but still sings "I love my India." The film's slogan is "American dream: Indian soul."

Hindutva has to confront a paradox in its policy toward disaporic Indians and the NRI. Many diasporic Indians are supporters and financiers of Hindutva policies (Rajagopal 2001), but Hindutva has to reorient its policy of Indianness to accommodate them. Proponents of Hindutva have attacked Muslims and Christians because the latter groups do not regard India as their *pitribhumi / punyabhumi* ("fatherland / holy land"), but for those in the diaspora, while India remains their *punyabhumi*,[30] it is only remotely their *pitribhumi*. This may explain the growing use of the slogan "*vasudhaiva kutumbakam*" ("the world is one family"), so while India may be one's fatherland and one's holy land symbolically, one does not have to live there to be Indian. Arvind Rajagopal (2001, 64–68) argues that in the United States, the Vishwa Hindu Parishad (VHP), one of the most virulently anti-Muslim Hindutva groups, has marketed itself not as Hindu nationalist, as it does in India, but as a global religious movement that is pro-family and celebrates traditional values.

While the Hindi film that wants to reach the diasporic market supports Indian nationalism, presented through the dominant Hindu symbols and forms, and risks alienating the Pakistani diaspora, it reasserts the inclusive identity of Indianness. Hindutva may be a powerful force in India and among those in the diaspora, but it cannot compete with global market forces. If the Hindi film wishes to keep its overseas audiences and to break through into the wealthy markets of Europe and America, it cannot be hostile to its minority communities and it is unlikely that it can benefit from the West's increasingly antipathetic attitudes toward Islam.

This brief look at Hindi cinema and Hindutva ideology needs to be conceptualized in a wider frame. Public culture in India is full of signs of the religious in its complicated interactions between visual culture, religion, and performance. These have been studied very little in the Hindi cinema beyond *darshana,* a hierarchical way of looking, which is acknowledged by many scholars of cinema yet not analyzed in depth (see note 13). This may be because this non-modern, culturally specific gaze contradicts other arguments about the lack of essential specificity in the Hindi film. Perhaps it is the fear of Orientalizing India by finding all manifestations of Indian culture in religion, which has contributed to the absence of scholarship on religion in Hindi cinema.

Although the relationship between other media and religion has been discussed in the Indian context, notably in Babb and Wadley (1995), this volume does not touch on important aspects of the public sphere and of politics. While the presence of religion in Hindi cinema continues unabated, its wider significance has yet to be interrogated. Although Rajagopal (2001) examines how television in India, notably religious soaps, brought Hindutva ideologies closer to the realm of public culture, existing theories of the public sphere provide few insights into the relationship between religion and Hindi cinema. While religion, as visuality and narration, plays a central role in "imagining the nation" (Appadurai 1997; Pinney 2000), its relationship to Appadurai's concepts of the cosmopolitan and the transnational as sites for public culture remains in question. It seems that here an emergent, uneven public sphere is splitting away from the national sites once discussed and the nature of the public sphere itself needs to be reexamined. It remains unclear how one might distinguish signs of Hindutva from that of "Indian values" in the present insecurity about pan-Islamic resurgence. This chapter rejects the widely held view that any depiction of Hindu practices in Hindi film is connected with the rise of Hindutva ideologies. However, while these signs are not inherent in the text it is possible that audiences and politicians may see them and manipulate these signs for such readings.

The striking absence of clear Hindutva images in the films constitutes a notable lack. It seems that market forces may account for this absence, as may industry personnel who do not embrace Hindutva ideology. However, pragmatic or economic grounds provide the clearest explanation of why producers are unwilling to risk problems with the censors or to alienate their established audiences. This high-risk, hugely expensive industry is unwilling to gamble on the kind of films it produces, preferring the tried and tested, and avoiding anything too political or controversial in order to reach the broadest possible audience. While it is unclear whether the values espoused by the films are those of wider society, it is significant that, although a BJP government was in power from 1996 to 2004, it had a slender majority and was far from gaining the votes of the majority.

In India, the dominant elite, the old middle classes, who endorse a secular politics, are anxious about the persistent presence of Hindu signs and practices in Hindi cinema. This chapter argues that Hindi films, while pervaded by religious ideology, depict it under the sign of Indian secularism, emphasizing plurality and equal respect for all religions rather than depicting their absence. Nevertheless, the worldwide growth of religiosity and its centrality to globalization; the shift in the boundaries of the public, the private, and the political; the growth of international markets and their dynamic relationship to the centers of cultural production all call for an urgent reexamination of religion in media studies, as well as in the Hindi film.

Notes

1. On the history of Indian nationalism, see Masselos 1991 and Chatterjee 1986; on Hindu nationalism, see Basu et al. 1993; Hansen 1999; Jaffrelot 1996; and van der Veer 1994.

2. See below under the section on censorship.

3. See Dwyer 2000a, chapter 2, one of several introductions to this topic.

4. Sadhvi Rithambhara's speeches are widely distributed on cassette tape, thus bypassing the need for a literate audience.

5. For a similar view, see Hansen 1999, 156.

6. See, for example, *Raja Babu,* directed by David Dhawan, 1994, in which female Congress party workers lift their saris suggestively throughout a dance number.

7. This is not to take one of the antisecularist positions critiqued by Amartya Sen, such as "non-existence" (of secular India), or "prior identity" or "cultural." See Sen 1998, but, more important, Hansen's view that "public spheres in India remained full of religious signs and practices, packaged and represented as culture, making up a nationalized central realm represented as unpolitical, pure and sublime" (1999, 53).

8. Including Amitabh Bachchan, Rajesh Khanna, Vinod Khanna, and Raj Babbar.

9. This naming of the industry is owing in part to the fact that the languages can be barely distinguished on formal terms in their *spoken,* colloquial form. Since filmmakers wish to reach the broadest possible audience, they tend to use a simple, widely understood form of Hindi-Urdu. Since Hindi is India's national language and Urdu is Pakistan's, this cinema is labeled "Hindi."

10. Different religious groups had different sacred and religious languages.

11. Few of these singers are Muslim, and not all are educated in Urdu literature although they are trained in Urdu pronunciation.

12. Available online at http://www.umiacs.umd.edu/users/sawweb/sawnet/news/fire.html.

13. This may draw on the religious practice of *darshana* ("seeing"), a term used most often in the context of religious worship, where it is a two-way look between the devotee and the deity that establishes religious authority. However, it is also used to establish social and political authority. It is a look that establishes an authoritative figure or icon and the space around him or her, assigning positions in a hierarchy although these are open to negotiation and change. See Prasad 1998, 76–77, which draws on Babb 1981 and Eck 1985; see also Vasudevan 1993, 2000b, 139–150.

14. The exposition of melodrama in Brooks 1995 [1976] and Elsaesser 1985 [1972] has been elaborated in Indian cinema in Vasudevan 2000b, n.d.

15. An English-language play based on the film was a great success in Britain in 1998. It ironically called itself *Fourteen Songs, Two Weddings, and a Funeral.*

16. Shyam Benegal, who was closely associated with the growth and development of "middle" or noncommercial cinema, directed three Muslim socials (see above) during the last decade: *Mammo, Sardari Begum,* and *Zubeidaa.* These three films, loosely autobiographical, were written by Khalid Mohamed, who also directed *Fiza* (2000), again a female-centered film (unusual in the 1990s), concerned with the search of a Muslim girl for her brother who became a terrorist after the riots of 1992–93.

17. One of the few films to engage with this issue was Gulzar's *Maachis* (1997), in which four young men become terrorists during the insurgency in Punjab in the 1980s.

18. This scene nevertheless caused the film to be withdrawn from cinemas in the north of England, where South Asian populations of Pakistani and Indian origins live in close proximity.

19. I was surprised to find that many British Asians of Pakistani origin enjoyed this film.

20. In Rajiv Menon's 2000 hit, made in Tamil but screened with English subtitles, *Kandukondein kandukondein,* the hero who was wounded fighting in the Indian Peacekeeping Force, says that Indian talks of Kargil heroes but has forgotten those who fought in Sri Lanka.

21. On the controversy surrounding this film, see Vasudevan 2000a.

22. Another film that attempts to address the issue of Kashmir is *Mission Kashmir* (2000), although it fails to do so.

23. Here I look at the films but in my public and private conversations with Mani Ratnam I have seen no manifestations of a Hindutva ideology.

24. *Roja* itself uses a composite of other mountainous scenery in India to represent Kashmir.

25. I am unsure whether the Hindi version of this song is a direct translation of the Tamil.

26. In his reading of this scene, Nicholas Dirks also sees references to public self-immolation suicides by students protesting against the Mandal Commission's affirmative action for lower castes.

27. A disturbing flirtation with violence was also present in Kamalahasan's earlier film contrasting modern-day corruption with the sacrificial heroism of the freedom movement (*Indian* [Tamil], dubbed into Hindi as *Hindustani* [1997]).

28. See Pinney 2000, on pleasure in Indian public culture.

29. See also Larkin 1997, on film among the Hausa in Nigeria.

30. According to Orthodox tradition, the Hindu loses caste on traveling overseas until he undergoes a ritual purification. The increasing number of temples in the diaspora and the regular visits of religious leaders has reduced, if not eliminated, the importance of India as the holy land. See Dwyer 2003.

References

Appadurai, Arjun. 1997. *Modernity at Large: Cultural Dimensions of Globalization.* Delhi: Oxford University Press.

Babb, Lawrence A. 1981. Glancing: Visual Interaction in Hinduism. *Journal of Anthropological Research* 37 (4): 387–401.

Basu, Tapan, et al. 1993. *Khakhi Shorts and Saffron Flags: A Critique of the Hindu Right.* Hyderabad: Orient Longman.

Bharucha, Rustom. 1994. On the Border of Fascism: Manufacture of Consent in *Roja. Economic and Political Weekly* 29, 23 (June 4): 1390–1395.

Brooks, Peter. 1995 [1976]. *The Melodramatic Imagination: Balzac, Henry James, Melodrama and the Mode of Excess.* New Haven: Yale University Press.

Chatterjee, Partha. 1986. *Nationalist Thought and the Colonial World: A Derivative Discourse?* London: Zed Books for the United Nations University.

———. 1993. *The Nation and Its Fragments: Colonial and Postcolonial Histories.* Delhi: Oxford University Press.

Dirks, Nicholas B. 2000. The Home and the Nation: Consuming Culture and Politics in *Roja.* In *Pleasure and the Nation: The History, Consumption and Politics of Public Culture in India,* ed. R. Dwyer and C. Pinney, 161–185. Delhi: Oxford University Press.

Dwyer, Rachel. 2000a. *All You Want Is Money, All You Need Is Love: Sex and Romance in Modern India.* London: Cassell.

———. 2000b. "Indian Values" and the Diaspora: Yash Chopra's Films of the 1990s. *West Coast Line,* Autumn 2000. Also in *Figures, Facts, Feelings: A Direct Diasporic Dialogue,* ed. Parthiv Shah, 74–82. Catalogue to accompany a British Council exhibition, November 2000.

———. 2002a. *Yash Chopra.* London: British Film Institute.

———. 2002b. Representing the Muslim: The "Courtesan Film" in Indian Popular Cinema. In *Imagining the Other: Representations of Jews, Muslims and Christians in the Media,* ed. T. Parfitt and Y. Egorova, 78–92. London: Curzon.

———. 2002c. Real and Imagined Audiences: *Lagaan* and the Hindi Film after the 1990s. *Etnofoor* 15, 1/2 (December), Special volume: *Screens:* 177–193.

———. 2003. International Hinduism: The Swaminarayan Sect. In *South Asians in the Diaspora: History and Religious Traditions,* ed. K. A. Jacobsen and P. Kumar, 180–199. Leiden: Brill.

———. 2005. *Filming the Gods: Religion and the Hindi Film.* London: Routledge.

Dwyer, Rachel, and Divia Patel. 2002. *Cinema India: The Visual Culture of the Hindi Film.* London: Reaktion.

Eck, Diana L. 1985. *Darsan: Seeing the Divine Image in India.* 2nd ed. Chambersburg: Anima.

Elsaesser, Thomas. 1985 [1972]. Tales of Sound and Fury: Observations on the Family Melodrama. Reprinted in Bill Nichols, *Movies and Methods,* 2:165–189. Berkeley: University of California Press.

Hansen, Thomas Blom. 1999. *The Saffron Wave: Democracy and Hindu Nationalism in Modern India.* Princeton, N.J.: Princeton University Press.

———. 2001. *Wages of Violence: Naming and Identity in Postcolonial Bombay.* Princeton, N.J.: Princeton University Press.

Jaffrelot, Christophe. 1996. *The Hindu Nationalist Movement and Indian Politics, 1925 to the 1990s.* London: Hurst.

Kapur, Anuradha. 1993. The Representation of Gods and Heroes: Parsi Mythological Drama of the Early Twentieth Century. *Journal of Arts and Ideas* 23–24:85–107.

Larkin, Brian. 1997. Indian Films and Nigerian Lovers: Media and the Creation of Parallel Modernities. *Africa* 67 (3): 406–440.

Lutgendorf, Philip. 1995. All in the (Raghu) Family: A Video Epic in Cultural Context. In *Media and the Transformation of Religion in South Asia,* ed. L. Babb and S. Wadley, 217–253. Philadelphia: University of Pennsylvania Press.

Masselos, J. 1991. *Indian Nationalism: A History.* 2nd ed. New Delhi: Sterling.

Merchant, Khozem. 1996. *The Television Revolution: India's New Information Order.* Green College, Oxford, Reuter Foundation Paper 42.

Mitra, Ananda. 1993. *Television and Popular Culture in India: A Study of the Mahabharat.* New Delhi: Sage.

Niranjana, Tejaswini. 1994. Integrating Whose Nation? Tourists and Terrorists in "Roja." *Economic and Political Weekly* 29, 3 (January 15): 79–82.

Pinney, Christopher. 2000. Public, Popular and Other Cultures. In *Pleasure and the Nation: The History, Consumption and Politics of Public Culture in India,* ed. R. Dwyer and C. Pinney, 1–34. Delhi: Oxford University Press.

Prasad, M. Madhava. 1998. *Ideology of the Hindi Film: A Historical Construction.* Delhi: Oxford University Press.

Rajadhyaksha, Ashish. 1993. The Epic Melodrama: Themes of Nationality in Indian Cinema. *Journal of Arts and Ideas* 35–36:55–70.

Rajadhyaksha, Ashish, and Paul Willemen. 1999. *An Encyclopaedia of Indian Cinema.* 2nd ed. London: British Film Institute.

Rajagopal, Arvind. 2001. *Politics after Television: Hindu Nationalism and the Reshaping of the Public in India.* Cambridge: Cambridge University Press.

Sen, Amartya. 1998. Secularism and Its Discontents. In *Secularism and Its Critics,* ed. R. Bhargava, 454–485. Delhi: Oxford University Press.

Uberoi, Patricia. 2000. Imagining the Family: An Ethnography of Viewing "Hum aapke hain koun . . . !" In *Pleasure and the Nation: The History, Consumption and Politics of Public Culture in India,* ed. R. Dwyer and C. Pinney, 309–351. Delhi: Oxford University Press.

Vasudevan, Ravi. 1993. Shifting Codes, Dissolving Identities: The Hindi Social Film of the 1950s as Popular Culture. *Journal of Arts and Ideas* 23–24:51–79 (plus appendix).

———. 1994. Other Voices: *Roja* against the Grain. *Seminar* 423:43–47.

———. 2000a. Bombay and Its Public. In *Pleasure and the Nation: The History, Consumption and Politics of Public Culture in India,* ed. R. Dwyer and C. Pinney, 186–211. Delhi: Oxford University Press.

———. 2000b. The Politics of Cultural Address in a 'Transitional' Cinema: A Case Study of Popular Indian Cinema. In *Reinventing Film Studies,* ed. C. Gledhill and L. Williams, 130–164. London: Arnold.

———. N.d. Another History Rises to the Surface: Melodrama Theory and Digital Simulation in *Hey! Ram* (Kamalahasan, 1999). Available online at http://www.sarai.net/mediacity/filmcity/essays/heyram.htm.

Veer, Peter van der. 1994. *Religious Nationalism: Hindus and Muslims in India.* Berkeley: University of California Press.

14 Impossible Representations: Pentecostalism, Vision, and Video Technology in Ghana

Birgit Meyer

This chapter seeks to unravel the nexus of religion and media by taking as a point of departure an understanding of religion as a practice of mediation (e.g., de Vries 2001; Plate 2003), creating and maintaining links between religious practitioners as well as between them and the spiritual, divine, or transcendental realm that forms the center of religious attention. This realm is constructed by mediation, yet—and here lies the power of religion—assumes a reality of its own. The question of how (if at all) sacred texts, images, or other representations are able to embody and make present the divine is at the heart of religious traditions. This question may give rise to vehement disagreements, as, for instance, in the iconoclasm of Catholic images by Protestants, who claimed to replace the worship of idols by thorough Bible study. That the accessibility of print media transformed Christian practices of mediation suggests that the introduction of new media, in particular, raises questions concerning their suitability and limitations in linking religious practitioners with one another and with God. If ideas are necessarily reworked through the particular technologies of transmission intrinsic to books, images, spirit mediums, film, radio, TV, video, or the computer, the question arises as to how the accessibility of a new medium transforms existing practices of religious mediation.

While a crude separation of medium and message, which makes it seem as if the message is an essence existing irrespective of a particular medium, is untenable, it is equally problematic to attribute a deterministic and message-overruling capacity to media, as implied in Marshall McLuhan's famous dictum "the medium is the message." What both options have in common is that, with their narrow focus on either message or medium, they remain stuck in partial aspects of practices of mediation without being able to fully grasp these practices themselves. There is need to move forward and assess how the accessibility of new media gives rise to new practices of mediation, and how these practices stem from and impinge on changing power relations, between followers and leaders, as well as between politics and religion. Hence the need to investigate religious change, and the changing place and role of religion in society, in rela-

Fig. 14.1. Gilbert Forson Art. Photograph by Birgit Meyer.

tion to the possibilities and limitations of new media technologies. This chapter explores the question of changing practices of religious mediation through a detailed investigation of the new public appearance of Pentecostalism in Ghana, where this brand of Christianity has become increasingly present in the public sphere since the turn to a democratic constitution which implied the liberalization and commercialization of hitherto state-controlled and state-owned media.

What is at stake can be powerfully evoked by a signboard advertising the shop of a roadside artist located at the Winneba-roundabout, Gilbert Forson Art, which captured my immediate attention when my colleagues Peter Pels, Marijke Steegstra, and myself passed through on our way from Elmina to Accra in early January 2003. While driving along the bumpy road, I was trying to sketch as poignantly as possible my research findings and thoughts on the apparent convergence of Pentecostalism and audiovisual technologies, as well as the dissonances arising when Christianity is processed through a video camera. The image at the roadside condenses what, albeit in a less articulate and coherent manner, is all over the place and forms the key concern of my research. It depicts a young man, dressed in a yellow shirt, who holds a video camera in his left hand without, however, looking through it, and, rather, I am tempted to say, gazing at the sky in a trance-like state. The camera is placed in the middle of the picture and directed toward an image of Jesus Christ, fair-colored with his eyes closed and sunken in prayer, not willing to be disturbed, let alone to look back. This somewhat old-fashioned image strongly evokes earlier traditions of mediating Jesus through painting, a representation reminiscent of the image of

Fig. 14.2. Impossible Representation. Photograph by Birgit Meyer.

Jesus in Catholic and Protestant popular prayer books and illustrated New Testaments. Around the image of Jesus there is some strange ethereal stuff, something like smoke, foam, or a cloud which is reminiscent of painted representations of divinity. Interestingly, however, here this substance seems to emanate from the camera in operation, targeting and at the same time blurring the image of Jesus.

While the man behind the camera is unable to see Jesus because the medium blurs his image, the whole scene is clearly visible to the outside observer. Jesus' partial invisibility is overcome, as it were, by the painting itself, which grants the onlooker a full view on both sides of the smoke screen separating the medium from the target of vision. The shop itself is a space where all sorts of representations—photographs of persons like Kofi Annan, Nelson Mandela, the former Ghanaian President J. J. Rawlings, and his successor John Agyekum Kufuor, images from TV, posters, religious icons—are re-represented in the medium of popular painting. Therefore this is a privileged location from which to start a reflection on how the accessibility of a new medium as video impinges on practices of religious mediation, and gives rise to new forms of spectatorship. Indeed, the picture offers a painted comment on the recent common use of video films in order to depict the divine—and, of course, the demonic—for mass spectatorship. Asked why he had painted this image, the young painter answered firmly and quickly: "I painted it because it is impossible." Thus, he told me, passers-by would be attracted to the shop just as we were; many people had come and commented that by all means it was "impossible to make a video of Jesus."

The most intriguing part of the picture is the ethereal substance emanating from the eye of the camera, which makes it impossible for the cameraman in the picture to see Jesus but which appears to outside observers like a smoke screen hiding, and at the same time hailing, the image of Jesus. Indeed, the painting makes visible to observers what remains invisible from the perspective of the cameraman. To be *in* the picture, as a subject seeking to visualize the divine, does not generate any true understanding of this practice of mediation; understanding, the painting suggests, can only be achieved by observers positioned *outside* the picture (cf. Weber 1996, 86).[1]

To me, the picture comments on—or at least can be made to speak to—the question of Christianity in the era of electronic (and even digital) reproducibility, popularized through the easy accessibility of video technology. It makes a painted statement about the aspirations and flaws of video and the new practices of religious mediation and forms of spectatorship to which it gives rise. Depicting the camera as a new technology colliding with the divine, the painting shows that the camera actually blurs, or even conceals, that which it sets out to picture. Interesting in this context is the absence of any pastor or institutionalized mediator. All that is, is the video-camera, engaged in a new way of mediating Jesus—as opposed to the old medium of painting—and creating a new form of public religiosity hovering around a camera-derived mystification.

In order to understand the role of new media in the public manifestation of Pentecostalism in Ghana, it is useful to take as a point of departure the question of technical reproducibility so brilliantly discussed by Walter Benjamin (1978). To what extent is there an analogy between the fate of the work of art and the seeming decline of its aura (but see chapter 12 in this volume) and the fate of religion and the problem of mediating the divine through new audiovisual technologies? In ways similar to the aura, understood as "the unique appearance of distance" (Benjamin 1978), camera-mediated representations of the divine seem to capture the divine in, or even *as*, an image, and yet at the same time fail to make present or embody the divine. Although Benjamin insisted that it is impossible to depict the aura as such, I suggest that in our painting the smoke depicts the aura of the divine, thereby tying into old representations of divinity marked by some cloudy substance around them. Of course, it is not visible as such to the subject *in* the picture, who seems to witness "the appearance or apparition of an irreducible separation" from the divine (Weber 1996, 87) but only to the outside observer, who is made to see that the aura here actually is a product of the camera, thus vesting divinity with its own mystifications. In this sense one may say that the picture condenses the full complexity of representing the divine, as well as the demonic, in the era of the electronic or digital moving image.

I have not portrayed this fabulous image as a prelude to an aesthetic analysis confined to the sphere of popular art (cf. Wolfe 2000), but because I read it as a critical comment on the interplay of Pentecostalism, popular culture, and new audiovisual technologies. The image speaks to representations of divinity and, by implication, the demonic in Ghanaian (and Nigerian) video films, which have become increasingly popular in the course of the last decade and which deliberately tie into Christian views (Meyer 2004). The painting is not a finished piece of popular art by and for itself but leads the viewer outside its own frame right into what may aptly be called Ghana's new image economy,[2] characterized by new infrastructures of exchange and exhibition of audiovisual products evoking contest and conflict, speaking to and feeding on people's imaginations, and highly dependent on apprehensive audiences. A key feature of this image economy is that much attention is paid to visualizing the divine and its negative, the demonic, leading to the articulation of a new public Pentecostalism in which the camera challenges existing forms of religious authority and gives rise to new forms of spectatorship.

The main theme of this essay, then, concerns the ways in which Pentecostalism, with its distinct practices of mediation, features in this new image economy. This image economy, I contend, plays a crucial role in designing a new public sphere replete with Pentecostal Christianity. My understanding of the public sphere is inspired by Negt and Kluge's (1974) critical formulation of an alternative to Habermas's all too narrow, elitist, and normative understanding (1990 [1962]; see the introduction to this volume). While Negt and Kluge (like Habermas) developed their theory with regard to Western societies, characterized by a high level of industrialization and, as a result, the penetration of the forces of production into the public sphere, their plea for a broader understanding of the public sphere, in terms of a "social horizon of experience" (1974, 18), is well taken and enables us to go further than a rather narrow focus on the political public sphere and to include the realm of the imagination or popular culture (cf. Bolin n.d.). Importantly Negt and Kluge insisted that, in order to grasp "what is of concern to everybody and only realizes itself in people's minds" (ibid., 18), it is necessary to pay attention to fantasy. Fantasy, in their view, is all too easily dismissed as "the gypsy, the jobless among the intellectual capacities" (1974, 73; my translation), especially by intellectuals who tend to emphasize rationalism.

This chapter pinpoints how, as a result of changes in state-society relations in Ghana, a new public sphere emerges that is not dominated by the state but rather critical about state politics of representation. Assigning a key role to Pentecostal religion, this new public sphere encompasses people irrespective of ethnic and denominational affiliations[3] and gives rise to new forms of consciousness and participation. Focusing on the nexus of Pentecostalism and new audiovisual media, this chapter addresses two interrelated issues. First, I show how changes on the level of media policy, incited by the turn to a democratic constitution, have facilitated the public articulation of Pentecostalism, while at the same time turning it into a lucrative resource for popular entertainment, such as the popular video-film industry. Second, I focus on this video-film industry and the changes stemming from the adoption of new audiovisual media, especially video, on Pentecostal practices of mediation. This chapter seeks to show that in the era of electronic/digital reproducibility, facilitated through video, Christianity is reconfigured. Its marked public appearance goes hand in hand with the genesis of new Pentecostal practices of mediation, which thrive on distraction in that they imply mass spectatorship and draw Pentecostalism into the sphere of entertainment, all attempts at recasting distraction as devotion notwithstanding.

Pentecostalism in the Public Sphere

In the course of the last decade, the place and role of Pentecostalism has changed tremendously. The year 1992 formed the watershed between a long period of military rule, in which the state dominated the media and society, and the turn to a new democratic constitution, which led to the gradual liberalization and commercialization of radio, TV, film, and the press. This turn occurred under the condition of neoliberal global capitalism, which granted market forces much more influence on domains hitherto managed by the state than ever before, and significantly curtailed its power and capacity to deliver the goods to its citizens (cf. Comaroff and Comaroff 1999). One implication of these developments, particularly relevant to this essay, concerns the incapacity of the state to fully control religion and media, and thus the politics of representation. Whereas, until 1992, the state could easily employ the media in support of its cultural policies favoring what became reified as "our African heritage," the situation became more diverse thereafter, when these cultural policies became increasingly contested by the Pentecostals, who promote a "complete break with the past" and tend to demonize local cultural and religious traditions (Meyer 1998).

In order to grasp the implications of these changes, it is useful to take as a point of departure a very concrete reconfiguration of urban space that pinpoints how Pentecostalism takes over hitherto secular realms: the conversion of state-owned as well as private cinemas into churches. One Sunday morning in late September 2002, when I had just returned to Ghana for a last stint of fieldwork on Ghanaian video films, my friend and colleague, Kodjo Senah, joined me on a car ride through Accra. On our route, unhampered by traffic jams which can be dreadful on a weekday, we passed by virtually all the cinemas in Accra: Olympia at Labadi, Regal at Osu, Rex, Opera, and Globe in Central Accra, Roxy at Adabraka, Orion at Kwame Nkrumah Circle, Oxford in Newtown, and Dunia in Nima. All were being used by Pentecostal-Charismatic churches, except Oxford which has been transformed into a department store. Already from afar one could hear the preachers displaying their virtuosity and eloquence in preaching the Word, the congregation praying in tongues, or the church's musical band playing swinging Gospel Highlife. In all this, loudspeakers were crucial mediators of the divine message, used not simply to reach the congregation inside but, above all, to communicate one's presence to the world outside. The fact that apparently "being heard" means "being there" indicates how Pentecostalism seeks to capture public space not only through images but also through sound.

While driving on, Kodjo told me how, as a child, he would go to watch films at Olympia, Regal, and Opera, often without his parents' consent, using his lunch money to buy a ticket. He explained to me that this marked appropriation of cinema space by churches and their noisy presence was quite recent and had come about as part and parcel of Ghana's recent turn to democracy. Although in the course of the 1980s Pentecostal churches, in particular, had become increasingly attractive, under the regime of J. J. Rawlings (1981–1992) they had more or less existed in a niche in society, not audible and visible as was the case now, but confined only to their places of worship. On the other hand, as a result of the spread of TV and, more recently, video, the cinemas had gradually lost their appeal to the audiences and were run-down and ill attended most of the time.

The appeal and public impact of these churches is only partly revealed by the last population census, which shows that 24.1 percent of the whole Ghanaian population regards itself as Pentecostal-Charismatic, whereas the figure is 37.7 percent in the Accra region (and, among all Christians in Greater Accra, the Pentecostals form 45.8 percent [Ghana Statistical Service 2000]). However, even the Orthodox churches have sought to accommodate Pentecostal views and practices so as not to lose members (cf. Meyer 1999a). Since most Protestant churches run prayer groups and the Catholic Church institutionalized the Charismatic renewal, it may safely be stated that Pentecostalism has become the main current in Ghanaian Christianity and at the same time has started to advertise itself outside the narrow confines of churches and congregations.

Significantly Pentecostal views, characterized by an uncompromising attitude toward local religious and, to some extent, cultural traditions (Coe 2000; van Dijk 2001), have become increasingly important in shaping the political public sphere. In many ways, in the wake of turning to a democratic constitution, Pentecostal-Charismatic leaders started to assert the necessity for Ghana to become a Christian nation (Gifford 1998, 85), and this entails the need to discard traditional religious practices, such as the public pouring of libation, as well as corruption. Difficult as all this may be from the perspective of politicians, clearly Pentecostalism is a power that cannot be ignored. In order to be elected, individual politicians from all parties struggle to show their commitment to Christianity and to their having been Born Again, and many do not hesitate to appear in one of the big Charismatic churches to publicly profess their faith, address the believers, and receive the blessings of the church leader.

Yet the presence of Pentecostalism reaches much further than political debate in the narrow sense in that it speaks to, and articulates, new social horizons of experience by linking up with popular culture as the prime arena for the work of fantasy. The churches' takeover of the cinema buildings is symptomatic of this broader development, instigated by the gradual liberalization of the media which implied the (albeit partial) commercialization of press, radio, TV, and cinema, and thus the retreat of the state from these media and an increasing fragmentation and privatization of the media scene. A case in point is the sale of the formerly state-owned Ghana Films Industry Corporation (GFIC) to a Malaysian television company in 1996 (Meyer 2001, 70). This sale was the result of the financial breakdown of the GFIC, which had been unable to produce a celluloid feature film for years, even at the time when it was under full state control. Film production, as well as importing suitable foreign films and maintaining the state-owned cinemas, appeared to be much too costly for the Ghanaian state, which spent a great deal of the limited media budget on TV. Also private cinema owners, for example, the Lebanese Captan family, found it difficult to maintain its cinema houses (all those cinemas mentioned above beginning with "O"), partly because of the increasing accessibility of TV and video in private homes and partly because of years of curfew in the early period of Rawlings's military regime which prevented people from going out at night. Even when the turn to democracy formally ended the previous "culture of silence," the old cinema industry was not revived again. Rather, its place was taken by the medium of video, which can be projected both on cinema screens and on TV.

When the Ghanaian video-film industry emerged in the late 1980s, the producers, usually self-trained persons who had been associated with the cinemas as film distributors or operators or simply keen spectators, sought to mimic the celluloid format, thus insisting that they made "Ghanaian *films*," not just videos. They fought for acceptance into the world of cinema, which was dominated by the old artistic elites associated with the GFIC and NAFTI, the National Film and Television Institute. As these groups more or less supported state cultural policies, the centrality of Christian images, and the demonization of local gods and spirits in video films, became a continuous bone of contention (Meyer 1999b). Eventually Ghanaian video films were screened in the cinemas, as well as in new smaller video centers set up in neighborhoods, with the help of beamers. Yet, in the late 1990s, a shift occurred, and now, for commercial reasons, videos are increasingly marketed as home videos and only after some time shown on TV. As a result, the cinemas became increasingly run-down and were ill-attended, standing instead as silent witnesses to a time when cinema still played a key role in structuring modern public space (cf. Larkin 2002) and offering access to a new public culture in colonial and early independent Ghana.

The Pentecostals were quick to assert their presence by occupying the deserted cinemas and buying airtime, thereby contributing to the emergence of a new public sphere characterized by the retreat of the state and the public presence of Christianity. Many of the big Pentecostal-Charismatic churches run their own media ministries, as does, for instance, Dr. Mensah Otabil's International Central Gospel Church. Otabil preaches on the Malaysian TV-station TV3 every Sunday evening, broadcasts his views on Radio Gold every weekday between 2:00 and 3:00 P.M., and produces and sells a broad range of audio- and videotapes (de Witte 2003). Other pastors run prayer programs early in the morning or late at night. If one flips through the stations on radio and TV, it is impossible to miss the programs oriented toward Pentecostalism, from talk shows to musical stations. And, driving through town, one is struck by the omnipresence of wall posters and bumper stickers advertising one or another Pentecostal-Charismatic church or event; some of the bigger churches, such as

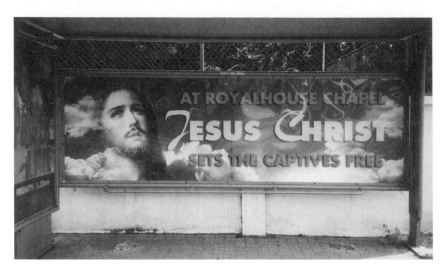

Fig. 14.3. Advert of Royal House Chapel. Photograph by Birgit Meyer.

the Royal House Chapel, even advertise themselves on large posters (depicting, among other things, Jesus peering up into the sky) put up at bus stops, thereby drawing an analogy between Coca-Cola, one of the major advertisements at bus stops, and Christianity.

Pentecostal-Charismatic churches owe much of their appeal to the fact that they easily, and seemingly effortlessly, tie into popular understandings and, in particular, take seriously anxieties about the evil machinations of demons and witches, whom they represent as vassals of Satan. These churches all share a projected notion of Christian modernity, which acknowledges the reality of all those evildoings, especially demons and other so-called superstitions, which a good Christian is supposed to "leave behind." In this way they mediate between frustrations and anxieties, and the wish for a better, more prosperous life. With God, it is said, all things are possible, and this cry underpins the claim of Pentecostalism to offer access to Christian modernity (Meyer 1999a, 141ff.; 2002).

The diffusion of Pentecostal views into public space also affects the realm of popular culture. Not only does Pentecostalism tie into, affirm, and recast popular notions, even formally independent media practitioners—from journalists to video filmmakers, from painters to musicians—have adopted Pentecostal representative forms. Recently, for example, the famous Ghanaian Highlife singer Kodjo Antwi publicly announced that he has been Born Again and feels attracted to the church of Mensah Otabil, and, in his new album, has included a number of Gospel songs. Similar public conversions occur regularly, often after an artist's reputation has been damaged by some scandal. While such a shift does not necessarily entail that artists truly perceive themselves as Born Again believers, it certainly indicates the crucial role of Pentecostalism in shaping Ghana's new image economy. Likewise many video-film producers adopt Pentecostal views and attitudes, although they may not consider themselves to be Born Again believers (some are even Muslim) as they know that affirming Pentecostal notions will assure a lucrative film. Thus movies usually thrive on an opposition of God and the Devil, in which the latter is shown to be powerful and yet is eventually overcome by the Holy Spirit; the ideal is a Christian version of modernity, centered on the nuclear family and on fresh notions of the subject separated from the extended family. Much use is also made of spectacular special effects, granting a voyeuristic look into the realm of darkness as well as the divine.

This return to Pentecostal notions, in my view, does not necessarily indicate an increase of religiosity in terms of deeply rooted inner belief but rather an expansion in space, on the surface of social life. Pentecostalism appears to conquer the public sphere through a centrifugal dispersion of audiovisual signs, and thereby purports a certain mood which binds people and to which they feel attracted because it connotes Christian norms and values (Meyer 2004). Of course, the commodification of Christian religion in the sphere of entertainment, and the proneness of Pentecostalism to thrive on this process, is not entirely new, nor confined to Ghana (cf. Moore 1994; Forbes and Mahan 2000). There are good reasons to agree with Lawrence Moore's suggestion that the successful presence of religion in modern societies depends on the ability to locate itself in the marketplace of culture. Indeed, Pentecostalism assumes a key role in feeding Ghana's new image economy, both by putting into circulation distinctly Pentecostal audiovisual signs and by contributing to the emergence of new infrastructures—religious programs on TV and radio, Gospel concerts, sale of music cassettes and sermons—along which these signs are diffused. In becoming ingrained in this new image economy, Pentecostal sounds and images spread like wildfire (a preferred simile for the Holy Spirit) but, above all, in terms of a presence to be seen and heard rather than a deeply felt state of being Born Again.

Pentecostals themselves are apprehensive about the possible devastating impact on Pentecostal religiosity by the adoption of new audiovisual media technologies and their association with an entertainment format. A question of much concern is whether people are truly Born Again Christians by displaying Christian bumper stickers or religious posters at their shops, or watching and listening to all the Christian subjects in the media. Some of the pastors I interviewed were critical of popular video films, because they fear that people watch them only to be entertained and fail to devote themselves to prayer and to changing their lives. Similarly pastors are at pains to admonish their congregation that attending church on Sundays entails more than showing off in lavish clothes, that what really matters is changing the inner person. This fear that superficiality may replace a depth of feeling signals that the public articulation of Pentecostalism, shaped by the exigencies of new media such as video and the urge to publicly profess one's faith to the world, risks a devaluation of meaning.

Further, as Pentecostalism becomes available outside the confines of churches, believers are addressed as audiences and consumers, and this, to a degree, recasts the religious experience (cf. De Witte 2003). This is not to say that there is no such thing as being Born Again but rather to stress that Christianity itself is being transformed by going public because it makes use of formats that are not of its own making and that can never be fully contained (cf. De Witte 2003; Van de Port 2005).[4] The public articulation of Pentecostalism takes it beyond the narrow sphere of religion (religion that is restricted to churches and targeting the inner person; cf. Asad 1993). By going public Pentecostalism recasts Christianity as distraction, both in the sense of deliberately adopting an entertainment format and dispersing the message without bounds. In doing so the Pentecostal message is dismembered into mediated religious forms and elements displayed everywhere in public urban space. The difficulty to ensure that those encountering these elements interpret them in line with Pentecostal understandings pinpoints that by spreading into the public sphere, religious authority over practices of mediation is, to some extent, undermined (see chapter 3 in this volume). Indeed, it seems that Pentecostalism cannot eschew the fact that distraction or *Zerstreuung*, as Samuel Weber (1996, 92ff.) explained in his reflection on Benjamin's use of the much more complex German term, is intrinsic to mass culture in the age of reproducibility. Simply put, the spread of Pentecostalism into the public sphere has a cost: it distracts from the genuine religious experience.

The Camera, Pentecostalism, and the Production of Vision

In the same way that Pentecostalism increasingly adopts entertainment features, so, too, does the realm of entertainment thrive parasitically on religion by representing itself through the format of talk shows on radio and TV and by employing top musicians in churches. Yet, on an experiential level, devotion and distraction—church and cinema—do not intermingle smoothly but instead rub against each other as two separate, albeit ever more entangled spheres. The transition requires deliberate action: a cinema must always be cleansed both literally and spiritually—by means of brooms and prayers—before being fit for use as a church.[5] This section examines the nexus of Pentecostalism, distraction, and mass culture by focusing on video films that are oriented toward Pentecostalism. The key concern is to show how video films confirm, lay bare, and to some extent destabilize Pentecostal practices of mediation, and for that matter Protestant practices as well, especially with regard to vision.

In order to understand how the medium of video relates to existing practices of mediation, it is important to briefly consider the complicated attitude of Protestantism toward images and its strong emphasis on the Word, both in the sense of the written Bible and oral preaching. Of course, it would be a mistake to take at face value Protestantism's alleged disregard of the image and iconoclastic inclination, which serves to express its difference vis-à-vis Catholicism's high regard of the image as a site of devotion (cf. Latour 2002).[6] As David Morgan (1998, 3) argues in his work on visual piety in America, "the act of looking itself contributes to religious formation and, indeed, constitutes a powerful practice of belief." He shows that, certainly in popular Protestant practice, images have a central role in that they reconfirm in a visual mode what people believe and think. The popular protestant aesthetic, to use his terms, "pivots on seeing as real what one has imagined" (26).

Morgan's plea to devote attention to "looking" as a practice constituting belief in Protestantism is well taken. While it is impossible in the framework of this essay to delve into a genealogy of looking in Ghanaian Christianity, it is useful to glance briefly at the way that mid-nineteenth-century Protestant missions introduced looking as specific Pietist practice. While the churches were kept sober and empty, and the missionaries were at pains to condemn local practices of idol worship, new religious images were introduced into converts' living rooms. For instance, the missionaries brought to Africa the famous lithograph of *The Broad and the Narrow Path*, which belonged to the popular culture of the Awakening and was cherished by African converts. This lithograph, still popular in Ghana and reprinted in numerous actualized versions, presents a very interesting relationship between image and word, as I have explained in detail elsewhere (Meyer 1999a, 31ff.). Juxtaposing images and biblical references, the lithograph focuses on a particular spectator who is made to look at the image and at the same time to look up the biblical reference in order to understand the former. Its first lesson is that the eye of God, depicted at the top of the image, sees everything and is able to penetrate the surface of the hidden. In order to be able to adopt His perspective, one has to submit oneself to His visual regime which entails that in order to see, one has to be seen. Here vision depends on divine surveillance. The second lesson is based on the juxtaposition of images and references to biblical texts and shows that, since images may evoke many confusing associations, it is only possible to determine their meaning by referring to the Bible. Thus, because there is little confidence in the power of the eye to genuinely understand an image, the lithograph offers a didactic device to practice the Protestant way of seeing the world. Here the Bible is presented as a key to allegorical interpretation, and thus limits the interpretative freedom stemming from the image. At the same time the lithograph, which, after all, is an image itself, acknowledges that the Bible alone is unable to create meaning, that images are needed in order to affirm the Bible's power to explain them.

While converts found it difficult to appropriate or even accept many new notions introduced by missionaries, it seems that they quite easily adopted Protestantism's popular visual culture and its acts of looking. At the same time viewing the world as an image to be understood by reference to the Bible alone was not enough for African Christians who were far more inclined than missionaries to obtain access to the realm of the invisible and to have visions. This urge to see, of course, links up with local religious traditions, which considered dreams and trance as means of acquiring access to the invisible world. The task of local priests was to communicate what they saw spiritually to those who were in need of support and could not see by themselves. It was this quest for visions which allow one to peek into what remains hidden to the naked eye (into the "spiritual world") and thereby make sense of the "physical world" that led to numerous conflicts between missionaries and African converts, and was the basis for the founding of African independent churches (see Meyer 1999a, 113ff.).

In Pentecostal-Charismatic churches, both vision and the Bible are central. Pastors claim to have visions, or even the Spirit of Discernment through the Holy Spirit—indeed this is often the basis of their power and even the reason why they broke away from another (more Orthodox) church to found their own—and refer to biblical passages so as to interpret what they saw in such a way that it becomes a revelation. In these churches pastors and believers invoke through their visions and dreams a huge imaginary space, the otherwise invisible realm of the powers of God and the Devil. The Bible is cited and called upon all the time, in a highly eclectic manner, in order to turn these visions (which are never confined to mere seeing but also imply hearing) into divine revelations and thus vest them with authority. In contrast to the more sober didactic representation of the act of looking as shown in the lithograph, which teaches that the visible can only be understood by referring to the Bible, here everything is geared to the production of vision itself, and the Bible is called upon to legitimate these visions.

For instance, in September 2002 I attended a Crusade organized by the World Miracle Church on the campus of the University of Ghana on three consecutive evenings. This church advertises itself as able to produce instant miracles on the basis of the leaders' capacity to see, and to hear messages from the Holy Spirit. As expected, night after night the Crusade drew a huge number of visitors, all eagerly awaiting the church leader, Bishop Agyen Asare, to perform a spectacular deliverance onstage—for example, prayers meant to free a person from indwelling spirits (cf. Meyer 1998). With full confidence he would announce that the "Holy Spirit just told me that there are twenty people in need of healing, come forward and I will pray for you," and indeed he would not rest until all twenty persons had stood up so that his vision had been proven right (even if he had to threaten with a story about a person who had once been called by the Lord but did not stand up, and right after the service died in an accident). People would race forward, howl, and throw themselves on the ground, thus participating in a complex spectacle of publicly casting out evil spirits (see chapter 2 in this volume). While other Pentecostal-Charismatic leaders may be a bit more moderate, they all have in common a strong emphasis on prophecy and vision, and frame the church service as a spectacular performance where the presence of the Holy Spirit can be witnessed.

Interestingly many video films also tie into this particular way of having and communicating visions as the central practice of Pentecostal mediation. Such movies are usually framed as confessions or testimonies, and make ample reference to biblical texts, either in the beginning or at the end, or state something like "To God be the Glory." Video films are often presented as *revelations*, thereby parasitically feeding on Pentecostal notions of vision. Movies construct spectators as Christians in need of vision, and seek to please them by offering them the privileged perspective of the omniscient eye of God, through a camera-mediated mimesis. Thus, by and large, there is little suspense in Ghanaian films, for the films themselves usually reveal to the spectators that which remains hidden from the film's main protagonists. Because spectators are addressed as witnesses, some find the films predictable and boring. However, for viewers with a strong Pentecostal inclination, especially women, the films offer audiovisual extensions and supplements to the Sunday sermon, and they are truly touched by what they see on the screen (Verrips 2002). Many fans of Ghanaian (and Nigerian) films told me repeatedly that a good movie definitely offers more than mere fun and distraction: it is not enough simply to laugh and clap and amuse oneself, certainly some hidden truths need to be revealed and certain morals taught or affirmed. Indeed, I noticed again and again that such movies would generate much audience response in the practice of viewing and trigger moral engagement. People would shout, sometimes even pray, in support of the good, and curse the bad with much vigor, thus practicing "devotional viewing" (cf. Gillespie 1995). Such movies are then discussed among friends or referred to in troublesome situations between friends or spouses ("Don't behave like this; haven't you seen such and such a film?"), and thereby popularize Pentecostal notions of the subject and of family life.

Some Pentecostal-Charismatic pastors whom I questioned as to their opinion of video films were concerned about the power of the image in itself; they feared that people might not even stay to watch the film to the very end and would be seduced by the power of the image alone, failing to notice the biblical quote and to realize the Christian orientation of the film. In other words, people would watch without adopting a Pentecostal way of looking and merely for the sake of fun, aestheticizing the invisible into witches, ghosts, evil spirits, and an occasional angel. Nevertheless, most of the pastors appreciated the medium of Christian film for offering powerful support to their sermons. One female pastor, Akua Adarquah-Yiadam, whose House of Faith Ministries hired the Opera Cinema for its Sunday and occasional weekday services, told me that although she somewhat disliked Ghanaian films because of their emphasis on occult forces (although in her church, too, pastors preached quite a lot about demons and the Devil), she certainly liked film as a medium. Some time ago she had shown a film to the congregation depicting how a dead man was raised from his coffin, which his widow had taken to the Crusade of a famous preacher in Nigeria. Such films, in her view, were able to document the power of God and were thus highly suitable to support one's faith with visual evidence.

Another Pentecostal pastor, Rev. Edmund Ossei Akoto of the Fifth Community Baptist Chapel (Madina, a suburb of Accra), was very much in favor of Ghanaian films. He explained to me that the Pentecostal-Charismatic churches had initiated a new mass movement in which the key term was "mass participation" in contrast to presenting Christianity to the congregation as a mere "program," as was the case with the Orthodox churches. In his view, as Pentecostals seek to extend their influence beyond the mere confines of the church service and to turn their members into full-time Christians, there is a need to reach out into the sphere of popular culture and the arts. Mass Pentecostalism requires all-round participation, and thus mass culture.

Before he was appointed pastor, Rev. Ossei Akoto and his wife would visit the Ghana Films Cinema at the GFIC, and now he often watched Ghanaian and Nigerian films on TV. In his view films "reveal the operation of the powers of darkness. They give ideas about how demonic forces operate, how to counteract evil forces with the blood of Christ, how to apply faith to counteract [the demonic forces]." Yet the films should not only portray evil forces but should make clear that it is God that overcomes these forces. Thus "to me, the ending [of a film] is the message. From here I make my own assessment and judgment." He therefore was not bothered about the depiction of occult forces, if in the end it was made clear that they were indeed evil. When I asked him how he knew that the demonic images would indeed reveal what happens in the invisible world, he emphasized that, in his opinion, about 80 percent of these visualizations were correct. He knew this, as he himself was much engaged in deliverance (i.e., practices of exorcizing evil spirits through the Holy Spirit); he saw how demons manifested themselves through people, and he also heard people confess, and "what they say matches with what the films show."

Thus, when his former schoolmate, the producer, director, and actor Augustine Abbey (alias Idikoko), asked him to play the role of a pastor in the film *Stolen Bible (Secret Society) I and II* (Idikoko Ventures 2001–2002), he accepted. *Stolen Bible* features a struggle between a secret society consisting of members who owe their wealth to a (spiritual) sacrifice of a beloved person, on the one hand, and divine power, embodied by a staunch Christian woman and a strong pastor, on the other.[7] The deliverance scene is intense, powerful, and highly realistic, and Akoto was at his best. He let himself go, as he usually does when he is in church. Knowing that many people would watch the movie, he wanted to preach a clear message. But this time it went even better than usual, because normally when he engages in deliverance he is tense, fearful, and cautious. In this situation, however, he experiences no fear and thus can perform very well. For him it was "great fun to cast out devils!"

Thus the power of a movie seems to derive from the extent to which it is able to appear as real, as a documentation of the spiritual realm, rather than just fiction. Viewers must be made to forget that they are merely watching a film (indeed, often the criticism of people who dislike a film is that it is too artificial). A good movie depends on eradicating any trace of the film as fiction and, instead, successfully featuring it as a revelation, thereby, with the help of the camera, convincingly bridging the realms of the visible and the invisible. In this sense films owe their power to their capacity to erase their own mediated nature and claim "im-media-cy" (Plate 2003, 7). Akoto's statement nicely captures the predicament of video-film production. While movies are organized as revela-

Fig. 14.4. Still from the video film *Stolen Bible* (produced by Great Idikoko Ventures).

tions of the struggle between divine and demonic forces, obviously they cannot simply record what goes on in the invisible realm. Rather, as Akoto's statement shows, they have to fake "the real thing" in order to make it seem as realistic as possible. Since the camera is a machine compelled to visualize (in Heidegger's words, to construct the "world as picture" [cf. Weber 1996, 76ff.]), it reduces even those matters that may initially resist or not lend themselves easily to audiovisual representation, to moving images (Meyer 2005).

It is precisely this gap between the camera as an image-producing device and its object that is depicted in fig. 14.1, which suggests that the camera, in attempting to capture the divine, mystifies rather than visualizes. The video camera cannot help but construct images of the divine, and thus mediate Christianity's invisible in line with the logic of film production, and yet these images can never be fully consonant with it. Thus the painting seems to infer that video films market their own visions, legitimize them with some biblical quote or Christian slogan, and invest them with a new aura, but all this amounts only to a camera-produced mediation of the invisible which is in no way superior to older attempts to mediate the invisible, such as devotional art. The impossibility of true representation notwithstanding, impossible representations are made all the time, yet carry with them the shadow of the very impossibility of their representativeness, which is a poignant, somewhat disenchanting comment on Ghana's Pentecostally loaded image economy.

At the same time, by depicting the aura as a product of the camera, the painting draws attention to the link between technology and enchantment. For there is more at stake than the realization that the video camera, though creating images by virtue of its technology and parasitically claiming to embody Pentecostal vision practices, is not the ideal medium of Pentecostal mediation that it claims to be. The relationship between camera and visual object is more complicated. While, for Akoto, the fact that there was no real exorcism at stake made him act even more impressively, Augustine Abbey, who played the role of the occultist to be exorcised, experienced the scene as more diffuse and strange, almost as if something actually was to be cast out. Adding to the confusion was that the snake, which was supposed to have been made visible through the power of the Holy Spirit in the film, went missing on location, which caused people to panic. This experience echoes the fears and experiences of actors and others involved in film production when they are engaged in the work of camera-mediated revelation.

In September 2002 I went on location with the crew and cast of the video film *Turning Point*. This film is about a woman who gradually becomes a Born Again Christian and thus is saved from her objectionable boyfriend, an occultist who wants to kill her as a sacrifice to his bloodthirsty god. When I spoke with Nina Nwabueze, the artist responsible for creating the occultist's shrine for the film, I quickly realized that distinguishing between fake and real shrines made little sense. Her job, she told me, required that she visit the very same "fetish markets" attended by real native priests. She would carefully examine all the items for sale so as to memorize their outlook, buy some rather innocent objects, and then build the major part of the shrine from other materials. Even when she built the made-up shrine, she would fast and pray beforehand, and then again go through deliverance prayers afterward. She explained to me that spirits would roam about in the air, always seeking another "image" (used here in a broad sense, encompassing paintings, pots, and statues) to dwell in. Hence one needed to be careful about all images, especially those that might resemble shrines, even if they were built merely with the intention to serve as a prop. Precisely because all the items manufactured for the film were to reveal the machinations of the Devil and demonic spirits, one had to be especially cautious, since the Devil would make every effort to disturb those who acted in or produced films that intended to show how he operates. The next day when we arrived at the place where the film shrine was to be set up, we could hear drumming outside, which was immediately identified as coming from a "real fetish shrine" next door. I jokingly remarked that the shrine scene could now be filmed with the sound of real fetish drums in the background. The actor who was to play the occultist retorted vehemently that he was not prepared "to get into the real thing," as that would be dangerous.

Later I talked about these observations with other video filmmakers. I learned that spirits may even have an impact on the camera, which, although a neutral technological device, could still be disturbed in its operation by spiritual forces. At times certain objects simply "refused" to be shown on camera; in the end, one never achieved the shots one had intended and sometimes nothing appeared at all (cf. Spyer 2001). Another video-film producer and director, Michael Akwetey-Kanyi, also explained to me that, even if a fake shrine were set up, that it was merely a copy was not a safeguard since spirits could still enter the shrine. He would always be sure to use as little original materials as possible in depicting the shrine and the rituals associated with it—water instead of alcohol, starch dyed with red coloring instead of blood—for after all, he remarked, "film is make-believe, so people will still take all this as the real thing." This statement aptly captures how video films claim to reveal what actually happens in the conjuncture of the physical and spiritual realms, and yet these "revelations" cannot be based on the use of original materials; because the use of original materials is dangerous, the films have to resort to fake representations— even though these, too, may be affected by occult forces. As there is no clear-cut boundary between reality and fiction, in the process of shooting a film simulation always entails the risk of mimesis, thereby affecting those who seek to represent "the spiritual" for the sake of revelation (cf. Taussig 1993).

This complicated relationship between fiction and reality, and the insistence that in order to make statements about the latter one has to make use of the former, reveals an important aspect of Pentecostal vision practices. For, in a sense, quite similar to the make-believe of video films, Pentecostal pastors, too, with their strong emphasis on vision as a sign of the Holy Spirit and a source of authority, need to develop techniques that make visions available in public at the right time. A successful Pentecostal service, as pointed out above, depends on a particular format: the Holy Spirit is to come down, here and now, enter the pastor, and give him visions that will make the service spectacular and thus lead more people to church. Clearly public visions are the product of a sophisticated set of spiritual techniques able to turn pastors into seers and give them a direct hotline to the Holy Spirit. In this sense pastors may be seen as a camera, and witnesses as spectators in the audience of a cinema film.

Hent de Vries (2001) has advocated dismissing the binary opposition of religion and technology, which may seem to make sense at first, and yet, when one delves more deeply into public religion to explore the interface between religion and technology, the suggestion is rendered dubious. For religion to articulate its message, it depends on mediation, and hence certain techniques and even technologies are required to make the invisible accessible. De Vries has eloquently shown how miracle and special effect, magic and visual technology, "come to occupy the same space, obey the same regime and the same logic" (28). In my view the danger of video technology haphazardly invoking occult forces testifies to the idea that video technology and Pentecostalism inhabit the same space and act in concert with each other. Since pastors and filmmakers both depend on certain techniques to mediate the invisibility of Christianity so as to make others believe, there is strictly no difference between miracles and camera-produced effects, between revelations in church services and those in films, between believers and spectators. That believers at times lament the blurring of the boundaries between the two further testifies to the extent to which the spheres of religion and entertainment are intertwined. In this sense video films lay bare the operation of Pentecostal mediation, with its emphasis on vision and spectacle (see chapter 2 in this volume). Moreover, that video technology is extremely suitable in bringing out the techniques that constitute the act of looking in Pentecostal circles suggests that Pentecostalism thrives on a cinematographic mode of representation. The linkage, therefore, between Pentecostal vision and video films is by no means coincidental but is implied and even, I dare say, prefigured in Pentecostal practices of mediation.

In this essay I have tried to show how, by understanding religion as a practice of mediation, Pentecostalism has increasingly "taken place" in the public sphere as a result of Ghana's turn to democracy, and the liberalization and commercialization of the media. Relatively undisturbed by the state, but all the more indebted to the emerging image economy, Pentecostalism has spread into the public sphere, disseminating signs and adopting formats not entirely of its own making and, in the process, has been taken up by popular culture. In the entanglement of religion and entertainment, new horizons of social experience have emerged, thriving on fantasy and vision and popularizing a certain mood oriented toward Pentecostalism. This movement of spatial extension, as I have tried to show, is criticized at times from within, as pastors and believers fear losing control.

Yet, that distraction and devotion are to be kept apart on the experiential level cannot be used in defense of a strict difference between cinema and church, entertainment and religion. At the same time it would be too simplistic just to write off, as mere entertainment, the public appearance of images derived from Pentecostalism, as if the entertainment format could completely absorb the religious and, in a sense, put an end to religion. The point is that, in Ghana, Pentecostalism is alive and kicking precisely because it casts religion in a new (postmodern?) form (cf. Martin 2002), a form geared to mass spectatorship and one intrinsic to distraction in the sense of *Zerstreuung*. *Zerstreuung* refers here to "the dispersed, centrifugal structure of mass phenomena" (Weber 1996, 94) which, as Benjamin (1978) showed, is condensed in the technology of film as it blows apart the prison of metropolitan space by "the dynamite of the tenth of a second" (236) and offers adventurous traveling among the ruins, putting together its images under new laws, laws that require novel ways of reception that parallel the process of recording (indeed, in German, both processes are described as *Aufnahme*).

The lament that devotion is opposed to distraction pinpoints the sense of loss evoked by the alleged impossibility of truthful representation, which is part and parcel of religious mediation, whether in a church or in the cinema. This problem of representativeness is depicted by the smoke in the painting shown in fig. 14.2, which, in the first place, is what intrigued me to write this essay.

Notes

The ethnographic material on which this chapter is based was collected in the framework of the NWO-Pionier research program "Modern Mass Media, Religion and the Imagination of Communities" (http://www.pscw.uva.nl/media-religion). Earlier versions were presented in the Pionier Seminar (February 2003), the Anthropology and Media Seminar at the School of Oriental and African Studies (London, March 13, 2003), and the Meeting of the Society for the Anthropology of Religion (Providence, April 24, 2003). I am most grateful to Augustine Abbey and Ashiagbor Akwetey-Kanyi for their tremendous help in doing fieldwork on the Ghanaian video-film scene, and Charles Hirschkind, Stephen Hughes, Bruce Knauft, Annelies Moors, David Morgan, Sudeep Dasgupta, Rafael Sanchez, Mattijs van de Port, and Jojada Verrips for their stimulating comments on earlier versions of this essay.

1. David Morgan drew my attention to Jan Gossaert's painting *Saint Luke Painting the Virgin* (1520). This fabulous painting depicts the virgin as surrounded by smoke and angels, so as to visualize her miraculous apparition. Saint Luke is shown to make a painting of this apparition with his hand being guided by an angel, since he is unable to see what spectators of the image can see. As in the painting described above, there is an image within the image which is only visible to the outside spectator. Gossaert's painting pinpoints the impossibility of depicting or capturing divinity straightforwardly in an image, and maintains that *religious* ways of seeing are necessary in order to make the image materialize. It seems to me that the roadside painting of the cameraman targeting Jesus can be placed in the same tradition, which pinpoints that representations of divinity can only be achieved through divine mediation. The image of the cameraman, however, goes one step further in suggesting that the camera employed in mediating the divine mystifies and conceals, rather than merely reveals.

2. This notion is inspired by Webb Keane's idea of representational economy, which is meant to "capture the ways in which practices and ideologies put words, things, and actions into complex articulation with one another" (2001, 85). I wish to highlight the complex articulation of images—painted, audio-visual, or photographed—with one another, hence the term "image economy." The notion of economy is important because it draws attention to the fact that these articulations depend on the logic of demand and supply in the market.

3. In Ghana ethnicity certainly plays an important role in the politics of belonging (Lentz and Nugent 2000); the point is that Pentecostalism crosscuts ethnicity.

4. Of course, the public spread of Pentecostalism does not occur at the expense of churches but is organized by them. Though many Pentecostals do attend church, the articulation of Pentecostal signs and symbols in public challenges the older forms of Christian religiosity as being confined to churches and the private sphere. Pentecostalism's spread into the public sphere raises questions concerning the maintenance of religious authority and the very nature of Pentecostal belief.

5. For instance, I witnessed and filmed how the House of Faith Ministries Church,

which held its services in the Opera cinema, transformed the theater from a place of worship back into a cinema by removing various lighting fixtures and decorations like plastic flowers and plants as well as the screen that rendered invisible the cinema toilets. The members of this church clearly saw the cinema as a smelly, dirty, and immoral environment, and it took some energy to transform it to a place of worship.

6. Usually this critique is backed by the Second Commandment's admonishment not to make images. Also 1. Cor. 13,9 comes to mind.

7. *Stolen Bible* is about a man, Ken, who is jobless, and his loving and beautiful wife Nora. Just when Ken is desperate about his situation, he meets his old friend Ato, who is fabulously rich and takes him to a secret society, Jaguda Buja, whose members obtain their riches by sacrificing the person they love most in life—an ongoing theme in Ghanaian and Nigerian films (cf. Meyer 1995). Ken tries to sacrifice another woman, Dora, who turned to prostitution because of poverty, instead of his own wife, Nora, but his plan fails, because Dora calls the name of Jesus in time. When he is forced to sacrifice Nora in a spectacular scene involving special effects such as a snake coming out of her mouth, he indeed begins to get rich and even obtains a high position in his church. Yet when the pastor is about to honor him in public, Nora's spirit returns and transforms Ken into a madman—"You cannot go to heaven with a stolen bible"—and makes him lose his riches. One day Dora, who now works for the Lord, finds Ken in the street and takes him to a deliverance session, where a pastor (Reverend Akokoto) prays over him until the evil spirit has left him as well as all the other members of the secret cult.

References

Asad, Talal. 1993. *Genealogies of Religion: Discipline and Reasons of Power in Christianity and Islam.* Baltimore, Md.: Johns Hopkins University Press.

Benjamin, Walter. 1978. The Work of Art in the Age of Mechanical Reproduction. In *Illuminations,* ed. Hannah Arendt, 217–252. New York: Schocken Books.

Coe, Cati. 2000. "Not Just Drumming and Dancing": The Production of National Culture in Ghana's Schools. Ph.D. dissertation, University of Pennsylvania.

Comaroff, Jean, and John Comaroff. 1999. Occult Economies and the Violence of Abstraction: Notes from the South African Postcolony. *American Ethnologist* 26 (2): 279–303.

Dijk, Rijk van. 2001. Contesting Silence: The Ban on Drumming and the Musical Politics of Pentecostalism in Ghana. *Ghana Studies* 4:31–64.

Forbes, Bruce David, and Jeffrey H. Mahan, eds. 2000. *Religion and Popular Culture in America.* Berkeley: University of California Press.

Ghana Statistical Service. 2000. *Population and Housing Census (Provisional Results).* Accra: Ghana Statistical Service.

Gifford, Paul. 1998. *African Christianity: Its Public Role.* Bloomington and Indianapolis: Indiana University Press.

Gillespie, Marie. 1995. Sacred Serials, Devotional Viewing, and Domestic Worship: A Case-Study in the Interpretation of Two TV Versions of the *Mahabharata* in a Hindu Family in West London. In *To Be Continued . . . Soap Operas around the World,* ed. Robert C. Allen, 354–380. New York: Routledge.

Habermas, Jürgen. 1990 [1962]. *Strukturwandel der Öffentlichkeit. Untersuchungen zu einer Kategorie der bürgerlichen Gesellschaft.* Frankfurt: Suhrkamp.

Keane, Webb. 2002. Sincerity, "Modernity," and the Protestants. *Cultural Anthropology* 17 (1): 65–92.

Latour, Bruno. 2002. What Is Iconoclash? Or Is There a World beyond the Image Wars? In *Iconoclash: Beyond the Image Wars in Science, Religion, and Art,* ed. Bruno Latour and Peter Weibel, 14–18. Cambridge, Mass.: MIT Press.

Larkin, Brian. 2002. The Materiality of Cinema Theatres in Northern Nigeria. In *Media Worlds: Anthropology on New Terrain,* ed. Faye D. Ginsburg, Lila Abu-Lughod, and Brian Larkin, 319–336. Berkeley: University of California Press.

Lentz, Carola, and Paul Nugent eds.. 2000. *Ethnicity in Ghana: The Limits of Invention.* London: Macmillan.

Martin, David. 2001. *Pentecostalism: The World Their Parish.* Oxford: Blackwell.

Meyer, Birgit. 1995. "Delivered from the Powers of Darkness": Confessions about Satanic Riches in Christian Ghana. *Africa* 65 (2): 236–255.

———. 1998. "Make a Complete Break with the Past": Memory and Post-colonial Modernity in Ghanaian Pentecostalist Discourse. *Journal of Religion in Africa* 27 (3): 316–349.

———. 1999a. *Translating the Devil: Religion and Modernity among the Ewe in Ghana.* IAL-Series. Trenton, N.J.: Africa World Press.

———. 1999b. Popular Ghanaian Cinema and "African Heritage." *Africa Today* 46 (2): 93–114.

———. 2001. Money, Power, and Morality: Popular Ghanaian Cinema in the Fourth Republic. *Ghana Studies* 4:65–84.

———. 2004. "Praise the Lord": Popular Cinema and Pentecostalite Style in Ghana's New Public Sphere. *American Ethnologist* 31 (1): 92–110.

———. 2005. Mediating Tradition: Pentecostal Pastors, African Priests and Chiefs in Ghanaian Popular Films. In *Christianity and Social Change in Africa: Essays in Honor of John Peel,* ed. Toyin Falola, 275–304. Durham, N.C.: Carolina Academic Press.

Moore, R. Lawrence. 1994. *Selling God: American Religion in the Marketplace of Culture.* Oxford: Oxford University Press.

Morgan, David. 1998. *Visual Piety: A History and Theory of Popular Religious Images.* Berkeley: University of California Press.

Morris, Rosalind C. 2002. A Room with a Voice: Mediation and Mediumship in Thailand's Information Age. In *Media Worlds: Anthropology on New Terrain,* ed. Faye D. Ginsburg, Lila Abu-Lughod, and Brian Larkin, 383–397. Berkeley: University of California Press.

Negt, Oskar, and Alexander Kluge. 1974. *Öffentlichkeit und Erfahrung. Zur Organisationsanalyse von bürgerlicher und proletarischer Öffentlichkeit.* Frankfurt am Main: Suhrkamp.

Plate, S. Brent. 2003. Introduction: Filmmaking, Mythmaking, Culture Making. In *Representing Religion in World Cinema: Filmmaking, Mythmaking, Culture Making,* ed. S. Brent Plate, 1–15. New York: Palgrave.

Port, Mattijs van de. 2005. Circling around the "Really Real": Spiritual Possession Ceremonies and the Search for Authenticity in Bahian Candomblé. *Ethos* 32 (2): 149–179.

Spyer, Patricia. 2001. The Cassowary Will Not Be Photographed. In *Religion and Media,* ed. Hent de Vries and Samuel Weber, 304–320. Stanford, Calif.: Stanford University Press.

Taussig, Michael. 1993. *Mimesis and Alterity: A Particular History of the Senses*. New York: Routledge.

Verrips, Jojada. 2002. Haptic Screens and Our Corporeal Eye. *Etnofoor* 15 (1/2): 21–46.

Vries, Hent de. 2001. In Media Res: Global Religion, Public Spheres, and the Task of Contemporary Religious Studies. In *Religion and Media*, ed. Hent de Vries and Samuel Weber, 4–42. Stanford, Calif.: Stanford University Press.

Weber, Samuel. 1996. *Mass Mediauras: Form Technics Media*. Stanford, Calif.: Stanford University Press.

Witte, Marleen de. 2003. Altar Media's *Living Word:* Televised Christianity in Ghana. *Journal of Religion in Africa* 33 (2): 172–202.

Woolfe, Ernie, III. 2000. *Extreme Canvas: Hand-Painted Movie Posters from Ghana*. Dilettante Press.

Contributors

Walter Armbrust is Lecturer in the Faculty of Oriental Studies at the University of Oxford, where he holds the Albert Hourani Fellowship in Modern Middle East Studies. He is author of *Mass Culture and Modernism in Egypt* and editor of *Mass Mediations: New Approaches to Popular Culture in the Middle East and Beyond* and of a triple issue of *Visual Anthropology* focusing on the Middle East.

Patricia Birman is Professor of Anthropology at the State University of Rio de Janeiro. She has published on gender-religion relationships in Afro-Brazilian religion, and Pentecostalism and religious pluralism in France and Brazil. She is editor of *Religiao e espaço público*.

Sudeep Dasgupta is Assistant Professor of Media Studies at the University of Amsterdam. His current research includes diasporic culture in the European context. He is editor of *Constellations of the Transnational: Modernity, Culture, Critique*.

Rachel Dwyer is Reader in Indian Studies and Cinema at the School of Oriental and African Studies, University of London. Her books include *Gujarati; All You Want Is Money, All You Need Is Love: Sex and Romance in Modern India; Pleasure and the Nation: the History and Politics of Public Culture in India* (co-edited with Christopher Pinney); *The Poetics of Devotion: The Gujarati Lyrics of Dayaram; Cinema India: The Visual Culture of the Hindi Film* (co-authored with Divia Patel); and *Yash Chopra*.

Faye Ginsburg is David B. Kriser Professor of Anthropology at New York University, where she is also the director of the Center for Media, Culture, and History, and the codirector of the Center for Religion and Media. She has been studying the growth of media in indigenous communities worldwide for the last decade. Her books include *Media Worlds: Anthropology on New Terrain* (co-edited with Lila Abu-Lughod and Brian Larkin).

Rosalind I. J. Hackett is Distinguished Professor in the Humanities at the University of Tennessee, Knoxville, where she teaches Religious Studies and Anthropology. She has published widely on new religious movements in Africa, as well as on religious pluralism, art, gender, the media, religion and human rights, and religious conflict in Nigeria. Her books include *Religious Persecution as a U.S. Policy Issue* (co-edited with Marc Silk and Dennis Hoover). She is President of the International Association for the History of Religion (2005–2010).

Charles Hirschkind is Assistant Professor of Anthropology at the University of California, Berkeley. His work focuses on the intersections of religious practice, rhetorical traditions, media technologies, and emergent forms of political community in the urban Middle East and North America. He has recently completed a book on the forms of media-based discipline through which Egyptian Muslims seek to cultivate ethical modes of sensory experience and appraisal.

David Lehmann is Reader in Social Science at Cambridge University. He is the author of *Democracy and Development in Latin America: Economics, Politics, and Religion in the Post-war Period* and *Struggle for the Spirit: Religious Transformation and Popular Culture in Brazil and Latin America.*

Birgit Meyer is Professor of Religion and Society at the Research Centre Religion and Society, Department of Anthropology, University of Amsterdam and Professor of Anthropology at the Free University, Amsterdam. Her publications include *Translating the Devil: Religion and Modernity among the Ewe in Ghana; Globalization and Identity: Dialectics of Flow and Closure* (co-edited with Peter Geschiere), and *Magic and Modernity. Interfaces of Revelation and Concealment* (co-edited with Peter Pels).

Annelies Moors holds the ISIM chair at the University of Amsterdam and directs the research program on cultural politics and Islam. She is author of *Women, Property, and Islam: Palestinian Experiences 1920–1990;* co-editor of *Discourse and Palestine: Power, Text, and Context;* and guest editor of a special issue of *Islamic Law and Society* (2003) about public debates and family law reform.

Ayşe Öncü is Professor of Sociology and the coordinator of the Cultural Studies Program at Sabanci University, Istanbul. Her publications include the co-edited volume *Space, Culture, and Power: New Identities In Globalizing Cities.* Her research interests include city cultures, cultural politics, and comparative media studies.

Dorothea E. Schulz is Assistant Professor of Anthropology at the Free University of Berlin. She is author of *Perpetuating the Politics of Praise: Jeli Singers, Radios, and the Politics of Tradition in Mali.* Her interests include West Africa, expressive culture and performance, popular culture, anthropology of media, anthropology of religion, and gender studies.

Batia Siebzehner is Research Fellow and the head of the Latin American Unit at the Harry S. Truman Institute for the Advancement of Peace at Hebrew University, Jerusalem, and Senior Lecturer at Beit Berl College, where she is also the head of the Department of Informal Education. She is author of *La universidad americana y la ilustracion.*

Patricia Spyer is Professor of Anthropology of Modern Indonesia at Leiden University. She is author of *The Memory of Trade: Modernity's Entanglements on an Eastern Indonesian Island;* editor of *Border Fetishisms: Material Objects in Unstable Spaces;* and co-editor of *Handbook of Material Culture.*

Jeremy Stolow is Assistant Professor of Communication Studies and Sociology at McMaster University, Ontario, Canada. His area of research concerns relationships between religious authority, media technologies, and popular culture in transnational perspective.

Index

cinema, 277–278; Shiv Sena in, 276, 277, 281; television in, 258–259, 263–270, 273–274; Urdu in Hindi film industry, 275, 286nn9,11

Indian (Hindustani), 287n27

Indonesia: and acronym SARA, 156, 159, 160, 163n7; Christianity in, 154, 161, 164n16; *Jawa Pos* in, 163n3; journalists on violence in, 2, 13–14, 152–162; *Manado Pos* newspaper in, 153, 154–156, 158, 160, 161, 162, 163n3; 1990s in, 248n3; Petrus killings in, 157, 158; *Radar Kieraha* newspaper in, 153–154, 156–157, 160, 161; radio in, 163n5; and *reformasi* era, 152, 155, 157, 164n13; Suharto regime in, 156, 158

Infotainment and religion, 15–19

International Monetary Fund (IMF), 152, 261

Internet: and ArtScroll Publications, 88n15; and Hindu Right, 18, 262; Öztürk on, 233; on Ramadan, 209

Iran, women in, 119–120, 121, 126n4

Iraq Gulf War, 259

Islam: Bosnian Muslims, 29–30, 39; cassette sermons in Egypt, 2, 8, 29–49; and *da'wa*, 31–32, 35, 49n5; debates on women and, 13; fundamentalism in generally, and media, 5–6; Haidara in Mali, 2, 10, 13, 134–135, 137–144, 145, 148nn24,27, 148–149n28; and media, 5–6; and music, 33–35; Öztürk on, 241–244; political Islam, 133–135; *Ramadan Riddles (Fawazir Ramadan)* television program in Egypt, 2, 16–17, 207–221, 221n2, 224–225n25; and "secular" Muslims in Turkey, 2, 17, 227–248; in South Africa, 172, 176, 181n18; in Turkey, 229–231, 241–244; in United States, 38–39; and women, 13, 115–126

Israel: air safety in, 109n9; Chabad in, 103; *haredism* in, 93, 94, 96, 99, 102, 105, 110n13; Hebrew as official language of, 78; kibbutz in, 66; official radio in, 93–94, 95, 109n8; pirate radio in, 1, 10, 94–101; popular music in, 95, 102; Shas Party in, 10, 92–93, 95, 96, 101, 103, 108; social enclaves and cultural divisions in, 91–92, 101; television in, 93–94, 109n11; tension between high and low culture in, 101–104; *t'shuva* movement in, 10, 92–95, 98–104, 106–108, 109n4; and West Bank settlers, 109–110n11, 127n14; Yitzchak in, 10, 102, 103–106

Israel Broadcasting Authority, 94

Isti'dhan, 32

Jameson, Fredric, 252, 259

Jardiwarnpa: A Warlpiri Fire Ceremony, 195–200, *197, 198*, 202–203n14

Jawa Pos, 163n3

Jews. *See* Judaism

Journalists: and changes in news media technology, 164n15; and transparency, 152–157; on violence in Indonesia, 2, 13–14, 152–162

Judaism: *Agudat Israel*, 9, 74, 75, 79, 81, 85, 87n5; and ArtScroll Publishers, 9–10, 73–87, 87nn1–2, 88nn13,15; Ashkenazim, 1, 10, 87n5; and Chassidim, 101, 109n5; and *haredism*, 9, 10, 74–87, 87n3, 88n13, 93, 94, 96, 99, 102, 105, 110n13; and *kiruv* movement, 80–81, 85, 88n9; London Jewish community, 81–87, 88n10; modern Jewish reading public, 76–79; as religion of the book, 9, 76–79; Sephardim, 1; in South Africa, 181n18; *t'shuva* movement, 10, 92–95, 98–104, 106–108, 109n4; and Zionism, 105, 109n1

Jünger, Ernst, 158–159

Kabhi khushi kabhie gham (K3G), 282

Al-Kafi, 'Umar 'Abd, 33, 42

Kandukondein kandukondein, 286n20

Kehilot, 76–77, 80

Keita, Modibo, 136, 148n16

Khan, Aamir, 275

Khan, Salman, 275, 276

Khatib, 42–46

Khomeini, Ayatollah, 128n19

Khutaba', 30, 36, 39, 42, 44–45

Kibbutz, 66

Kiruv movement, 80–81, 85, 88n9

Kishk, 'Abd al-Hamid, *33*, 36, 39–40, 42, 45, 47

Konare, Alpha, 137, 146n1, 147n5

Kuch kuch hota hai, 279

Lagaan (Once upon a Time in India), 282

Langton, Marcia, 196, 203n15

Lee, Bishop Peter, 171, 182n39

Literacy. *See* Education

London Jewish community, 81–87, 88n10

Lubavitch Chassidim (Chabad), 102–103

Maachis, 286n17

Macedo, Bishop, 56, 64, 65

Mahabaratha, 18

Maimonides, 102

Mali: ADEMA in, 137, 146n1; AMUPI in, 137, 140, 142–143, 145, 148nn18,25; *Ansar Dine* in, 134, 139, 140; *arabisants* in, 133,

Passion of the Christ, 1
Pentecostalism: and Bible, 302; compared
with *t'shuva* movement, 106–108; format
of Pentecostal service, 302, 307; in Ghana,
2, 11, 18–19, 70n15, 290–309; in Latin
America generally, 70n14, 107; and media
generally, 5–6; and miracles, 56, 62, 302; in
Nigeria, 2, 70n14, 174; prophecy and vision
in, 302–303; in public sphere, 295–300, 308,
309n4; Universal Church of the Kingdom
of God (UCKG) in Brazil, 8–9, 52–68; and
video-film producers in Ghana, 2, 11, 18–
19, 290–309; and video-film producers in
Nigeria, 2
People's Communication Charter, 178
Peterson, Nicolas, 194, 201nn1,4,6, 202nn9–
10,13, 202–203n14, 203n15
Pintupi Revisit Yaru Yaru, 190
Pintupi Revisit Yumari, 190
Pirate radio: and Ashkenazi in Israel, 94;
finances for, 97; government closing of,
95–97; and intimacy with audience, 99;
Kol HaChesed as, 98–99; Micol Halev as,
97–98, 99; and Sephardi in Israel, 1, 10, 94–
101; and *t'shuva* movement, 98–101; and
women, 99–100
Politics: aestheticization of, 256; identity politics, 11–15
Poverty in Rio de Janeiro, 56–57, 67–68
Presbyterian Church, 69n11
Public sphere: and *da'wa* movement, 31–
32, 35–48, 49n5, 49–50n8; female public
spheres, 121–122; Habermas on, 3–4, 11,
120, 123, 126n3, 127n13, 132–133, 135, 141,
145–146, 146n2, 192, 253, 257, 269–270,
294; Hindu nationalism and return of aura
to, 251–270; indigenous public sphere in
Australia, 198–201, 203n16; and media, 4;
modern Muslim public sphere, 115–116,
119–126; Negt and Kluge on, 294; Pentecostalism in, 295–300, 308, 309n4; politics
of difference and religion in, 11–15; and religion, 3–6, 11–15; Salvatore on, 6, 7, 49n6;
and Universal Church of the Kingdom of
God (UCKG) in Brazil, 67–68; and women,
119–126, 126n3

Quran: Haidara on, 141–142; and music, 33–
35; Öztürk on, 241; on Ramadan, 209; reading of, forbidden in Turkish schools, 49n7

Rabin, Yitzhak, 97, 99
Radar Kieraha, 153–154, 156–157, 160, 161
Radio: in Africa, 180n6; and air safety in Israel, 109n9; in Ghana, 297, 300; Haidara's
use of, in Mali, 13, 141; in India, 258; in
Indonesia, 163n5; legal status of radio sta-
tions, 97; official radio in Israel, 93–94, 95,
109n8; pirate radio in Israel, 1, 10, 94–101;
preference for, over television, 107; *Radio
Islamique* in Mali, 142–143
Ramadan, 207–209, 214–215, 220–221, 221n3,
221–222n6, 223n14, 233
Ramadan Riddles (Fawazir Ramadan), 2, 16–
17, 207–221, 221n2, 224–225n25
Ramayana, 18
Rashtriya Swayamsevak Sangh (RSS), 262,
264, 281
Ratnam, Mani, 280–281, 287n23
Rawlings, J. J., 292, 296, 297
RBP (Religious Broadcasting Panel), 14, 170,
171, 172, 176, 181n13, 182n30
Religion: decline of, 4–5; and entertainment,
15–19; new publics for mediated religion,
6–11; and politics in the nation-state, 68–
69n3; politics of difference and public
sphere, 11–15; and public sphere, 3–6, 11–
15; relationship between media and gener-
ally, 1–20, 166. *See also* Hinduism; Islam;
Judaism; Pentecostalism; Religious freedom
Religious Broadcasting Panel (RBP), 14, 170,
171, 172, 176, 181n13, 182n30
Religious freedom: in African countries, 168–
169, 178; in Brazil, 69n6; Moosa on, 178; in
South Africa, 178
Representational economy, 309n2
Rio de Janeiro. *See* Brazil
Rithambhara, Sadhvi, 285n4
Roja (Rose), 280–281, 287n24
RSS (Rashtriya Swayamsevak Sangh), 262,
264, 281

Saatchi Synagogue, London, 84–86, 88n16
SABC (South African Broadcasting Corpora-
tion), 14, 167, 169–180, *173, 175, 177,*
180n11, 181nn16,26, 182nn29,40
SACC (South African Council of Churches), 170
Saint Luke Painting the Virgin (Gossaert),
309n1
Salamandra, Christa, 222n9
Salvatore, Armando, 6, 7, 49n6
Sami, Muhammad, 207–208
Sandall, Roger, 190, 191, 193, 194, 195, 199,
200, 201n4, 202n8
Sardari Begum, 286n16
Sarfarosh (The Willing Martyr), 279
Satya, 279
Schach, Rav, 94, 109n7

322   *Index*

Senegal, 135
Sephardi: and educational system in Israel, 92;
  pirate radio used by, in Israel, 1, 10, 94–101;
  and Shas Party, 92–93, 95, 96, 101, 103, 108;
  and t'shuva movement, 10, 108
Serbs, 29–30
Sermon tapes. See Cassette sermons
SET (Sony Entertainment Television), 259, 269
Seth, Swapan, 265–266
Al-Sha'arawi, Muhammed Mitwalli, 42
Shahin, 'Abd al-Sabbur, 42
Shari'a, 31, 167–168
Shas Party, 10, 92–93, 95, 96, 101, 103, 108
Shiv Sena, 276, 277, 281
Siegel, James T., 155, 157
Sikkhs, 279
Singh, Yashika, 174, 181n26
Soares, Luis Eduardo, 69n5, 146n2
Sony Entertainment Television (SET), 259, 269
"Sonya," 207–208
South Africa: and African Renaissance move-
  ment, 175; African Traditional Religion
  (ATR) in, 175–177, 177; challenges for tele-
  vision broadcasting in, 174–176; Christian
  programming on television in, 169–175,
  179; examples of television programs in,
  172–174; Hinduism in, 181n18; Human
  Rights Commission in, 176; Independent
  Forum for Religious Broadcasting (IFRB)
  in, 170–172; Islam in, 172, 176, 181n18; Judaism in, 181n18; Media Development and
  Diversity Agency Act in, 178; as rainbow nation, 178–180; reapportionment of airtime
  for religious groups in, 1–2, 14, 166–180,
  173, 175, 177, 181n14; Religious Broadcasting Panel (RBP) in, 14, 170, 171, 172, 176,
  181n13, 182n30; religious freedom in, 168–
  169, 178; rights culture of, 168, 169, 171,
  176; statistics on religions in, 181n18
South African Broadcasting Corporation
  (SABC), 14, 167, 169–180, 173, 175, 177,
  180n11, 181nn16,26, 182nn29,40
South African Council of Churches (SACC), 170
Soviet Union, collapse of, 228–229, 263
Speech, freedom of, 168–169, 178
Spitulnik, Debra, 166–167
STAR Network, 259
Starrett, Gregory, 216, 223n19
Stolen Bible, 304–306, 305, 310n7
Sufism, 128n20, 135, 148–149n28, 215,
  216, 275
Suharto regime, 156, 158
Sunna, 33, 40, 49n4
Syria, 222n9

Tafsir al-Qurtubi, 216
Talmud, 102
Al-Tayyib, Nadir, 222n12
Teer-Tomaselli, Ruth, 169, 182n29
Tehran, 119–120
Televangelism, 3
Television: advertising in "flow" of, 211–213,
  217, 222n10; advertising on Egyptian television, 211–217, 219–220, 224n22; advertising
  on India's television, 258, 265–267; in Australia, 196, 198–200; Bourdieu on, 179; British television, 170, 212; and call to prayer in
  Egypt, 214–216, 223n19; and DTH (Direct-
  to-Home) technology, 264, 267; in Egypt
  generally, 222n11, 223n15; in Ghana, 297,
  300; in India, 258–259, 263–270, 273–274;
  in Israel, 93–94, 109n11; and kidnapping
  of television mogul's daughter in Brazil,
  58–59; MTV music video on, 251–252,
  252, 265; musalsal on Egyptian television,
  223n17, 224n23; preference for radio over,
  107; Ramadan Riddles (Fawazir Ramadan)
  in Egypt, 2, 16–17, 207–221, 221n2, 224–
  225n25; relationship between knowledge
  and, 231; in South Africa, 1–2, 14, 166–180;
  super-subjects on, 231, 248–249n9; in Syria,
  222n9; talk show with Öztürk in Turkey,
  17, 231–248; in Turkey generally, 17, 227–
  232, 228–231; in United States, 3, 22n16,
  212–213; and Universal Church of the Kingdom of God (UCKG) in Brazil, 52–54, 59,
  67, 110n17; West African beauty pageant
  on, 142–143, 148nn26–27; Yitzchak's campaign against, in Israel, 103
Terrorist, 280
Thackeray, Bal, 276, 277, 281
Time-Warner's CNN, 259, 264
Tomaselli, Keyan, 169, 170, 178, 182n29
Torres Straits Islander Studies, 190
Touré, Toumani, 137, 143, 146n1
Transparency and journalistic practice,
  152–162
Traoré, Moussa, 136–137, 140
T'shuva movement, 10, 92–95, 98–104, 106–
  108, 109n4
Turkey: AK (Justice and Development Party)
  in, 247–248; Alevi minorities in, 230; CHP
  (Republican People's Party) in, 247; conflict
  between Kurdish dissidents and Turkish
  military, 229, 231; Directorate of Religious
  Affairs in, 229–231, 244–245, 247; Islam in,
  229–231, 241–244; and neoliberalism, 228–
  229, 245; newspapers in, 232; parliament in,
  247–248; reading of Quran forbidden in

schools of, 49n7; "secular" Muslims in, 2, 17, 227–248; television in, generally, 228–232; television talk show with Öztürk in, 17, 231–248; televisual moment in, 228–231, 245, 247, 248n1; women in, 121
Turning Point, 306
Tutu, Archbishop, 180

Ubuntu (community), 179, 182n28
UCKG. *See* Universal Church of the Kingdom of God (UCKG)
"Umm Kulthum," 223n17
Umma, 31, 37
UNESCO, 163n2
United Hebrew Congregations of Anglo-Jewish Orthodoxy, 82
Universal Church of the Kingdom of God (UCKG): in Africa, 65; in Bahia, 65–67; and Bishop Crivela, 64–67; and cathedrals of faith, 52, 53, *53,* 60–64, *63, 64,* 67–68; and CDs by Bishop Crivela, 66–67, 70–71n21; and chains of faith and transnationalization, 59–64, 67–68; characteristics of members of, 67–68; charitable organization of, 69–70n11; compared with, 107; creation of labor market for followers of, 71n23; and dress of pastors and church workers, 67; evangelical label for, 57; and exorcism, 55, 56, 57, 58, 60, 70n15; and Fire of Israel ritual, 62–64, *63, 64;* and land possession, 66, 70n20; media reaction to, in Brazil, 55–57, 69n6, 71n22; and miracles, 56, 62; newspaper of, 59, 60, 67, 70n15; and poverty, 56–57, 67–68, 69–70n11; and public space, 67–68; ritual practices of, 60–64, 67–68; and television, 52–54, 59, 67, 110n17; war against Africa-oriented cults by, 8–9, 55, 60, 69n5
Upadhyaya, Deendayal, 20
Urdu in Hindi film industry, 275, 286nn9,11
Urry, John, 182n41
U.S. State Department, 180n1, 264
USAID, 163n2, 223n15

Vasudevan, Ravi, 280, 281, 282, 286n14
Veer Savarkar, Ambedkar, 282
VHP (Vishwa Hindu Parishad), 284
Video and audio cassettes: cassette sermons in Egypt, 2, 8, 29–49; and Chabad, 102–103; Haidara's use of, in Mali, 13, 140–144, 145; Yitzchak's use of, in Israel, 10, 103–106. *See also* Films and videos
Violence: in Brazil, 56–57, 58; journalists' rep-

resentations of, in Indonesia, 2, 13–14, 152–162; in Nigeria, 167–168; Siegel on, 157; statistics on, 163n6; against women in Palestine, 127n8
Vishwa Hindu Parishad (VHP), 284
Vries, Hent de, 166, 307

WACC (World Association for Christian Communication), 179
Al-Wahab, Muhammed ʿAbd, 42
Walbiri Fire Ceremony: Ngatjakula, 190, 191–194, 195, 199, 200, 201nn4–6, 202n13
Warlpiri fire ceremony, 14–15, 190, 191–201, *191, 197, 198*
Warlpiri Media Association, 193–196, 200
Warlukurlangu (Warlpiri Artist's Association), 197
Warner, Michael, 145, 244
West Africa, 135. *See also* Ghana; Mali
West African beauty pageant, 142–143, 148nn26–27
WHO (World Health Organization), 65
Williams, Raymond, 212, 215, 217, 222n10
Windhoek Charter on Broadcasting 2001, 178
Women: *chador* worn by, 121, 128n19; and *daʿwa* movement, 35, 49n5; dress of, in Muslim countries, 118, 121, 123–125, 128nn16–17,19, 210, 223n21; education of, in Muslim countries, 123, 128n17, 140; and family law debates in Palestine, 115–126, 126n1, 127n8; and gender segregation, 121–122, 127nn12,14; *hijab* worn by, 118, 128n19, 210, 223n21; homo-social interaction among, 121–122, 127n14; in Iran, 121; and Islam, 13, 115–126; Muslim women's learning circles in Mali, 140; and NGOs (nongovernmental organizations), 116–118, 126n5, 127nn7,9; in Palestine, 116–126; and pirate radio, 99–100; and public sphere, 119–126, 126n3; and sufism in Algeria, 128n20; in Turkey, 121; violence against, in Palestine, 127n8
Women in the Sun, 117–119, *119,* 122, 125, 127n8
World Association for Christian Communication (WACC), 179
World Bank, 18, 259, 265
World Health Organization (WHO), 65
World Miracle Church, 302
World Trade Organization, 265

Yemen, 126n1, 127n14
Yitzchak, Amnon, 10, 102, 103–106, 107

324 *Index*

Yosef, Ovadia, 99, 102
Yuendumu, 193, 201–202n7, 202n9

Zee TV, 259, 269
Zimbabwe, 180n7

Zionism, 105, 109n1
Al-Zobaidi, Subhi, 117–119, 127n9
Zohar, 105–106
Zubeidaa, 286n16
Zulu independent church, 182n40